HANDFULS OF PURPOSE

HANDFULS OF PURPOSE

Gleanings from the
Inner Life of Ruth Bryan

"First the blade, then the ear,
after that the full corn in the ear."
—Mark 4:28

Reformation Heritage Books
Grand Rapids, Michigan
2006

Published by
Reformation Heritage Books
2965 Leonard St., NE
Grand Rapids, MI 49525
616-977-0599 / Fax 616-285-3246
e-mail: orders@heritagebooks.org
website: www.heritagebooks.org

originally published in 1866 in London by W. H. Collingridge

10 digit ISBN 1-60178-003-6
13 digit ISBN 978-1-60178-003-4

For additional Reformed literature, both new and used, request a free book list from Reformation Heritage Books at the above address.

CONTENTS

Preface ix
Sketches of life xi
Diary:
1822
Early religious impressions—Mourning over a hard heart—
Halting between two opinions—Illness of her father 1
1823-28
Prayer for sanctified affliction—Father's death 7
1829
Self-acquaintance—Commencement of spiritual warfare—Earnest
longings after a living faith—Hope springing up 12
1830
First communion—Doubts and uncertainty—Waiting for
a sense of pardon—Becomes a Sunday-school teacher 21
1831
Anxiety about family prayer—Self-mortification hard to bear .. 27
1832
Begins the year with an Ebenezer—Visit to Normanton—
Cholera at Nottingham 29
1833
Declining health—Much spiritual darkness and trying
Providences—Last illness and death of her uncle 34
1834
Journey to Birmingham—Looking into self—Consequent
depression—Glimpses of the grace of Jesus 41
1835
Bearing the cross—Deep heart-exercise—
Temptation to infidelity 47
1836
Fervent wrestlings—Distinction between root and fruit—
Hears with interest a Caffre chief 52

1837

The Scriptures precious—Helps by the way—Riots in
Nottingham—Loss of a book—Striking answer to prayer
in connection with it—Lukewarmness lamented 57

1838

A profitable conversation—After perplexities—A blessed "assurance
of faith" given—Sin a burden—Rejoicing—Symptoms of a fatal
disease—The world a snare—Felt helplessness 66

1839

A close walk with God—Bodily weakness—Fresh manifestations
and love visits from Jesus—Foretasting glory—Deep sense of
sin—The Savior her hiding-place—Living in Christ—The flesh
subdued—Fasting and feasting 76

1840

Renewed dedication of body, soul, and spirit to the Lord—
Remembrance of past mercies—Shortcoming—Searchings of
heart—Victory through the blood of the Cross 99

1841

Soul discipline—Diving teaching—Under a cloud—Felt distance
from her Lord—Pressing after a life of faith—Restored to communion—Much tried respecting the publication of her letters 108

1842

Large requests—Perfect freedom—The Proverbs of Solomon
full of Christ—Groaning under felt corruptions, yet glorying in
the Lord—Pecuniary straits 119

1843

Earnests of the inheritance—Her watchword, "More of Christ"—
His Person unfolded by the Spirit, through the Word—Sorrow
and joy—Self-loathing—The fight of faith—The chastening of
love—Kissing the rod—Spiritual arithmetic 133

1844

Risen with Christ—Blessed views, by faith, of a glorious Christ—
Feeding upon the Word—Poor and needy—Leaning upon the
Beloved—Jesus her daily Sabbath—Still panting after further
revelations of His glory 158

1845

Eternal union with Jesus—Fiery darts of the wicked one—The
precious name of Jesus—Lesson from a spider's web—Temporal
mercies lent by the Lord—Fresh anointings from the Holy One—
Singing of mercy and judgment 171

Contents

1846
The illness of her mother—Anxieties and pleadings on her behalf—New discoveries of the beauty of Jesus—Serving Him without fear—Grace abounding—Her mother's death—A sparrow alone—The Lord also her Comforter 182

1847
Not alone—Visit to the grave—Communion with glorified saints—Pressing cares—Walks by faith—Timely deliverance—Visits the House of Refuge 196

1848
Peculiar straits—Looking unto Jesus—Longing for the salvation of souls—A cry from the depths—Feasting at the King's table—The triumph of faith—Prayer and fasting, with thanksgiving—A great answer—Emboldened to wait upon the Lord—Singing His praise 213

1849
The Lord's faithfulness—Temporal and spiritual help bestowed—A visit to Ockbrook—Great weakness of body—Beams of the coming glory—Rejoicing in the great salvation—Laboring in the vineyard—A public fast—Continued trial in temporal matters, yet cleaving to the Lord and to His promises 243

1850
Christ her all in all—Favored with access to the throne of grace—Blessed fellowship with Jesus—Matlock blessings—Teachings of the Spirit—The spread of Popery 272

1851
A day of darkness—A "time of refreshing" from the presence of the Lord—Fatigue and sharp conflict—Great Malvern—Journeying mercies—Increasing sufferings, but new songs—A happy Christmas Day 292

1852
Rumor of a French invasion—Trusting in the Lord—Heart-wanderings—A peculiar trial—Meditations on the Word—A day of humiliation—Friday evening meetings—Prayer to know God's will in little things 306

1853
Seeking brighter evidences—Sensible comforts diminished—Faint, yet pursuing—Sojourn in Edinburgh—Feasting in Famine ... 321

1854

Yearning over the soul of a sick friend—Good Friday a hallowed season—The mystery of the blessed Trinity unfolded—Lessons from the Scriptures—Thanksgiving for a plentiful harvest—A time of war—Fellowship with Christ in His sufferings 335

1855

Thoughts upon death—A day of national fast and humiliation—Much exercised about seeking further medical advice—Passion week—A time of Jubilee—Sips from the fountain—A glorious view of a suffering Christ—Resurrection blessedness—Justification by faith—Christmas-eve 347

1856

A time of temptation—The Bible a wonderful book—Perplexing letters spread before the King—National rejoicings on account of peace restored—The blessings of Calvary—Martha and Mary—A visit to Filey—Self-examination—"The Word made flesh" .. 377

1857

The Spirit's word—Redemption price—Pantings after Jesus—A banquet with the King—The coverings of the tabernacle—A second visit to Filey—Divine love—Watching for the Lord's hand on the top of Mount Carmel 398

1858

A New Year's motto: "Looking unto Jesus"—The Refiner's work—Longing for the "better land"—The debt paid, and the Church eternally free—The blessedness of union—No birthday portion—The sun in a mist—The furnace 417

1859

Tribulation—Disease progressing—Death of Mr. T—.
—Preciousness of the blood of the Lamb—Jesus as the High Priest—Christ delighting in His Church—A feast-day 427

1860

Much bodily suffering—The enemy harassing—Christ in the types, Psalms, and Prophets—The realization of the presence of Jesus in the furnace—Safe in the Ark—The Lord of hosts for a crown of glory—The last entry 436

Letters to Miss W— 445
Letters to A. T— 456
Letter to Miss A— 464
Letter to Miss P— 468

PREFACE

Reader,

This little book is sent forth with much prayer, that the anointing of the Holy Ghost may distill upon thy soul in reading it; and that the faithful testimony it bears to the eternal love of God the Father, the redeeming grace of the Lord Jesus, and the sanctifying power of the Holy Spirit, may be the means of encouragement to many tried and tempted souls. It breathes throughout of a full, free, and unconditional salvation to "the poor and needy."

JESUS, as the Alpha and Omega, was the one theme of the writer. He was as the dew to her soul; she had so beheld His glory, that she could truly say, "Thou art fairer than the children of men: grace is poured into thy lips." "All thy garments smell of myrrh, and aloes, and cassia." "His mouth is most sweet: yea, he is altogether lovely. This is my beloved, and this is my friend."

May the savor and fragrance of His precious name be "as ointment poured forth" to you.

"Do not grudge to pick out treasures
from an earthen pot."

"All may of thee partake:
Nothing can be so mean,
Which, with his tincture, for thy sake,
Will not grow bright and clean."

"They shall speak of the glory
of thy kingdom, and talk of thy power."
—Psalm 145:11

SKETCHES OF LIFE

"Who hath despised the day of small things?" was a question put to the prophet in days of old. And again, to the same prophet, it was declared, "Not by might, nor by power; but by my Spirit, saith the Lord of hosts." In blessed keeping with this testimony, the apostle in after days says, "God hath chosen the weak things of the world to confound the things that are mighty…; and things which are despised hath God chosen, yea, and things which are not, to bring to nought things that are, that no flesh should glory in His presence." We have abundant proofs still that the Lord, in the exercise of His divine sovereignty, for the display of His own wisdom, *does* choose and make use of instruments, apparently the most unfit and unseemly, to carry out His own eternal purposes, that glory may redound to His great name.

None who were acquainted with the disposition of Ruth Bryan, naturally so diffident and retiring, could have supposed there was within her so deep and privileged an insight into God's Word, qualifying her in an eminent degree to impart to her fellow-pilgrims the sweetest and most glowing views of the "truth as it is in Jesus." Taught as she had herself been by the Holy Ghost, in a clear and most experimental way, she was thereby fitted to minister from her own heart to the hearts and consciences of others. Moreover, the scenes of trial and deep soul-exercise through which she was called to pass, from her earliest years, prepared her all the more to "weep with those that weep," and "to rejoice with them that do rejoice."

The subject of this brief sketch was born in London, July 6th, 1805. Her father was at that time engaged in trade, but was soon after providentially called to Nottingham, to preach the everlasting gospel.

Almost from infancy Ruth became the subject of religious impressions. Her mind opened as it were unconsciously. So gentle was the work of the Spirit in His early operations, that in speaking of it she would say it was like Mark 4:26. The seed had sprung and grown up, she knew not how. Hence the after work and the whole course of her future life was the more conspicuously of God. Without doubt, the very tender way in which the Lord first began to deal with her, tended to produce the like spirit which so specially characterized her daily life. As in her own case, there had been, "first the blade, then the ear, then the full corn in the ear;" so she in turn was ready to watch and wait patiently for the buddings and blossomings of grace in others: feeling peculiarly jealous of cutting off any in whom she perceived the faintest breath of spiritual life.

Although her education was adapted to the position she occupied, Ruth had a mind far above the measure of instruction she had received. She possessed a quickness of mental perception, combined with striking originality of thought, which plainly proved her to be a person of no ordinary capacity.

This high order of mind is evinced by her letters and meditations, which are remarkable throughout for clear arrangement of ideas and power of expression. No doubt the lack of intellectual culture, of which she was conscious, led her to depend more entirely upon the teaching of the Spirit of truth, who by His grace did develop and mature these His natural gifts. Had it not been so, she might have been more easily drawn aside from the simplicity which is in Christ, by one or other of the many specious devices and ensnarements with which Satan in these last days seeks to entrap unwary souls (2 Tim. 3:1-7).

From early youth, when as yet she "knew not the Lord," Ruth showed great tenderness of conscience, which was observable even in her intercourse with her school-fellows. Among other things, she would shrink from the trifling use of scriptural expressions, while at the same time she tried to influence her companions to do likewise; thereby manifesting the benefit of careful and godly training.

It has been said that hers was emphatically "the life, walk, and triumph of faith." But be it remembered, that this was not the lesson of a day; ere such a blessed life could be attained, self must be brought low. The process was a painful one. Many years of darkness were appointed her, during which time she had to wade through deep waters of heart-exercise, while groaning under the bondage of the law. She had occasional gleams of hope, but her usual frame of mind was one of doubt and uncertainty, to which many experienced Christians can bear witness who then knew her. She had not yet learned to follow that wise counsel—

> "Pore not on thyself too long,
> Lest it sink thee lower."

The heavy cloud at length passed away; Ruth's jubilee day dawned. After sixteen years of soul anguish, Jesus Himself proclaimed liberty to His captive one. "The word of the Lord came *expressly* to" her soul, and she was free indeed (John 8:36). From that happy day of her great deliverance, she may be said never to have become "entangled again with the yoke of bondage."

Let it not be thought, however, that her conflicts were over. It was far otherwise. She groaned daily under *felt* corruptions, and was ofttimes sorely harassed by the enemy; yet was she enabled by precious faith to hold fast the beginning of her "confidence stedfast unto the end." Neither did she rest satisfied with the mere knowledge of her acceptance "in the Beloved." She was ever seeking fresh revelations of His glorious person, and pressing after closer communion with the adorable Trinity; and that with wrestlings and watchings, yea, even with fastings.

We must not pass over the Lord's providential dealings with His child. She had naturally a sensitive and clinging heart, which made home associations very dear; and seemed to unfit her to bear the brunt of the storms which gathered round her path. But He saw it good to sever these earth-born ties, by calling away the loved parents to whom she was wont to look for help and sympathy. Thus was Ruth left "a sparrow alone," to trust in her *best* Beloved.

From the following pages of her Diary, it will be seen how she was brought sometimes into great straits as regards temporal provision; doubtless, for the trial of her faith. At her mother's death she was left with a small income, which from different causes gradually diminished, so as scarcely to supply her necessary wants. Under these circumstances she did not eat the "bread of idleness," but sought to increase her little store by doing needlework. Yet, in spite of her endeavors, she was often in painful extremities, at which times she indeed proved that "it is better to trust in the Lord than to put any confidence in man." Her expectation was from Him, therefore to Him alone did she confide her pressing needs, carefully keeping them secret, even from those friends who were on terms of the closest fellowship with herself, and who would have esteemed it a privilege to minister to her wants.

On one occasion, when called, like Israel of old, to pass through "*a place of straits*" (in the Hebrew, "Pihahiroth"), such was her importunity, that she spent five hours on her knees, wrestling with the Lord. Like Daniel, she set her "face unto the Lord God, to seek by prayer and supplications with fasting" (Dan. 9:3). Nor did she wait for Him in vain. He speedily sent the needed help, granting her the very sum for which she had been led to plead. By such deliverances was her faith strengthened, and she was emboldened to flee with every difficulty to the mercy-seat.

But Ruth had other cares than these to occupy her mind, she was far from being engrossed with her own sorrows; for grace had given her—

> "A heart at leisure from itself,
> To soothe and sympathize."

And it was truly her delight to fulfill the apostolic exhortation, "Bear ye one another's burdens, and so fulfill the law of Christ." She was often mourning her unprofitableness, but gladly embraced every opportunity of witnessing for the Lord, or of helping His tried and afflicted people. For many years she had a weekly meeting, for prayer and spiritual communion, in her house. This was frequently felt to be a peculiarly sacred season. And there are some who cannot forget the sweetness and savor of her soul-breathings on those occasions. Her prayers were the pleadings of a child, the solicitations of a friend, the entreaties of a spouse; in a word, it was Ruth over again, coming often "softly," when it was in feeling "midnight" with the soul, laying herself at the feet of the heavenly Boaz; and, in answer to His "Who art thou?" exclaiming, "I am Ruth, thine handmaid; spread, therefore, thy skirt over thine handmaid, for thou art a near kinsman." It was, perhaps, more especially to individual cases she was most helpful, both by word and letter. The weak plants in the Lord's vineyard were her special care. She loved to lift up "the bruised reed," nor would she willingly quench "the smoking flax," while she ever sought to direct the eyes of such little ones to the great Burden-Bearer, and to "the word of his testimony." It might be here adduced, as a striking proof of her intimate acquaintance with the deceitful workings of the human heart, that her prayer had often been, that, if blessed to the conversion of any, she might not know it, lest she "should be exalted above measure." It was so. She was not permitted to wear this "crown of rejoicing" here; on which very account, she would sometimes grieve, failing to recognize herein another request granted.

"The happy Gleaner," a name by which she often called herself, was peculiarly exempt from all party spirit. She felt union with all who loved the Lord Jesus in sincerity, but her heart was *most* closely knit to any in whom she saw His image *brightly* reflected. She was diligent in attending the means of grace where her lot was cast, having been nourished in "a field which the Lord had blessed;" she scrupled not, however, to glean from *other* fields any parched ears of corn, which were reached her by the Lord's reapers.

It will be apparent to the readers of these pages, that, as Ruth neared the promised land, her Lord seemed to be ripening her for glory; but it was in "the furnace of affliction" that He continued to try this precious daughter of Zion, "comparable to fine gold." She had for some time discovered symptoms of the painful and lingering disease of cancer, which ultimately caused her death. From feelings of delicacy she forebore to make it known, until the marked progress of her disease made it necessary to have recourse to medical aid. When the tidings of her approaching dissolution were first disclosed, her heart was saddened and depressed. She shrank from the prospect of the sufferings appointed her, and avoided any reference to the subject. But soon she was brought into blessed submission to her Father's will, and enabled to glory in her infirmities, while she lay passive in His hands. At such times she would say she needed no sympathy, it was but the beckoning hand of her Beloved, saying, "Come up hither." From the trying nature of her disease, irritability might have been expected; but no, the power of the indwelling Comforter kept these earthly tempers in abeyance, and the lessons she had so long been learning at the feet of Jesus were now evidenced by the patience and forbearance which characterized this latter stage of her pilgrimage. She could never be persuaded to resort to opiates, even in the most distressing moments, lest she should lose her powers of mind, and consequently her spiritual joys. In this she seemed to have her Lord's example in view, when He refused the vinegar, and rather desired thereby to have personal fellowship with Him, "filling up that which was behind of the afflictions of Christ" in her flesh for His body's sake, the church.

And now nothing remains, but to tell of the transplanting of this "lily among thorns" from earth's barren waste into the "paradise of God." As in life, so also in death's dark valley, she sought to be *alone with Jesus*. Hers was not a triumphant death-bed. No excessive joy was manifested there, but a quiet waiting for the Lord's best time to call away her ransomed spirit from the body of its humiliation, to see Him "face to face," whom not having seen she loved. His sweet peace was keeping (*garrisoning*) her heart; and to the very last she enjoyed blessed communings with her Lord.

On the night before her decease she refused the presence of any friend to watch by her, lest it should disturb this holy converse with the King of saints; but she was overheard pleading with Him, just prior to the shining into her soul of the beams of the eternal day.

Early on the morning of July 27th, 1860, she was found unconscious, and, in less than an hour after, she sweetly fell asleep in Jesus, to wake up after His likeness.

Thus have we endeavored to trace the outline of the quiet life of Ruth Bryan, with some of her heart aspirations. It will be perceived she was one of the Lord's favored children, often privileged to walk in His sunshine, and to dwell under His shadow. But be it remembered that the *beauty* of her character was all of *grace*. Without its wonder-working power, she would have been but a cumberer of the ground, a stone in nature's quarry; but the Lord, in His divine sovereignty and matchless love, took her from thence, to cleanse, and clothe, and consecrate her for Himself: and, under the hand of the Great Refiner, she was prepared and adorned to take her place among the *living* stones in His heavenly temple.

This little work is now committed to the care of the heavenly Husbandman; who alone can sow the precious seed, and, when sown, is able to give the increase.

> "For ever to behold Him shine,
> For ever more to call Him mine—
>   And see Him still before me:
> For ever on His face to gaze,
> And meet His full assembled rays,
> While all the Father He displays,
>   To all the saints in glory.
>
> "Oh, how the thought that I shall know
> The Man who suffered here below,
>   To manifest His favor:
> To me, or those whom most I love,
> Or here, or with His saints above,
> Does my delighted spirit move,
>   At that sweet word—'for ever.'
>
> "Not all things else are half so dear
> As His delightful presence here—
>   What must it be in heaven?

'Tis heaven on earth to hear him say,
As thus I journey day by day,
'Poor sinner, cast thy fears away—
    Thy sins are all forgiven.'

"But how must His celestial voice
Make my enraptured heart rejoice,
    When I in glory hear Him:
While I before the heavenly gate
For everlasting entrance wait,
And Jesus, on His throne of state,
    Invites me to come near Him?

"Come in, thou blessed, sit with me,
With my own life I ransomed thee—
    Come, taste my perfect favor:
Come in, thou happy spirit, come,
Now thou shalt dwell with me at home—
Ye blessed mansions, make him room,
    For he must stay for ever.'

"When Jesus thus invites me in,
How will the heavenly host begin
    To own their new relation:
'Come in, come in,' the blissful sound,
From every heart shall echo round,
Till all the crystal walls resound
    With joy for my salvation."

"Thine eyes shall see the King in His beauty."
—Isaiah 33:17

DIARY

I am going to aim at keeping a kind of *diary*, to write down my feelings, thoughts, and the occurrences of the days as they pass away, in hopes of finding it beneficial. May the Lord grant His blessing!

Sunday, September 1st, 1822 — Attended the seven o'clock prayer-meeting this morning for the first time. The affectionate prayers which were offered up for my dearest father affected me. May they be answered! Seem to have some feeling about divine things; but, alas, this afternoon am as stupid as usual. Nothing, nothing will break this hard heart. The services of another Sabbath are over; how have my privileges been abused! I feel this evening I cannot tell how; I know not which way to turn. Oh, that I may be directed by the Spirit of truth to the right way of happiness!

Monday, 2nd — Have spent this afternoon at a friend's. Alas! Alas! I have still to mourn my insensibility to serious things; indeed, I seem not to have any desire.

> [Reader, this may appear a strange expression from a quickened, living soul; but hast thou known nothing of having been brought so low, under the power of unbelief, and the entanglements of worldliness, carnality, and sin, as to be brought to halt—to hesitate—to doubt, and, in thy inner heart to sigh for even a *desire* after spiritual manifesta-

tions, and such tokens of mercy as thou hadst once hoped were thine? Was not the prophet here when he said, "My strength and my hope is perished from the Lord"?]

I fear that I am not affected as I ought, and have only a faint desire to become a Christian; and that merely to escape hell. Lord, have mercy upon me! Lead aright; break this hard, hard heart! Thou, Lord, knowest what I would have, even the forgiveness of my sins. During service was as cold as a stone. Oh, when will this vile heart be melted and subdued by divine grace?

Tuesday, 3rd — Have been more light and trifling than usual to-day. I not only indulged the spirit, but encouraged and courted it. How have I to lament every day my sinfulness. I am afraid I have been in some measure trusting to what I hoped to do; but the more I strive to do something acceptable, the shorter I come. I know the right way, but find it hard to depend only on Christ, and to exercise faith. I have no faith, no humility, no sense of sin, no confidence in the promises, no fear of the threatened punishments; nor anything that I ought to have. Oh, what a picture!

This evening heard a sermon from St. John 2:11; but, alas, felt next to nothing. O Lord, break this heart into ten thousand pieces! Oh, I would sooner suffer all horrors and terrors imaginable, and be saved at last, than be in my present awfully-secure and stupid state. Break— break, oh, break my heart, and make me give it entirely to Thee, thou blessed Savior!

Wednesday, 4th — This evening have been to a friend's. No profitable conversation, nor did I wish for any; but joined in the nonsense, and seemed almost to forget I had a soul. What shall we say to these things? Every night I have to look back upon a day spent in folly and sin. Alas,

I fear, and with too much reason, that I never felt the plague of my own heart. Oh, for all the sorrows imaginable, sooner than indulge in such wickedness! Lord, forgive, and rouse me from this worse than death. Oh, what a hypocrite I am!

Friday, 6th — Went with Miss B— this morning for a walk. Enjoyed it very much. She seems to think there is good hope even for me. Surely I have not deceived her. I think I told her all I felt; but hope and encouragement seem almost impossible. I have been informed by one of my companions that Miss B— has with pain observed in me a spirit of censoriousness and sneering. *I* sneer! the last person in the world who ought to do it, feeling so guilty myself. I am afraid I did not receive the reproof in a proper spirit; but felt hurt, as it came from those younger than myself. Lord, subdue the abominable spirit of pride which I feel, and enable me to overcome the censorious looks which are observed in me!

Sunday, 8th, Evening — I have enjoyed or understood a little of what has been delivered to-day; but now it seems to have gone from me, and I am the same stupid creature again. Oh, how long shall I groan under this worse than Egyptian bondage? Oh, that I may be enabled to look to Christ for deliverance, and to wait patiently His good time!

Tuesday, 10th — The day has passed as usual; we have little variation, and my feelings vary almost as little. I am generally as cold and dead as the stones in the street. This evening heard a sermon from Psalm 50:13. Felt a little encouragement to hope that I should some time be delivered from my burden; but then, when I thought of feeling what was said, and looking upon myself as a sinner, it came into my mind, "Oh, thou hypocrite! Thou whited sepulchre!" From whence it proceeded I know not.

Saturday, 21st — I have this day been rather more still than I am sometimes; but must take shame and confusion of face to myself for all the events thereof. O Lord, make me humble, and suffer me not to depend upon anything it is in my power to perform. Oh, keep me humble, keep me from self-deception, begin the good work, if it is not yet begun. Oh, may I not be a castaway! Break, break this stony heart! How long, Lord, how long? Make me *feel*. Oh, leave me not to this insensibility! What argument can I use? Oh, leave, leave me not! Suffer me not to perish! Mercy, mercy is all my plea; for Christ's sake, have mercy on me! Oh, precious, precious Christ Jesus, be Thou my Savior, Husband, Friend—*my* Jesus, and my all. Jesus! Jesus! Oh, that Thou wert precious to my soul!

> [To a mere novice in divine things, or speculators in religion, these heart-exercises would appear strange and anomalous; but by such as have been brought into the school of Christ, and are set by the divine Teacher to the study of the human heart, the struggles—the contention—the warfare between flesh and spirit—that which is from beneath, and that which is from above—will be perfectly and practically understood.]

October 25th — My dear father has been severely exercised with pain; for five hours he endured such agony as he never felt before. My distress during that period was such as I cannot express. The fear that I should soon lose such a dear parent, and the misery of hearing his groans without being able to afford relief, exceeds all I ever felt; but, thanks be to the Lord, my father is fast recovering. Here is cause for a fresh Ebenezer. Oh, I can never be sufficiently thankful! O Lord, grant that both my dear parents may be spared many years, unworthy as I am of them.

October 31st — Have just returned from a prayer-meeting. My dear father gave us a sweet address from the words, "I know it shall be well with them that fear the Lord"; but, alas, it was not for me—I cannot say that I *fear* the Lord in the manner described. Everything I hear seems to add to my distress; to hear of the high privileges of true believers, to long to enjoy, and yet to be left almost without hope, is trouble. What shall I do? The door of mercy seems eternally closed against my petitions. I am ready to give up all for lost; but, Lord, make me pray! Never let me neglect the means. Oh, sometimes I feel as though I never should give up crying for mercy. I think, if I am cast into hell, I will still cry to Jesus for mercy. Oh, that the Lord would appear for my relief! How long wilt Thou hide Thy face from me?

November 1st — Alas, this has been another day of sin. I have given up writing in this book for some time, till this week, for fear it should be *pride;* but my father says it is a temptation; but I write *sin, sin*, all *sin*, nothing but *sin*. Lord, have mercy! A week since to-day, my ever dear father suffered unutterable anguish; I cannot be thankful enough to the Lord for restoring him. I have to engage in prayer to-night;* may the Lord help me! But, alas, I tremble.

December 22nd, Sunday — For the last month, or more, my feelings have been tried indeed. My dear father has been, and still continues under severe affliction. This is the fourth Sabbath he has been confined from his usual labors, but he has enjoyed sweet peace under his suffer-

---

* Her Friday-evening meetings (of which she often speaks in the course of her Diary) were commenced with one or two Christian friends, at or about this time; and were continued till within a few days of her death.

ings—no fear of death—but he has been enabled to bow to the will of his heavenly Father. He said to me one day, "I care not what pain I suffer, or what affliction, if I could but *preach*"; the tears came into his eyes, and he was much affected. He longs again to be among his little flock, and to preach to them Christ crucified. May the Lord, if it be His blessed will, soon restore him! But, alas, how stupid and dead have I been under this affliction; my natural feelings have been keen, but, as to spiritual things, I remain unimpressed and cold. Lord, rouse my stupid affections! Leave me not to myself! but take some means to rescue me from that destruction to which I am rushing with impetuosity.

1823

January 19th, Sunday — My dear father preached this afternoon from "God is love"; evening, "Mary hath chosen that good part, which shall not be taken away from her."

March 9th — My dear father preached from the words, "But where are the nine?"

March 22nd — My father has this week, again, been reduced very low, and little hope entertained of his recovery; but to-day he has revived, and our expectations are again raised. May the Lord continue the work He seems to have begun. The night before last, my dear father began to think "it was all over," and that he should soon be at rest; but we would wish, if it were possible, to keep him a little longer. May this affliction have its due influence on my mind. Hitherto, I have been very stupid, cold, and dead; prayer has been almost a burden; and at times all religious exercises could have been dispensed with. O Lord, arise and shine upon my benighted soul! Arouse my sleeping powers! Give me to see the multitude and magnitude of my crimes, and to fly to Jesus Christ for refuge. To-morrow is the Sabbath; may the divine blessing attend our engagements!

March 23rd — My dear father is again very low and weak; the Lord only knows what will be the result of this long affliction. Talking to Mr. —, my father said, "Mercy!

Mercy! All is mercy on this side of hell; it is a mercy *I* am out of hell." Lord, restore him, hear and answer our prayer, if Thy divine will.

March 30th — This hard heart! Sometimes I cannot pray, and, when I do try, the heavens seem as brass to my petitions; surely there is no mercy for me. My dear, dear father gets weaker every day; he seems still to think he shall get better—Lord, grant he may! Oh, take him not away! Leave, oh, leave me not fatherless! My father said to some friend, "I wonder at myself; for I have been thinking that I know the happiness and glory of heaven, and yet am not, as it were, rushing into it." At another time he said, "I should be happy to continue to work in the vineyard, if my Master would hire me." And must we part, my father, to meet no more? and shall I read this when I am a desolate orphan, and my father is singing the praises of the Lamb, and has joined the multitude which no man can number? I fear I shall. Oh, it is almost more than nature can bear! If we might meet at last, it would alleviate the pang; but, oh no, I fear we shall be for ever separated.

April 1st — Yesterday, my dear father was much worse. Kept his bed all day. I was not at home until evening. About eight o'clock, he was seized with violent pain, which continued, I should think, two hours—when, enduring great agony, my dear father said, "Now for the Fountain!" I had read to him in the early part of the evening his favorite chapters, Psalm 51, Isaiah 43, 1 John 1 and 2. He feels much better this morning; he said to Mr. U—, "Farewell; if I never see you again (and waved his dear hand), I shall soar with the lark; may the Lord bless you!" Yes, my dear father, you will soar above us all; if we do but follow, it will be well. To Mrs. T— he said, "My dear, dear friend, whatever you do, let your soul be your chief concern."

Thursday — My dear father has had a restless night; he told Mrs. C— that he now derived comfort from the truths he had preached; he said, "I am firm as a rock. I am a poor sinner falling into the arms of mercy. I think I may, with propriety, look *home* now." Seeing my mother weep, he said, "Do not give way, only pray that I may wield the sword to the last." Perhaps, this time next week, I may be an orphan! Oh, is it possible? is it not a dream? Ah, no, it is but too true! Surely, I cannot live.

Sunday Night — My dear father is no better; the doctors give no more hope, but I cannot give him up: he said, when asked how he was, "Oh, I am going full gallop home"; to several he said, "I cannot say much, only look to Jesus, think of Jesus"; he remarked, "I could not have thought the frame could be so much reduced, as to shut the mouth of a Christian," alluding to his own weak frame, and inability to talk. When any one prays with him, he says, "Pray for strength, that I may be kept fighting and wielding the sword to the last." My dear father said to me this evening, "The Scripture says, 'a threefold cord is not easily broken'; but you know it may be broken now; the Lord is about to break our threefold cord, and then it will be a twofold one. The happiness of life consists in unity; I commend to your care your dear mother. Make her life as happy as you can; she has been one of the best of wives and mothers. What a comfort it is nothing can dissolve the union between Christ and the soul." He often repeats Hebrews 6:18.

Monday — My dear father no better, but rather worse. To my mother he said, "We shall soon all see Jesus as He is." "To be a member of Christ, His body, His flesh, and His bones, an *inseparable* member." "To-day, Satan came in very slyly, saying, 'You are not worthy'; I answered, 'Christ came into the world to save sinners, of whom I *am chief*,' and I was at liberty in a moment."

Tuesday — My dear father is still alive; he laments very much that he cannot say more now, but hopes he shall be able before he goes. This afternoon he said to my uncle and self, "The Lord is our King, the Lord is our Lawgiver, and the Lord Jesus Christ is our Savior; we have affronted Him as our King, broken His law as our Lawgiver, but have access to Him as our Savior."

Wednesday — My dear father appears to be going very fast; after taking some water, he said, "As cold water to a thirsty soul, so is good news from a far country; good news of salvation to poor sinners!"

Wednesday, 23rd — Since I last wrote, death has entered our family. Yes, my father, my own dear father, is no more! The funeral solemnities are over, my brother gone, and we left to mourn our desolate condition. On Thursday, the 10th, the happy spirit took its flight, at five minutes past eleven, in the morning. My dear father was sensible to the last. We were both with him: about five minutes before his departure, my mother said, "Are you happy?" He replied, "Very! I was just wishing I could speak. 'Salvation is of the Lord' and not from the hills and mountains of creatures; it is solid:" his voice was failing in death, and he spoke with much difficulty. About a minute after, my mother saying something to him, he said, "Don't talk *just now*"; which were the last words he spoke.

My dear father's remains were interred on Monday, the 14th, in a vault beside the pulpit, where he has so often preached.

May 4th, Sabbath — Have attended a prayer-meeting this morning, but without deriving benefit. I daily feel the loss of my dear, dear father, more and more; every place reminds me of him, whom I shall see no more. Oh, how shall I bear up under this heavy, overpowering weight? It is indeed too true, he is gone; he has taken his seat in the mansions of bliss; no more shall I hear his sweet voice encouraging me to look to Jesus, and assuring me I should not be cast out; now that voice is silent in death, and I am indeed an orphan. May this solemn event be sanctified to my soul's good! A bitter cup!

> [Here, of necessity, a break in the Diary occurs, as a number of pages in the MS. are missing. From what follows, however, it will be seen that her conflicts between hope and fear—her warfare between flesh and faith—had by no means ceased. It was by a most gradual process, and only after the most prolonged contention between faith and feelings, she was brought to that blessed soul-establishment to which she was at length permitted and privileged to attain. It appears, from memoranda made in the interval above referred to, that Miss Bryan formed an attachment, in which it was difficult for her to trace the approving hand of God; and this, without doubt, led to much of her subsequent conflict, and to that strife between light and darkness, which is so observable in the annexed pages. The whole, however, issued in a considerable amount of self-knowledge, and a clearer apprehension of Christ's glorious person and work: thus she lived to prove, that "all things work together for good to them that love God, and who are the called according to his purpose."]

1829

January 4th — The first Sunday in the year 1829 finds me having made but little progress in the ways of God; still, still, I am halting between two opinions, and seem as if I could not give myself up to the Lord. May grace be given to enable me to do so, and the close of this year find me united to Him in an everlasting covenant!

April 5th — Oh, that the Lord would be pleased to imprint gratitude on my heart for the mercies with which He does favor me; and make up every deficiency by bestowing on me a new heart, and enabling me to devote myself to His service. I long to come out from the world, and avow myself a disciple of the Redeemer; but, alas, I am persuaded that I never felt the regenerating influence of divine grace; sin has still the dominion over me, and I can truly say,

> "The more I strive against its power,
> I sin and stumble but the more."

I do wish to resist it, but have such an evil heart, that, at times, it seems my element. Gracious Lord, deliver me by Thine almighty power, for nothing short of Omnipotence can rescue me. I have been much exercised lately about the Trinity, and have no experienced friend to open my mind to, in whose judgment I could confide, and who would meet my difficulties; perhaps the Lord

Himself will be my Teacher. I wish to examine the subject in humble dependence upon Him.

May 24th — This has been a Sabbath of much darkness, and deservedly so, for, during the last two days, I have sinfully indulged in building castles of worldly happiness; I have been hewing out to myself "cisterns, broken cisterns, that could hold no water," though at the same time my conscience told me I was wrong. How then can I expect comfort in religion when I am seeking it in the world? I am now plunged in gloomy doubts and dejection; my sin weighs heavily upon my soul; I am bereft of hope, and afraid to pray, because I have sinned presumptuously, and contrary to much light and knowledge. Oh, when shall I be enabled to give my whole heart to the Savior, to resist the devil, and fight the good fight of faith? Descend, Thou divine Spirit! Renew my heart, and give me strength to mortify and subdue the lusts of the flesh, to which I am now in subjection. How miserable is my state at this moment! My inward corruptions, and the enemy of souls, are strongly urging to sin and indifference; while conscience and past experience, amply testify that sorrow and distress will be the sure consequence. Lord, deliver me from this bondage!

July 5th, Sunday — I trust I can say that it is my anxious and chief desire to be found walking steadily towards the heavenly Canaan; but, alas, I am so distressed by the powerful corruptions of my wicked heart, that I often fear I am going the downward road. I can truly say, "That when I would do good, evil is present with me." I am at this time in a state of much anxiety about my immortal interests. I have begun to read "Romaine's Life of Faith." I feel much interested in it, and see more of the nature of faith than before; but find myself lamentably deficient, and think that my want of this *precious* faith in the dear

Redeemer is the cause of my overwhelming distress. Oh, that I could view Him as my "Law-fulfiller." Holy Spirit, be pleased to open my eyes, to see clearly the finished work He has wrought out; be pleased to grant me a sweet view of Jesus as a Savior, who is able and willing to save all who come to Him; and enable me to come, to be ever coming in the midst of all my darkness. Oh, grant me faith—strong faith! May I every day live nearer to Thee, and be more weaned from the world. I hunger and thirst after righteousness, and such Thou hast said shall be filled. "Lord, may I be constantly looking for and expecting the fulfillment of Thy promise. Amen."

July 6th, my Birthday — Twenty-four years have I sojourned in this wilderness, and find additional proof, every succeeding one, that this is not my rest! The last year seems to have passed more quickly than any one in my life. Oh, that I may be enabled to devote myself from this time to the Lord! Dear Jesus, and thou, Eternal Spirit, graciously enable me to do so, and seal, oh, seal my wandering heart to things divine. May I come out from the world and be separate, and be able to say, "All is well," whether Thou hast ordained life or death for me during the next year.

> [The reader is especially requested to observe the ardent soul-breathings of the beloved Ruth of *faith*. Constantly she cries through these pages, "Lord, increase my *faith!*" and to every unprejudiced mind it will be obvious how graciously and condescendingly the Lord answered this her prayer. During the latter years of her life, *faith*, in its simplicity and its power, shone so conspicuously in her whole character and conversation.]

July 7th — I have been reading the memorandum I wrote on my birthday last year, and desire to raise an

"Ebenezer" of gratitude to my gracious Redeemer for bringing me out of the anxiety and distress by which I was then surrounded. Bitter indeed was the cup I was drinking, but it was a deserved one. On this day twelve-months I was all but in despair. I thought the Lord had forsaken me, that He would never more be gracious, and all things were working against me; but now, blessed be His name, I can say He has been better to me than all my fears. I have experienced a wonderful temporal deliverance. Oh, that it may be only a prelude to a spiritual one! I do hope the Lord has, in much mercy, turned my face toward the heavenly Jerusalem, for it is now my chief desire to deny the lusts of the flesh, to live to His glory, and enjoy communion with Him. Yea, thou ever blessed Jesus, I long for a sweet view of Thy reconciled countenance. I long to live by faith upon Thee, to pass my time here as a stranger and pilgrim, and have my affections set entirely on things above. Oh, grant the desire of my heart!—send me not empty away, but enrich me with the graces of Thy Holy Spirit, and enable me from this time to be Thy disciple.

July 19th, Sabbath — During the past week, I have, I trust, been led to see a little more of the nature of the Christian warfare, and daily taking up the cross, than ever before. It appears to me now, to consist not merely in abstaining from those outward transgressions which are obvious to the view of others, but steadfastly resisting, in the strength of the Lord, those inward corruptions which are daily and hourly striving for mastery; and, also, in endeavoring to deny and subdue those sins, which, from habit and constitution, are as dear as a right hand, or a right eye. This is, indeed, a cross which we ought to be carrying; the moment we lay it down, and *allow* ourselves in any carnal indulgences, or sinful pleasure, that moment we bring guilt upon our souls, and lose that sweet peace, and serenity of mind, which is only found in reconciliation *to*, and communion *with* God.

July 26th, Sabbath — Since writing the above, I have proved it true, indeed, by bitter experience. Within the last few days I have been more indifferent to spiritual things; those sins of my heart, to which I am so prone, have again, in some measure, gained the ascendancy, and I am now miserable indeed; my heart is cold, my conscience alarmed, and I have lost those sweet desires and longings after the bread of heaven, which I before felt; the privilege of prayer, which was becoming one of my sweetest enjoyments, is now a task. I have but little inclination; and, when I attempt to pray, guilt flies in my face, and I fear to approach the Majesty of heaven. Oh, how hard it is to keep a "conscience void of offence"; religion appears to me one of the most difficult things in the world, and I very much fear I shall never attain the true enjoyment of it. There must be something essentially wrong, or I should not be so easily and frequently overcome of evil. Oh, thou Holy and divine Spirit, thou Comforter, thou Enlightener, thou Sanctifier of thy people, be pleased to descend in all thy mighty influences, and begin a work of grace upon my soul! I am ignorant; instruct me. I am dark; enlighten me. I am sinful; apply the precious blood of Jesus to my guilty soul. I am altogether an outward-court worshipper. Oh, renew me in the spirit of my mind, and grant that henceforth "the life that I live in the flesh, I may live by the faith of the Son of God." Oh, that I may be enabled to overcome the temptations of the devil, to subdue the lusts of the flesh, and live daily in nearer communion with the Lord! Oh, blessed Savior, be pleased to rouse my sluggish heart! Cut deep and close, rather than suffer me to deceive myself, or to go on in a lukewarm, indifferent state. Make me lively in Thy cause, spiritual in Thy service; and may my heart and affections be constantly in heaven, while my body is on earth.

August 23rd, Sabbath — Some five or six weeks ago, I had some hopes that the Lord was turning my feet Zionward, and that I should be enabled to cleave to Him with purpose of heart; but now, alas, I have reason to believe I was deceiving myself, for my iniquities have again taken hold of, and conquered me. I have lost those earnest desires after the enjoyment of religion, which I before experienced. I am at a loss to account for my strange variety of conduct and feeling, and fear I am entirely given up to work the desires of my wicked heart. At times I feel a perfect hatred to sin, delight in the privilege of prayer, reading, and meditation, and seem to desire nothing so much as to grow in grace, and press forward in the divine life. But soon my besetting sins gain the advantage, Satan represents these in the most captivating light, my heart is ensnared, and I sink into carnal ease and indulgence; then prayer becomes a burden; spiritual exercises lose their charm; and I am brought into dreadful bondage by the terrors of an accusing law, and a guilty conscience. Oh, that I knew the secret of real religion, but I fear I never shall. I have so often indulged the hope that I was in the way to its enjoyment, and been disappointed, that I now know not which way to turn, and shall, I believe, sink in deep despair, or give myself up to work iniquity with those that know not God. May divine mercy be extended, and I, forcibly, snatched as a brand from the burning. But, ah, I dare not hope, for my heart seems still to love and cleave to its iniquities; and the Scripture declares, "*If* I regard iniquity in my heart, the Lord *will not* hear." Misery and despair are my sad portion.

October 10th — Most feelingly can I say with the poet—

> "Strange and mysterious is my life,
> What opposites I feel within";

for at times my whole mind and soul seem absorbed in desires after spirituality, and the enjoyment of the divine presence; the world sinks into insignificance, and its enjoyments and pleasures lose their power to charm. But soon, perhaps ere one short day has passed away, some temptation is presented suited to my corrupt inclinations; and, catching the bait, I grovel again in the dust, and give up my soul to the pursuit of trifles. Whence arises this inconsistency? Can I dare to hope that I know anything savingly while I am the subject of it? It is certainly very discouraging, and at times I quite conclude my hopes have been all a delusion; but there is a something whispers, Would the Lord have shown me these things if He had meant to destroy me? I think not, and must still hope, even against hope. I do think the cause of my giving way to temptation, and bringing so much guilt and distress upon my soul, is my not looking sufficiently out of myself; for when I am in some measure restored from my distress, and favored with a more comfortable and spiritual frame of mind, I immediately hope all is right, and think I shall never fall again: but, alas, I soon, very soon prove that my own strength is *perfect* weakness. Blessed and divine Spirit, be pleased to enlighten my dark understanding! What I know not, teach Thou me! I am weak and ignorant, be my Teacher and Supporter! Grant me copious outpourings of thy sacred influences! Take of the things of Jesus, and show them to me, and enable me to be constantly going out of self, and looking to Him who is the Author and Finisher of faith!

> [Reader, here appears to be the first dawning of that great and glorious light in which she afterwards so sweetly rejoiced.]

November 22nd — Within the last day or two our dear kind pastor has called upon us, purposely to converse with me on becoming a communicant at the Lord's table, which he very much wishes me to do. It is a subject upon which I have not allowed myself to think, always concluding, without hesitation, that I was not a proper character. I have stated my objections to Mr. S., but he does not think them sufficient reasons, and still urges me to come forward; he thinks it a very refreshing, strengthening ordinance, and that it is our duty to avow publicly our attachment to the cause of Christ, and devote ourselves openly to Him. I feel no hesitation on this part of the subject, but think I could declare myself on the Lord's side before an assembled world, were I *sure* I had experienced a change of heart, and was under the influence of the Holy Spirit. May my fears be dissipated, and my doubts banished by the Lord Himself! And, oh, that I may be enabled to devote myself to Him wholly and unreservedly, and be determined through His grace to forsake all false refuges, and cleave to Him alone. Amen.

November 30th — Yesterday attended sacrament, as a spectator. Felt my mind in some degree impressed with divine things, but did not enjoy that clear view of the loveliness and all-sufficiency of Jesus which I long for. I see clearly the guilt and depravity of my nature and practice, and at times am almost overwhelmed with the sense of my grievous heart-backslidings, but am not at present favored with a faith's view of the precious Savior. I cannot say "My beloved is mine and I am His"; and, though I acknowledge Him to be the "chiefest among ten thousand and the altogether lovely," my heart is not so attracted and won by His charms as I wish. Ah, no, the world occupies too much of my affections, and often, alas, excludes the Redeemer from my thoughts. When shall the day dawn and the shadows flee away? When will the Sun of Righteousness arise and dissipate, by His refulgent beams, the thick mists of unbelief and carnality which envelop my grovelling soul? Hasten, dearest Lord, the happy time! I do long to give myself entirely to Thee. Enable me to do so, and accept the worthless offering.

December 6th — I am still undecided as to whether I should immediately make a public profession of my faith in Christ. I feel more desirous of doing so than at any former part of my life; but am very fearful of rushing unbidden to the feast of the Lord. I consulted a friend last week, whose opinion I much value; she quite advised me to do it, and thought I should consider Mr. S.'s invitation as a voice from God. Could I once be quite sure that this was the case, I should not hesitate a moment, but cheerfully obey the divine mandate. May I be more importunate and constant in prayer, and at length be enabled plainly to discover the mind of the Lord! I have to complain of much languor and unprofitableness in heavenly things. Oh, that the gracious Spirit of truth would descend and kindle in my cold heart a flame of love divine! Would that things temporal might no more so absorb my thoughts; but all my affections and desires be swallowed up in contemplating my glorious Redeemer.

> "Prone to wander, Lord, I feel it,
> Prone to leave the God I love;
> Here's my heart, oh, take and seal it—
> Seal it for thy courts above."

1830

January 3rd — Through the kind providence of God, I am brought safely to the commencement of another year. Numberless temporal mercies have attended me through the past, and I trust also I have been favored with some spiritual refreshments. I desire to raise a fresh "Ebenezer" to the goodness of the Lord, and long for faith to trust in Him more unreservedly: but, alas, how painful is the retrospect of the past year as regards myself, and how much cause have I for *deep* humiliation and self-abasement. Often have my feet wandered from the right way, and often have I hewed out to myself broken cisterns which could hold no water; but I humbly hope the Lord has not left me entirely to my own ways, and that He will enable me to be more completely devoted during the remainder of my pilgrimage; for, notwithstanding my frequent backslidings and wanderings of heart, it is my chief desire to be His alone. Be pleased, dear Lord, to grant me during the present year more of Thy gracious presence, more tenderness of conscience and fear of offending Thee; more humility, stronger faith, and more entire devotedness to Thy cause. Enable me to leave my temporal concerns entirely with Thee, to walk by faith, to have my treasure in heaven, and to manifest by my conduct that I am Thy disciple. Let me not grow cold or lukewarm, but may "I lay aside *every weight* and *the sin* which doth so easily beset [me], and [may I] run with patience the race set before [me], looking unto Jesus. Amen."

January 30th — I have to-day, for the first time, commemorated the dying love of our dear Savior, at His own table; but have not had that comfort and enjoyment of His presence which I hoped for. I am, in consequence, very, very much cast down. I do desire to wait patiently the Lord's time, and trust in His mercy, but I seem, instead of getting nearer to Him, to be further off; it is, indeed, a bitter cup; but, if I could know the Lord had a favor to me, and was leading me by the right way to a city of habitation, I think I could bear it. It is the fear, that for my very great and terrible sins and backslidings, He has cast me off, that makes my burden so heavy. Oh, where shall I go for peace? Jesus alone can be the source of true peace, but I have not faith to behold Him. Precious Savior, look upon my distress, and support me; grant me patience and faith, and in Thine own time, oh, do mercifully bring me into the liberty of the gospel. It is dark night, indeed, and I have neither sun nor stars.

> [It is clear, from her soul-pantings, that she knew *where* she was, as personally struggling with sin and corruption; and *what* she wanted—namely, a *realizing sense* of the pardon of sin—of the Lord Christ saying unto her personally, "I am *thy* salvation."]

February 24th, Thursday — I trust, during part of this week, I have had a little foretaste of that comfort the Lord bestows upon His own people. On Monday evening I suddenly felt a sort of impulse and desire to look to Christ for deliverance from sin; and it was in a way I never experienced before. I was convinced that the impression proceeded from something independent of myself, and therefore hoped, that in following its dictates, I should receive strength to withstand temptation. The result proved it to be so, and I afterwards enjoyed serenity of mind, to which I am usually a stranger. I cannot be sufficiently thankful for this gleam of comfort, and I am inspired with a strong hope, that it is but the pledge of a more full manifestation in the Lord's own time. Yes, I do hope, unworthy and vile as I am, that I shall one day say, with sweet appropriation, "My beloved is mine, and I am his." How I long for the glorious period! I expect next Sabbath to approach the table of the Lord; perhaps He will then graciously *shine away my fears,* and grant me a glimpse of His lovely countenance. Oh, that it might be so, but if not, I hope resignation will be given, and I be kept waiting, longing, and praying. "Come, Lord Jesus, come quickly"; to the rejoicing of my soul.

May 2nd — I have been much distressed for some days with the fear that I am only a hypocrite in Zion. I seem to make no progress in the divine life; and, indeed, have much reason to fear that I am only a cumberer of the ground. May the Lord search and try me; and, whatever it may cost, make me alive and lively in His service. I long to be more devoted to Him, but cannot attain to it.

May 9th, Sabbath Evening — A day of guilt and uneasiness has this been to me. In vain do I attend the ordinances of the Lord's house, and in vain hear the delightful sermons of our valued pastor, if Jesus hide His face, and leave me to my own heart. Oh, when shall the day dawn and the shadows flee away? When shall I be made fruitful in Zion, and be enabled to live entirely to the glory of the Lord? I long for the joyful period, and have many, many fears that it will never arrive, but that I shall prove a self-deceiver—may the Lord forbid!

May 16th — After service, I was much surprised by a young person asking me whether I should object to become a Sunday School teacher, as they were much in want of them. Of course I could not decide immediately, but said I would think of it. I have named it to my mother, who will not be an obstacle in the way, if I think it my duty. I have lately thought much of my inactivity in the Lord's vineyard, and wished to be more useful. An opportunity now presents itself, and shall I—can I—refuse? I think not. Perhaps it was the Lord Himself who excited the desire, and who has now shown me how I may, in some little measure, promote the interest of His cause upon earth. If so, may He incline my heart to the work. I wish to be as clay in the hand of the potter. While thinking on the subject, these words occurred with some weight: "Why stand ye here idle all the day?" "Because no man hath hired me, Lord." "Go work in my vineyard." May I have direction from above! I feel myself very incompetent and unfit for the engagement, but know that the Lord can make use of the meanest instruments. "Guide me, O Thou great Jehovah!"

June 7th, Sabbath — I entered last Sabbath on my new engagement of instructing the young, and felt, on entering the school, most distressingly agitated, partly from an overwhelming sense of my unfitness for the work, and partly from the natural timidity of my disposition, most of the teachers being strangers to me. The Lord, however, mercifully supported me; and I think, when more initiated into the rules, I shall feel much pleasure in the work. Oh, that my mind might be enlightened from above, and my humble instrumentalities made use of, to promote the Lord's glory, and the good of His church!

July 6th — I have this day attained my 25th year. Through many difficulties and dangers the Lord has brought me. His hand has been ever over me for good, and hitherto by His help I am come. Here, then, I would review the mercies of the past year—erect an "Ebenezer" to His goodness—and, with lively gratitude and increasing faith, gird up my loins and go forward. Since my last natal-day I have solemnly given myself to the Lord and to His church, and also entered upon the responsible duties of Sabbath School teacher. How ought these additional obligations and privileges to weigh upon my mind, increase my seriousness and desire to be wholly the Lord's! But, alas, as dear Mrs. Graham says, "backslider is still my name"—still I am prone to slight my best Friend. I would, Lord, leave my body and temporal circumstances in Thy hands, nor wish to dictate in the smallest particular; but for soul prosperity, I desire to beg hard for the Holy Spirit to quicken and invigorate. May a spirit of fervent and earnest supplication be poured out upon me, and may I be brought much nearer to the blessed Jesus!

August 27th — I had this morning a most delightful and refreshing season. My soul was sweetly led out in prayer, and I clearly saw my interest in a precious Jesus. Oh, how precious was He then to my soul, and how amazing did it appear, that one so vile and worthless should be interested in His love—never, I think, did I enjoy so much, and here I would set up an "Ebenezer" for the same. Dear, dear Savior, repeat the visit so divine! This glimpse of Thy favor only makes me long for a greater manifestation.

September 5th — I have this week been favored with a more abundant manifestation of the Lord's love to my soul than I ever before experienced: my heart has been sweetly led out in prayer while sitting plying my needle; and I have had such delightful witnessings of the Spirit, that I could not doubt my interest in a Savior's love. Amazing that such a vile sinner should be a chosen vessel of mercy! I stand astonished, and can hardly believe the delightful fact, and yet I have had such clear intimations, that I dare not dispute it. Oh, how sweet to have a foretaste of the joys above; a smile from Jesus and whisper of His grace! How insignificant then is the world with its pleasures and honors! May it ever appear to me as it has done during some part of the last week. Ten thousand thanks to Thee, dear Lord, for Thine amazing goodness. Oh, may I be watchful and prayerful, and very fearful of grieving Thy Holy Spirit; do continue Thy favor—what I have tasted makes me long for more; and I hope it is only the earnest of what is in store for me, for I do desire to live near Thee, and have much of heaven on earth; grant this, dearest Jesus, for Thy mercy's sake!—"Ebenezer."

November 21st — While thinking this afternoon of some friends who have been running eagerly from one place to another after a celebrated, and, I suppose, most interesting preacher, this idea forcibly struck me—why manifest such undue anxiety after *streams*, when we have the *Fountain* always accessible? I can, in my humble cottage, approach the footstool of the Father of mercies, and enjoy the manifestation of His love.

1831

January 10th, Monday — I am at this time much perplexed on the subject of family prayer. Since the death of my beloved father, it has been quite neglected, which has long been to me a source of regret; but I cannot decide whether it is my duty to propose it, and engage in so important a service. The Lord alone can give me courage for it, and till I am convinced that it would be in accordance with His heavenly will, I dare not attempt it. May He decide the doubtful case, and cause clear light to shine upon the path of duty, which at present appears enveloped in thick darkness.

May 17th — My mind is this morning much depressed; I do not attain to that *establishment* in the faith which I long for, and two very pious friends have informed me that they think I do not seek it sufficiently, and that I refuse consolation, and cast comfort from me. Surely, did they know the conflict I endure, and the anguish which frequently oppresses my afflicted bosom, they would not think I should refuse that comfort which alone can hush the storm into a calm. I think those who are enjoying full assurance cannot enter into the feelings of trembling, tempest-tossed souls like mine: if, however, I have been guilty on this point, may the Lord convince me of it, and make the reproof very profitable, though it has painfully wounded my comfortless heart.

July 18th — I have just had to endure a severe mortification. The day before yesterday I entreated the Lord to send mortification and disappointment, if He saw it for my spiritual good; but, alas, I find it is easier to *talk* about than to *bear*. The flesh is as rebellious as ever, and would fain persuade me that such contrary things can never work for my good. Shall I then withdraw my plea, and supplicate for ease? Ah, no, but rather that my rebellion may be forgiven, and patience granted to suffer all the Lord's will, and consider all these trials but light and momentary, looking not at *them*, but at the eternal and exceeding weight of *glory* which is in reversion.

1832

January 1st, Sabbath — "Here I raise my Ebenezer." Thus far the Lord has brought me. Though the past has been a year of multiplied transgressions and backslidings, I trust, through His abundant mercy, my face is still Zionward, and that my prevailing desire is to be devoted entirely to His service. Take me, dearest Lord, and form me for Thine own glory. I feel much bodily weakness, and writing seems more laborious than I ever knew it. Oh, that through the crevices of this frail tabernacle, I may see some of the glories of the eternal world!

March 4th — I am like a mariner on a tempestuous ocean, without any haven to think of; or a traveller in a dreary wilderness, without any home to anticipate at the end of it, having no assurance that I am in the way to the home of believers. Dark, dark is the night, but, if an eternal day dawn at the end of it, it will be worth a *life* of darkness here below.

May 10th — "He [Satan] goeth about like a roaring lion," and last night he seemed to have permission to worry my poor soul almost to death. I was very weak and ill in body, and the agony of my mind was indescribable. It seemed to me my hope was quite cut off, and I must perish for ever. I lay weeping most bitterly, nor could I obtain any gleam of comfort. It was indeed passing through the fire. May the Lord bring spiritual good out of the gloom and horror which so frequently surround me, for they cannot be without His permission. I feel this morning very poorly, and have still to mourn the absence of Him whom I *desire* to love above all created objects. Come, precious Jesus, chase away these thick clouds, and let me behold Thy lovely countenance, and be so captivated with Thy charms, that I may never more give my heart to earthly objects.

May 11th —

> "In darkest shades, if Thou appear,
>   My dawning is begun;
> Thou art my soul's sweet morning Star,
>   And Thou my rising Sun."

During the past night I have again been called to suffer much bodily affliction and very severe pain, but was favored with such sweet comfort from my precious Savior that it seemed light; nay, methought I could willingly bear a *life* of such suffering, if I might constantly enjoy His presence. Oh, how delightful was the hope of an eternity of glory, and how sweet the thought that when life's journey was ended, the veil would be drawn aside, and no cloud ever again intervene to hide from my soul, even for one moment, the lovely countenance of my adorable Jesus. Ten thousand thanks to Thee, dearest Savior, for this manifestation—continue to be gracious! I long for more tokens of Thy love, and thirst for more constant communion with Thee. Be pleased to preserve me from resting in my feelings. Such is my frailty, that I am ever prone to sin. Oh, lead me to see that darkness and light are both alike with Thee; and, that though Thou dost hide Thyself, Thy love is unchangeable, and, "Thou wilt perfect that which concerneth me."

May 28th — A friend this morning reminded me of the following sentiment of Legh Richmond's: "Never impute a bad motive to a person, if you can find a good one." May I not only remember it, but act in accordance therewith.

June 2nd — Very weak and languid in body. I know not how it will terminate.

June 23rd — My bodily health much improved yesterday and to-day.

July 6th — Again the Lord has brought me to the morning of my birthday, and through the past year has followed me with lovingkindness and tender mercies; for, though I have been visited with bereaving strokes and personal affliction, I believe it is all in covenant love; and, during my own illness, I have enjoyed more spiritual comfort and calmness of mind than I have known before. The Lord make me grateful, and, as He is about to restore my health, oh, that I may be devoted to His service, and live more constantly sensible of my weakness and dependence upon Him!

August 13th, Monday — Through the kind protection of my heavenly Father I arrived safely at Normanton, the day before yesterday. I was much fatigued, and still feel very poorly, much more so than before I left home; but I am favored with more calmness and serenity than I have lately known. I hope, while enjoying this secluded retreat from the world and its bustle, to be favored with the presence of my Savior, and cheered with the whispers of His love. May my visit be a profitable one! Oh, divine and almighty Spirit, be pleased to descend and exercise me in spiritual things; open the sacred Scriptures to my understanding; take of the things of Jesus, and reveal them to my soul: and grant, oh, grant, that while in retirement I may have delightful foretastes of the joys above, and ravishing views of the glory of the celestial world! Hast Thou not said unto me since I left home, "According to thy faith be it unto thee"? I must reply, "Lord, increase my faith."

> [The reader will observe, not merely the simplicity, but the earnestness, with which the beloved Ruth pleads with the Lord. She ventures to remind Him of His promise, and to entreat for its fulfillment, and such is in perfect accordance with the Lord's mind and will, for He says, "Put me in remembrance; let us plead together." Reader, be it yours, in common with Ruth, thus to plead; be assured that every wrestling Jacob shall, in due time, become a prevailing Israel.]

September 4th — I have the last few days been very uneasy about my dear mother, understanding that that dreadful disease, the cholera, is proving very fatal in Nottingham. I long to be at home, and I trust the Lord will bring me there in peace and safety. Oh, for stronger faith! I am never so happy as when I can give all my concerns into the Lord's hands. May I be humbled and penitent on account of the sins, the aggravated sins, of our country, which are bringing upon us the signal chastisements of the Almighty. Oh, that the people may learn righteousness, and turn to the Lord with weeping, fasting, and supplication; but, alas, at present His voice is disregarded. I desire to be among the number of those who sigh and cry for the abominations committed. Surely, surely, if ever we had cause to be spiritually minded, and to be upon our watch-tower, it is now. Almighty Spirit, be pleased to vouchsafe Thy powerful influences; solemnize my mind, and enable me to live every day as if my last!

September 10th — Bless the Lord, O my soul, for His lovingkindness and tender mercy to one so unworthy! He has in His abundant goodness brought me in safety to my own dear home, and restored me to my friends, in peace. Oh, that He would, as He has heard the voice of my supplication, and been better to me than all my fears, now enable me to give to Him my whole heart as a sacrifice of praise and thanksgiving, graciously accepting the same, and forming it entirely for His own glory! Do, dearest Savior, be pleased to make me live to Thee alone, and vouchsafe much of Thy delightful presence.

1833

January 18th — My health is very much declining again. I endeavor to say as little about it as I can, not wishing to grieve my dearest mother; but I begin to think there must be something seriously wrong. Temporal circumstances are dark and trying, and my soul much distressed; the conflicts of the last week have been very severe; storm, tempest, and horrible darkness have been my experience. And why? Because for some time I have been walking at a distance from my Lord, grown remiss in private duty, and at length indulged in one of my besetting heart-sins, thereby giving Satan an advantage; and when I would have roused myself, he let me know that I had opened the door of my heart to him, and it was out of *my* power to close it against him; for, when I strived to humble myself before the Lord, confessing my sins, and longing to forsake them, he presents temptations to my soul with such power that I am thrown into confusion, and sometimes know not whether I have yielded or not, being only able to say, "Jesus, save, Jesus, save," over and over again, as quickly as I can repeat the words in my mind, the temptation passing through it at the same time with equal rapidity; and I afterwards feel all the guilt and distress of having taken part with the tempter, though I am sure I do not intend to do so. I am indeed in a woeful state, and the Lord hideth Himself from me; but it is most just, and I do not suffer a thousandth part of what I deserve. Whenever I am inclined to yield to my sinful inclinations, may I read

Diary entries for 1833

this, and remember the bitterness of the draught, and take warning; and oh, may the Lord in mercy condescend to look upon my sore distress; sprinkle my conscience with cleansing blood; seal home a sense of forgiving love upon my soul; and enable me to walk humbly before Him the residue of my days, fearing nothing so much as His frown.

February 23rd, Sabbath — I have for sometime been walking in darkness, but last Sabbath eve was much relieved. We received a letter from Birmingham, containing a disappointment with regard to money matters; instead, however, of depressing me, comfort seemed to flow into my soul. The Lord's ways towards me are wonderful indeed; the past week my mind has been somewhat calm, but not rejoicing.

May 10th — I have suffered more from extreme weakness the last week than at any former period of my life; and Satan, my cruel enemy, has taken the advantage of it during the night. When unable to sleep, I have been almost in the "belly of hell"; and my mind at times so confused by temptation, that I have not been able for a season even to *cry* for relief. The Lord has, however, in mercy partly restored my health, and delivered me from the violent assaults of the enemy. I have been much blessed in reading an old book ("The Life of Elizabeth Cairns," written 1752), at which I have often before looked, but never thought it interesting—the set time for me to enjoy it was not come.

August 4th — Temporal things appear dark and distressing. During the past week my mind has been much exercised about my present employment, not knowing whether I am in the path of duty, or whether I ought not to seek a more lucrative one. May the Lord direct me! For myself, I do not desire great things, and shrink exceedingly from the idea of entering more into the world; quiet and retirement I much prize, but I wish to follow the leadings of Providence. May the present darkness be removed from my mind, and my way made clear. I have at this time nothing at all to do; but the Lord has done wonders for me, and I would not distrust. Spiritual things are at a low ebb with me. I am reading Dr. Owen, on "The Glory of Christ"; he is an author I much value; his writings are very searching; I find I have been too anxious about worldly things for some time past, to the neglect of spiritual duties, and in consequence have to cry, "My leanness, my leanness!" May the Lord restore me; it is *He* alone that *can* bring me with weeping and supplication to His footstool. Alas, alas, how little reason have I to hope that I am a Christian indeed! "Oh, for a closer walk with God!"

August 12th — Again favored with employment, for which I desire to be thankful, and take it as a token that I am in the right path of duty; but, if not, may the Lord convince me of my mistake, and lead me in the way He would have me go. My heart is hard and unfeeling; Lord, revive me; I long to walk *cheerfully* in Thy ways, enjoy daily communion with Thee, and bring forth fruit to Thy glory; but begin to think I never shall, until I am more dead to the world. I believe the indulgence of a carnal spirit is the bane of my happiness. Divine and almighty Spirit, condescend to deal with my poor dead soul; enable me to crucify the flesh, deny self, forsake the world, and be spiritually minded—

> "I would not always live
> At this poor dying rate."

August 14th — My feelings are most tried; last evening my dearest mother was so poorly, that she was obliged to come out of chapel. Oh, how is my heart agonized at the very thought of losing her, and the slightest indisposition which attacks her occasions me the severest distress; thanks to the Lord, she is much better this morning. "Bless the Lord, O my soul." I know not what is in the womb of Providence, whether my dearest parent or myself will first be called away; but, from my present feelings, I should think I could not endure the anguish of losing her. I know "with God all things are possible." May He bestow upon me a submissive spirit; and, if it be His will, long spare my dearest mother.

September 1st — Feel much darkness and ignorance in my mind respecting the life of *faith*. I fear mine is a life of *sense*. May the Holy Spirit condescend to instruct me on this important subject, and may the life I henceforth live in the flesh be by the faith of the Son of God. I am longing for a revival, but feel much deadness, and not that spirit of prayer I wish. I have again this week written to my friend, and pressed eternal things upon her notice. May the Lord bless the message! My soul yearns over her, and often do I mourn over her condition, for she is evidently given up to fashion and worldly pursuits and pleasure. "Oh, that [she] might live before Thee!"

September 8th, Evening — Dark and distressed indeed. Surely, I am one of those who are ever learning, but never coming to the knowledge of the truth. In reading Dr. Owen, on the "Glory of Christ," I am led to fear that my profession is hypocritical. I do not find that beholding of Christ by faith which he describes, nor that longing to depart, that I may fully behold it. Oh, that the Lord may show me my real state, and not suffer me to deceive myself or others. I am at this time truly wretched. My heart is cold and carnal; my thoughts trifling; and I cannot pour out my complaint before a throne of grace. I chatter like a crane or a swallow. I am at *home* in the body, and *absent* from the Lord. Oh, that I may have some word this evening suited to my case, for I am in a miserable condition, and deserve, *richly* deserve, the lowest hell for my abominable ingratitude and sin.

October 15th — No tidings from Birmingham; perhaps we shall be disappointed in both the legacies which have been left us, and obtain neither of them. May we have grace to say and *feel*, "Thy will be done." My mind is deeply exercised and much distressed. I find it very difficult to rise above temporal things; nay, it is impossible in my own strength. Lord, vouchsafe me Thy grace, and enable me to view things in the light of eternity, and to feel myself a stranger here. I am sure I have been making myself too much at home in the body; and, whatever disappointment may await me, it will be all in justice; and, if it is sanctified, I shall have reason to rejoice. We are mistaken in thinking that our happiness in any measure depends on outward circumstances: I know from experience, that, when favored with the light of the Lord's countenance, and enjoying His smile, I can be happy in the midst of trials and afflictions. Why, then, so much anxiety about temporal, and so little about spiritual prosperity? Pardon me, dear Lord, and enable me (as dear Mary Jane Graham says) to put a blank into thy hands regarding outward things, for Thee to fill up as Thou pleasest. I did profess and desire to do it some years ago, and petitioned that I might have decision and prosperity in spiritual things. I would now "renew my blank," and so do, Lord, as seemeth Thee good; but, ah, I find another principle crying, Give, give temporal ease and comfort. Oh, of what conflicts am I the subject, so that I cannot do or think the things I would. Lord, strengthen the new man in me, and subdue the old; and, in Thine own time, shine in upon my soul; till then, give patience and a praying spirit.

October 18th — My dearest mother very poorly; my mind is much distressed on her account. May the Lord in mercy restore her. He has been very gracious in sparing her so long. I think it has been in answer to prayer. I wish to feel grateful.

October 19th — Family prayer re-established last night.

October 22nd — My dearest mother is still poorly. May the Lord restore her, and in mercy sanctify the present dispensations of His providence, which appear very dark. Oh, how has my poor mind been tempest-tossed and agonized lately. I feel a little more calm, and am more anxious to have trials *sanctified* than *removed*. This is a desert land, but I have been expecting to find it a place of ease and rest, forgetting "In the world ye *shall* have tribulation."

November 29th — I have found much profit this evening in perusing my memoranda, written July 19 and 26, 1829, relative to the cross. Indeed, what I have written has proved so particularly useful afterwards on different occasions, that I am encouraged to proceed, though often disposed to give it up, and burn what is penned, fearing I have been actuated by wrong motives. I have hard fighting just now; the corruptions of my nature are very headstrong. May I be kept from laying down arms, to which I feel sinfully inclined; yea, even to make a truce with my deadliest foe, and that which formerly robbed me of my peace. The Lord have mercy on me, for I feel that, of myself, I can do nothing but sin.

December 30th — Uncle W— is much worse, apparently dying—quite insensible. I hope it will be a glorious change when he leaves the body. My dear mother had an accident on Thursday, but I hope, though her foot is much bruised, it will not be very serious. May the Lord support us, and sanctify all dispensations.

Afternoon — I have shut myself up, that I may not hear my poor uncle, who is struggling and gasping for breath. May the Lord in mercy ease him, though, as he is insensible, I suppose he may not be conscious of suffering; but, ah, we know not what dying is. My mind is much solemnized. I do not doubt his safety, and think him enviable. He is just on the threshold of Heaven. There may we meet — *A quarter to Four:* My dear uncle has just departed.

> "In vain my fancy strives to paint
> The moment after death."

1834

January 19th — The conclusion of the last year and commencement of this have been marked by trial and anxiety. May the Lord sanctify it. I am ashamed to acknowledge backslider is still my name, but past mercies encourage me to hope the Lord will again restore my soul. I expect to go to Birmingham with my beloved mother to-morrow. The Lord protect us, and our habitation, while absent from it, and grant us that degree of prosperity which will be most for our spiritual interest and His glory, and bring us home in peace and safety. My mind is somewhat depressed. "Lord, increase my faith."

February 2nd — When I view the mercies received during the last fortnight, I am lost in wonder, and wish to have my heart melted with gratitude. We have been taken to Birmingham, and brought back in safety. Our habitation has been preserved in peace during our absence. We have been treated with much kindness by those with whom we sojourned. My dear mother has been wonderfully supported under a considerable degree of anxiety and fatigue, and we have obtained payment of the legacies left us by my uncle J—, which will add considerably to our temporal comforts; and I trust my beloved mother will have more rest and ease than formerly. Oh, may the Lord fill our hearts with gratitude, and add His blessing to what He has given, for without this I should tremble at the possession of it. Dearest Lord, grant us grace to live to Thy glory, to "set [our] affection on things above, not on things on the earth"; and grant us much communion with Thee, conformity to Thee, and enjoyment in thy ways and worship. I am now ashamed of my former distrust. "Ebenezer."

March 16th — I have had a season of temporal bustle, and, alas, of much spiritual deadness. The Lord revive me! I have heard the Word preached with very little profit since we came from Birmingham. I do not wish to condemn the preaching; I fear the cares of this world have had a bad influence on my soul. During the last day or two, I have suffered fearfully from the old temptation, in another form; the Lord preserve me from yielding! But alas, I did yield in the first instance. I tampered with temptation; gave the reins to my inventive and sinful imagination; and then, when I would have retraced my steps, that which had been imaginary was partly realized; and what I am indulged in fancy and for amusement, became, through coincident circumstances, the constant and tormenting inmate of my breast, showing me the danger of being off my watch-tower. May the Lord pardon and deliver me from the temptation, and say to the storm, "Peace, be still." I know He can, and do believe He will. Mr. B—'s text this morning, was, "The heart knoweth his own bitterness," &c.; very suitable to me. My sin, and its punishment, being both mental, no creature knows; but the eye of my heavenly Father is upon me, and I hope, by making my sin its own punishment, He is teaching me a valuable lesson, and will bring glory to His own name, and humble me in the dust. His ways are mysterious, and He brings good out of evil.

March 23rd, Sabbath — Much calmness of mind, morning and afternoon, but dreadfully tempted and distressed this evening; the billows have, indeed, gone over my soul, and the proud waves wellnigh overwhelmed me. May the Lord deliver, specially support me, and, above all, preserve me from yielding to temptation.

March 29th — My mind mercifully relieved of its burden; may my heart be filled with gratitude, and my tongue with praise.

April 20th — May the Lord direct my path, and enable me to bow in silence when He says, Resign! He only knows the feelings which agitate my bosom, and, I believe, He will not be an unconcerned Spectator. May I commit all to Him in faith, and wait with patience the development of His will.

August 3rd, Sabbath — Much depressed. Behold, I am vile and full of sin and unbelief. I cast my helpless soul on Jesus for life and salvation, but do not feel that confidence of my safety which I desire, seeing He has said, "Whosoever believeth on him shall not be ashamed." I do believe; Lord, help against my unbelief, and enable me to receive the testimony of Thy Word, without looking at *feelings*. I want to realize that darkness and light are alike with Thee, and to believe Thou *lovest* me, even when Thou *hidest* Thy face.

Evening — While mourning over my barrenness, it has just struck me, that I am thinking more of *fruit* than of *Jesus Himself*; that I want to bring forth *fruit* to rejoice in, instead of glorifying in *Christ alone;* and that Habakkuk 3:17, 18, may apply—viz., When quite barren in ourselves, we will rejoice. If this is a right view, the Lord strengthen me in it.

> [Those who know the plague of their own hearts are deeply conscious of the absolute necessity of the "line upon line, precept upon precept" ordeal. It is

this, and this alone, under God, produces the rooting, the grounding, and settling in the truth. In the foregoing sentence, is, as it were, the first budding forth of that sweet germ of grace, which afterwards so beautifully and conspicuously shone in this plant of the Lord's right-hand planting. None, perhaps, were ever more clearly shown the distinction between *root* and *fruit*, than the deeply-taught, and subsequently highly-privileged, Ruth Bryan. During the perusal of the Diary, we would have the reader keep this prominently before him, as it is evident the deep exercises of her heart were all, in the issue, to tend this way; leading to a humbling of the creature, and to the setting of the crown upon the right head; Jesus, at length, being so sweetly her all-engrossing theme.]

August 4th — Favored with a wonderful manifestation of the love and grace of Jesus last night, after service; my soul was, indeed, filled with rapturous delight. What condescension! May I be thankful, and bless His name.

August 13th — Darkness has veiled my mind; my Savior has withdrawn, and my soul is mourning His absence. Nothing on earth can fill the vacuum in my soul, nor do I wish it should; but long, though in the dark, to hold fast my confidence; to this I do not attain: my heart is timorous and fearful, lest all should not be well at last. "Lord, increase my faith."

August 14th — My dear mother rather poorly yesterday, but better this morning. She was taken this afternoon with sudden and violent pain, which has much alarmed me; the Lord grant restoring mercy, and prepare us both for the whole of His will. How does my heart tremble at the thought of losing my beloved parent. Lord Jesus, increase my faith; let me recognize Thy hand, and say, "Thy will be done." Precious Savior, make me less fleshly, and more spiritual; restore, if it please Thee, restore my dearest mother.

August 19th — I awoke last night with a violent fit of coughing; my breath quite went, and had not the Lord granted relief, I must in a few seconds have been in eternity. I felt afterwards much agitated, and could not realize that my soul would have been safe, had the veil of mortality been drawn aside. Precious Jesus, leave me not in uncertainty. Come and show me my real situation, strengthen my weak nerves and weak faith. Thou mayest call me suddenly into Thy presence; but, whatever may be the messenger, oh, meet me on the banks of Jordan, and then I shall not fear the swelling tide. Absent not Thyself, precious Savior, when my heart and flesh fail, and the world is receding from my view. Oh, *then* come, come to be the strength of my heart, and my portion for ever. Thanks to Thy name, O Lord, for sparing mercy; write gratitude upon my heart for Thy distinguishing favors.

August 28th — I trust the Lord is doing "great things for me, whereof I am glad"—viz., bringing me now into the liberty of the gospel, and showing me more of its simplicity. The Word says, "He that believeth shall be saved." I *do* believe in the dear Lord Jesus. I cast my naked, helpless soul on Him for salvation; He is my only hope and refuge, and will He send me empty away? No; He is a tried stone, a sure foundation, and I believe (not without intervals of doubt) that He will get glory to His great name by saving me, vile, abominable, hell-deserving me! Thanks and praise to Thee, adorable, precious Savior, for this hope; however weak my faith, let me trust Thee implicitly, love Thee supremely, and be with Thee eternally.

October 28th, Sacrament Sabbath — Not favored with enjoyment under the Word preached, but enabled at the Lord's table to lay hold, as it were, of the Lord Christ, and with importunity to cry to Him, and, though He seemed to hide Himself from me, and appear to deny my request, still I was kept pleading, and did He not Himself enable me to do so? Yes; and I bless Him for it. I am resting upon the promise, "Him that cometh to me, I will in no wise cast out," but not favored with a sensible manifestation of my interest, yet believing, vile, abominable, and guilty as I am, I shall never perish; because I am enabled to cast my soul upon Christ for salvation, and to believe He will never suffer a soul to perish at His feet. I long to hear Him say, "I have loved *thee* with an everlasting love."

November 30th — Much blessed in reading a letter from the Rev. Ralph Erskine to a Mr. Fisher, in which he plainly shows the difference between *faith* and *feeling*. How often do I stumble here.

> [It was this most important distinction our departed sister was to learn by her protracted exercises; and as the reader proceeds with her memoranda, he will perceive how blessedly the Lord brought out His servant in her clear definition of faith and feeling.]

December 25th — My Savior hides His face, and I am troubled, and my mind dark and distressed. Heard Mr. S— this morning, a very spiritual and simple discourse: I trust I have been profited, but want a fresh manifestation of my Redeemer's love. I desire to bear patiently the chastisement of the Lord, because I have sinned against Him, but I cannot be *satisfied* with His absence. "Return, O Lord, how long?"

1835

January 1st — To-day the outward cross is very heavy, and, with Jacob, we feel as if all these things were against us; our temporal circumstances are very adverse, but "it is well." I feel so much dross that I need *hot fire*—dear Jesus, sit by as the Refiner, then it will not be *too hot*. I believe Thou dost (though to me generally unseen) give patience, and enable us to journey on, anticipating rest above, not expecting it here.

January 14th — The Lord knows how to put a nail in the right place in the process of flesh crucifixion, viz., through some carnal affection that is growing too strong; it will be inexpressibly painful to the flesh, but it is possible for the spirit to bow in submission, and see that it is in answer to prayer while the flesh is struggling and suffering.

February 23rd — Lord, appear for us, keep us from our own spirit, and direct us by Thine; can it be so, that in this large town we are in the midst of churches and chapels, and yet nowhere can we hear profitably? If it is from a captious, critical spirit, condescend, Lord, to convince us of it, and humble us for it; but if, as we think, the preaching is not sufficiently in the simplicity of the gospel, and unaccompanied by the demonstration of the Spirit, condescend to hasten the dawn of a brighter day;

and, in the meantime, favor us with the spirit of fervent supplication on this behalf.

April 17th — I can say with David, "it is good for me that I have been afflicted," and I desire to record the faithfulness of my God with thanksgiving, for He has been mindful of my low estate, and visited me with His reviving mercy. "Bless the Lord, O my soul"; trust Him evermore; walk in His strength; be willing to be nothing, that Christ may be all in all; and *then* wilt thou find settled peace; but, oh, this being *nothing*, we take much discipline to bring us to it in reality; much emptying from vessel to vessel, much afflicting, much purging. How much have I had, and yet how *self* rises; and how do I seek something to glory in, or lean upon, beside Christ. Dear Jesus, bring me more and more into the simplicity of the gospel, and let me lean more and more upon Thee.

May 4th — I cannot describe the experiences of my mind; surely none of the Lord's people feel as I do. The greatness of Jehovah and my own insignificance contrasted, overwhelm me; and yet to Him alone, through Christ Jesus, can I go; I have no other refuge. "Out of the depths do I cry unto thee, O Lord." "Bring my soul out of prison, that I may praise thy name." But still enable me patiently to endure temptations, and the hidings of Thy face, because I have sinned against Thee.

May 6th — My mind is relieved of its heavy burden by reading this evening 1 Corinthians 1:18 to the end, from which I was led blessedly to see that Christ crucified was, indeed, the power and wisdom of God to them which believe. The preaching of the cross is to them which perish foolishness. How clear it is, that natural wisdom cannot understand the things of God; and wherever it exalts itself in the mind, it brings darkness, confusion, and distress. "Bless the Lord, O my soul," for light again shining on my path.

May 10th, Sabbath — "Bless the Lord, O my soul," for a throne of grace, and for the access with which thou hast been favored to approach it this afternoon. Sweet indeed are the moments when enabled by the Eternal Spirit to pour out our soul in prayer and praise. "Oh, for a heart to praise my God" for this privilege.

June 25th — I have been favored with much enjoyment under the preached Word; but, alas, after the sermon I have returned to my own sad place, and still carry my burden of unbelief and sin; my heart is very heavy, and I wonder how I could hear such truths, and not be comforted. All seemed to rejoice but *me*; but why do I wonder? I am sure the power must be of God, and not of man; and, without the weight is taken off my soul by the Eternal Spirit, human efforts will avail nothing. May I then use the means in simple dependence on His blessing.

July 5th — A dark, unbelieving, infidel heart; surely I am not born again, and have no part in the matter. To describe my feelings is impossible. The Bible, Christianity, God, Christ, Christians, are all to my mind enveloped in confusion, obscurity, and doubt. Awful state! the Lord condescend to deliver me; and, though in the depths of distress, yea, of *infidelity*, I must cry to Him as my only Refuge.

[Reader, mark the depths down into which some of the Lord's hidden ones have to descend, in order that thereafter they may have to testify, in common with the Psalmist—aye, and with the Psalmist's Lord *too*—"He brought me up also out of an horrible pit, out of the miry clay, and set my feet upon a rock, and established my goings. And he hath put a new song in my mouth, even praise unto our God."]

July 13th — The sermon, last evening, was much blessed to my soul; I am now sure there is a heaven, a covenant God, a precious Savior, and a comforting, teaching Spirit. Oh, what a relief! Hope has again shed a ray or two on my path; and there seems a possibility I may yet see that good land. Ebenezer!

August 22nd — From the various opinions and sentiments of persons whom I believe to be Christians, added to my own ignorance and darkness, my mind has fallen into a most distressing state of confusion and perplexity; never did I more feel the need of divine teaching. I long for Jesus to say to me as He did to the disciples, "To you it is given to know the mysteries of the kingdom." May the Eternal Spirit be my Instructor. He alone teaches to profit, because He alone has access to the heart.

October 4th — Crucifixion of the flesh and deadness to the world is what I pray for; but, when the Lord puts his hand to this work by embittering my enjoyments, putting quite out of my reach what I most anxiously wish for, keeping my purse in His own care, giving me enough only for my present needs, not desires, then my heart rebels, and my case seems hard; and I wonder why I am thus dealt with, thinking it impossible the Lord can intend my good.

November 8th, Sabbath — Much deadness of soul lately, and much discovery of my extreme ignorance in divine things; I long exceedingly for the Holy Spirit's teaching; I am sure He alone can *reveal Jesus in my soul*. To have the understanding informed will not satisfy. I want to *feed* upon Christ, to *live* upon Christ, to *grow* up into Christ, and to be *rooted* in Christ, esteeming all things but dung and dross for the excellency of the knowledge of Him; instead of which, day after day passes, and I seem encrusted with earth and enveloped in carnality. I feel not this morning the spirit of the Sabbath. May the Lord come suddenly to His temple.

December 20th — I have for the last two days welcomed bodily affliction, because by it the awful corruption of my nature seemed kept down. The past has been a week of sin, temptation, and severe exercise, such as I could describe to no mortal; and to my own feelings, my way has been hid from the Lord, except as He has viewed it in a way of judgment. Sometimes I have felt, that though I may cry and shout, He has shut out my prayer from Him; and at others, have had no inclination to approach the mercy-seat. I fall at Thy feet, O Immanuel: loathsome, corrupt, and abominable, crying for free, unmerited mercy. I come to Thee, O Almighty Spirit, begging for the sake of, and through, what Jesus has done and suffered, that Thou wouldst be my Teacher, and, whatever it may cost, lead me into the truth, and reveal Christ in my soul the hope of glory. Before the Father, I fall self-condemned, having nothing to say why sentence should not be executed upon me, but that He so loved the world that He gave His own dear son to die for sinners (of whom I am the very chief), to whom, I pray Him, to look for a sacrifice to atone for my sins, and a perfect righteousness to cover my guilty soul, that so He may be well pleased with me for His righteousness sake. When will the day dawn and the shadows flee away? Lord, make me thankful for a faithful, searching ministry, and keep me from overestimating the instrument.

1836

January 3rd — Precious Jesus! grant me a fresh manifestation, another token for good. Eternal Spirit, pour upon me the grace of supplication, for I cannot pray but as Thou dost dictate. Oh, then, pity my abject condition, and bring my soul out of the prison of unbelief, in which it is confined. Oh, that this may be a year of deadness to the world and close walking with God. Remember, Ruth, the flesh will not like this; do not present this petition and calculate upon outward ease in the fulfillment of it, or you will be disappointed.

January 10th — I want to realize in my experience that I am dead to the law by the body of Christ. Precious Immanuel, give me that faith which shall enable me to lay hold of Thee as my righteousness, and to run into Thee as my city of refuge, receiving the sweet assurance that I am safe. Oh, come as the heavenly Boaz, and wed Thine abject handmaid; black and filthy as I am, give me to know that Thou viewest me all fair in Thine own robe, which Thou puttest upon Thy bride. Tell me Thou hast paid all my debts, and relieve me from the constant anxiety and distress which I feel, lest I should be taken away to prison and to judgment. Assure me, also, that Thou hast provided for the future, and that Thou wilt not allow sin to have the dominion over me, mine enemies to destroy me, nor mine adulterous heart to provoke Thee to jealousy by seeking after other lovers. Thus, dear Jesus, condescend to comfort me; it is long since Thou didst kiss me with the kisses of Thy mouth, and cause me to lean on Thy precious bosom; long since Thou didst call me Thy love and Thy dove, enabling me to respond, "Thou art fairer than the children of men," yea, the chief among ten thousand, the altogether lovely. I know my sin has caused Thine absence, I confess it with shame; but, oh, come in the sovereignty of Thy love, and melt me with Thy free favor; come skipping over the mountains of my sin, leaping over the hills of my unworthiness, and cause me to rejoice in Thy precious salvation. Dear Jesus, hear my cry; grant me a manifestation, if it please Thy divine Majesty. "Come, Lord Jesus, come quickly."

March 22nd — Much struck with hearing this passage read this morning: He will "keep them alive in famine" (Ps. 33:19). I thought it was often fulfilled spiritually, the Lord keeping the souls of His people alive, when to their own feelings they are in the midst of dearth, and cannot obtain a morsel of spiritual bread; that is, I mean, when there are no enlivenings in the soul, no love-visits, no openings of Scripture, no savor in the preached Word; in short, the streams seem cut off from their mouth, and they think all hope must be given up. Still it is wonderful to observe, and more wonderful to trace, in one's own experience, how the spark of divine life is invisibly and imperceptibly fed, so that there is a breathing, a panting, a longing for another taste of the Paschal Lamb; and, though there may be no fire to be seen, the smoke keeps rising from the smoldering embers, and the soul is kept alive in famine.

August 7th — Much struck with a remark of Mr. Huntington's which I have just read; speaking of a certain author, he says, "He seemed to be more earnest for *fruit* than for *engraftings*, and, I believe, would be better pleased with a *crop of leaves* than with a *good root*." It immediately occurred to me, how much more we hear about the fruits of a holy life and an upright conversation, than about the root from which alone *real holiness* can spring. The Savior told us not to expect grapes from thorns, and I think I never saw so clearly that the most beautiful moral works from a natural heart are not acceptable in the sight of God, who will only accept the fruits of faith, which are wrought in the soul by the Holy Spirit, and cannot be appreciated by the unregenerated, though there will be the outward effect of a good conversation, &c. May I thus be made more and more fruitful.

September 11th — The past week has been one of distance and darkness. I am now, and have been for some time, in a miserable condition, from extreme nervous depression and irritability, together with active corruptions, carnality of affections, hardness of heart, and, indeed, everything which is contrary to what I *would have*. I look at my friends, and envy them their spirituality, cheerfulness, and sociability, often concluding there is not another being on earth so wretchedly miserable and sinful as myself; for such is my state lately, that I cannot look, speak, walk, work, hear, read, or think, without sin—manifest sin, abominable sin; and such sin as brings me into the very depths of distress, shame, and self-loathing, but yet unaccompanied, as I fear, with true repentance and godly sorrow. I am sometimes almost desperate to find myself in such an awful condition, and yet, as it seems to me, so utterly without power to extricate myself from that which I hate. Oh, that the Lord Jesus would stretch out His almighty arm, and deliver me from the infidelity, unbelief, and other abominations of my evil heart, which seem to triumph over me. I often wonder what the Lord intends to do with me, and fear I am only drying, as it were, for everlasting burnings! The very vitals of my soul seem scorched up by the heat of temptation and corruption, so that I shrivel in selfish misery, and would sometimes be shut out from society, because I am unfit for it. None, or very few, drink the same bitter cup as myself, the most noxious ingredient in which is, my own *sinfulness;* for, as Moses burnt the calf, and ground it to powder, and then made those who had sinned by it to drink it, so it seems with me, my sins are my daily and sorrowful portion. The Lord have mercy upon me, and pardon my ingratitude, murmuring, and unbelief, for Christ's sake.

September 25th — I have taken the Sacrament this afternoon, and surely there was not another communicant so vile: unless the Lord Jesus put forth His almighty power, sink I must into despair, carnality, and sin.

> "Other refuge have I none,
> Hangs my helpless soul on Thee."

Leave me not to myself, for my wicked heart is longing after fleshly indulgence! I want, dear Immanuel, to be Thine alone, but *cannot*. Oh, no; I cannot! A divided heart Thou wilt not accept. I fall a dead weight on Thy sovereign, undeserved mercy, by which, if I am not caught, I must continue falling until I reach the lowest, hottest place in Tophet, which is my merited portion. But, blessed Jesus, take me for Thine own, and magnify the riches of Thy grace in my deliverance! "Lord, save, or I perish!"

December 4th — My flesh and unbelief have been insinuating that it is in vain to wait for the Lord any longer; but with considerable sweetness, and some power, the following words came to my mind: "*They* shall not be ashamed that *wait* for *Me.*" Dearest Lord, carry on Thine own work in Thine own way, and keep me waiting *on* and *for* Thee!

December 25th — Christmas Day and Sabbath — A very heavy snow descending; the face of nature is wrapt in a mantle of most beautiful whiteness. May my poor soul be so covered with the spotless robe of Immanuel's righteousness; that wedding garment, without which I shall be "speechless" before Him. It is our Sacrament to-day. May Jesus be there, and we enabled by the precious Spirit to follow Him from the manger to the tomb, and by faith recognize our individual interest in all that He did and suffered, eating His flesh and drinking His blood; thus having a taste of fat things. Then would this be a Christmas-day to be remembered. It may be the last I shall spend on earth. The Lord carry on and perfect His own work in my soul, and all will be well, whether for life or death.

December 26th — I was much gratified in hearing a Caffre chief and a missionary describe the work of grace which has been carried on in the souls of the Hottentots and Caffres in Africa; but, oh, how ashamed do I feel of my want of zeal; and I am ready on this ground to question whether I am the subject of that new birth which produces in the poor heathen such fervor of love and devotion.

1837

January 1st, Sabbath — Text this morning, Jabez' prayer, particularly applied to the cause of Zion. This new-year's day findeth me sad at heart, and much inclined to pass it in silence, only I find that on each returning period I have a desire to converse with, and look back upon, my former self; and I am gratified to learn how I felt this time last year, with what feelings I looked at the future, and how my fears or hopes have been realized, &c. As this *black book* is to meet no human eye but my own, I do with freedom put down those strange cogitations of my sinful heart to which I imagine others are strangers, and also those reliefs and deliverances which they would think insignificant or fanatical, but the retracing of which has often encouraged my sinking heart. Pen then, O daughter of the dust, thy present sinful condition with self-loathing; and may this new-year's day be the last which shall find thee so overpowered by the corruptions of thy deceitful heart. On reading the past, I am distressed to find, that instead of *close walking with God,* for which I prayed, I seem to have been more than ever harassed by temptation and my own evil propensities during the last year. Much have I desired that on the last day of 1836, or first of 1837, I might review my backslidings and miscarryings with heartfelt sorrow, confess them without reserve, and receive a token of forgiveness and promise of future support; instead of which (awful to say), on the very last night in the year, my old enemies made a sudden effort, found me off my guard, and I was carried a prey (and a willing one too, at the time) by those heart-sins which have their seat in my fallen nature, and have been so often the bane of my peace. Here, then, I am on new-year's day, miserable enough, and waiting to hear what the Lord will say to me. Surely, if I were His child I should have some victory over sin. May He have mercy on me. I begin this year a poor, broken, shattered vessel, not knowing of what spirit I am, nor to whom I belong. I *would* walk closely with God, but fear I never shall. I *would* be conformed to the image of Christ, but can only trace marks of the black tyrant. Lord Jesus, condescend to save even me. Precious Spirit, whisper forgiveness through the blood of the Lamb; pour upon my dry soul a spirit of confession, supplication, and thanksgiving, also for the many mercies with which Thou dost surround me, to my frequent amazement. A leper! Unclean, unclean! Jesus, have mercy; say, "I will, be thou clean." I tremble passing through another year so cold, carnal, and unbelieving.

February 18th — I must mark down, and that with extreme thankfulness, one new mercy which thus far in the new year I have been privileged to enjoy, viz., that of perusing the precious Word of God with calmness and pleasure, not being so hunted by temptation, disrelish, and want of interest, when I attempt to read it, as was the case, generally, last year, and, indeed, for some time previous. Oh, *it is* a mercy most valuable to be able to read calmly, and have some little gleams of light on the sacred page, which is now dearer to me than ever. Methinks, those who have never been shut up in this respect cannot enter into my feelings; however, the Lord knows them, and I bless Him for the change, and pray it may continue. Surely, this is ground to erect a "stone of help" upon. Ebenezer!

March 19th — Oh, for a manifestation of precious Jesus

to my soul, a revelation of Him by the Holy Ghost as *my own* Beloved! Methinks I trace some "stately steps" towards me in Providence which are encouraging, but this will not satisfy. I want close communion with a covenant God through an adorable Jesus, by the influence and drawing of the dear, sacred Remembrancer, the best and infallible Teacher. I have a gleam of hope that deliverance from the heavy burden of the last eight months is at hand. Trust evermore.

April 2nd — In reading, this morning, of the Israelites passing over Jordan, I was struck with the circumstance of the priests' feet touching the brim of the waters before they divided, and thought it is sometimes so in afflictions—the waters overflow their banks. Cross we must, our feet touch the wave, and, to the apprehension of sense, we are just about to sink in the swelling flood, when, lo, the stream suddenly divides! We find firm standing-ground, and pass through the dispensation with overwhelming astonishment and gratitude. Such displays of the power of a covenant God are majestic indeed, but not unfrequent; and blessed are those who are led to observe them, for "they shall understand the lovingkindness of the Lord."

April 25th — My timid heart is much moved this evening, by hearing there are some beginnings of riot in our town. The Lord protect us! He is my only refuge; and I feel some little calmness in the hope that He is my God. Oh, that the suffering poor may be relieved.

April 26th — All quiet again for the present. The Lord be praised!

June 14th, Evening — Heard an excellent sermon from Mr. I— (1 Samuel, 6:13, last clause), by which I have been cut up, and almost cut out, but in which was described the very state I am longing for, stretching out after, and, of late especially, desiring, viz., the liberty of the gospel.

June 18th, Evening — I seem to tremble lest the privilege of hearing Mr. I— should pass away without any real profit. I long for the great truths he advanced to be *wrought into* my soul by the Holy Ghost. I believe there is a state of establishment and stability, which he described, and most ardently I desire to be brought into it. Lord, condescend to manifest Thy power on my behalf!

June 25th — Awoke this morning with "The soul of the diligent shall be made fat." Oh, may *true spiritual diligence* be wrought in me by the power of the Holy Ghost! I am convinced of the sinful sloth which has prevailed over me.

July 7th, Evening —
"God, on my thirsty, barren soul,
Some mercy-drops has sent."

Oh, that it may be the harbinger of a plentiful shower! I am thankful for the longing desire I feel.

September 5th — I have been exercised for some time past with successive perplexities, which, though apparently trifling, work painfully upon my susceptible and too-easily excited nerves. I am now distressed about a valuable book, which was lent us by a friend; another friend saw it, and wished to borrow it; she was in a distressed state of mind, and it seemed very suitable, therefore we ventured to lend it. She has now had it for some time, and, when applied for, it could not be found. I cannot describe the painful anxiety I have suffered about it the last few days, because it is one of a set of volumes which, by its loss, would be spoiled; nor is it possible to replace it in the same form. It is also on other accounts valuable to the family; what to do I know not: I have laid it all before the Lord, but at present He does not appear to interpose, which again adds to my grief, because I have found much comfort in believing that nothing is too trivial to bring before Him, and I expect His direction and deliverance; and, if obliged to give this up, shall lose my chief support and comfort in the trials of life. I know I am prone to be impatient, and dictate when the Lord *should* appear, which is very wrong. May He give me a waiting spirit, and, in His own time, show that he has heard my cry, by delivering me in this trial. 2 Kings 6:5, is my encouragement to bring this matter to Jesus, who is the prophet in gospel days.

September 8th — Not yet relieved, but favored with much of a wrestling spirit, and think it has been in this respect a blessing, as my soul has been constantly kept supplicating for some time. Still, however, I much desire the Lord would condescend to bring to light the lost book, as unbelief and Atheism threaten to gain much ground within me, by proving from this, that it is not right to spread such trifling circumstances before the divine Majesty, and that He will not regard them. Oh, what sharp struggles have I had, and, how does my heart tremble, lest it should lose the sweet solace of telling out all the minutiae of its woes at a Throne of Grace; but I must yet hope that He who *has* delivered, will yet deliver.

September 10th — Oh, for another Ebenezer stone, another pillar of gratitude for divine interposition! What jealousies and misgivings does my poor heart experience, because the Lord *delayeth* to appear. I have been privileged with a spirit of wrestling and importunity at the divine footstool almost constantly during the past week, in which my only temporal request is the restoration of the lost book. All other outward things I have been led to give into the Lord's hands, to be by Him ordered as seemeth Him best, so that His divine glory may be manifested through me, and my soul made healthy and fruitful. It seemeth that to these last-mentioned things I must hold fast, being thoroughly tired of my lukewarm state. In the midst of this exercise something has been occasionally prompting me very powerfully to believe that it is all delusion, excitement, and imagination which has agonized my soul; but then, again, I have thought, if this is *not* the work of the Spirit, I can only go afresh to Him to discover to me what *is;* to lead me into it, and preserve me from the delusions of Satan, and the workings of my own flesh; so that this has proved, at some seasons, fresh matter for prayer and supplication. The Lord condescend to look at my case, carry on His own work with power, exercise me Himself, deliver me from temptation and the power of the tempter, and thus bring glory to His own name, by making such a vile, ignorant creature a vessel meet for His use, and which shall sound forth His praise.

September 12th — "When the desire cometh it is a tree of life";—verily God hath heard me; adorable Jesus has condescended to the low estate of His handmaid! *The lost book is restored;* and, oh what jealousies and misgivings are removed from my heart, for unbelief was ever and anon taunting me with this affair, suggesting that Jehovah did not, as I conceived, listen to such trifling requests; but, ah, with what fresh confidence can I approach the sacred footstool, and spread out all my cares! My soul is lifted up within me with rejoicing, because of this *manifest* answer to my petition. May I be humbled under a sense of my sinfulness and distrust, and be kept from sinking into a careless frame.

The lost book was restored to the bookshelf of the lady to whom we had lent it, quite unknown to her, by whom she knows not; but one of the family came downstairs, exclaiming, she had found the book upon the very shelf which she had searched over and over again. The Lord has all hearts in His hand, and no thief can hold when he says, restore.

> [Reader, we cannot allow this incident to pass, without asking you to admire and acknowledge the good hand of God toward His servant. Whilst, on the one hand, by this simple record, we see the simplicity, the teachableness, the earnestness of her faith, do we not, on the other hand, see how graciously the Lord honors that faith which honors Him! It is as true to-day as it was of old, "In *all* thy ways acknowledge him, and he shall direct thy paths."]

October 8th — The former part of last week I was favored with a supplicating spirit, and some outgoings of soul more than formerly; on Thursday, carnal security attacked me, on the heels of which came vanity, about an article of dress I was altering; I had not recourse to the shield of faith, the "sword of the Spirit," or the powerful weapon of "all prayer," but deluded myself in thinking I would finish as quickly as I could the alteration of my bonnet, and then pray, hoping to feel more at liberty. Ah, foolish creature, my iniquity prevailed, prayer was neglected, and a guilty conscience the result; since which I have not had that nearness of access as before. The Lord give me a broken heart, and then come and heal it: the Lord keep me from sinking into unbelief and sin: the Lord speak pardon!

October 15th — A spirit of careless security in what I have received was again the inlet of sin, and now what shall I say? May the Lord melt this *stony* heart, wash this *filthy* heart, bring back this *wandering* heart, and *some-*

how, by almighty power, make me more watchful against those sins which most easily beset me.

December 21st — Last night the wind was awfully tempestuous, and howled around our dwelling most fearfully; sleep fled from my eyes, and the fear of being suddenly called into eternity agonized my spirit, for I could obtain no sense of interest, and knew that fire unquenchable was my just desert. The horrors at the fear of dying out of Christ are, I think, felt by few; but few are so guilty and unbelieving as I.

December 31st — The 31st of December come again! How rapidly are the wheels of time revolving and bearing me on to a boundless eternity! Another year closing, and of what do its "gone-by" periods testify? Why! of aggravated transgression and ingratitude on my part, and most astonishing mercy and longsuffering from a covenant God. The past year has, I think, been one of more manifest spiritual favor than any former one in my life. My undeservings have been as great as ever, but the Lord has condescended to speak to me with more power than formerly, having permitted me to come into straits, and then poured upon me a spirit of importunate and unceasing wrestling at His footstool, which has been, in itself, a blessing, as well as the harbinger of either support or deliverance; added to this, He has enabled me to love the precious Bible, and read it with calmness; also, at times, to feed therein, of which privilege I was before deprived by reason of sore buffeting from the enemy. The Word preached has also, at times, come with power and sweetness into my soul. The dear precious Jesus has, I hope, in some little measure, been endeared *to* me, and revealed *in* me; and, though I have not had the full revelation of Him for which I long, yet I take this as an earnest, and look for more. There has, also, been granted more laying hold of Christ, and, when sensible of sin, more running to Him for pardon and cleansing, and, as it were, hanging upon him in my desperate case, and, if I perish, to do so at His feet. All this, with much more, I take to be very, very great mercy, and much alleviation of my case; but, oh, the dark tale of my own sin which has also marked this year—it is too black to be told. Ingratitude, murmuring, carnality, worldliness, unbelief, backsliding, and a thousand other evils, make up a list which ought to sink me into shame and self-abasement. The almighty Spirit condescend to melt me into real contrition, that having received much, I may love much, and having sinned much, I may have much forgiven. I am so astonished at the near access I have at times enjoyed; the answers to prayer which have been given, and the spirit of communion occasionally vouchsafed, that it is impossible to express my feelings. It seems worth much more suffering than I have gone through, and is all of mercy, free mercy, sovereign mercy, surprising mercy. The Lord make me thankful, and then accept the gratitude He gives. I cannot help hoping for more. The Lord seems to draw out my expectations that He *will* bless me; and, though it still be through the outward cross and flesh mortification, *it shall be well!* I am sure the flesh is no friend of mine, and as I have not resolution to cut off its right-hand, and to pluck out its right-eye sins, it is most merciful of the Lord to do it *for me;* and, though I often cry out from pain, the spirit says, Go on, Lord, deal with me as Thou wilt, only support and bring me to walk *closely* with Thee. Ebenezer!

1838

February 3rd — Most unexpectedly favored with a call from Mr. S—. The Lord condescend to fix deeply in my soul his most encouraging conversation. May the Holy Remembrancer bring it back with power, in so far as it was God's truth.

February 11th — Since Mr. S — called upon me, my soul has been exceedingly exercised. His coming was unsought and unexpected, having had no communication with him for more than two years. His converse was addressed to me, and as much in point to my state as though in the habit of frequent intercourse. His aim was to show that I am looking more at my faith than its object, and am more anxious about frames and feelings than to be established in the knowledge of Him from whom all spiritual gifts come, with much more which, to my sorrow, I have forgotten. Oh, how blessedly did he discourse on the privileges of a believer in Jesus, and how much do I long to realize that living by faith which he described. Here is the question, Did the Lord send him with a message to *me?* If so, may the Holy Spirit open my heart to receive it. Was what he advanced the truth of God? If so, may the Holy Spirit seal it upon my heart. Is living upon Christ *above* and *in* all frames attainable, and is this the true life of faith? If so, the Lord bring me to it, in spite of sin, Satan, and myself. But, then, most of the Christians I know, though more experienced than

I, seem to think we cannot properly realize interest in Christ when under desertion, temptation, the power of indwelling sin, or a sense of fresh-contracted guilt, and that being influenced by feeling produces the closest walking with God, the most tender conscience, and the greatest fear of sinning. Now this variety of opinion in the Lord's children exceedingly perplexes me, because they each point to the Bible, and there do seem passages to favor both. I have been much tossed about in this matter, the last three or four years, and was just lately leaving it more, desiring the Lord to lead me as would most promote His glory, and my close walking with Him, though certainly inclining to think the doubting path the most safe and humble. I am now, however, on the search again to know the Lord's mind; may He condescend to teach me, and suffer me not to be deceived by Satan, unbelief, or creature opinion.*

February 18th — Encouraged considerably to believe in and on the dear Lord Jesus as *my* Savior, because I think if I were not interested in Him, I should not have been brought to hang upon Him the whole weight of my soul's salvation. If this is the work of the Holy Spirit, may it be confirmed; if a fleshy confidence, may the Lord in mercy knock it out of me, cost me what it may.

February 26th — Privileged yesterday with a most blessed assurance of my interest in the person and work of Jesus, and such confidence of my eternal security in Him, that I could sing with Toplady—

---

* This page was endorsed, under date July 1839: "Oh that dear Mr. S— knew what I am now enjoying! It was a true report he brought of the land of promise, and now my feet have reached it, my eyes see it, and my mouth tastes its milk and honey."

> "More happy, but not more secure,
> The glorified spirits in heaven."

I desire to bless the Lord for this high favor, though last night and this morning, the enemy, together with my own unbelief, have thrust sore at me. The Lord enable me to *trust* firmly in Him, even though He hide His face.

February 28th — Yesterday morning was favored to taste the *joys* of salvation by Jesus, and triumph in Him as my portion; but have since been sorely buffeted by Satan and unbelief, who join in telling me it is a fleshly faith which I am persuading myself into, and not the work of the Holy Spirit. These things are most bitter and trying, but still the Foundation is sure, and I trust I am fixed on it, and shall, to the confusion of my enemies, be made more than conqueror through the blood of the Lamb!

March 22nd — I am much perplexed by the different opinions of *real* Christians—some urging to look to and trust in Jesus, without regard to *feeling*, and declaring this the way to stability and comfort; others continually directing me to what is felt within as a ground of comfort, and condemning the faith of the former as presumptuous. May the Holy Spirit be my Teacher! I desire to look to Him more constantly, and to pray Him to carry on His own work in my soul with power, let who will oppose. Afresh I fall helpless and ignorant on Jesus for salvation; and will He cast me out? Ah, no, no! "Him that cometh I will in *nowise* cast out." "Lord, increase my faith."

March 25th, Sabbath — This day month I was favored to mount upon the high places, and, while I sat in the house of God, to triumph in Him as the God of my salvation, rejoicing with exceeding joy to realize my interest in the person and work of Jesus, so that I thought I was keeping a Christmas Day in my soul, seeming to realize there the birth of Jesus as my Savior. How different this morning! I sat under the Word cold and insensible, feeling fully what I am in myself, and proving afresh that in "my flesh dwelleth no good thing." In this sad state I fly to Jesus as my only refuge. I expect to sit down at His table to-day. Oh that the depth of my sin and misery may be overcome by His rich grace, that with Mary I may weep at His dear feet, and love much, having much forgiven.

May 18th — Most exceedingly distressed by my sins, and lately have been much fearing that I must be wrong, because of my unfruitfulness. I feel the need of Jesu's precious blood every hour, but it has seemed to me like esteeming it a light thing to be making such constant application, and yet again constantly defiling myself. May the dear sacred Spirit teach me out of His own Word, for I am in much confusion, and feel afraid of trusting any human author. I want a supply from the Fountain!

June 10th — Since Mr. S— called upon me, I have been much desiring the jubilee trumpet to be sounded in my soul—that is, I long to be brought into gospel liberty. I believe some of the Lord's people are favored with it; but, for myself, I only seem to see it at a distance. Conversing with a minister on that subject which is my daily grief and perplexity—indwelling sin and its activity—he said, "What do you think of sanctification?" Having told him, he asked, "Do you think it has anything to do with the flesh?" I replied, "To subdue and mortify"; but he rejoined, "Do you expect the flesh made holy?" "Not in my judgment," I answered; "but I really begin to think I am expecting in my experience what my judgment disallows." "I thought so," said he, "and that was the reason I asked the question; remember that 'that which is born of the flesh is flesh, and ever will be.'" He then showed that the believer's perfection is *in Christ*; that while in the body we shall never be free from sin; but while groaning on account of it, we may be enabled by the Holy Spirit to recognize interest in the covenant, and deliverance through Christ, as Romans 7:24, 25. This seems just what I want, and, if for the divine glory, I trust it will be given. During the above conversation, my mind was forcibly struck with the conviction that I had been looking for something from and in my flesh which the Word of God does not warrant me to expect; if so, may the Holy Spirit deliver me from this error. I feel exceedingly confused, and full of ignorance. Oh that He may condescend to teach me, and lead me to look straight out of self to a glorious Christ!*

August 5th — A Mr. P— preached. Great and marvellous are the heights and depths, lengths and breadths of God in Christ, into which he seems to have entrance. My soul listens and longs, wondering much that some of the Lord's dear ministers get so into the marrow and fatness, while others are always cracking the bone; but "every man in his own order." Inasmuch as the things I am now hearing are *the* truth of God, insomuch may I— poor, sinful, hell-deserving creature as I am—be led into them. My soul *thirsts, longs intensely*, to know more of a glorious Christ, and live more upon Him, for He *is* the bread of God. May the Holy Ghost breathe again upon my barren heart. Most Holy Comforter, most solemnly do I entreat Thee, as the Teacher of Thy people, to lead me more deeply into heart acquaintance with divine truth, and into communion with a Triune Jehovah, making me lose all things outward, and count them as dung and dross in comparison with this. Oh, let me not continue

---

* I do *now* believe that the first blast of jubilee in my soul was on February 25th, preceding this memorandum, though *here* I do not seem yet to have fully recognized it as such, but events have quite proved it.

on the surface, but bring me to swim in, and take large draughts of, the water of life. If thy servant's ministrations are dictated by Thee, stamp them on, root them in, my soul; if not, for the sake of a precious, glorious Christ, keep me from receiving them, and from all error. Oh, come, divine Spirit, with demonstration and power, that "my faith may not stand in the wisdom of men."

August 7th — Mr. P— is condemned as a mere letter-preacher by some. Methinks divine power did accompany his words to my soul. May the most Holy Spirit condescend to prove it by sealing the savor afresh home with unction upon my soul, or, if not His truth, taking it quite away. I want to be Spirit-taught, Spirit-led, Spirit-fed.

August 11th, Sabbath Morning — I heard again last evening of some condemning Mr. P— as a letter-preacher; this takes me afresh to a throne of grace, to beg that the Holy Ghost will bear witness to His *own* truth in my soul, and not suffer me to be deceived by any false light, but rather strip me of every atom of comfort I think I have received; instead of which, I have again this morning been wonderfully favored with inflowings of light, peace, and power, showing me that Mr. P— has told a little, but not one-half of the glories of a precious Christ, the boundless love of a covenant God, the sweet communion of the dear Comforter, and the stability and security of the everlasting covenant. Oh, these are indeed soul-strengthening, establishing truths: I feel them such, and, while others are caviling, I am in secret feasting and rejoicing. May many others of the Lord's dear people be thus favored. Perhaps some heavy trial will follow these high enjoyments. The Lord give support and submission, and make me very, very thankful for what I now taste and handle of the word of life. Ebenezer! Hitherto the Lord hath helped.

August 19th — By reason of sinful yielding to worldly care, my mind has been brought into guilt and darkness; the Lord deliver me—He only can. May He bestow upon me that penitent, broken heart which I desire, but cannot procure. In fact, I find I must come to Him for all—sorrow for sin, pardon for sin, cleansing from pollution, deliverance from a guilty conscience, and the renewal of peace there through the application of atoning blood; yea even a longing desire for these things must be given, or I shall lie in cold and stupid apathy. So desperate is my case— one just fit for the interference of a glorious Christ, who, by undertaking such objects and doings all *for* and *in* them, gets much honor to His great name. May He again appear for me and to me. Ah, I do believe He will, ungrateful wretch though I am. May the eternal Spirit reveal His own truth in my soul, and daily establish me more in it, that I may discern things that differ. Soul-agony, horror, and bondage have been long my portion; but I do believe there is in this life a realizing of solid peace, through knowledge of interest in the everlasting covenant, union to Christ as a living Head, and in receiving out of His fullness all needful supplies. To this I much long to be brought. If I am wrong, may the Holy Spirit undeceive me at any cost; if right, lead me onward, onward, till grace shall be crowned with glory; and I, even I, through sovereign mercy, be brought to swim in the ocean of love to all eternity. "Perplexed, but not in despair."

October 5th — I have just witnessed the death of a neighbor's child: I trust her end was peace. She was most conscious she was dying; she kissed her friends, and wished them all good-bye, and was constantly in prayer for mercy, which I hope she found through that dear Savior on whom she called. May the Lord sanctify the stroke to the family, and to us also. Death has come very near.

October 7th — My mind dwells much on the death-bed scene I lately witnessed; the dear child's incessant cry of "Lord, have mercy on me," was very striking, as also the earnestness with which she once said, "I *believe* He will," and ejaculated, "Amen, amen, amen," to every sentence of petition which fell from those around her. I trust it was the work of the Holy Spirit on her soul, and that she is in the presence of dear Jesus. She is a beauteous corpse; never but once did I see death in so lovely a form. The Lord awaken the dear parents by this visitation. I am much distressed about my own death, fearing I should die out of Christ; or, if I am indeed built upon Him, that He shall be absent when I come to the confines of mortality. Oh, dearest Savior, increase my faith, speak comfortably to my heart now, and be with me manifestly in my last struggle. "Bochim!"

October 30th — Found much sweetness this morning from Isaiah 49:23, last clause, and Psalm 31:22. The Lord be praised for the divine dewdrops. Lord, increase faith and patience.

December 3rd — Arose this morning heavy and sin-burdened, but favored at family worship with near access, wrestling faith, and a sense of pardoning love. Wonderful! Wonderful! Who is a pardoning God like Thee? "Truly, to the Lord our God belong forgivenesses, though I have sinned against Him." My naughty, carnal nature is very active to-day. What a monster of iniquity and a monument of mercy! Surely I am, as the apostle says, a "pattern" that none may despair.

December 11th, Morning — The former part of last night quite sleepless. "Lord, all my desire is before Thee, and my groaning is not hid from Thee." Oh, deal not with me according to my sins, which are known to Thee, but condescend manifestly to appear for my deliverance. Oh, renew former mercies.

Evening — Is it vain to expect the Lord's special guidance in matters of providence? The conversation of a Christian friend this evening seemed almost to intimate as much, and that we must be guided by circumstances; but my own experience says, the Lord *does* notice the most trivial of His people's affairs, by means of which He communes with them. I desire, however, still to wait, watch, and pray. I am sure I shall be no loser by that. The conversation of our friend, being an old Christian, has certainly added to my burden; but here, again, is fresh occasion to go to a footstool of mercy for teaching and relief. Few, I think, have such conflicts. I suppose they must have stronger faith. The Lord grant special mercy in the special time of need.

December 12th — Much comforted to-day with views of precious Jesus, as my dear, almighty Savior, engaged to do all *for* and *in* me. Faint indeed are these glimpses compared with what I desire, but are they not earnests of more? I verily believe they are, and that, though a vile, hell-deserving sinner, I shall shout, Victory through the blood of the Lamb! and join the ransomed throng in casting at His dear feet our blood-bought crowns. Who should louder sing than I?

December 24th, Christmas Eve — Shall I see another on earth? Why—oh, why do I wish it? Have strong reason to believe that the Lord has sent the messenger of death to begin sapping the foundation of my tabernacle, and soon I shall fall a prey to a painful and fatal disease—*cancer*. I am most uneasy; I feel too much clinging to life, and much shrinking from the furnace that I think is preparing for me. My dearest Jesus appear for me, conforming my will to His, and separating my affections more from earthly objects, to which they seem to cling faster since I have had the prospect of leaving them. No one yet knows my forebodings, or the ground of them. Much mystery in my outward path—contrary, most contrary, to flesh and sense. The Lord prepare me for all His will, and manifest in its development that it is all covenant love to me, though I verily believe that henceforth sorrow and suffering are my appointed portion—I mean outward. I feel inclined to name this dark place "Jehovah Jireh." If prompted to do this by the Spirit the Comforter, I am sure I shall see it fulfilled, though it may be through the destruction of all my fleshly projects. If spared to see another Christmas Eve, which I do not now expect, I think I cannot spend it in more dejection than I have done this; but, "why art thou cast down, O my soul? hope thou in God; for I shall yet praise Him." A little gleam darts through the gloom. Oh, yes; I hope "I shall yet praise Him."*

---

* The event has proved *fully* this was of the Lord.

1839

January 27th, Sacrament Sabbath — Oh, what manifest outward mercies have I been the subject of since this time last month; how does my cup run over, and how am I astonished at it, often exclaiming, "Why me? Why, oh why am I so distinguished?" Dear Jesus, sanctify the temporal mercies Thou hast given; let me enjoy Thee in and with them, or they are all nought. Prepare me for *all* Thy will; if death is hastening, presence Thyself when I pass through the "dark valley." Oh, then let me *feel* that Thou hast taken the sting out of death, and permit me to go to sleep on Thy dear bosom. Precious Jesus, I think I can neither live nor die as I would without Thee. Oh, then, if Thy holy will, manifest Thyself in the hour of dissolving nature; but if I must long sojourn here, give patience, give direction, set me apart for Thyself, and let me have much of Thy presence, to keep me from the evil of the world. I desire solemnly to yield up myself afresh to Thee, for time and eternity, desiring to be Thine alone. Oh, enable me to say, "Thy will be done." The Lord keep me from sinfully desiring to depart, but surely the upper house hath more exalted joys to which we must aspire. A debtor indeed to sovereign, unmerited mercy.

February 8th —
> "Did ever trouble yet befall,
> And He refuse to hear my call?"

Ah, never, never! May I now, then, "trust and not be

afraid." Though at present in thick darkness as to the future, I do believe He, the God in whom I trust, will yet appear.

Evening — Writing to my friend, Mrs. H—, I felt cold, barren, and empty; but before I concluded, which I was going to do very briefly, the precious Comforter came, and I had again such ecstasy in the foreviews of glory as I cannot describe; but I have frequently had such lately in the midst of deep conflicts. To what it is a prelude I know not. The enemy says, "Perhaps a dark death-bed, or some heavy trial." Well, I leave it to that dear Lord who sent this beam of glory. It is an earnest of the future, whatever may come between. "Praise the Lord, O my soul."

February 16th — The dear Lord has condescended again to appear in His wonderful character, as the Hearer and Answerer of prayer. Oh, what miracles of mercy to such a wretch! Now, precious, lovely Savior, I look up to Thee for support. Mortify and crucify the flesh as Thou wilt, only sustain and comfort. I have waited, but not in vain.

February 22nd — I am exercised much with felt barrenness and coldness. Mr. Romaine might well say, "It is like leaping overboard in a storm, to venture on Christ alone for salvation, under coldness"; and so I find it, but desire afresh to cast myself upon Him—all empty, sinful, and barren as I feel. I am not more so in reality at this time than I always am in myself. It is *His* light, and love, and power which glow in my bosom when my case is revived; and, perhaps, it is because I have counted these gifts *my own* that they are withdrawn. Afresh, then, precious Jesus, I do venture on Thy person and work, Thy blood and righteousness, for salvation, and desire to wait with longing and wrestling till Thou shalt again appear.

February 26th — Disease seems to be decidedly fastening

upon the walls of this clay tabernacle. Well, it is condemned; come down, it must; the time and means I leave with my dear Lord. I have felt much of cloud on my mind, through sin and clinging too much to some earthly objects. The dear Lord pardon, restore, and snap the ties which bind me down to earth. Oh that my dear friends might be wings to me, instead of fetters.

March 3rd — What will be the issue of my present exercises I know not, but have lately experienced much hot fighting, considerable outward perplexity, and seem to have "Ichabod" strongly stamped on all created good; with which I have had also mingled sweet views of Christ as my own precious, precious Savior, my Law-fulfiller, my Surety, my Head, my All; and also such ecstatic sips of glory as have made my poor soul pant and long to be away to the full enjoyment of it. Never did my heart so bound at the thought of being absent from the body, and present with the Lord, as lately. If this is the Holy Spirit's work, may it increase; if from the flesh, may the sacred Comforter take it away, cost what it will. Afresh I commit myself into the hands of a covenant God in Christ, for either life or death, sickness or health, as shall seem good to Him; only praying to be set apart more for His service, and to be brought to walk closer with Him. Still, my soul seems to cling to an early dismissal and an abundant entrance; but, says something, "How dare you hope for such favor?" All through the person and work, love, blood, and righteousness of my most precious Redeemer, on whom I now again fall for full and free salvation. The Lord pardon what is mine, and strengthen what is from Himself.

March 11th — The sun shines cheerfully, and all looks smiling around, but it is nought to me, for my Savior is absent, and my soul joyless. Disease seems advancing, and I am agonized with the fear that, after all my cries, I have been left to myself, and must henceforth walk in darkness.

March 17th — The tempter foiled, my Savior faithful, and my poor soul relieved. The storm has subsided, but its effects are not quite gone; the foaming and dashing of the waves are over, but still they ripple; and though their sound is dying away, it at present prevents that calm view of my danger and deliverance with which I hope yet to be favored. I see enough, however, to adore my most precious Savior; and, though the most cowardly creature that ever fought under His banner, I believe He will get honor to His great name by gaining me the conquest, and then crowning me with victory. Oh, wondrous Savior, to do the work, bear the suffering, and bestow upon me the reward. Give, oh, give me a heart to praise, love, and adore Thee. Holy Comforter, come again, come again, and speak peace through blood. Oh bathe me in that living, healing, cleansing stream. Breathe, oh breathe, on this dry, barren, cold heart! Have I grieved Thee? oh, melt me into penitence, and then seal home pardon. Hope revives.

March 20th — This poor tabernacle seems fast weakening. Do I wish to live? Not for anything on earth, but I do want the light of my heavenly Father's countenance. Jesus, my own precious Savior, is absent, and all is cheerless to my soul. Oh, come, come and visit and comfort me. Thou art faithful, and wilt not suffer Satan to triumph, but he does taunt and buffet me; and it is hard to bear it in the dark. Well, cheer up, poor soul; be not so cowardly: this is the place for fighting, and the Captain of thy salvation will yet show Himself more than a match for thine enemies. Oh that it were morning. My Savior is with me, but I want to see Him.

March 25th — Wonders, wonders of grace and mercy! The dear Lord revealed Himself to me again this morning, as my covenant God in Christ. I would praise Him for renewed tokens of salvation and temporal mercies, coming as covenant blessings. The Lord bless my blessings, and only give what He will bless to me.

> [Sweet expression, "The Lord bless my blessings." Dear reader, is this the language of thy heart?]

March 26th — A beam of heavenly sunshine, a ray of glory has been mercifully let into my soul this morning; the devil told me it would never come again; but Jesus is faithful, though I am most ungrateful. The harp in tune.

March 27th — This naughty, naughty flesh is here yet, and distressingly active; the dear Lord be pleased to subdue it. Oh, my precious Savior, come and conquer Thy and my enemies. I want to be Thine alone, without one wandering desire; but, ah, it is not so. I want again the balsam of blood.

March 30th — Never had any one so rich a Banker, so kind a Husband, so tender a Shepherd, and so forbearing a Captain, as I have in my glorious Christ. The more I venture, the more He encourages; the bolder I am, the kinder He grows; the more I expect, the more He gives. I cannot tire or wear Him out, for He is full, yea, *fullness* of grace, mercy, love, and compassion. The one-half of His glory has never been expressed by mortal tongue, nor the thousandth part of His ravishments and condescension conceived by those who have not felt them. This, this is my—oh, yes—*my* Beloved, and this is my Friend. Haste the day when in His full-orbed glory I shall lose my sorrows and my sins for ever. Oh, what mercy to have another glimpse. Praise, oh, praise God, my covenant God; join me, ye saints on earth, and in heaven, to adore and magnify Him for His mercy—amazing mercy—to a vile Magdalene. Hallelujah. Amen.

April 3rd — Blessed beyond measure with comfort, peace, and joy—all flowing through the bleeding heart of Christ, my Savior, Husband, Friend, Surety, All. The desire to be with Him in glory continues and increases; wherefore there is hope in this thing, that my Beloved is about to consummate my happiness. Dearest Jesus, give patience. Pardon what is mine; strengthen what is Thine; accomplish Thine own purpose in this frail tabernacle; and then fetch me home! Come with Death, precious Christ. I tremble at him without Thy presence. Oh, come, and let me breathe out my soul on Thy bosom, in Thine embrace. Much for *me* to *ask*, but not too much for *Thee* to *give*. Thy kindness makes me bold. For Thine own love's sake, grant my request, or give submission; and, if not seen, support secretly. Darkness and light are both alike to Thee; and if it is a dark going to sleep, it will be a bright awaking. Help me to feel "Thy will be done." "Bless the Lord, O my soul." Saints and angels, join me to praise Him. Creation, animate and inanimate, I would ye were all in tune to praise *Him* who has done so much for me. Eternity is coming, and then I shall never tire; but shout, methinks, louder than all the blood-washed throng, "He loved me and gave Himself for me." I wait, Lord, Thy will.

April 5th — Tempest-tossed again! Enabled this morning to commit my case afresh to Jesus, the "Wonderful Counsellor"; and am waiting for Him to break the temptation.

April 8th — My Beloved is come again over the mountains of my sin and guilt. I can now shout, Victory, victory, through the blood of the Lamb! Oh, the sweet, blessed visits my dear Lord pays me! Pen cannot write it, tongue cannot utter it. Praise Him, oh, praise Him with and for me!

May 4th — Since writing the above, I have been confined to my room by illness; and oh, the sweet, blessed season it has been to my soul, none can conceive but those who have felt the same. My most precious Savior has made all my bed in my affliction, sensibly communed with my soul, and revealed Himself in such glory and majesty, that it seemed nothing but an entrance into His immediate presence could satisfy me. Oh, what delightful views have I had of the stability of the everlasting covenant, and the safety of my, and every, soul hanging on the blood and righteousness of Jesus—the faithfulness of Jehovah being pledged for their security; and what can go beyond that? It is indeed "strong consolation." Bodily strength seems a little returning. It will be hard work to come into the world again. The Lord give submission.

May 23rd — My health apparently improving. I wait the will of my dear Lord, who will do the best, the very best for me. He has given Himself to me for time and eternity, and what can He withhold? Still, to enter again into active life, or at least the prospect of it, has been the severest disappointment I ever met; for I thought my feet were on the very threshold of my Father's house, and with ecstatic joy, inexpressible by mortal strains, I did in spirit join the bright host above in Hallelujah to Him that sitteth upon the throne, and to the Lamb who was slain! Oh, yes, indeed I did seem to catch the strains of celestial harmony, and fragrant breezes from the everlasting hills were breathed around me. How could I, then, but long to be away? My own precious Savior, I bow to Thy will; only keep me from dishonoring Thee, and use me for Thy glory. I tremble—how do I tremble at myself; but afresh I throw myself into the arms of covenant love, to be preserved from all evil. I cannot tell half the sweet mercies of my affliction. *Ebenezer!*

May 24th — Again last night favored with some of the joys of heaven let into my soul. The ecstatic rapture, the full-flowing tide of felicity with which I have last night, and to-day, drank of the cup of salvation, is inexpressible. What shall I—what can I—render? My own dear Jesus, Thou art most sweetly spoiling me for earth; and what then? Ah, Thou knowest; but methinks home is the best place for a *spoiled* child. Go on, blessed Immanuel, with Thy work of love; triumphantly I resign all created good for Thy embrace. Prepare me for Thy will, and give submission. Make use of me for Thy glory, and keep me from my own evil ways, and for the rest "Thy will be done"; but oh, Thy smile, Thy embrace, Thy unveiled presence; nought else can *fully* satisfy a heart so blessed as mine. I thank, laud, and magnify Thee, O my covenant God, for what I have received, through precious Jesus, by the Holy Comforter, and wait expecting more.

May 26th —
>   "Now let my songs abound,
>   And every tear be dry,
>   I'm marching through Immanuel's ground,
>   To fairer worlds on high."

Then, O my soul, droop not because thou must stay a little longer here, but take up thy cross and follow, closely follow thy Lord—happy, beyond expression, in my precious Jesus. Oh, Thou adorable Prince of Life, and Thou Eternal Father in Christ, Thou hast condescended by the power of the Spirit to absorb my soul, engage my affections, and, as one says, "Were all creatures extinguished, I am happy beyond conception in the enjoyment of Thy love." Jesus Christ is come in the flesh; here is the ground of my confidence, joy, triumph: Christ Jesus, my Savior, has lived righteously, died willingly, lovingly, and conqueringly. Yes, "He conquered when He fell," has risen triumphantly, ascended gloriously, and sent down the dear Holy Comforter into my soul, to witness all this that has been done for me—accepted by the Father, *my* Father, for *me*—to say that Jesus lives for me—now, and will ever live; and "because He lives I shall live also," being a part of Himself, His flesh and His bones. Oh, wonderful, incomprehensible, soul-ravishing truth! One with Jesus, one with the Father, heir of God, joint-heir with Christ: must I not praise, adore, and magnify my most glorious covenant God in Christ? Oh, yes, I must; the year of jubilee is come; the tabernacle of God is with men! In Christ we are restored to that state in which God can walk with us in the cool of the day, and commune with us of covenant love and purposes: which are not trusted in our hands, but deposited in Christ, the precious Treasury, and from Him dealt out to us as we need. "Thanks be unto God for His unspeakable gift"; thanks unto Him that we, poor bankrupts, are not set up with a stock to try again, but have an inexhaustible fortune placed in the keeping of a loving, kind, bountiful Banker, who will not let us want any good, or trust us with too much at once. Oh, it is sweet to grace, though mortifying to nature, to live on His bounty; to come every moment for more strength, more patience, more faith, more love—everything we want. He loves large requests, and is honored by great expectations. I bless and glorify Thee, Thou immaculate Prince of Life; and Thou, almighty Abba, Father, in Christ Jesus; and Thou, holy, blessed Comforter, my near, kind, faithful Friend. I adore and thank Thy divine Majesty, the one triune Jehovah, for all I have received and enjoyed of Thee; and I humbly, believingly, for Christ's sake, in Jesu's name, ask, long, and wait for more. Oh, nought, nought but the Fountain Head above can satisfy the thirst of love. Happy, happy Sabbath morning, a foretaste of the eternal rest-day, rejoicing-day, Sabbatic-day, on which my spirit longs to enter in my Lord's time. Well may I wait, when heaven is sent into my soul on earth; hallelujah! Hallelujah! "The Lord God omnipotent reigneth," "Thy kingdom come." Amen. Hallelujah!

May 29th — A bleeding heart! I have only returned to life afresh to agonize and suffer in the flesh; but do I repine? Ah, no; "my spirit rejoices in God my Savior," and now says, "Thy will be done." My own dear, precious Jesus, Thou art mine; there is ecstacy in the thought; amputate right hands, pluck out right eyes, where Thou seest needful. Love will guide the knife, and, though I suffer, my spirit cries, "Go on, dearest Lord; separate me from all that keeps me from Thee; give Thyself in close communion, and all is well." God is my refuge, and I shall not be destitute; the enemy may taunt in my weakness, but he shall not triumph. God, who is my strength, will arise, and I shall yet—yea, I do *now*—praise, adore, laud, magnify, love, and give myself joyfully to Him; yes, I do it *now*, in this low, low place. Oh, for fresh sensible realization of blood, love, and righteousness, to wash, robe, and crown me.

May 30th — I seem to have found something of the blessedness of living upon Christ, and I want it more fully; I dread the very thought of *living myself* again. It is a wretched life, but the happy, happy one is, "not I, but Christ liveth in me"; and the life I now live in the flesh, I live by the faith of the Son of God, who loved me and gave Himself for me. Oh, wonderful, for *me*; transporting, soul-ravishing truth; to live thus is indeed blissful, solid, and scriptural too; the Lord grant it me, more and more!

[Reader, it is clear that all the teaching and training to which the Lord had been subjecting His servant was to bring about this gracious end—the "ceasing from man"—the crucifixion of the flesh; or, as she here significantly expresses it, the "living myself." She was sensibly to "die daily," in order that Christ, in His glorious person and perfect work, should become more manifestively her "wisdom, righteousness, sanctification, and redemption"; yea, her *all and in all.*"]

June 1st — "Behold, I am vile." I have sinned, sinned against love, mercy, and favor unspeakable; my heart is torn with anguish at my ingratitude, and weakness; but I fly to that dear heart which was torn with deeper anguish for this very sin. Oh, yes, to Jesus I *must* go, deep and dark as is the character of my guilt; for to despair of mercy would add another stain. O Jesus! Thou canst pardon my sin, and I believe Thou wilt—Lord, speak, comfort, cleanse, restore—

> "Foul, I to the fountain fly,
> Wash me, Savior, or I die."

How does it agonize my soul that I have sinned against a Father, a dear kind Father, who loves me, loves me so as to give His well-beloved Son for me; loves me so that nothing can sever me from that love, not even my vile transgressions. Forgive, Holy Father; for Christ's sake, forgive; Thou dost, Thou hast forgiven me all sin. I cannot, dare not doubt it; but I want remanifestations of Thy pardoning mercy, as new guilt arises. Oh, yes! I want Thy love again to flow through the bleeding heart of my precious Savior, and, by the unctuous power of my most Holy Comforter, applied to my soul. I ask it humbly and believingly (oh, pardon every atom of unbelief), for Christ's sake, in Jesu's name.

June 2nd — Are pardon and peace again mine? Oh, yes, thanks to the Holy Spirit, my faithful Friend, who will "not suffer sin upon me" without sharp reproof; thanks, most divine Comforter, that Thou hast enabled me to confess my sin, with all its aggravation, known and unknown; yes, and the evils of my whole life, with the pollution of my nature, upon the head of Christ's most perfect sacrifice, and by faith to receive cleansing in His precious blood, and justification in His perfect righteousness. Thanks to my reconciled Father for pardon, through His dear Son, my dear Savior—thanks for calmness; but yet I want the kiss of communion, close, actual, soul-absorbing communion. I ask it, Holy Father, in the name of Jesus, by the power of the Spirit, nor shall I ask in vain! Praise for salvation by grace! It is hard work to trust sin with Christ, felt sin, fresh sin, Spirit-revealed sin; but it is very safe and very relieving; for in the ocean of His blood it sinks, never to condemn us. Oh, for a clean conscience, ever purged, constantly purged by blood; it is healthy to wash often, and not allow sin to grow hard upon the conscience, for that affords food for unbelief and triumph for Satan. Oh, did the dear people of God live nearer the fountain, and more frequently apply to it, we should have more rejoicing in the camp of our Israel. The Holy Ghost revive His work.

June 4th — A sweet feast from 1 John 5:13, which came in this way, "I have written unto you that believe in the name of the Son of God, that ye may know that ye have eternal life, and that ye may believe"; that ye may know ye are safe, but not rest satisfied, saying, I have believed, but still go on believing, "that ye may believe"; how sweetly did it show the continuation of the life of faith, that as far as the believer is healthy, it is a continual believing, living on Christ. The Holy Spirit bring me more into this single-eyed faith, that every day I may know I have eternal life, and may believe. The first epistle of John has been to me lately a garden of most fragrant sweets and delicious fruits; thanks for the Holy Bible, and the Sacred Spirit shining on its dear contents.

June 9th — Thanksgiving, adoration, and praise to my covenant God for the blessed sermon the sacred Comforter has preached *into* my soul this morning. Oh, I never had such Sabbaths in my life. This morning my feast was from Galatians 2:17-20, whence was given such a view of gospel liberty and *living* Christ as I think I never had, showing, from that and Romans 7, how the believer may, even in this body of death, and while groaning under it, be free from condemnation, dead to the law as regards justification, and dead to sin, even while feeling it alive in him, and hating it too; and all through recognizing himself complete in Christ, who has for him fulfilled the whole law; yes, magnified it to the utmost extent of its righteous claims, and for him also atoned fully for his every breach of it, so that now, what can the law say to him? He is dead to it and alive to God, and now brings forth the fruits of love, which are richer and riper far than any produced by "do and live." *Live* and *do* is blessed work, because it is "not I, but Christ who liveth in me"; and "I can do all things through Christ, which strengtheneth me." Dear Comforter, Thou condescending Teacher, be pleased to seal home Thy truth in my soul, that I may not only see it and rejoice in its light, but feel it and live in its power. I am not afraid of sin gaining more power while I am viewing Christ *with both eyes*, and believing on Him for justification. I verily think our slips come not from looking at Christ instead of our way, but from looking at our way, or our feet, instead of Christ. When the eye of faith is steadily fixed on Christ, I can trust Him to keep my feet even; but as soon as I begin to square them myself, that I may take some graceful step, and then look at Christ, and see how He is glorified thereby, down I come; and in the dust must hide my blushing face, ashamed of not being pleased as the Eternal Father is, that "*in Him* should all fullness dwell," and from Him should we receive it. Lord, teach me to live Christ!

> [Reader, mark the saying: it contains volumes. Until we are brought to "live Christ," we shall never know what real gospel rest is.]

June 14th — Dearest Jesus, I leave my case in Thy hands. Oh, be much with me in communion, until Thou shalt call me up to be with Thee for ever. My heart aches. What a poor soldier! Sure of victory, and yet shrinking from the contest. Lord, pardon—but oh, I must desire to be where my heart is already.

June 16th, Sabbath — "I have found Him of whom Moses in the law and the prophets, did write,"—precious, dear, adorable Jesus; and, with Him in the arms of my faith, I can say, "Lord, now lettest Thou [Thy handmaid] depart in peace, for mine eyes have seen Thy salvation." It seems to me that the Holy Comforter is showing me more and more beauty and comfort in a life of faith on the Son of God, which is continual living out of self on Christ; also, intermixing the same with sweet foretastes of another life, still more delightful, viz., the life of glory above; the former I long to be getting deeper into while here, but the latter, in the full beaming presence of my glorified Lord, is what my soul intensely longs for. Make haste, my Beloved, and cut short the hours of Thy delay; but still, what is sinfully impatient I pray Thee to pardon and subdue. Ten thousand thanks for the sweetness I find in Christ under every circumstance. Reveal Him more and more fully, almighty Spirit, that I may continually rejoice in the Father through Him, and thus commune with the Three-One Jehovah. Oh, for more of Christ! All things else are sinking into shadows; and my soul, absorbed with

His overwhelming majesty and grace, would forget that earth and creatures still enfetter me. Oh, did dear Christians see half the beauty and holiness of Christ I now behold, they would press with more eager anxiety to walk very closely with Him; indeed, it is worth any sacrifice. May the most Holy Comforter descend with more manifest unction, that we, who are "risen with Christ," may "seek those things which are above."

June 18th — My heart is full of happiness in Christ, who is all, all to me. How do I mourn to find so few dear children of God *living Christ,* and forsaking all for Christ. I have an intense desire that my own dearly-beloved mother may have Christ revealed in her soul, and walk in the sense of union to Him. Holy Spirit, condescend to show the sweet simplicity of the Gospel; enable her to embrace Christ under the deepest sense of her miseries, and she will—oh, yes, she will—feel the virtue come out of Him. Dear Jesus! I never thought to find such a heaven on earth as I now enjoy in Thee; and then the Heaven of heavens! Oh, wonders of rich, sovereign grace! Vile, helpless, guilty as ever in myself, but finding a perfect salvation in a perfect Christ. Ebenezer! Praise ye the Lord!

June 19th — On first waking this morning I trembled exceedingly, as I usually do, lest I should dishonor Christ, and begin to *live myself* again. Felt most sensibly my weakness, and the pollution and depravity of my whole nature, and longed to find refuge in Christ; and feared lest I should sink into myself, and dishonor my precious Savior, by unbelievingly viewing the disease greater than the remedy, when these words came, "He will not suffer thy foot to be moved." Oh, how sweetly suitable! I long, every day, to lose my life for Christ; that is, count upon, wish for, no enjoyment but Him, and to lose myself in Christ; taking up the cross He appoints, and only desiring to feed upon, grow up into, and be absorbed with Christ. Lord Jesus, I plead before Thee the promise Thou hast given; accomplish it, to the glory of Thine own name, in which the Father and the Spirit are also glorified, and the one Triune Jehovah honored.

June 23rd — I have fed and feasted richly upon Christ the last week; to ballast me, I have, last night and to-day, had strong temptations. Satan envies my happiness, and, because sin is still in me, would have me again in bondage; but my trust is in the Lord my God, and, though in deep conflict and a vile sinner, I am not destroyed, and shall lose nothing in the furnace but dross. Jesus, my own Savior, sits by, though not so visibly; His heart sympathizes, while mine is agonizing; and He will—oh, yes—He will deliver. I think I am willing to live, fight, suffer, or do anything (but sin), so that my dear Jesus may be glorified in me. Oh, I want to live Christ now, henceforth, and for ever! There will be no fighting soon; it will be (oh, happy thought!) all communion. "Lord, increase my faith." It is a mercy, when one is in darkness, that it is a darkness which may be felt; the darkness which is not felt must be the darkness of the dead; but the very feeling it is proof of life. "Rejoice not against me, O mine enemy: when I fall, I shall arise; when I sit in darkness, the Lord shall be a light unto me."

June 25th — Yesterday, and last night again, exceedingly harassed by Satan and the flesh; but found the cross of Christ my place of refuge, and from a dear, once crucified, but now glorified Savior, did receive strength in the battle, sympathy in the suffering, and assurance of victory through His blood. Oh, the sweet wonders of a life of simple faith in Christ! From what little I know, I am sure it is the most flesh-humbling, sin-subduing, world-crucifying, Satan-defeating life in the world. Unbelief is the source of my misery. "Lord, increase my faith." Precious Jesus, Thou art full as ever; the more I enjoy Thee, the more I see yet to be enjoyed. The larger draughts I drink of "salvation by grace," the more overflowing seems the fountain; and the more I get into its depths, the more unfathomable seems that delightful ocean. Thanks, thanks to a covenant God for a salvation planned, accomplished, and applied.

June 30th — From the present appearance of my health, it seems I have longer to live in this dreary wilderness than once I hoped. I cannot tell what is the meaning of my blessed Savior; I thought He intimated to me the contrary, by the soul-ravishing views of glory with which He favored me; but, however, I am nothing shaken as regards His faithfulness. I am quite sure that not one word of all He has promised shall fail me. Should it prove otherwise, it was my ignorance which misinterpreted the voice of my Beloved, and not His alteration of either purpose or promise. Blessed be His name, "He is the Rock, His work is perfect." Much in temptation the last few days, and unbelief sorely buffeting me. How I detest and tremble at this old enemy, which has been allowed so much quarter that it now makes desperate efforts; but my precious Savior stands by me—yea, fights for me; I only fail when I go forth in my own strength. I have had some jealousies, because the actual and near communion which I enjoyed has been withholden; but, however, I find in my living Jesus all I need; and when it will be for His glory and my good, He will again beam upon me the bright rays of His life-giving countenance. Lord Jesus, I am Thine. I long to see Thee, but submit to Thy will, and again unreservedly lay before Thee myself, with all I have and am, to be at Thy disposal, and used for Thy glory; only crucify self, and live Thou in me henceforth and for ever! Amen.

July 6th, my Birthday — The mercies which have followed me through the past year are overwhelming and astonishing. "Bless the Lord, O my soul, and all that is within me bless His Holy name." Most precious Jesus, I desire through Thee solemnly now to take hold of Thy covenant, into the bonds of which Thyself hast brought me. In it Thou promisest to "put Thy fear into Thy people's heart, that they shall not depart from Thee." I plead for the fulfillment of this in my experience, and entreat that I may be Thine manifestly and entirely, henceforth and for ever; to be by Thee used for Thine own glory, as a vessel polished for Thy service, and to reflect Thine image. Whatever fire-and-water exercise may be needful for this polishing, I humbly yield myself thereto, leaving all I have and am at Thy disposal. I do now fearlessly and joyfully surrender myself to Thee (oh, happy privilege!) as the purchase of Thine own blood, and, therefore, Thy undoubted right. I am no longer my own, but Thine; and Thou, O precious Jesus, art mine for ever! Cause me, by Thy Spirit's power, continually to abide in Thee, and walk closely with Thee. It would be pleasant to be at home, but the length of my sojourn here I leave with Thee, only be Thou glorified in me, by life or death.

August 12th — I have been hearing such glorious things from Mr. T—, about my glorious Christ and His Church, that quite astonish and delight me. Truly, "I am of yesterday, and know nothing," but still am not discouraged thereby. I bless and praise the dear Comforter, that He has taught me that Christ is mine, with all He is and has for His Church. I wait, therefore, at His threshold, and seek further entrance. Holy Teacher, what I know not teach Thou me; from Thyself I must receive it. *What*, oh, what am I born to possess and enjoy in knowing Christ! The thousandth part was never told me. Though a very babe, I can praise, bless, and adore my covenant God for what I have received, and still cry, "More of Christ, more of Christ!"

September 1st — "I am as a wonder unto many, but Thou art my strong refuge." Some look at me with wonder of pleasure to see me brought back for a little space from the gates of death. Some look at me with wonder of admiration, to see the poor prisoner set at liberty, and "the tongue of the stammerer speaking plainly." Some look at me with wonder of jealousy, "lest, having begun in the Spirit, I now am expecting to be made perfect in the flesh." Others look at me with wonder of expectation, thinking the feast will be over, and I shall "return to my own sad place." And I look at myself with wonder of amazement and overwhelming delight, because a monument of saving, sovereign mercy. Happy, happy, unspeakably happy, with Christ in my heart, the hope of glory! Wonder, O heavens, and be astonished, O earth, for the Lord Himself hath done it! "He hath comforted His people, and will have mercy upon His afflicted."

September 2nd — A letter to-day from dear Mr. T— so full of the glories of my precious Christ. What am I, that such "handfuls of purpose" should be let fall for me? Ah! it is what Christ is. From Him come all my blessings and blessedness. One with him, as He is one with the Father. Amazing miracle of superabounding love! The dear Lord bless Mr. T—, in return for his kindness to poor Ruth, the Moabitish damsel.

September 11th — Ah, dearest Jesus, it were easy *to burn for Thee* when Thy *sweet love burns hot in me.*

September 16th — Bless God for the Bible!

September 29th — O my Christ, Jehovah, "Thou hast triumphed gloriously, for the horse and his rider hast Thou cast into the sea." Yes, even Satan, my strong enemy, who was tempting me to doubt Thy divinity. Awful, terrible insinuation; but with this passage Thou hast foiled Him: "And let all the angels of God worship *Him*"; and this from the eternal Jehovah, who thus commands my Christ to be worshipped. Here, then, is my authority; higher there cannot be. Oh, how my soul does dance and sing; it is safe, very safe, to give Satan with his blackest lies into the hands of Jesus. Here *we* are sure of victory, *he* of defeat; and, whatever he may suggest to us, he is obliged to bow at that mighty name, and to acknowledge, "I know thee, who thou art, the Holy One of God!" Victory is mine, through the blood of the Lamb.

November 4th — "My feet had almost gone; my steps had well nigh slipped"; looking too much at "things seen," and listening to the flesh, under circumstances which are very contrary to it, I was seized with deep depression; but have just been much refreshed by sitting down on the Ebenezer-stone erected September 14. The dear Lord has inspired me with new vigor, and again I yield my all to His disposal, acknowledging with shame, that it is my unbelief and fleshliness that are the *cross* of the cross; Dear, precious Savior, pardon and restore; I tremble lest I should sink down into self again! My Jesus, prevent it, by Thy mighty power. Holy Comforter, teach me how to live Christ at all times, in all conditions. Christ is my *day*, and *I* am my own black *night*. When I walk *in* the day (*in Christ*) I stumble not, but when I walk in the night (*in self*)—ah, then it is I stumble, then I fall; but where do I fall? Oh, into the arms of my beloved Jesus! When He has taught me my weakness, then again He bears me up in His own strong arm; and, ashamed of my folly, I would hide my blushing face, and desire never, never, to try or trust self again.

November 16th — "The Lord is my light and my salvation; whom shall I fear? the Lord is the strength of my life; of whom shall I be afraid?" A time of especial trial, but Jesus is my support. He does bear me up. To His honor I acknowledge that, "having trusted in Him, I am helped." My Christ, my own loved and loving Jesus, to Thee I look; take Thine own way, but continue to succor. What I now feel of Thy supporting power is beyond all I could have hoped for, but Thou must go on, I still hang dependent upon Thee; nor wilt Thou prove unfaithful. "Choose Thou the way, but still lead on." Implicitly, unreservedly, and entirely, I give all I have and am to Thy disposal; only glorify Thyself in me, and then glorify me with Thyself! "Thy will be done."

Saturday Evening — Here closes a week of superabundant mercies.

November 17th — My Christ, Thou hast heard and answered my prayer and my groaning, and I desire "to praise thee with joyful lips." Lead on, dearest Savior; leave me not to myself or Satan. I fall my whole weight upon Thee, and go forth at Thy charges, nor wilt Thou disappoint me. It is indeed a "verity," that none who wait on Thee shall be ashamed. "Lord, increase my faith!"

December 22nd — Again I have abundant reason to bless my God, that He hath inclined and enabled me to put down His dealings with me. With affection, I remember, it was my own dear father who recommended this practice to me; and very, very profitable have I found it. This very day my soul hath been energized by perusing a former memorandum. I have discovered I was growing fainthearted and cowardly, and have been encouraged to put my whole trust in the Lord, and expect my whole happiness in Him, in the midst of all outward contradictions and crosses. Verily, I am ashamed that these should have moved me an inch. "Lord, increase my faith." Lord, subdue my unbelief. Lord, pardon my cowardice. Lord Jesus Christ, my dear Savior, be Thou my courage, Thou my victory, Thou my all in all. Most unreservedly I do again commit my all to Thee, roll my all upon Thee, not desiring to seek outward alleviation, but embracing Thee as my all, and praying Thou wouldst glorify Thyself in me. Though tempted not vanquished, though cast down not destroyed; a conqueror in my precious Jesus, though the battle has been lost a hundred times in myself. "Return unto thy rest, O my [wandering] soul."

December 31st — Another inch of time concluding, and oh, what loud and lofty songs of praise should sound from my heart, for the supereminent mercies and lovingkindnesses with which I have been crowned this year. It has almost been as the "beginning of years" to me; and yet I do remember the last was rich and favored. Oh, what shall I render? I can only "take the cup of salvation," desire larger, larger, and yet larger draughts, and call joyfully, thankfully, adoringly, upon the name of my God. Oh, ecstatic, ravishing, delightful sound! *My* God! It is full of unutterable and inexpressible delights to me, who for so long was shivering and shrinking before His presence, as my august, tremendous Judge. Hell seemed to gape upon me; corruption boiled within me; temptation hotly pursued me; the world was gloom around me; and oh, what would I not have given to have been without a soul, a never, never-dying soul! So filthy, polluted, and distressed, I had at times no hope of mercy. But, ah, my Jesus watched me through those shades; and, though unseen, unfelt, He bore me up, and, in His time of manifested love, He brought me out in His own light, to see Him as my Lord, my righteousness, my life, my all. And during this year, with fullness, glory, and nearness unknown before, He has been pleased to shine upon me; and, also, when the rays of glory were withdrawn, He has by the dear sacred Comforter taught me somewhat of a life of simple faith upon Him, in which I have been made to renounce joys, comforts, enlargements, deliverances, self and creatures, in point of dependence, and hang completely my whole weight upon Jehovah-Jesus. More of this blessed life I long to know, for I do find it flesh-mortifying, world-crucifying, Satan-defeating, sin-subduing, and soul-invigorating— "Lord, increase my faith," subdue my unbelief. A poor, weak, guilty, hell-deserving creature, I fall at Thy feet, my Jesus; "Thou hast redeemed me by Thy blood; I am Thine." Oh, use me for Thy glory; prepare me for Thy will; reveal Thyself still more unto me. By faith I would embrace Thee for more gratitude, love, faith, submission, patience, courage, and all I need, while in this dreary desert (which Thou alone canst cheer); for all must come from Thee. Accept a thousand thanks for this sweet year of mercy, and crown me with lovingkindness, though still the cross and conflict must attend. Faithfulness {Ebenezer, Dec. 31, 1839} Mercy.

1840

January 1st — Most dear and precious Christ, I had not thought to see another new-year's day, but hoped ere now to have beheld Thee face to face! Like him of old, who was possessed of a legion, I besought that I might be with Thee; but for a season Thou hast seen good to withhold the full answer to my request. "Thy will be done"; but glorify Thyself in me, and be much, very much with me, till Thou shalt say, "Arise, my love, and come away," to be with me for ever. I desire most humbly and unreservedly, in Thine own strength, to yield to Thy divine disposal all I have and am, and to lose my wish and will in Thine continually. I would lay at Thy feet all creatures and created good, with every seeming evil, and embrace Thee, my Jesus, as my joy, portion, happiness, wisdom, strength, peace—yea, my all in all—for the coming year, or so much of it as I tarry upon earth; and then my joyful, blissful portion through eternity! Oh, lead me, Holy Comforter, more into Christ and out of self; I have had much of blessing, but I long and pray for more; in Jesu's name. Enlarge my expectations more, I pray Thee, and more I shall receive—"Lord, increase my faith."

January 15th — A full cup of consolation has my precious Savior vouchsafed me to-day, and that in much bodily pain and faintness. A child at school is delighted with a letter from home, reminding him that the vacation is near; so my affliction seemed like a note, a glowing, loving, heart-burning note, from my most dear Jesus, saying, "The discipline of the wilderness will soon be ended, and thou shalt enter into my immediate presence."

> "Ah! then, in the full tide of bliss,
> My soul shall see Him as He is;
> And prostrate fall before His face,
> And shout the loudest, '*Grace, free grace.*'"

"Bless the Lord, O my soul," for this remanifestation of covenant love; I long to praise, in strains more suitable, my covenant God. O divine Comforter, do tune my heart, and teach my lips to praise. It seems as if I knew not how. Lord, warm my heart with living fire, and give me more ability to speak it out.

January 26th — Hot temptation, fiery darts, sharp conflicts; but Jesus is all-sufficient. In myself, weaker than the weakest, and quite unable to bear the present heart-aching anguish, or stand against the traitorous foes of my own house; but in Christ, my Head, even now a conqueror.

February 16th — Praise, adoration, and thanksgiving to my covenant God for this day's mercies; especially that the soul of my dear, dear mother has experienced an unusual melting. I trust it is an earnest of good things to come; how do I *long* that she may be comforted. My Jesus, Thou hearest, knowest all; glorify Thyself in me and mine. Ebenezer!

May 3rd — Heard a sermon upon the cross of Christ—a special time of love to my soul this evening. Surely, "His left hand is under my head, and with his right hand He doth embrace me." Yes; vile, guilty, abominable as I am, my own Jesus bathes me in His blood, robes me in His righteousness, puts upon me His beauty, and then says, "Thou art all fair, my love; there is no spot in thee." Oh, the wonders of His love! my heart is ravished and overcome, and I would be away to enjoy the full fruition; "I charge you, O ye daughters of Jerusalem, that ye stir not up, nor awake my Beloved till He please."

> "My happy soul would stay
>   In such a frame as this,
> And sit and sing herself away
>   To everlasting bliss."

May 13th — A triumphant faith my heart longs for; not only for a submitting, confiding, wrestling faith, but a triumphant one; and what for? Oh, to honor Jesus; and not to rest in, but to go straight out of all the victory, the triumph, and the joy, into Him, the one object of my soul's desire; and with that same triumphant faith to "crown Him Lord of all." Rich indeed is the feast of my Jesu's love again. This very day I banquet with the King, and cannot tell a thousandth part of what my soul enjoys; free, free mercy, sovereign favor; "grace, grace unto it."

May 18th — The minister supplying for us, very unexpectedly called this morning, and methinks the alabaster box was broken amongst us, for my soul blessedly caught the fragrance of my Beloved's good ointments; before I had been burdened and buffeted, though certainly recognizing rest in Christ, and Him to be my resting-place.

May 29th — Jesus is come, and my soul rejoices. We have been painting, papering, and cleaning our little parlor, but I could not enjoy it till He had sanctioned it by His presence; for nothing is aught to me but as He is in it, and approves of it; and this very evening He has come and communed with me most blessedly, granting me the desire of my heart. Many tears have I shed this week, under a sense of my deep ingratitude and shortcomings. But Jesus will conquer; He will pardon; He will bless; and in His smile I am—I must be—happy! Oh, what wonders, and the consummation to come yet! "Bless the Lord, O my soul."

June 14th — Since the dear Lord has seen fit, in holy sovereignty, and contrary to expectation or desire, in some measure to restore my health, and longer to keep me in this drear wilderness, I have regretted and wondered that I did not put down that first blast of the jubilee trumpet which was so blessedly blown in my soul, that I might thereby be refreshed in future seasons of trial. It was on this wise. During the week these words followed me with some encouraging effect: "If the Lord had meant to destroy us, he would not have shown us such things as these"; and, on the following Sabbath, which was February 25, 1838, Mr. S— took for his text Judges 13:23. I was surprised at the coincidence, and began to listen with interest to the sermon. The Lord, however, was pleased to manifest His power and sovereignty by taking me aside from the means, while under them, and teaching me Himself, apart from human instruments; for, though I liked what I heard of the sermon, no power attended it, but the Holy Ghost did, quite separate from it, reveal Christ in my soul as my own precious Savior. He was pleased to lead me to recognize Him as born in my soul, and mentally to exclaim, "Unto *me* a Child is born, unto *me* a Son is given"; also, to behold Him going through His whole life on earth for me, as my Head, Surety, and Representative; in every part of it obeying the holy law of God, fulfilling all its righteous requirements: the eye of infinite justice following Him through every avenue, and finding no flaw; and all this, not for Himself, but for me. I felt it as fully so as if no other had interest therein. Then His crucifixion, His offering Himself once for all; there was the atonement for all my guilt, the satisfaction for all my breaches of the law; and here, again, I saw justice fully satisfied, my debts being honorably paid, and my soul lawfully acquitted. As a proof of this, I was privileged to behold the resurrection of my glorious Christ: seeing, that having had all my guilt laid before Him, He must have drunk every drop of wrath and curse due to it, or He could not have burst the bars of the tomb, and taken again that life which He said He "laid down of Himself." Then His ascension to His Father's right-hand was blessedly set forth to me, as a token that the infinite Jehovah had accepted all He had done and suffered as on my behalf. I can only describe the view I had of the ascension of my Christ into heaven by recognizing the eternal Father thereby putting "settled" to my *long black bill* of sin, guilt, and law breaches, and sending down the dear sacred Comforter to witness and seal home the same most comfortably in my conscience; according to the promise of Jesus, "I will pray the Father, and he will send you another Comforter, that he may abide with you for ever"; and again, "the Comforter, the Holy Ghost, whom the Father will send in my name, he shall teach you all things, and bring all things to your remembrance, whatsoever I have said unto you." And truly thus it was with me, this ever-to-be-remembered morning; for the most divine Spirit did "take of the things of Christ, and show them unto me," putting, as I call it, individuality and personality into them all; so that I, who had entered the chapel with the sentence of condemnation round my neck, signed with my own hand as just, did come out with a free pardon in its place, signed by the infinite Jehovah; also feeling myself robed in a spotless, seamless righteousness, in which I knew He accepted me, well pleased for His righteousness' sake. I, who had often been longing to have no soul, because of the judgment I saw impending, could now bless God for a soul to know and love Jesus, who had first loved me. My burden was gone, and I came home full of happiness. But as it hath generally been my lot to fight every inch of ground, so all this was questioned by unbelief and Satan that very night, and my soul agonized with sharp and bitter conflict. But it was *done*, and *done for ever*; nor can the howlings of all the monsters in my own fallen nature, or hell itself, ever undo it. Obscured from my view it may be by darkness, or fierce attacks of my enemies; therefore, while thankfully recording and gratefully remembering it, I humbly desire ever to place my whole dependence, and hang the whole weight of my salvation, upon the glorious Person and finished work of my dear and precious Lord Jesus Christ, and not merely upon the revelation thereof in my soul. For I do find that every part of experience, however clear, and every manifestation, however glowing and triumphant, may be questioned, and, for a time, made to appear a delusion, by unbelief and vigilant Satan. But when, by the power of the Holy Ghost, I am enabled to rest simply on Christ—though in myself as helpless and empty as at first—to venture on Him, and plead His blood and righteousness alone before the divine footstool, and in the face of all threatening foes—ah, then comes the victory; for the battle is the Lord's, and unbelief and Satan are obliged to fly before Him. May I ever remember this, and, while retracing these marvellous displays of His condescension and love, go through them all to Him, the immovable foundation of my soul, and the inexhaustible source of my happiness; in whom I may still safely confide, should all the streams of manifested comfort be for a season withdrawn. May the dear Lord keep me from dishonoring Him, by making more of His *gifts* than of *Himself!* May He also keep me from questioning those gifts, through the power of that hateful and hated enemy, unbelief. Many a dark night and dreary day have I passed since the fore-mentioned dawn of gospel liberty, which I can now clearly see that it was, though, by reason of sore buffetings, I was not for some time convinced that it was, a blast of the jubilee trumpet for which I had been so long listening. Slow have I been to learn that life of simple faith upon Jesus, which honors Him, and makes us in Him more than conquerors, even now. But here I am, pressing after it, longing for it, and blessedly tasting a little of its sweetness; and, by the good hand of my God upon me, I continue to this day a monument of sovereign, saving mercy, and free rich grace. "Bless the Lord, O my soul," for all His amazing benefits to the very chief of sinners! Oh that I could praise Him a thousand thousand times more! Giving myself up to Thee afresh, at this time, most precious Christ, to be wholly at Thy disposal and under Thy direction, I humbly crave that Thou wilt condescend to be exceedingly, increasingly glorified in me, whilst Thou continuest me here; and that my short remaining span may be one glow of praise and love, kindled at Thine own fire, and kept alive by Thine own Spirit. In remembrance of Thy miracles on my behalf, I here erect a stone of help. Ebenezer! Praise the Lord!

August 23rd, Sabbath — Of what wonders do I live to be the happy partaker; and all in Christ, through Christ, and by Christ! "Bless the Lord, O my soul." Having heard that some dear friends were grieved by my not receiving Mr. B—'s ministry, I began to fear lest I should be a stumbling-block to them, and might have done wrong in absenting myself. I went therefore to hear him this morning, for the sake of others, and that I might in no way dishonor that precious Jesus who has done so much for me; and truly the Lord was present indeed; and of a truth, "the Word came in demonstration of the Spirit, and with power"; and my soul was melted in love, gratitude, and astonishment. What Mr. B— advanced was deeply searching; but I desired to be searched to the very bottom, cut to the quick, and then healed by the blood of Jesus, and thus made thoroughly sound. I love to hear of the obedience of faith and the fruits of faith, as well as the joy of faith. The doctrine, experience, and precepts of the Word are dear to my soul—my Christ being to me the life of the doctrine, vitality of the experience, and the activity of the practice; from Him is my fruit found, and there will be no lazy walking, flesh feeding, or sin loving, as we are brought by the Holy Spirit to "abide in Him." Blessed be the Lord, who daily loadeth me with benefits.

August 26th — It has never been by looking at circumstances, but by looking to Jesus, that I have conquered. The Lord teach me this again, at this very time, and give me a song of victory through the blood of the Lamb!

October 8th — With thanksgiving and the voice of melody would I record the mercies of my God and Savior, in that He has condescended to appear for me most manifestly, in a circumstance connected with my employment; proving that He is a God who "revealeth secrets," and that He doth as manifestly give wisdom now, as when He fitted Bezaleel and Aholiab to devise curious works for the tabernacle.

October 31st — This ever-memorable night I must mark down; for this very evening, on hearing a dear friend read the last illness of Caroline Smelt, my heart hath been broken to pieces to find that the joy, ecstacy, power, glory, and blissfulness which she experienced, I too have known; and have bathed almost in bliss ineffable, while caged in mortal clay. But here hath been the bitterness, the grief, the wound, the anguish—my deep, deep ingratitude. My Jesus took her home, me He restored to tell His own wonders, sound His praises, shine His glory forth. But oh, how have I sunk into myself, and creatures, and dishonored Him, my loving and glorious Lord. My heart doth bleed, and to the very quick is pained; but all my pain is nothing to the cause of it, my wicked, shameful slothfulness and selfish sinfulness. Oh, pardon me, my

Jesus, and in Thy power restore; and, whether long or short be my life, let it henceforth be Thine, and Thine alone. Amen, most solemnly so be it; O Lord, Amen.

December 4th — It seemeth to me that Christ is the stooping-down of Jehovah; the arm of Jehovah, on which we can lean; the heart of Jehovah, of which we feel the sympathy; the eye of Jehovah, of which we can bear the glance—yea, whose look is love; the glory of Jehovah, upon which we can gaze unconsumed, and, while we gaze, are changed into the image thereof by the Spirit of the Lord; the voice of Jehovah, which is music, melody, and peace; the revealing of Jehovah. Oh, infinite abyss of love and joy, and peace, and grace, and truth, and holiness! my Christ, what is there not, what have I not, in Thee? In vain I try to ascend the wondrous heights, and explore the mighty depths! I am lost, overwhelmed, absorbed in love and Thee—almighty, boundless, matchless, endless love; "for God is love," and in this dwelling-place I would rest for evermore.

1841

January 1st — Goodness and mercy, lovingkindness and longsuffering, have hitherto surrounded me. The past year has been marked with love; but, methinks, actual communion has run in a lower channel, which sometimes makes my heart jealous. Lord, keep me close, very close to Thee; and, whether faith or sight will most honor Thee, mark Thou the way, and give submission. But, if Thy will, continue my loved seclusion from the world. Bless the Lord for the mercy-seat! Oh, the great, great privilege! Would it were more enjoyed and valued! Ebenezer!

January 6th —
"Thy mercy, my God, is the theme of my song,
The joy of my heart, and the boast of my tongue;
Thy mercy is more than a match for my heart,
Which wonders to feel its own hardness depart;
Thy mercy is matchless, most loving and free,
How great is that mercy extended to me!"

January 20th — Passing under cloud and depression, but "the Lord is my light and my salvation"; and, "though now I see Him not, yet believing, I rejoice," even in sorrow, and know He still is faithful, even though He hide His face. I much long to know what it means, whether a chastisement for sin, or a trial of faith, for its strengthening and increase. May the Lord speak—actual communion and love-embraces, my soul longs for, but fears to be impatient.

January 30th, Saturday — The Lord hath dealt wondrously with me this week. He first condescended to show me that I was unduly anxious about my work, which has much pressed upon me lately, from Hebrews 12:5, and 1 Peter 5:7; He then enabled me, after a sharp struggle, to cast all the care of it upon Him, and to prefer His will to the accomplishment of a portion of work, which I had thought very desirable for the accommodation of the owner. After this, when I had quite given it up, He most wonderfully gave me ability to accomplish it with ease, to my own astonishment; thus proving again, that in what we forego for His sake we shall be no losers. I believe my over anxiety was one cause of the cloud I have been under. He does, indeed, lead poor, blind me in a way I know not; but it leads to a city of habitation. "Bless the Lord, O my soul." Proverbs 22:15; blessed correction.

February 8th — I have been travelling rather heavily, my soul often bowed down in me because of the distance of my Beloved; that is, as to manifestation; for I know His eye is upon me, and His heart ever towards me, and that all discipline is love. I believe the Lord is dealing with me to humble me and empty me of self, which is what I long for; therefore, though painful the process, I can trust the hand of love; for it is love, almighty love, which lets out the life-blood of self. I have been exceedingly harassed by the fear that my extreme anxiety to live to the Lord, and be used for His glory, has arisen from self-seeking, and a desire for self-exaltation. The Lord teach me the right way; I am sure this case is "too hard for me." I almost think I shall not write here again for the present, lest this also be self. Well, now, if I stay away from the mercy-seat because of this my sinfulness, and wait till (through the power of the Spirit) I am enabled to walk more closely with God, and then approach because my conscience is less burdened, what will have become of my sin? It may for a time be forgotten, but will not be the less, and may arise again, to my extreme anguish. Nothing can safely put away sin but blood. Oh, then, away to the Fountain at once, though Satan or unbelief suggest it is presumption, and that I should wait till I am better. I cannot "find out the Almighty," but He can reveal Himself to me. That may be unfolded to me which never could have been found out by me. I am formed capable of receiving, but not of acquiring. "Bless the Lord, O my soul," that He could descend where I could not ascend, and raise me to where I could never climb (John 17:24). Infinite fullness can fill a finite being (Eph. 3:19), and a finite being be brought to dwell in Infinite fullness (1 John 4:15, 16).

> [Reader, mark this momentous distinction, "Found capable of *receiving*, but not of *acquiring*." This cuts up, as it ought to do, our poor fallen Adam nature, root and branch. Reader, art thou made willing to such a flesh-and-blood-crushing ordeal? If so, blessed be God for what He has done, both *for* thee and *in* thee.]

Some ministers seem most taken up in delineating the features of Christ as reflected in the church; others rise up into the personal glories of the Beloved, and, almost forgetting mortality and creatures, gaze upon "the perfection of beauty"; and, while they thus gaze, that beauty is, and must be, most clearly seen in them. *No fear of crooked walking while the eye is fixed full on Jesus.* I know my flesh must be crucified, but I was never told how many nails should be put in. So as one after another comes, I have no right to say, There are too many. Have I not been too contracted in my ideas of communion, thinking it must be ecstacy, delight, and pleasurable sensations? May there not be communion in patience, faith, submission, waiting, trust, venturing, &c.? The less I am, the more room there will be for the largeness of other people; but as self-importance swells me out, so their importance annoys and offends me. Real humility will pity the pride of others, but not take offence at it; because, always wishing to be least and lowest, it will easily concede what the other demands, and thus there will be nothing to contend for.

February 16th — A time of love this evening; that is, a nearer approach of my Beloved than that with which I have, of late, been favored, though not that close and ravishing communion which my soul longs for, and which I *have* enjoyed. Oh, that the fires of almighty love would descend and melt my frozen heart, and unloose my icebound affections, that they may glow and flow towards their source and centre. "If ye see my Beloved, tell Him I am sick of love." Ebenezer, for one more visit in this far-off country.

March 28th — Much blessed in living on the fullness in Christ during the last few weeks; I was tempted to-day to think that this continual victory in Christ was not right, and that the faith-embracements of Him to which my soul is brought were all fancy. I was enabled to take this matter simply to the Lord Jesus, entreating to be searched to the bottom, probed to the quick, and separated from all false peace, and the Spirit's work in me still further confirmed. This has been done by 1 John 5:4, from which I plainly see that the work has been of God; and I am led to desire still more constant baptism "*into* Christ," and more venturing acts of faith upon Him as my whole salvation, by the power of the Holy Ghost. "Bless the Lord, O my soul," that Satan is again foiled by Jesus; it is his constant aim to get something, *anything* between me and Christ. The Lord prevent it.

April 9th, Good Friday — After all I have received, I bless the Lord I have not had, or known, a thousandth part of Christ yet; it is still above and beyond me; and out of all I have had would I rise into Him "in whom dwelleth all the fullness of the Godhead bodily," to whom, with the Father and the Spirit, be glory evermore. Amen.

April 20th — I do find it in my heart to entreat earnestly and anxiously that no future circumstances of life may experimentally separate between me and my precious Jesus or cause me to walk at a greater distance from Him. I plead not exemption from the trials of life, or the mortification, crucifixion, and continued disappointments of the flesh; but I do plead, that in and through all I may be brought to closer, closer walking with Him who loved me, and gave Himself for me, and that nothing may be suffered to intervene to bring leanness of soul, or that dreaded coldness, lightness, and worldliness of spirit, at the thought of which I tremble and recoil. Oh, hear me, precious Jesus, and grant my one request—to be more like Thee, and more with Thee, and that Thou mayest be more glorified *in* me. Thou hast, Thou dost, Thou wilt deliver.

April 25th, Sacrament Sabbath — A good day in Christ. I have to-day blessedly seen how He is my Brother, born in my nature on purpose for adversity; for it was the adversity of His "sister spouse" which brought Him down to bear her woes. Oh, what love and fullness do I find in Jesus; may I go on to know Him more. Precious Christ, I embrace Thee as "my life and the length of my days"; in Thyself the good land into which Thou hast brought me, and in which, experimentally, Thou alone canst keep me. I do now, irrespective of outward circumstances, give myself again to Thee, imploring that Thou wilt be more glorified in me and mine. The weakest, lowest, vilest of all Thy family, I embrace Thee as my energy, ability, life, and righteousness—my all in all; and do close this book,* this page of my life, acknowledging the mighty mercies which have surrounded me hitherto, and the Ebenezers which crowd my path; and, had I room, would here erect an Ebenezer of Ebenezers—a pile of stones of help!

May 4th — A blessed and refreshing shower of unction from the Holy Ghost upon my soul to-day, leading me to fresh faith-embracements of Jesus, in whom I lose my sins, my sorrows, and myself. "Bless the Lord, O my soul," and still cry after, and seek for, more Christ.

May 30th, Sabbath Morning — The Lord has been very gracious to me through the past week, not suffering the pressure of circumstances to overwhelm me, but accomplishing for me wonders therein. I have felt at times like a ship becalmed, having the sails spread, and waiting for celestial breezes from the Holy Ghost; but feeling that, because of my wanderings, they were in justice withheld. Again, however, sacred gales have sprung up, wafting sweet odors of my Beloved, and carrying me forward towards the desired haven, under a melting sense of pardoning love and restoring grace. How precious and blessed is a life of faith, wherein everything spiritual and temporal, providential and circumstantial, minute and important, becomes matter of exercise and medium of communion. And how great a privilege is the use of the pen, whereby these things are recorded, and reverted to again and again. I cannot tell the solace and profit it has been to me. No doubt my dear father well knew its pleasures, since he recommended me very early in life to commence this system of mental bookkeeping, if I may so call it; and truly I have found my account and profit in so doing.

---

* The Diary was written in separate books. This closed one of them.

June 16th, Wednesday — My dear mother was in bed nearly all yesterday, but I trust she is better to-day. May the Lord be glorified in this sickness, and may she be comforted. I think I have found it profitable, though very painful; it has been like loosening the earth about me, that I might cleave less to it, and shaking my comfort in the creature, that I might find it all in Jesus; and truly I do find it there most richly. He has this morning shone on me with love, and is now very near to my spirit. "Bless the Lord, O my soul," for light in a dark place.

June 18th — My mother is better, the Lord be praised! This affliction hath been a very merciful one to me, giving fresh opportunity for the display of the love of Jesus, which hath sweetly flowed into my soul, proving that He is better to me than all earthly mothers, fathers, husbands, brothers, or any other. Oh, what have we in our precious Christ! Heart cannot conceive it, tongue cannot utter it; He is all love and loveliness, all glory and majesty. He is Jehovah manifested, communed with, and delighted in; it is heaven begun to dwell in His embrace—yes, heaven—while fettered in mortality, surrounded by creatures, and roared at by Satan too. Oh, for higher, loftier strains of praise to the Three-One Jehovah, my all in all.

July 6th, my Birthday — I desire to give myself more unreservedly than ever to be the Lord's alone. Thine I am, O Jesus; Thine, thou Son of David. Oh, stamp Thine image on me; breathe Thy fragrance through me, and be exceedingly glorified in me in life and death. Thanks and praise be to Thee for the great mercies of the past year; thanks that I was ever born to know Thee, and thanks that I am born to live for ever; thanks and praises, endless and ceaseless, to my covenant God in Christ, for being in Him who loved me and gave Himself for me. Ebenezer!

July 25th — Amidst the changes of this changing world, O Lord, give us to find sweet repose in Thee, in Thy unchangeability, who art ever the same! May Jesus be the Alpha and Omega of the coming week and month.

July 31st — I humbly trust Jesus has been the Alpha and Omega of this week, and the one object of my desire and pursuit. I have been much blessed, and have had some gracious bedewings and anointings of the Spirit, and *that* in "holy sovereignty"; for my undeservings have indeed been manifest, and I am constrained to say, "Grace, grace unto it."

August 8th — The past has been a week of manifested mercy; it began with fears and faintings, because of things cross and contrary; but the Lord hath been my stay, bearing me up, through, and above all, in Christ! He has also, this week, vouchsafed me an outward token of His faithfulness, which has been precious. Some months since, He put it into my heart to do without a dress I wanted, that I might give the money to a saint of His, united to me in the flesh and in the Lord, and who was in want. This was a privilege, and so I esteemed it; but the dear Lord would not be behind in payment, for He has now sent me, through a dear relative, a dress and a shawl too. To Him be the praise and glory of all I receive; also that every occurrence in life affords matter of intercourse and communion with Him, and fresh proofs of His faithfulness. Oh, to trust all with Him, and to forsake all for Him more and more! "Bless the Lord, O my soul," for the privilege of thus beholding a part of His ways.

August 15th — Lord, increase *practical* faith in my soul,—

"For I am but a learner yet,
Unskillful, weak, and apt to slide."

August 22nd, Sabbath Morning — If the richness and riches of Jesus shall roll over, rise above, and come through the poverty of the instrument to-day, my soul will rejoice; and He shall have the praise who holdeth the stars in His right hand, and makes them sparkle forth His glory, according to His own will.

September 12th — I do not now wonder that Satan did formerly press me so heavily, hunt me so closely, and tempt me so fearfully about the divinity of my precious Christ; for, as He is dishonored and rejected by unbelief, the soul is kept weak, dark, and uncertain; but as He is received by faith, through the Spirit's power, no mortal tongue can express the benefits, the blessedness, the glory we find in Him. I know it, for I prove it; and though it be contradicted by those who have never tasted or handled, yet the fact remains the same, and in it we do, must, and will rejoice. "Lord, increase our faith."

September 19th — It is not all *eating*, even when with Jesus, as Matthew 15:32: how much of the three days they fasted, is not said; but so much, that they were in danger of fainting, if not refreshed. Let me not, then, be cast down by fasting times, even though long; they are often the prelude to a blessed and miraculous supply, when and where least expected; neither let me think, as Satan would insinuate, that because I am not enjoying, Jesus is not with me. He is here as much to regulate the length and effects of the fast, as to bless, give out, and enliven the feast.

September 30th — A most blessed feast of love, and glimpse of glory to-day; my soul ravished, and lifted in enjoyment far away from all earthly objects. Somewhat of the grace-fullness and glory-fullness of Jesus revealed to my wondering, admiring soul; but more is yet behind to be unfolded. "Praise the Lord, O my soul." The glory came in writing to Mrs. —.

October 22nd — A blessed interview with Mr. D— this morning, one of the Lord's dear ministers; and truly a heart-warming season it was to me. Oh, why, why am I so favored? The dear Lord does melt me with kindness. Mr. D— seems to know blessedly the power of "love and blood," and the efficacy of prayer; he said, very sweetly, "If you can say nothing else at the footstool, cry, *Blood, blood*!"

> [Reader, nothing disturbs the devil like the cry of "Blood, blood!" He has no answer for the glorious testimony—the sinner's last and only plea—"The *blood* of Jesus Christ his Son cleanseth us from *all sin*."]

October 29th — I have been completely shaken this morning by a letter from dear Mr. T—, in which he tells me that he has sent my last for insertion in the "Gospel Magazine." I cannot describe the distress it occasioned me. Publicity is so completely contrary to my wish and inclination; seclusion and hiding are what I love. But it is done, and without my knowledge. What the Lord intends by it, I know not; my heart aches, but still I would not dishonor Him, for the sake of five times, nor a hundred times, the anguish. I do know I have given myself, and my feelings, to my precious Jesus, to be used for His honor, as He sees best; and shall I draw back when He says, "Come forth?" No, Lord; if it be Thy voice, I submit, though clean contrary to my natural feelings; but if it be an act of the creature, contrary to Thy will, I beg and entreat that Thou wilt frustrate it. I know well, that in writing that letter, Thou didst bear me up into such bliss and blessedness as no language can describe; it came from Thee, therefore do as Thou wilt with Thine own. I remember Vashti, who refused to come forth at the king's commandment, and I tremble; for though my precious Jesus will never divorce me, yet His absence in anger, and the frown of His displeasure, are more terrible than death. Oh, pity Thy trembling one; let the cordial of Thy love and blood keep me from fainting; and again, in Thy presence, solemnly do I say, "Thy will be done," though it cuts closely and keenly, and I sensibly feel the smart, for I would be shut up from human observation to my life's end, Thou knowest; and yet I would joyfully be a witness for Thee to the world's end.

October 31st — Reading this morning Luke 8:22, 23, &c., it struck me thus: Why, Jesus knew, when He entered that ship, what a storm would come on the lake; and He knew, when He went to sleep, in His human nature, how that sleep would draw forth the fears of His disciples; and yet He did all this to show forth His glory, and exercise their faith; and so, when I wrote that letter to Mr. T—, and Thou, blessed Jesus, didst lift me up so blessedly in communion with Thyself, beholding Thy glory, Thou knewest what would come out of it, though I had not such a thought; therefore I do trust it with Thee, and commit it to Thee. Bring out of this event Thine own glory, and my soul will be content, though I suffer deeply in my feelings. Now is the time of the storm, but Thou art controlling its waves and its billows, and I am safe amidst its tossings; and, when a calm will honor Thee, it shall come at Thy command, nor would I desire it one moment sooner.

1842

January 1st, New Year's Morning — My dearest mother seems somewhat better; but, while thankful for it, I dare not trust in it, or in anything short of the will of Jesus—that is my safe abiding place. And now, precious Christ, I come with a large request for 1842: it is that Thou wouldst be the "Alpha and Omega" of it; dost Thou not say, "Ask what I shall give thee"? *Thyself, Lord!* Thou hast most blessedly given Thyself to me: but I find sweet liberty to entreat more unfolding, revealing, and opening of Thy glorious person, amazing work, and matchless love, than I have yet had; and more losing and treading down of self, too, that I may be lost in the fullness of Thee, and forgotten and forsaken in Thy soul-absorbing glories. Oh, raise me higher, draw me nearer, that I may daily die, and Thou in me more manifestly live. I just give myself to Thee, to live on Thee, to live in Thee, to live for Thee, more and more than heretofore, and that by the power of the Spirit resting on me, through union to Thee; for Thou hadst the divine anointing, without measure, that all Thy members, in measure, might receive the sacred unction. I humbly ask that mine may be a large and still-increasing portion; that, under fresh anointings, Thou, most lovely Jesus, mayest be more fully known, more loved, more served; for it is to Thee the Holy Spirit leads, of Thee He testifies; and as, by Him, we are brought to honor Thee, the Father too is honored, and thus the Holy Three-in-One adored and worshipped. Oh, do make this a large, rich, full year! Thou being increasingly honored in me, and I increasingly lost in Thee, and made an increasing blessing to Thy dear people. An Ebenezer for past mercies becomes me; large and magnificent have been Thy bestowments; bountiful and constant Thy favors to me, a poor worthless nothing! "Bless the Lord, O my soul: and all that is within me, bless his holy name."

January 2nd — The extreme selfishness of one of my friends has of late pressed heavily upon me; but something this morning has said within me, "Is it not my own selfishness that makes me feel it?" Were I in the proper spirit, should I not be ready to distribute, willing to communicate to her, all the attentions of Christian friendship, even without receiving much in return, especially as I am receiving so much from Christ? Oh, Thou precious Jesus, pardon me, and make the very pain I have felt a corrective to my own *self-love,* seeing that is the hateful principle which has been grumbling about the want of attention from my friend; so that what I have condemned in her, has, in the very condemnation, been prevailing in myself. Oh, kill and crucify this self in me—this hateful, hated idol! Come in, Thou precious Christ, and make it fall before Thee. To Thine own discipline I yield myself. I would be Thine, to serve and honor Thee, in comforting and profiting Thy members; but without Thee can do nothing. Oh, use me for Thy glory, and this new year let self be lower laid, and Thou exalted more: and Thine shall be the praise!

January 8th — A full cup of love and glory have I enjoyed in Christ to-day; it has been one of the days of heaven to my soul, an *antepast* of glory and *high tide* of bliss, and all in Christ, who is the boundless, fathomless fullness of it, and all to His praise; for I am a most undeserving, or rather hell-deserving nothing; but He, my Head and

Surety, has had my deserts, and I most blessedly have His. He has endured my *hell*, and I enjoy His *heaven;* and in Himself, my heaven of heavens, do I find substantial bliss. Oh, why am I so favored? why taste so sweetly, drink so largely, of overwhelming joy? It is so because my Father *wills* it, in "holy sovereignty." To Father, Son, and Holy Ghost, be all the glory, and endless, boundless praises, evermore. Victory, victory is mine, through the blood of the Lamb!

January 9th — Eternally freed from sin, as one with Jesus; what a liberty, what a freedom! It is so, and so for ever— it cannot be undone. "Wonder, O heavens! be astonished, O earth." I myself do wonder, with great admiration, at the glorious blast of the jubilee trumpet, which has just reached my ear, and touched my heart. It was the voice of my Beloved, which said, "Thou art all fair, my love: there is no spot in thee"; free from sin, being dead with Christ to it, "In that he died, he died unto sin once" (Rom. 6:10), and we died to it in Him—free from sin, in being risen with Him, to live unto God for ever. Paul knew this freedom (Rom. 6:7). Romans 8:1, 2: "There is therefore no condemnation [then there can be no sin, for where sin is condemnation is] to them which are in Christ Jesus, who walk not after the flesh, but after the Spirit." John knew it (1 John 3:6): "Whosoever abideth in him sinneth not"; and 4:17: "As he is, so are we in this world"—that is, must be perfect, and without sin; not in our *nature-self*, but in *Christ*, and in that which is born of God and sinneth not (3:9). But why, then, do I so often feel myself a transgressor? Because I build again, by my legality, what I had destroyed by faith, viz., justification by my own doings; and thus make myself a transgressor (Gal. 2:18). This is not walking after the Spirit, but after the flesh, and it tendeth to bondage. The Spirit points to Christ, the flesh leans to self. In Christ we have perfection, without spot, in which we can lift up our head with joy; in self we have spots and no perfection, which must needs make us ashamed!

January 11th — I am finding the Proverbs of Solomon exceedingly rich, they being full of Christ, and describing, blessedly, a life of faith upon Him, with its benefits. But it is the Holy Spirit alone that can unlock these secrets, and bring out the hidden treasure: once I knew them not, and never thought to find them here; I am now only beginning to discover their fullness. The best is all to come.

January 30th — As I was this evening mourning my shortcomings, it struck me that there was sufficiency in Christ to make up for all deficiency in me; and then it came, "Divers weights are an abomination to the Lord," and I saw very plainly that I was not acting uprightly, but was attempting to put divers weights into the scale—viz., *Christ and self*. "A false balance is an abomination to the Lord" (Prov. 11:1, and 16:2). What is a just weight in God's account? Only righteousness in which there is no defect; an obedience which reaches to every jot and tittle of the law, and an atonement which fully satisfies for every breach of it. These are the weights of the bag, which are His work, and His delight (Prov. 11:1), and are only to be found in His Christ, who is not to be put into the scale to make up our deficiencies, for He is the one *full weight and just measure;* and it must be a *whole Christ*, and *Christ only*. Nor are the fruits brought forth in us, by Him, to be added. These are for His honor, not for our justification, He is *that*—made so of God unto us, "wisdom, righteousness, sanctification, and redemption" (1 Cor. 1:30). Oh, what a full-weight Christ has the Father given, and the Spirit revealed in us: so that, being made to feel our nothingness, we need not fear, for *Christ* is all we need. But, truly, it is one thing to confess we are nothing, and another to be content to be nothing, and make no account of ourselves. I see plainly that I am more frequently engaged in *fraudulent* practices than I was aware of. The Lord give me to forsake them, and hold fast Christ (my integrity and uprightness), since self has been weighed, and found wanting—yea, proved to be less than nothing and vanity.

March 5th — Rich and full have been the bestowments I have received in my soul last evening and this; proving, blessedly, that the religion of Jesus is one of power; and that in Him is an inexhaustible fullness of love, blood, and free-grace salvation. How *near* have I been drawn, and how intimate and endearing has been the communion I have enjoyed; it is wonderful, most wonderful! "Bless the Lord, O my soul!" "Grace, grace unto it!" I am nothing, have nothing: it is Christ is all and in all. My heaven has begun, and the eternal Sabbath has dawned on my wondering soul, while dwelling in mortality. The days of darkness may yet be many, for God has set prosperity and adversity, the one over against the other; but the full consummation will come, "as sure as the earnest is given," whatever may lie between. Eternal praises to the great Three-One!

March 23rd — I, through free and sovereign grace, shall leave the ante-room of faith-communion, and enter the presence-chamber of sight-beholding and love-unfolding.

April 3rd — A good day, and day of goodness, and all in Christ; He is the fullness of my enjoyment, which hath been most sovereignly vouchsafed by the power of the Holy Ghost, without instrumentality, except that the minister spoke of our being chosen in Christ before we fell in Adam. And then my soul was led away in views, most glowing and glorious, of the life we have in "second

Adam," as infinitely superior to that we lost in the first. It was, indeed, an ecstacy of triumph in Christ, which made poor weak mortality shed tears of joy; and if such be the glory of a little apprehension and revelation of that eternal life, just gleaming through the crevices of our prison, what—oh, what—will be the full unfoldings and open beholdings thereof? I cannot tell what it will be; mortality, I am sure, could not endure it, but "mortality shall be swallowed up of life." And, when at these high entertainments, I think it will be soon, and am ready to say, Surely I cannot. Bless the Lord, for more heaven on earth, this blessed 1842. My sole desire now is to honor Him who has done so much for me, but, poor feeble worm, I can do nothing; He must, He will, work all my works in me, and glorify Himself in the work of His own hands. I feel, with others of the living family, the achings, sinkings, sinnings, and sufferings of the flesh; but I do find in Christ support, pardon, deliverance, and victory. No tongue can tell *what* we have in Him, in whom "eternal fullness" dwells. Oh, for more entrance into Him, by the power of the Spirit, and more abiding in Him, by faith, by the same almighty power! The more power we have, the more we want; for power seeks power, and never, never can be satisfied with form.

April 10th — The day my dear father was emancipated from a body of death and a world of sorrow; and, though nineteen years have rolled away, I still cherish his memory with affectionate tenderness and lively interest. But oh, what mercy have I to tell of since we lost him; truly, our God has been the Husband of the widow, and the Father to the fatherless. To His name be the praise for all the spiritual and temporal favors we have received. I feel a desire spring up afresh, to commit myself unto the Lord this day, for all that yet awaits me in providence and grace, humbly desiring, more than ever, to be devoted to

His service; more than ever to live upon His Christ; and more than ever to reflect His image and glory.

April 21st — Last evening heard, with much unction, a minister of the Spirit. How clearly did he describe a form of godliness without the power, and how forcibly did he speak of the power also; but oh, the wonder of wonders is, that I had, most blessedly, the witnessing of the Spirit with my spirit, that *I am in the power*, and *the power in me*. And this morning my soul is on the wing for glory, longing "to leave dull mortality behind, and fly beyond the grave." Oh, what can I render, for such sovereign displays of sovereign love and favor? How do I feel it has been put into me, without any act of my own, and how am I amazed that I should be taken, and others left. To the Holy Three-One, by whom I have been loved, chosen, and saved, be all the praise!

May 8th — A day of extreme depression; it has not been reaping, but sowing, and that "in tears."

May 17th — I have just seen the clay tabernacle of a dear sister laid in the dust, and that "in sure and certain hope of the joyful resurrection." Glorious prospect, when this mortal shall put on immortality, and this corruptible incorruption; then shall "death be swallowed up in victory," and all to come, be endless, blissful life, for evermore! I love that term, "swallowed up"; it is so triumphant and expressive. The believer's life is victory, his death is victory, and his eternity is victory—but not in himself; himself is all defeat and loss, *Christ* is his gain, and crown, and never-ending triumph. Hail, liberated sister, happy spirit, from clog and fetter free, thou knowest the joys of presence, and dost behold Him, without a veil or cloud to intercept His glory. Well—

> "But a little, and we know,
>   Happy entrance shall be given;
> All our sorrows left below,
>   And earth exchanged for heaven."

June 19th — "Mortality swallowed up of life," has just been very sweet to me in this way—I am mortality, Jesus is life; I want to be swallowed up of Him, in Him, with Him—not merely at death, not merely when I wake up in His glorified likeness, but now, now, precious Jesus, absorbed and lost in Thee, yes, "swallowed up." Strange as it might sound to the natural man, my spirit glows at the thought, and longs to launch out into, and blend with, eternal fullness: and thus be absorbingly lost, yet blessedly and joyfully found, in God, the great Ocean of love.

July 3rd — On this last Sabbath in my thirty-seventh year, I do desire most solemnly to dedicate, or yield up, myself afresh unto the Lord, for more peculiar and complete devotedness than heretofore; to be more blessed, and make a greater blessing. Nehemiah 11:2, seems what I want, to dwell in Jerusalem; to forsake all earthly interests; to give up all earthly and fleshly delights and self-pleasing; so that, in all I do, I may be seeking the Lord's glory—and that thus even my lawful engagements and avocations may be sanctified. It is a great and blessed thing I seek; but He who has given Himself to me, can do it for me. Oh, precious Jesus, grant me this request; I do not honor Thee, love Thee, praise Thee, serve Thee, half enough. Oh, what unworthy returns have I made for Thy great kindness towards me! What pride, baseness, foolishness, and worldliness, have prevailed in me; do anoint me afresh with the Spirit that descended and remained on Thee, that I, in union to Thee, might receive thereof. I ask a large, large measure of Thy glory—my deeper abasement and Thy people's good.

July 6th — Thirty-seven years have I sojourned in this wilderness, and would now solemnly erect an Ebenezer, and thankfully say, "Goodness and mercy have followed me hitherto." Under the Spirit's power, may I, afresh, renew my trust in the Lord for all the future; still seeking, most earnestly, to live more to His glory. I long that I may, by faith, again take hold of that blessed covenant, which suits me so well: "I will not depart from doing them good; but will put my fear in their hearts, that they shall not depart from me." Lord, fulfill it in me. I painfully see how much I have lived in and for self. May I henceforth come to be nothing, and Jesus to me be all in all! Ebenezer!

July 7th — Glory, glory hath, this morning, filled my soul. Last Sabbath I "sowed in tears," to-day I "reap in joy," and long for the fullness of the glorious harvest in eternal glory. The first three months of this year were most glowing, so that I named it the blessed 1842. It began with this, on New Year's day: "Light is sown for the righteous, and gladness for the upright in heart." Christ is my righteousness and uprightness, and in Him I have it all. The second three months I had much blessedness and many blessings, but not such positive, close, and soul-ravishing communion; also, more mingled with chilliness of soul, and depression of spirit. I am now getting on in the third three months; and what—oh, what—am I waiting for? The Lord to "crown this year with His goodness." Yes, crown it, precious Jesus! crown it now with Thyself; and give me again to "crown Thee Lord of all." More love, more joy, more heaven; for truly, this last two or three days, I have at times had heaven upon earth in my soul, and it does seem as if I must soon burst mortality, and "be ever with the Lord!" I long to behold Thee "with eyes made strong to bear the sight." Come, come quickly, Thou dear Lord Jesus! in Thine own good time: but *come*, do not *send*. Oh, I cannot meet death without Thee! Thou art indeed "the death of death." Oh, come, then, Thou eternal life, and be honored and glorified in this body till, and when, it falls asleep in Thee. Be thou crowned with shouts of triumph, victory, and praise, while Thou beginnest to crown me—poor little me—with glory. Hallelujah! Amen.

August 27th, Evening — Precious Jesus! I embrace Thee as my Way, my Strength, and my Guide for the coming week; it looks very dark, but in darkness Thou wilt be light about me.

September 4th — What am I now learning? Methinks, how to be abased, for most painfully is now being developed my cross and crooked nature, so that I am hateful to myself, and sick of myself, and seem unfit for society; so ignorant, weak, unamiable, and timid, unlike all around me, and I just seem more fit than ever to be secluded from all but my Jesus. A good deal of shade during the last week, and my Beloved not present in manifestation. Oh that I could honor Him in all states! This is the great grief, that He is in me so much dishonored.

September 18th — A high look and a proud heart the Lord will not suffer, and yet these two abominations met in me this morning; and where? Ah, monster that I am, on entering the house of God! I felt the evil, and the rebuke of conscience; the Lord pardon. It is said, "He knoweth the proud afar off," but this I cannot bear; I must press near, if it be to receive the stripes of love, and have my pride beaten out of me.

September 27th — A good deal depressed in spirits today —a time of weeping. I feel I am preparing to go down into the valley of humiliation, in outward circumstances; all things seem tending that way. May Jesus support, and be glorified, and it shall be well. It is astonishing how every thing I have to do with, both great and small, seems blighted by my touch; and I have constantly contrarieties and crosses in the flesh. I have thought of Job. Perhaps the enemy has envied my happiness, and obtained leave to afflict me; but, if so, I know he is bounded, and cannot go one step farther than he is permitted. Almighty love is overruling; and, if but my Jesus be honored, it is worth the smart. I cannot, yet, feel anything like wrath in all that befalls me, but believe I am in the arms and heart of love; and, "though he slay me, yet [would] I trust in him."

October 2nd — My beloved mother again very ill; seized with an unusual coldness yesterday. It lasted all day, and during the night she was so ill that I was much distressed, and feared the dreaded period of separation was really come; and, what was most agonizing, she was rambling in her mind. I dare not sleep, but kept painful and solitary watch; but the Lord heard prayer, and my dear mother is this morning herself again, though very poorly; still, I hope, a little better. Dearest Lord, spare, oh, spare her a little longer, if it may be Thy will and for Thy glory; and, above all, shine upon the soul of my loved parent.

October 12th, Wednesday — My dear mother gradually improving. What shall I render for such mercies? But still I wait for more power and light in her soul.

October 13th, Thursday — My dear mother was taken this morning with giddiness and sickness; but the Lord is still my confidence, and, though He slay, I must trust in Him.

October 16th — I rather think the above-mentioned relapse was for the trial of faith; and a fiery trial it was, for my beloved mother was so ill, and my faith so weak, that I really thought my former expectations were quite cut off; and much I feared the enemy would triumph, because we had given this matter simply into the Lord's hands, on Monday. He has, however, taken care of His own honor, and, though shaken, we are not destroyed. Again she is better, and has this morning gone up to the Lord's house, to praise Him for His great mercy. I feel now to "rejoice with trembling," and to walk fearfully, and carefully, as if it were uncertain ground—I mean as regards my dear mother's life. I wish to hold it *in* and *for* Jesus, not, not for myself. I trust her recovery may be perfected, that unbelief and Satan may get another throw-down, and we be encouraged to trust and pray more and more; and, also, I would be seeking submission. I fear that I have been too much distressed; for my heart seemed really almost broken, when I thought how she was declining. The Lord pardon any dishonor I have done Him in this matter, and bring me to perfect absorption in His will. I think there is a little breaking in my beloved parent's mind, and have strong hope that the light will come. I have borne my dear mother before the Lord in supplication, and have carried her heavily in my heart, many, many years, very long before I knew liberty myself—yea, even in my childhood, I have groaned and cried to the Lord for her; and I think the reaping time will come. I am sure the breathing of the Lord's Spirit will be answered. May all mine that has been fleshly, be forgiven. Ebenezer! Jehovah-Rophi!

November 18th, Friday — A blessed prayer-meeting this evening, and a season of power, very great power, in pleading for J. B. R—, with sweet whispers in my soul of future good things to come for him (Mark 5:19, 20; 1 Sam. 9:25-23, 24; Acts 27:25). Oh, precious Jesus, Thy name is wonderful, Thy ways are wonderful, and the instruments Thou usest are wonderful; for they are very little, and very mean in themselves, and Thou makest them of the "vine-tree, of which men will not take a pin to do any work" (Ezek. 15). Go on to be glorious in the eyes of Thy own servants, and still do wondrously before them.

November 20th, Sabbath — My beloved mother is better, and has gone to chapel alone to-day, for the first time. "What shall I render?" I feel just now like Esther 5:1-4, venturing into the presence of King Jesus, and supplicating Him to come and banquet with me. And what for? Oh, that I may plead with Him against that enemy which hath caused lately a distance between Him and me. I know not yet what it was, but He can discover it; or, I can plead against an unknown foe, and say, "Let Thine enemies perish, O Lord." Come, Beloved, let the King come to the banquet, bringing His royal dainties and royal state with Him. The dark cloud has gone. On Friday evening it was removed. All day I kept fearing, lest Jesus should not come, and this word seemed to answer me, "Be not faithless, but believing"; and He did come, and the shadows of darkness fled at His presence. Oh, then, come again, precious Christ, if it may please Thy divine Majesty, and explain the cause of Thine absence, and let the Haman be destroyed at Thy commandment. Afresh, I do this morning make a full resignation of myself and my all to Thy disposal, that thou shouldst be honored in me in Thine own way, even as Thy love and wisdom dictate.

November 22nd — I rather think the darkness I was under last week might be covenant discipline, and the stripes of love, for the inordinate distress I felt in prospect of losing my dearest mother in her late illness. Perhaps precious Jesus has been saying, "You shall try whether your mother's presence will make up for *My* absence." Ah, no, dear Lord, it would not; but *Thy* presence would, I know, supply the place of every creature, and make up the loss of them. Oh, pardon, pardon me, in that I have dishonored Thee; and restore me to the simplicity of living to, and for, Thee. Destroy this propensity of overrating and clinging to the creature, with every other which separates me from Thy manifested love.

December 26th — The Lord, my Lord, is indeed crowning the year to me with His love and with Himself! Much darkness have I felt the last few months—that is, at times, but it is all gone; my soul is now light in the Lord, and I have so much of Christ, that I long to be away to full fruition. "Bless the Lord, O my soul."

1843

January 1st — Precious Jesus! a new-year's blessing my soul craves of Thee. Oh, deny me not, but shine and smile, and give an earnest of good things to come during this 1843. For my dear mother, spared and restored, I praise Thee, and for the ten thousand other blessings with which Thou hast blessed me, I would adore Thee; but most for Thyself, in whom all things are blessings to me. I humbly erect an Ebenezer for the past, and for the future crave earnestly, longingly (but not half earnestly enough) more, much more, of Thee, my Jesus, that I may live in Christ. *9 o'clock* — The glory, power, love, sweetness, and ravishing communion I have this evening enjoyed, are inexpressible in mortal strains; I think it almost exceeds anything I have ever before known; but, however, it was truly heaven begun, and still I cry, "More of Christ," till "mortality shall be fairly swallowed up of life."

January 15th, Sabbath — "I have loved the habitation of thy house, the place where thine honor dwelleth." These words are much on my mind this morning; and, though I know Christ is the fullness of them, still they seemed to bear upon the outward sanctuary as they pressed upon me.

Noon — It has not been vain to wait upon the Lord. He has blessed me, above the instrument, by Himself, through a passage which was only quoted; it was, "The heaven of heavens cannot contain thee." What bliss and glory do I see, in that the heaven of heavens could not contain Jehovah, because of *love* as well as of *greatness*. Love brought Him down; love made Him stoop—yea, made Him bring His heaven to earth, and raise His earth to heaven. "Bless the Lord, O my soul," and give me, precious Christ, to dwell in Thee, for Thou art love and heaven. Oh, may my soul in these blessed fires kindle and burn for evermore. Truly this dull body cannot long contain this enraptured soul; but it will burst out of prison to be absorbed in Thee—Thee, oh, precious Three-One Jehovah, its glorious all in all, revealed in Christ by the Spirit, to the glory of the Father.

February 19th — I felt yesterday, and feel to-day, that I could just be one of the poor widow's mites which were cast into the treasury in God's temple. My dear mother is a widow, and I am a *mite* indeed; but into God's treasury, for God's service, I would, and must, be cast. Nothing less can satisfy my longing soul than entire and unceasing dedication to the Lord, and deadness to earth. In all my powers and faculties I would that He might be honored. O Lord, accept this little humble mite for Thine own use, and let me be for Thee alone, and not another's with Thee.

February 24th — It is a great thing to be brought to joy in God; but it seems greater still to apprehend that God joys in us: this was with power made known in my soul last evening. A sense of this is overwhelming indeed, not only to have our hearts full of joy in God, but sensibly and feelingly to know that He joys in us; and thus be able to say, not only, "I am my beloved's," but also, "His desire is toward me." Oh, wonder of wonders! the feeling of it did melt my heart indeed. "Bless the Lord, O my soul."

February 27th, Sacrament Sabbath — I expect to-day to commemorate the love of our dying Lord at His table;

and, in seeking His presence in so doing, I have just been led to see an evil, of which, I believe, I have been the guilty subject—that of resting in, and being taken up with, certain feelings and sensations experienced by me, rather than with Christ Himself, the *Substance* of the feast; and thus my feelings become more the object of my pursuit and desire than His glory. Both in praying and reading the Holy Scriptures, I seem to have been thus beguiled from simplicity, having feeling and enjoyment more in view than Him from whom they come. And so, when favored with a sensation of comfort, peace, and joy in my reading, I have the next time come to the Word searching for that same sweetness again, more than for Christ, the source and fullness of it. Many dear Christians might not see what I mean, but I see plainly, and beg to be delivered from this seeking the gifts more than the Giver, which is unbecoming *to*, and not allowable *in*, a state of liberty. Oh, my Christ Jehovah, how hast Thou been dishonored by worthless me; so blest, so favored, and yet so prone to rest in Thy bestowments rather than Thyself; do pardon, and restore to that simplicity which is alone in Thee. Oh, do it for Thy love and honor's sake!

Evening — Most blessedly was I privileged this afternoon to triumph in Christ above feeling, and to prove that what we forsake for Him we shall find most abundantly in Him, which I did, till my body was well nigh overwhelmed with the love and glory in my soul—one of love's secrets for the abasement of self and exaltation of Jesus. To the Lord be all the glory!

> [We venture to detain the reader for one moment; first, to call his attention to the fact of our departed sister's very marked "growth in grace, and in the knowledge of Christ Jesus her Lord," in His divine Person; and, secondly, to the very clear way in which she now—in contrast to her former inability

so to do—distinguishes between faith and feeling—gifts and the Giver! Christ Himself, in His most lovely and adorable Person, has now become her theme—her sole object and subject! Reader, is this the tendency of *thy* experience? There is something wanting in everything short of it.]

March 10th — How sweet and powerful hath the Holy Ghost been in me this morning, as a Spirit of adoption, and with what endearment hath my soul cried, "My Father!" It seems that I could with delight be all day at the footstool, repeating the rapturous sound, my God, Abba, Father; and, oh, what love my Father hath, to give me to Christ, and Christ to me, and to "bruise Him" for my worthless sake. "Wonder, O heavens! and be astonished, O earth! for the Lord hath done it." An eternity is before us to dive into, and to explore this matchless love.

March 19th, Sabbath Morning — Much sweetness and power in reading Psalm 91, and this promise seems mine, "There shall no evil befall thee, nor any plague come nigh thy dwelling." The Lord fulfill this, in every sense.

Noon — Truly my soul has been in heaven, and heaven in my soul, this morning. I do not know whether great power has been felt by minister and people; that is with the Lord, and He will work in His own way; but I do know that I, the most unworthy of all, have power and powerful love vouchsafed to me, and still feel we shall be blessed as a people, and by this minister. All that is from Thee, O Lord, establish and fulfill; all that is of the flesh, pardon and crush.

March 26th — I heard with much power this morning, though under the deepest abasement, on account of sin—it almost breaks my heart to feel it working so powerfully, and then I am led to see that my Jesus has borne it, and that I am dead to it, through union to Him, and that breaks it again. The meltings and dissolvings of love none can know but those who experience them; and, methinks, those who feel sin most, feel love most. It is so amazing and so humbling to find love, blood, and salvation abounding over the aboundings of felt iniquity; the Lord only knows how I have been broken under the evils of my nature this week, and how I have longed to be released from the body, that I may sin no more.

March 28th — How tremblingly do I venture on this day, and how gladly would I leave this polluted body, and be away in the full perfection of glory, love, and praise. Oh, my dear Jesus, how precious art Thou to me, and how willingly I would be with Thee, and be like Thee, and dishonor Thee no more, Thou knowest. "Thy will be done."

April 2nd — Truly it is very blessed, safe, and profitable to take a gift from Jesus in the dark, all shut up in mystery, and not being able to see what it is, but trusting the Giver, taking it because He gives it; and for His sake content that it should be to us that measure of cross and that measure of comfort which will glorify Him; this is very flesh-puzzling and humbling, but it will turn to good account. "Bless the Lord, O my soul." Jesus in His person, Jesus in His work, Jesus in His love, has been my feast this morning, and I know not how to leave off writing of His wonders. St. John might well say, "And there are also many other things which Jesus did, the which if they should be written every one, I suppose that even the world itself could not contain the books that should be written." And so it seems, if my soul was indulged, I should write page after page, and book after book, and so spend my inch of time, and atom of energy, in trying to speak well of His name, and, after all, say nothing in comparison of what is to be said; for what can poor feeble *I* say of infinite majesty, infinite holiness, infinite love, and infinite condescension? Oh, I can only acknowledge that, having enjoyed much, I can say nothing; but desire to launch quite out of self, into the eternal fullness treasured up in Christ.

April 10th — On this 10th day of April, 1843, I, Ruth Bryan, do most humbly and solemnly desire to devote myself afresh to the Lord, in His own way, praying that He may be pleased to be more glorified in and by me than heretofore. I know most feelingly that I have no capabilities for this. I have lately been very sensibly realizing that I am nothing; and thus, worthless and helpless, I cast myself upon the Lord, who will be very greatly magnified, if He will condescend to be glorified in me.

April 12th, Wednesday Evening — Returned from hearing Mr. C— preach from Psalm 143:8; the text itself was enough for me, being most suitable to my present state. I have just read 2 Chronicles 20, and find it in my heart to ask the Lord to fulfill it in me, on the subject which has much harassed me for some days; that He would be pleased to fight the battle while I look on, though the very subject of the conflict; and then bring me by His mighty power to the valley of Berachah. Oh, yes; I do want to praise Him on this very ground, where flesh and Satan have so sharply troubled me. So be it, Lord. May I "stand still and see Thy salvation," and rejoice in it too, though it cut the flesh all to pieces.

April 14th, Good Friday, Noon — I have had a season of great power and blessedness in reading John 19, and pleading at the footstool with my dear mother, since breakfast. Why does the Lord so bless and favor me? In holy sovereignty, and because I am one of the most uncomely members of Christ, and have, therefore, put upon me more abundant honor, whereby I am humbled and Jesus much exalted. The fifth verse of the chapter was very powerful to me, "Behold the man!" crowned with thorns, that the woman, His bride, might be crowned first with lovingkindness, and then with glory, and that she might have ability and privilege to crown her glorious Bridegroom with praise—yea, "crown Him Lord of all." And He stoops to hear her low notes, and to receive her feeble adoration; and there are, even here, such mutual endearments and communion, that no carnal mind can conceive. Thoughts of the crucified Immanuel much dwelling in my soul, at this time the sun was darkened; may I be privileged to view by faith the mystic wonders of that scene, which the light of nature could never reveal, nor the eye of nature ever behold. Precious, precious Jesus, once crucified, but now glorified, do give me a season of power in Thy sanctuary to-night. May love and blood flow richly round to the redeemed, and let minister and people rejoice together.

April 15th, Saturday — Why me, why me so favored? Surely my heart will be right down broken with love and mercy. Just received a note from my sister-friend, to say it is on her mind to come and unite in supplicating for large power to-morrow—"a pentecostal season." And what is this but an answer to the Spirit's breathing on Sunday evening? The Lord keep us waiting and praying.

April 16th, Sabbath — It is mine to endure sharp temptation just now, almost constantly, notwithstanding what I enjoy. Sometimes the bodily frame sinks under the soul exercise of joy and sorrow, which do much exhaust poor nature.

April 18th — "The backslider in heart shall be filled with his own ways." A bitter, bitter portion, but most richly deserved.

April 22nd — Much powerlessness, much fleshliness, and much heart-coldness have been mine this week. I dreaded our little Friday meeting, nor could I think there would be a blessing; but there was one. My heart was broken, and brought close to the mercy-seat, under the prayer of my dearly beloved Mrs. F—. Now mercy and power followed, and truly it was a season of solid profit. The Lord be praised, and His name glorified.

April 30th — My heart broken to pieces under the sermon this morning—text, Isaiah 42:2. Surely it was my privilege to weep at the feet of my faithful and ever-loving Jesus, to whom I have made such unworthy returns; and I believe He will come and heal the broken heart, and restore me to that intimacy and endearment of friendship which I have enjoyed with His divine Majesty, and thus defeat Satan, who is trying to mar it, and crucify my flesh, which has lately been so busy. Some power and sweetness in partaking of the Lord's Supper; and, near the close, a most powerful and melting assurance that the dear Lord Jesus is about to come into us more manifestly, and bless us more abundantly in that place. Lord, confirm and fulfill all that Thou hast spoken. I am astonished Thou wilt speak to *me*, and whisper Thy sweet secrets; but it is because of union, as we were told, "Communion springs from union." Oh, though I, and union springs from love—yea, I think love is union; it is, as it were, the root of it; where we love we are united really, whether present or absent. One in spirit, there is union of soul; manifestive union springs out of this, and the communion succeeds; thus it was that "everlasting love" in the heart of Jehovah was the origin of our union to Jesus—that is, in the sense in which it had a beginning. We were loved, chosen, united; and neither earth nor hell can separate us. We had a being in Christ before all time, but we began *to* be, or really existed, in our flesh-and-blood nature in time, first representatively in Adam, then consciously in our own persons, when we were born into the world: in Adam the first we lost all creature holiness and perfection, and in our own persons we experimentally prove the loss; we feel our distance from God, and our estrangement from Him, and we think we are undone for ever, and all is gone; but the secret has to come out, the secret of love and union, and it does come out in the Lord's time, and love comes in, "and because we are sons, God sends the Spirit of His Son into our hearts, crying, Abba, Father." The divine Spirit communicates a new nature, born of God, one with Jesus, which cannot sin, because it is born of God; and He makes us know also that this body and soul, which fell in the first Adam, were redeemed by the second from all iniquity, corruption, and misery, of which they are now the subjects, and also from the curse due to that iniquity. He makes us know that we are the chosen bride of Christ, notwithstanding "our low estate"; that He has betrothed us unto Himself from all eternity, and that even then His delights were with us, and He rejoiced in us (Prov. 8.) Thus we discover a relationship we never thought of; union where we could not have conceived it; and love which was so beforehand with us, as to provide a patrimony which we can never waste, riches which we can never spend, holiness which we can never mar, purity which we can never sully, a life which can never die, a crown which we must wear, and an inheritance which we must enjoy for ever! Oh, the wonder of union to Jesus, *really* before time, *manifestly* in time, and its consummation in eternity! It is very moving and melting, as revealed in the soul by the Holy Ghost, who does further and further develop the mysteries and privileges thereof, as we go on in the divine life. Truly, union is *of* love, and communion is *in* love; and soon love and communion will absorb and overwhelm us for ever and ever!

May 2nd — A little drop of love let into my soul at the family altar this morning. Come, my Beloved, and overpower me again by Thy glories, as in former seasons.

May 3rd — Oh, this hateful and hated apathy, how it strives to gain upon me! I cannot bear not to *feel*. Dear "Caroline Smelt" just made again very arousing to me. I have returned to life from such joys as were to her the immediate prelude of glory. But oh, the unworthy returns! My heart is deeply grieved. How *can* I honor Jesus? How can I be useful and profitable to my dearest mother, and my much-loved Christian friends? How can it be? The Lord only knows. May He anew baptize me with the Holy Ghost, that my converse and actions may be full of power. I often think that the sands in my little glass of life are nearly run out. Oh that Jesus would take all that are left, for His own use and honor.

May 6th — Our Friday evening most exceedingly and solidly profitable to my soul; fresh closing with Christ, and fresh actings of faith upon Christ, brought about in my soul by the Holy Ghost, of which my dear Mrs. F— was the medium, by proposing some queries on 1 John 3:7. "Bless the Lord, O my soul!"

May 10th — My heart sorely grieved that I honor Jesus so little in my daily life. The moments are rapidly flying over, and how little are they redeemed. Truly my spirit mourns within me. Oh for new baptisms of the Holy Ghost! "Lord, what wilt thou have me to do?" Can it once be that I can live to Thy glory? I know it must be by Thyself alone; and I now desire afresh, by faith, to take Jesus only as the answer of my earnest request, expecting from—yea, in Thee, O Beloved, all fruit and fruitfulness. Read Daniel 1 at family worship this morning. Felt a good deal of power then, and since, from verses 8 and 12.

Daniel's desire is mine; and as he on *pulse*, so I on *Christ*, would live alone, henceforth and for ever; so be it, Lord. Do Thou say so too. "Prove me now herewith, I beseech Thee." Cause me to take Christ for my all, in time and eternity. Keep me from that beguiling by which I have been so robbed; and then I know I shall honor Thee more, and more reflect Thy glory. Oh, let it be so! My poor heart pants and thirsts for this high privilege.

May 22nd — Enjoying much; whether it be a preparation for trials on earth, or speedy glory in heaven, the Lord only knows. I am seeking to have no self, but Christ instead, since *it* with Him was crucified. Oh, the overwhelming happiness of being yielded up by the Spirit's power to Christ alone, and to daily crucifixion in all that the flesh loves and longs for!

June 4th — Much blessed this morning; not from what was said, but from a sweet view of Psalm 23, especially verse 4, compared with Romans 7:24. This present flesh-and-blood state of existence, with all its sins and sorrows, seemed to me "the valley of the shadow of death"; and very triumphantly did I see and feel that, as we experimentally abide in Christ by faith, we may walk through it and "fear no evil." "He turneth the shadow of death into the morning." It was truly blessed. I seem now to give myself up afresh, to seek that hidden and mysterious life of faith, so little known in the fullness of its privileges. I would just be watching daily at the gates of Christ, the true Wisdom, and waiting at the posts of His doors. I would only know His righteousness, and in that walk before God and man; so be it, Lord, to me, a poor sinner in myself, but a sinner saved by Thee; so let it be, for Thine honor, that I may be experimentally saved into Thee.

June 11th — My dear mother has been out this morning,

but she seems very ill, and has a great deal of internal fever. Part of my exercise in the house of God has been trusting my dear mother with Jesus, as able to do for us all we need and desire. My struggle is to rest in His will, however contrary to my flesh, and to look at Him more than circumstances. May we both know the triumph, as well as the trial, of faith.

Evening — Come, precious Jesus, and wind me up to the climax of love, as Thou before hast done, and then it is impossible to withhold anything from Thee. Life, love, health, friends, circumstances—all are given to Thee; and Thou art sweetly proved to be infinitely more than all. Nearest and dearest—all must give place, that Thou mayest have the nearest, first, best place in the soul's affections. So be it, Lord, my loving and all-lovely Jesus; so be it to me, and to my dearest parent, for Thy glory, in and by us. Then, come life, come death, if Thou art but honored, and we behold Thy glory and feel Thy love. Methinks earth is not long my country, for surely my soul catches celestial breezes, and almost rises into the overwhelming love of Deity, which, in the glories of its fullest radiance, would overpower mortality.

June 15th — My dearest mother once more raised up to moderate health. The Lord be praised! His mercies to us are very great. I am groaning under extreme powerlessness of mind, as if all energy and vigor for meditation, or other spiritual exercises, were dried up. Surely the Lord will restore it, for thus to live, yet not to live, would be an affliction indeed; and to slip out of life without a word from Jesus is what I shrink from.

June 16th — Mercifully relieved from the above-mentioned powerlessness this evening (Friday) at our little social meeting; to the Lord be all the glory!

Diary entries for 1843

June 19th — My mind a good deal solemnized by finding I have spit blood. Feel no alarm. Blood is a peaceful sign. When the destroying angel sees it on the lintel, he passes by; when it is applied to the conscience, it proclaims peace; and, should it now be a token of the speedy laying down of this frail tabernacle, it is peaceful still. For to be "absent from the body" will be to be "present with the Lord." Still, I would hereby be led to the footstool for deep heart-searching, to seek that Jesus may be honored in the residue of my life, and exceedingly magnified in my death. Death, did I say?—rather laying down mortality—going to sleep. Death is all gone. Jesus had that, and "abolished death, and brought life and immortality to light by the gospel." Oh, glorious, conquering Savior may I, by the Spirit's power, abide in Thee by faith. Then shall I, experimentally as well as really, be conqueror too. May Revelation 3:11, 12, be fulfilled in me, whether a speedy dissolving or a longer sojourning be appointed me. "To depart and be with Christ is far better."

June 25th — The subject of much depression to-day; no power in hearing; and Hosea 2, first clause of verse 2, with Jeremiah 11:15, seem my sad sentence, under which I fall, willing to receive the deserved stripes of dishonored love, but begging to be restored to that life of simple faith from which I have too much departed, as shown me by the above passages. Some little whisper of the Spirit in my soul this afternoon, prompting me to rise above effect into cause, and to be more engaged in looking at and believing in Jesus, than in looking at the fruits of so doing; and here, methinks, I have got wrong. The Lord restore me and teach me, for I am a poor ignorant thing. I would now surrender myself afresh to the instruction of the Holy Ghost, to learn to live Christ and walk in Him, trusting Him with consequences, and rising above effects, however pleasing, into Himself, the glorious cause.

Lord, condescend to teach me this mysterious, flesh-crucifying life of faith, so little known or preached about. Very plainly do I now see how I have failed, and how prone I am to think more of the fruit than of Him from whom it comes. For example, supposing I have some experimental victory, how am I wrapped up in it, instead of in the Conqueror? If I find that, when walking uprightly in Christ, no good thing is withholden (Ps. 84:11), anon, I get delighting in the good things, and then does the stooping infirmity creep upon me again, and they are withholden, for my correction, and to teach me that Christ must be more delighted in than His benefits. In a thousand other ways I have been beguiled, so foolish am I, and so ignorant; and such a narrow path is the highway of holiness, that it must be all Christ; there is not room for one bit or scrap of self. This whisper from the blessed Comforter is like a gleam from afar. May it shine brighter unto the perfect day. May Christ increase, and *I* decrease, till again I am nothing, and He all in all, experimentally. I do loathe myself, O Beloved, for my wanderings; be pleased to work in me till I not only hate self, but forsake it also. I feel what a hard thing I am seeking, "but all things are possible with God," and "all things possible to them who believe." "Lord, increase my faith," and give me now to venture out upon Christ for the desired blessing. I write this because I see I have got wrong. I trust the Lord is about to restore me, and I would have this a word of warning and caution in some future day, if I live to need it. I seem afresh now to see that as faith is kept, by the Spirit, in continued actings upon Christ, there will be much emptying, purging, and purifying; not making the flesh better, but purifying from the flesh, and purging from dead works. The old nature will remain what it was, not a whit improved, but it will have starvation; for I am quite certain that, as faith is feeding upon Christ, there will be more flesh-denying and crucifying than in any other way. But in the word before mentioned (Jer. 11:15), "holy flesh" is spoken of. I have wondered what this meant; it has just now opened beautifully to my mind while at the footstool; and seems to be explained by Leviticus 27:9, 10, 21, and last clause of 28th verse; from which I now see that a thing is holy because it is devoted to the Lord, without any real intrinsic holiness of its own. Would that I could express all the fullness and beauty I see here, but I cannot. It is partly thus: The spouse of Christ is His, in her body as well as spirit, for He has redeemed her body, though it is now the subject of sin; well, when Christ is revealed in the soul, and we are brought into liberty, finding to whom we belong, and what He has done for us, we are led to devote ourselves wholly to the Lord; or, at least, thus it has been with me again and again; not expecting our flesh to become righteous (that is, when in my right mind), but giving it to Jesus, earnestly craving that it may be the instrument of His glory; and, like the Gibeonites, devoted to be "a hewer of wood and a drawer of water for the house of my God." Now, this being the case, my flesh is not my own, but the Lord's: doubly so—His by purchase (1 Cor. 6:20), and His by a loving and entire surrender (Rom. 12:1), being made willing thereto in the day of His power; and thus it is holy (not righteous), being dedicated to the Lord (Lev. 27:28), either for doing or suffering, and, most assuredly, for crucifixion (Gal. 5:24). Being brought to this state, my proper and only legitimate life is that of faith on, by, and for the Son of God, who is that holiness, in which I see the Lord, and whose glory is now to be the object of my constant pursuit. Nor am I to choose whether it shall be promoted by my passing through the fire, or through the water; lying down in green pastures, or tossing on the foaming billows; eating rich fruits, or keeping solemn fasts—circumstances and feelings must all be considered as secondary and subservient to the glory of Jesus, by me. Here seems the "holy flesh" (not holiness of the flesh), entirely set apart to the service of that Master to whom it belongs (2 Tim. 2:21). Now, if after this I draw back, and through self-love seek to spare the flesh from suffering, or seek self-honor, self-ease, or self-satisfaction, then shall I know what it is, experimentally, to have the "holy flesh" pass from me—that is, the devoted thing employed to unlawful use; and the Lord then says, "What hath my beloved to do in my house," seeing she hath preferred her own? How much this is my case, the Lord knoweth; I know, to my shame, that I have been sadly seeking my own things, instead of the things of Christ; and my gratification, instead of His glory. Humbly I would seek restoration to a simple life of faith upon Jesus; and with trembling ask that I may be henceforth for Him alone. Lord, be pleased to lead still further into this mystery.

> [Reader, be it yours and ours to prayerfully weigh the foregoing observations. They are full of importance. In fact, within the last page or two, is what may be termed the summary of that deep and special teaching for which Ruth Bryan was remarkable. There is no disguising nor denying that hers was a standard in the truth to which but few, even of the Lord's living ones, are privileged to attain. Whilst they are, for most part, in the lowlands, entramelled by self and sin, Satan and the world, Ruth was fed and nourished upon the high mountains of Israel. What she so constantly craved, she as constantly enjoyed—namely, a living out of self, above creature-changes, in and upon the person of Christ. None more sensibly felt the truth of His words than she did; "Without me ye can do nothing," and "From me is thy fruit found"; but she at the same time correspondingly gloried in the fact that Christ was hers, and that Christ was all she wanted. Hence she

was, so to speak, *lost in Him!* "Not I, but Christ liveth in me," was her watchword; this her theme, this her triumph and her boast. Thus it was, as she so constantly expressed it, she "lived Christ." This she craved, when she so coveted *"the abiding"* of which she so frequently speaks.]

July 1st — A providential return of income-tax to-day, which proves, afresh, that it is very safe to trust in the Lord in the dark, and go through any difficulty, leaning upon Him alone. I was led to act thus in this matter, not going to any creature; and the answer has come when I did not expect it. There are also other bills filed in the High Court above, which will have answer in the time appointed. The Lord teach me more of a life of faith; not merely for its own sake, or for its benefits, but for the honor of Jesus, its Author (Heb. 12:2). And methinks this is one of its secrets, to be pressing after the glory of Jesus, more than any other thing whatsoever; so that, however painful the circumstances, we cannot seek so much for their alleviation as the glory of Jesus in them; and however pleasing the circumstances, the glory of Him, our Beloved, *by* them, is much more pleasing still. I see it, Lord, a little. Oh, bring me to it, experimentally, more and more. Ebenezer! Trust, and be not afraid in what lies darkly beyond.

July 2nd, Evening — My experience this day has been that of seeking from my precious Jesus the restoration of a life of faith upon Him and for Him, from which I fear I have been considerably beguiled. I too often forget that the life of faith is to be as much *for* Jesus, as *on* Him and *by* Him. I want to live on Him for my own advantage, but this will not do. He must be Omega as well as Alpha. O Holy Comforter, teach me this practically, as well as in my judgment.

July 9th, Sabbath Morning — The Lord be praised for all the mercies of the past week; the dark and the light has all been love; I feel it so; my spirit has been as much refreshed by the outward trials we have had, as my body is, when weary and thirsty, by a cup of cold water; so that I can say it is "very good to be afflicted," though not pleasing to the flesh. I trust the Lord is hereby bringing me a little lower, and teaching me, more, how unimportant are outward appearances, and how secondary outward possessions.

July 20th — Outward circumstances still tending downwards. The Lord teach us to descend, and make us willing to come as low as He pleases. How am I plagued by my unamiabilities! Surely very few of the Lord's people ever dwelt in such a *crusty* piece of flesh; and few were ever more painfully aware of it, or loathed themselves more completely. I would be what I am not, and do what I do not. How can the Lord Jesus be honored in this matter? Is it possible? I long to find in Him the remedy of this malady, the healing of this malignant sore—my reserved, unkind, and selfish self. Oh that I could "glory in mine infirmities, that his power may rest *upon*," and be manifest *in*, me. Methinks, if precious Jesus might be honored in the cure, it would be better than being whole in myself. But what if He sees fit I should not be cured? and will be glorified by my bearing the hated part of my disposition or temper all my life? Then it is a grief, and I must bear it. But, Lord, "if Thou wilt, Thou canst make me whole." Would it not honor Thee to subdue *myself*? Thou only knowest what I feel, and how I groan and mourn, that I do not honor Thee more in my exterior. "Lord, if Thou wilt, Thou canst." Do speak to me on this subject. I inquire of Thee, "What wilt Thou have me to do?" Let faith go out upon Thee, my unseen Deliverer, for a yet unfelt deliverance. That I am not more amiable, in myself, will be well, if Thou wilt gain glory thereby—Thyself being manifested, and I subdued, and kept out of sight.

July 26th — How very sensibly do I discover the workings of the two natures at this time—the spirit rising ardently upward, the flesh clinging to earth and creatures; but "the elder shall serve the younger"—Jesus shall prevail, and the works of Satan be destroyed.

Noon — Afresh, precious, precious Jesus, I resign this body to Thee, for doing or suffering, for living or dying. Wilt Thou accept it? Wilt Thou use me for Thy glory more than heretofore, that Thou mayest have some little return for all the benefits Thou hast done to me? Oh, do grant this request; my heart longs for it, my spirit pleads for it; and "if thou wilt, thou canst." Thou knowest the hot temptation of which I am the subject. Bring Thy glory out of it, and keep me from the evil, and it shall be well.

August 1st — My precious Jesus! Thou art worth more than a thousand worlds to me, in sorrow as well as joy. When friends frown, and circumstances frown, and the heart is bleeding, how precious then Thy love and sympathy! So I feel it now, and find it very sweet to trust Thee still, though much outwardly is dark, and rough, and painful. Thou wilt make the darkness light, the rough places plain, the crooked things straight before us (Isa. 42:16). It seems a strong word, *"Thou wilt";* but Thou hast said it first, and I only echo it back to Thee again; it does not come with felt power to me, but I plead it. Thou hast said it. fulfill it for us.

Evening — This day my heart has been weeping, though no tears have been shed; but through all, my broken, softened spirit feels that love prevails; and if my sweetest Lord Jesus should blight outward things, I must still love the hand that smites, and crops, and withers, for He is all love and loveliness—which thought melts my soul before Him, and I find such deliciousness in Him, that all the bitters on earth seem as nothing in comparison.

August 13th, Sabbath — Rose this morning sorely beset with the trifles of earth; and oh, it seemed as if there were scarcely any rising above them; but the Lord kept me crying, and at the family altar the blessing came; for I felt it was like the poor woman with the issue—the sore was running, and the crowd hindering, but it was for faith, by the Spirit's power, to press through all to Jesus; and so it was, I trust. And now—

> "Dissolved by the sunshine, I fall to the ground,
> And weep to the praise of the Jesus I've found."

September 9th — Had unexpectedly a conversation with Mr. — on Monday, in which something was said about faith. It appears to me that he thinks it entirely passive, and I humbly conceive it to be active; then, on Tuesday, while preaching on the subject, he said, "faith is only a receiver." I was a good deal exercised, and went to the Lord, not to have *my* view of the subject established, but to be taught by Him what is right. To-day (Friday) this word has come with power, "As ye have received Christ Jesus the Lord, so walk ye in him" (Col. 2:6). We received Him by faith, we also walk in Him by faith, and walking must be active; faith in itself has not power—Christ is its power to walk, fight, overcome, &c., and it gives Him all the glory. Then I saw the three stages mentioned in 1 John 2:12, 13. Now if faith be passive in the little children merely receiving the forgiveness of sins, it certainly is not in the young men; for it is said, they "have overcome the wicked one"; and it is by faith we overcome both the world and the devil (1 John 5:4, 1 Peter 5:9, and James 4:7, compared with Ephesians 6:16). I also see plainly how the Lord has taught me the activity of faith, by experimentally bringing me into it. It is not in my soul a matter of theory, learned from books, but it is the mysterious life, walk, fight, and triumph, which I much long to know in the power of it, but am very slow in learning, because it is so contrary to myself; and yet I must thankfully acknowledge that the Holy Ghost has led me into a little of its blessedness and privileges. I am now thankful the above has transpired, although it made me tremble lest I should be wrong, and sent me to the Lord to be searched and proved. May Mr. — have as much blessing from it as I have; and to the Lord shall be all the glory. He can speak and teach, when and where we least expect it.

September 17th — Why was wine lacking at the marriage feast in Cana of Galilee? To open a chasm for Jesus to fill up, and just make a way for His power and glory. So it is with us; and it is worth feeling the want, to receive supplies from *such* a hand.

September 18th — Last evening, Jonah 4:7, met my eye, and it made me tremble. The Lord prepare me for His will, and preserve me from resting in His gifts instead of in Himself!

September 21st — Very great glory have I felt and seen this evening, at our prayer meeting, in these words, "The righteousness of God in him"; and more especially those two words, "in him," did sweetly echo in my soul again and again.

September 23rd — A circumstance occurred to-night very mortifying to my flesh; and I have since been exceedingly buffeted on account of it. It was respecting one of the gifts sent us last week; and I just now see it to be in accordance with that word (Jonah 4:7) which so much struck me last Sabbath evening. But am I angry for the gourd? The Lord forbid! If I am, in the leastwise, I do not well indeed; rather, precious Jesus, would I surrender all I have on earth, to be withered by Thy touch, if Thou seest it a needful discipline. Give me grace to say, "Thy will, not mine, be done"; and faith to take refuge in the unchangeable Giver, till these calamities be overpast. A Saturday evening gloomy indeed; the Lord get glory out of this unexpected exercise, and it will be worth the smart. How singular that the verse about the gourd should catch my eye, and that I should feel as if it had some reference to me.

September 24th — Heard a sermon this morning from St. John 3:7, and much was said against living above feelings. The Lord be judge between Mr. R— and me, for I verily believe the Holy Spirit Himself has taught me a little what it is to live upon Christ, the source of true spiritual feeling, more than upon the feeling with which He favors me; and great stability have I found in so doing. Mr. R— seems to think that to live above feeling is to live without it. How mistaken he is; for truly I find that it flows most sweetly and constantly when I am not so much delighted and taken up with it, as with Him from whom it comes. But I would go to my Counsellor and infallible Teacher, and spread the matter before Him, begging Him to confirm what is His own, and deliver from what is error, either in Mr. R— or myself.

October 20th — My soul much exercised, and also distressed, by a fearful threatening, from Jeremiah 17:4, that I shall experimentally "discontinue from the heritage" the Lord has given me. I wait to know whether this sentence is from Himself, or the voice of an enemy.

October 21st — Some comfort this morning, in thanking my Father for "His unspeakable gift," and also in realizing that the atonement *is* made, the obedience *is* accomplished, the salvation *is* finished, let my feelings vary as they may. I trust I found a little of the "rest of faith," which is the most solid and lasting relief we can be favored with. I trust also the sentence which has seemed to threaten me, will not be executed; real separation I have not feared—that is impossible; but experimental distance, with apathy and powerlessness of soul, is what I have trembled at, and that the Lord should lay me upon the shelf as a thing not in use, and withhold from me entrance into His Word, into His Christ, into His love, and into His glories, seems to me the worst evil that can befall me. The Lord avert it in love, though He might afflict me with it in justice. "Bless God for Jesus Christ."

October 22nd — Again I am taught that what we ask in and for the flesh, if it be granted us, will very often be *with*, or *as*, a cross to the flesh which desired it. I think I did ask the Lord for a temporal thing, a year or more since—I thought I wanted it; it came not, but it has come lately, and it is a withered gourd, for the flesh is mortified by it. Oh, may I at length learn to be content with Jesus only, and not be importunate for any outward thing, but just take what He gives.

November 5th—It just now strikes me forcibly how very few of us have got so far in spiritual arithmetic as to "reckon ourselves dead to sin," even when we sensibly feel its workings. I feel my own deficiency, and seem now afresh to embrace Christ as my ability thus to reckon more continually than I have ever yet done.

November 7th — Happy, oh, so happy, in the love of Jesus—yea, in Jesus Himself; for it is in Him I begin my heaven, and have my all. Much privileged at the family altar, and very loath to leave it. "Bless the Lord, O my soul." How the world has lessened and deadened to me lately I cannot tell. It seems a very nothing, and vanity indeed; and to see the living ones gathering its golden dust, and playing with its tinsel toys, is monstrous. Oh, come away, ye foolish ones, and leave the dunghill, and rise into Christ—your rich inheritance and your eternal riches! "But I have no power." And are you digging for power under those clods of the valley, where you seem to be exhausting all your energies? What find you there, that you work so eagerly? When you have dug out and heaped up a mountain of shining dust, will you have more power then to rise with Jesus? Think you it comes that way? Preposterous! It is like saying I cannot get fire, and then plunging the last warm coal you possess into water.

November 20th — My cough is nearly gone, and my health better; but I seem to think the sappers and miners have begun their operations in my constitution; and, if so, the effect will ere long manifest itself. "This mortal must put on immortality, and this corruptible must put on incorruption"; and then will death be manifestly "swallowed up in victory." This body must go to sleep for a season; the Lord only knows how soon. Oh that He may be more honored in it while in its present state of animation!

December 3rd, Sabbath — I have this morning given myself afresh to the Lord, in His house, feeling much affliction in my body, and not knowing but that more may await me. I am enabled, however, to leave that with the Lord, only begging that He will be glorified in me. I belong to Jesus, and have just yielded my whole self anew to Him, embracing Him as my strength for whatever may be coming upon me. Dear Lord, I am all emptiness, powerlessness, and weakness: in Thee I must, and do, cast all the cost and charges of this affliction, whether it be long or short, light or heavy; nor do I believe Thou wilt refuse or disappoint me, but carry me triumphantly through in

Thine own arms of love and power. Accept, sweetest Jesus, this offering of my poor self, which is of and from Thine own free will—not mine. "Praise the Lord, O my soul," for such a privilege! To be His in eternal love and purpose, and His by free surrender, through the sweet constrainings of His own Spirit!

December 15th — I think the Lord is teaching me that I shall not only "have no other gods but Him," but also that I shall have no other goods but him; and that if I pursue any object, whether minute or important, for its own sake alone, or my own gratification, my purposes shall be frustrated, and disappointment sent. Last week I planned about my work, and thought to accomplish much (for my profit, not for the Lord's glory), but this week a lock has been put on the wheel, and I have moved slowly—yea, labored, as it were, in the fires. I bless the Lord for what He is teaching me, and feel much humbled under His mighty hand.

1844

January 28th — I have found that I have been beguiled from the "simplicity which is in Christ," and have been grieved and troubled. This morning I was seeking for Christ to come on my soul like rain, and like the showers that water the earth; and, some time after, this word sweetly breathed upon my spirit, "I will be as the dew unto Israel." The Lord fulfill and restore!

February 4th — Much entreating for restoration this week, and I trust the Lord is granting my desire, and showing me where I have got wrong—in seeking to have, in myself, what my Father wills I shall have *in Christ*. Much blessedness now in being made willing to have and enjoy *all in Jesus* alone. This morning I opened these words, "Thou shalt eat bread at my table continually" (2 Sam. 9:7). Precious Jesus! this is just what I want; then it will not matter who preaches or talks against living upon Thee, above feeling. I shall prove it a reality—yea, I do now—and prove also, that to live above feelings is not to live without them; for then they flow most blessedly, when kept in their proper place as *effects*, and I living upon Christ Himself, for His own glory. The Lord further restore and unfold the secrets of liberty!

February 18th — I find Jesus my wisdom, my life, and my all: "He restoreth my soul"; and that not to rejoice or rest in the *restoration*, but in *Himself* alone. It is safe to live in the cause; then effects are sure to follow.

February 28th — "Mark the perfect man, and behold the upright: for the end of that man is peace." A light seemed to beam on my mind which I had never seen in this passage before. It appeared to allude to those who are *perfect in Christ*, and to those who are walking uprightly in Him, their perfection. It was a comfort to my heart; for, since the Lord has brought me into liberty, it has been very often suggested to my mind that, having so much joy in life, I certainly should have darkness in death. But the Lord make me upright, knowing nothing but Christ, and keep me so: for the end of such is peace. *Evening* — I have just seen a new beauty in Genesis 49:11, the first clause. May the Lord open it more fully.

March 17th — I am proving, blessedly, by experience, the liberty, privilege, and triumph of a life of simple faith, and also enjoying sweet communion with dear M. C—, who is indeed brought into the good land, flowing with milk and honey; her enlargement has been a blessing to me. "Bless the Lord, O my soul." Would that I could bless and praise *my Jesus*. How do I long for more triumphant strains! My heaven is begun, and yet my notes so low, my praise so poor and inadequate. Lord, if Thou willest it, grant me enlargement in praise.

March 22nd — "The name of the Lord is a strong tower: the righteous runneth into it, and is safe." Never did I enjoy the fullness of this word so much as this morning, at the family altar. When my soul had felt convicted of lightness of spirit and heart-wanderings from Jesus, the above word came, and I saw this was the name, "Jehovah our Righteousness"; and I was then running into it, and found safety, in the midst of my own sin and shortcoming.

April 3rd, Good Friday — Some melting sense of the wonderful cross and glorious Sufferer who endured my death, and who is my eternal life. My precious Jesus is more and more precious, as faith goes out upon Him, by the power of the Spirit. Dearest mother is better, but much weakened. A *good* Friday to me.

April 7th — Sorry to find that many dear friends object to have Mr. T— to preach for us, because they think he is getting beyond the truth of God and the experience of His people; but they misjudge. The perfection, glory, and continued happiness which he speaks to us of are *in Christ*, and as we are one with Him. And did ever sin and death touch that life and union, or can it ever do so? I trow not. Our brethren admit this as a doctrine; they own we have a completeness in Christ which can never be marred, a life in Him not subject to death or change; but when the Lord makes this glorious doctrine present *experience*, and brings us to rejoice continually in the triumph and liberty of it, immediately they are afraid and offended, and think we go *too far*; but how can we, when the Lord Himself has brought us here? Truly, I can say from my heart, that what little I know of this glory was not taught me by any man, but it came by the revelation of Jesus Christ in my soul; and the light and glory increases in the same way. I am not moved as to the triumph of faith above flesh, sense, and circumstances; I know it, I feel it, and long for more; and "I cannot but speak the things which I have heard and seen." May the Lord be pleased to make the doctrine of complete perfection, safety, and victory *in Christ*, one of daily experience to our dear friends; then will they not fear to say, with joy, that in Christ they are experimentally raised, even now, above sin, Satan, the world, and themselves, and do triumphantly sit with Him in heavenly places.

April 10th — Twenty-one years since my beloved father was removed from us by death, and how faithful and forbearing has our covenant God been with us, during that period, cannot be told; truly, "goodness and mercy have followed us," and we have lacked no "good thing." My father was dearer to my heart than words can express, but Jesus has more than made up the loss; and I have much greater reason to praise than to repine. My dear mother still remains to me, and that is a great favor; she is my earthly all, but I must not, I would not, withhold her from Jesus. If He call her away, He can then support and comfort me. Although I do seem the most unfit in all the world to stand alone, perhaps I shall then see great miracles. What want I for the future? Only more faith to apprehend and know more of Jesus; to be continually going out upon Him, never resting *on* or *in* self one moment, nor in the creature either, but Christ be all in all. May the Holy Spirit work thus in me by His power, for the glory of the Three-One Jehovah. Amen. For mercies past, "praise the Lord, O my soul."

April 29th — "Grace, grace unto it." To the Lord be all the glory of my salvation, and my present enjoyment of it too. It is wholly unmerited by me; I have not procured my enjoyments, I do not deserve them, and I cannot by my own power retain them. Sovereignly, as the rain descends upon the unconscious earth, even so, sovereignly, does the Holy Ghost descend in showers of blessing upon my conscious, wondering soul, which, surprised by love, sinks into abasement, crying again, "Grace unto it." "Not unto me, O Lord, but unto Thy name be all the glory." Glory to God in the highest; for on earth His peace is felt, and His goodwill enjoyed by the very least of His chosen ones.

May 9th — Sweet Jesus! lovely Jesus! what do I find in Thee? Thou art all fair, all glorious, all loving; and Thou art mine, and I am Thine. "Bless the Lord, O my soul!" I cannot express what Jesus is to me.

May 14th, Tuesday — I have been the subject of very sharp, though short affliction, the last few days. During the extreme pain, I had not the triumph of faith, or inflowings of love and peace, although not in darkness or soul distress. I trust the exercise has been salutary, and very humbling. I have learned afresh that, after all I have received and enjoyed, I am as helpless as ever, and cannot *bear* or *do* anything without divine power. My soul says, with renewed feeling, "Without Thee I can do nothing," and "it is good to be afflicted."

May 17th, Afternoon — 2 Corinthians 5:1, has been very sweet to me this day. "We know," by the revelation of Christ, by the witnessing of the Spirit, by the Word of God, by the testimony of love in our conscience—"We know" that if this earthly house were dissolved, and when it shall be, we have a building of God, an eternal house, a house provided and prepared. Blessed, comforting knowledge! Short the storms of life, the inconveniences of the lodging-house, and the coldness of this foreign clime; soon the welcome sound from our Beloved, "Arise, my love, my fair one, and come away." Even so, come, sweet Lord Jesus, quickly come.

May 19th — Dearest Lord, if Thou wilt restore me to health, oh, let it be double health; let my soul prosper, let me come forth in Thee, walk in Thee, abide in Thee alway, during the rest of my journey. Let me be lost and hidden, and Thou only seen; let me be dead, and Thou alone my life. Oh, let me not again be defiled with my own works or inventions, or myself (Ps. 106:39), but be Thou all in all. This only can reconcile me to the wilderness—that I should be nothing, and Jesus only seen, and heard, and exalted.

May 27th — Proverbs 8:21, last clause, has been very sweet to me this afternoon, and it came in this sense: I,

Wisdom—or Jesus—I, *myself*, will fill their treasures; not merely putting in something valuable, but myself will be the fullness of their treasures; so, whether we have much or little outwardly, if Christ fills it, and is the fullness of it, we are rich indeed. Precious Christ, fill Thou my heart, my life, my lips, for Thou art all I want; and, having Thee, I am rich, if stripped of all beside.

June 12th — "All things work together for good to them that love God."

> "Ye fearful saints, fresh courage take!
>   The clouds ye so much dread
> Are big with mercy, and shall break
>   With blessings on your head."

Very solid and consolatory has the above been to my mind this morning. A good deal of outward storm, and from such a quarter, that I can open my heart-ache and sorrow to none upon earth. But Jesus is enough; He knows it all. His glory I humbly desire, and also strength and patience to carry my daily cross, deny myself, and follow Him; yea, and to triumph in Him, too, all the while. "It is well," and a mercy, to feel thorns where we try to nestle on earth. How plainly is the Lord showing me, that when we cling too closely, and hold any outward comforts too fast, we shall be pierced by them. Seeing where I was wrong, surely the deepest humility and submission become me, now that I am smarting.

June 16th — A little more of the wonders of love and of union to Jesus breaking upon my soul, with some insight, in a little measure, into our separation from the first Adam, and the evils of his fall; yea, it seems to me real joy (perhaps more than I should express), that the creature bank did fail, and the shadow give way to the Substance, the second Adam, the Lord from heaven, our own dear Treasure, in whom our all is stored. But the millions who had all their stock in the creature-head! Ah, there is mystery deep and unfathomable! But the Judge of all does right. To His sovereignty I bow, wondering much that He provided amply for me in Jesus Christ the Righteous. To God be all the glory! As an instrument of His own forming, may I be tuned to sound His praise.

July 7th — Yesterday I completed my thirty-ninth year. So long have I sojourned in this drear wilderness; and, indeed, have abundant reason to erect an Ebenezer, and confess that very abundant have been the Lord's mercies to me. The future is shut up in mystery, nor would I lift the veil, but renew my trust upon the Lord, and live upon Him by the moment. It is truly wonderful to feel that He is my portion, and that, for time and eternity, I am provided for in Jesus. To "live Christ" is blissful indeed, whatever be the outward circumstances. When He is all, we have all, even though we should seem to have nothing.

> [Reader, this is the only solid and really happy way of living "upon the Lord, and by the moment." Strictly speaking, we have nothing whatever to do with the morrow. Distinctly we are told to "take no thought" for it, but "let the morrow take thought for the things of itself."
>
> "'Tis enough that *He* should care;
> Why should *we* the burden bear?"]

July 28th — A feast this morning from one word—"Passover." It broke into many parts with much sweetness, and I see how Christ, our Passover, was sacrificed for us, and how He is our Passover, as I never saw it before.

August 8th — Our morning reading was in Nehemiah, and very plainly did I see from thence that one great aim of our enemy is to put us in fear, while our Lord continually says, *fear not, dread not,* nor *be afraid*. "Thou shalt not be afraid of them," &c. I see that fear often goes before fainting, and that our souls are thereby much weakened, and the Lord also dishonored, who says, "Fear not, *I* will be with thee." Surely that is enough, let what will betide. Oh for more of the confidence of love, and trust of faith! I feel my soul energized and encouraged.

August 25th — Memorable day thus far, five o'clock, happy Sabbath, and such a feast of love at sacrament as I rarely enjoy on that occasion—it was all Jesus. Oh, sweetest, dearest Lord, I cannot tell a *tithe* of what I find in Thee: death to death, and life to live eternally. Thou didst take my nature, that my poor, fallen creature-life might die with Thee upon the cross; and Thou hast given me Thy life, that I may never die, but live in Thee, and with Thee, my Life, for ever and ever; a joyful, never-ending "for ever!" Hosannahs to Thee, my glorious Deliverer! I would praise Thee if I could. Oh, when shall it once be? The golden harp, the immortal strains of love and harmony, will never reach Thy worth, Thou wondrous, glorious Savior. Immanuel, the name so dear, so fragrant to my ravished soul.

September 19th — I have lately thought much, and somewhat with melting, of the condescension of our divine Redeemer, in His act of washing His disciples' feet, and I see how we are to follow this, by ministering to the comfort of His people; and I see it to be a greater honor to minister to the meanest of His members than to rule an empire. Oh, for humility and ability to be thus engaged; my heart weeps, and I loathe myself that I do it so little.

September 29th — "My cup runneth over." "His paths do drop fatness," and He rewardeth me "according to my cleanness in His eyesight"; not according to my own doings and deservings, but the doings and merits of my glorious Surety. It is marvellous in my sight!

October 14th — "He turneth the shadow of death into the morning!" Very great fullness and power beam upon my soul in this precious word, of which I do, experimentally, feel the truth, and find such joy and blessedness, and love and glory in Jesus, as words cannot describe.

October 19th — How mysterious are the ways of my dearest Lord. Our friends consented to invite Mr. T— to preach when he came to Leicester; this evening to my extreme disappointment, I was informed that he had been to Leicester. I do believe that my precious wonder-working Lord will somehow turn this shadow of death into the morning. Perhaps He saw me too much anticipating this enjoyment, with my eye upon the creature; and so He kindly cut off the creature-stream, to oblige me to go away to the Fountain. I thank Thee, oh, my precious Christ, that Thou wilt be nearer than the nearest, and dearer than the dearest, and that not even this, Thy and my beloved, shall be between me and Thee; but Thou wilt be "All in all." Even so, for "so it seemeth good in Thy sight." I humbly take Thee anew as my all, and I shall have no lack in Thee. Oh that more of Thy loved ones were lifted up in love, and found the heaven of delights which is in Thee! But why me? Here is the unanswerable question, the wonder of wonders! I, a weak, low, vile, wandering worm, filled with Thy love! ravished with Thy beauty, and absorbed in Thy glory, and finding that Thy very crossings are infinite, boundless love! It is all of grace! To God be all the glory!

October 20th — Surely such a poor worm, and such rich mercy, great glory, and sweet love, did never meet together before!

October 25th — "To the upright there ariseth light in the darkness." This word was on my mind this morning, and, I think, has been fulfilled to-day. What, do I call myself upright? Nay, verily, but Christ is my uprightness, and in Him I am so dealt with.

October 27th — Oh, my precious Lord, I am overwhelmed in, and by, Thy love! Thou hast freed me from my sin and its punishment, by taking them upon Thyself; and Thou hast prepared me for Thyself, by putting Thy perfect comeliness upon me. Thou hast overcome me, Thou dost ravish my heart.

November 10th — How precious Thou art, my Jesus, no word can tell. All empty, poor, and nothing in myself, how free, how blest I am in Thee, I cannot find out. I know a little, a very little. Oh, teach me more. Anew, this Sabbath evening, I cast myself on Thee, to care for me, that I may only care for Thine honor, and seek Thy glory. My cup does indeed run over. Thou loadest me with benefits; but it is Thyself that art my glory and joy. I would crown Thee, my precious Jesus, with glad Hosannahs, Lord of all. I expect dear Mr. T— shortly, and wish not to think of it, but to think only of Jesus. I am sure that, at first, I anticipated it too much; it was, therefore, kind of the Lord to disappoint me. My Jesus must, and shall be, all in all. "Bless Him, O my soul."

> "And when I see Thee as Thou art,
> I'll give Thee nobler praise."

November 16th — My Jesus, my absorbing, all-lovely, loving Savior, how precious art Thou to Thy poor handmaiden! Sharp have been my temptations this week; but the Lion of the tribe of Judah does, and will, prevail. Thou knowest all, and Thou only. Let not Satan succeed; let not the flesh conquer; let not creatures deceive; but rule

Thou in the midst of Thy and my enemies. My cup still runs over with love and mercy, and I richly prove that "Godliness with contentment is great gain." Thou, dearest Lord, art more precious to me this morning than the gold of Ophir.

November 18th, Monday — No morning is so dreary to me as Monday morning. I love to feel the Sabbath coming, but cannot bear to awake and find it gone. But yet, Jesus is my every-day Sabbath. Oh, yes, indeed He is, and in Him I find happiness and peace all the week, and all the year, when I am kept abiding. This is all I want, never to wander more, or expect any good from anything or anybody, but look for all in Jesus, in whom I now find heaven begun.

> [Reader, can you say, with Ruth, "Jesus is my every-day Sabbath?"]

November 19th — Happy in Jesus, more so than tongue can express! It is, indeed, heaven begun. My Beloved is to me a "Fountain of gardens, a well of living waters and streams from Lebanon." What awaits me I know not; perhaps much that is dark and dreary; but that will not be in Jesus. He is all light, and "in Him is no darkness at all"; and the joy and gladness I now have in Him is wonderful. "Grace! grace! unto it." Thine, O Lord, be all the glory.

November 23rd, Sabbath — The chief part of last week has been very glowing and triumphant; but all in Jesus, and He is above it all. "Bless Him, O my soul," and rise into Himself, above all His bestowments. Dear Mr. T— comes on Tuesday. My heart trembles, and something would persuade me my feast is over; but this cannot be, for Jesus is the substance of it, and "He is the same yesterday, to-day, and for ever." Something threatens to be contrary, but I fly to Jesus; in Him all will be well.

Diary entries for 1844

November 28th — Our dear Mr. T— is here, and what a blessing we have had; what a feast! What loves! What a Jesus! Praise Him! Praise Him! Our beloved friend goes to-morrow. I do feel it painful to part with him, but it is well; for Jesus must be all, and He shall be; and He shall take His own way to accomplish it. Hallelujah to God and the Lamb!

November 29th — What a night was the last! Very little sleep, but such inflowings into the soul, as were ten thousand times better; teaching me more how Jesus must be all. The Holy Remembrancer brought back very much of what dear Mr. T— has been telling us; it was a second benefit. "Bless the Lord, O my soul."

November 30th — My spirit thirsts with intense and increased ardency, for unfoldings of the personal glories of my precious Christ, who is, indeed, "more precious than rubies."

December 2nd — This seems to be my word to-day, "The peace of God, which passeth all understanding, shall keep your hearts and minds through Christ Jesus"; and my dear Lord seems to say, "Fly to my bosom for peace: expect it nowhere else, desire it nowhere else, seek nowhere to rest thy head and thy heart but here." Precious Lord, Thou art my rest, my happiness, and Thou art all-sufficient. Hold me to Thee, nor let me wander more.

December 13th — What a Jesus! What grace, love, glory, and liberty I find in Him; and yet I know but as nothing of what He has, and what He is; still He says, "Open thy mouth wide, and I will fill it." Ah, precious Christ, nothing but *Thyself* can fill this mouth, this heart, which Thou hast made to thirst and long for Thee!

December 23rd — My soul is intensely longing to be led, as the Eastern sages were, to the place where Jesus lay. The wonders of the incarnation I long to be led into, in meditation deep and sweet. Much blessed in Jesus, who is to me more excellent than "mountains of prey" or "hills of frankincense and myrrh." Himself is my glory—Himself is my happiness; and He makes me rejoice with exceeding great joy. To God be all the glory. Amen and amen.

December 29th — Sabbath, and a glowing one, too, a crowning one, at the closing of this blessed 1844. "Bless the Lord, O my soul," for the wonders, the secrets of love, made known to love's object, in love and by love, for love's own glory. "God is love," and He my blissful dwelling-place for evermore.

1845

January 7th — "Blessed is the man to whom the Lord will not impute sin." How did those words sound in my soul, and break my heart last night. He will not impute sin to us, then who or what can condemn us? He will not impute sin to us. Keep back, ye sin-lovers, who know not these wonders in experience. Here you cannot lawfully tread; but here we, pardoned, justified, brokenhearted ones, may tread and triumph. Bless the Lord, my pardoned soul.

February 2nd — The past has been a week of much love and mercy, and many heart-meltings; and I increasingly see that when the eye is singly fixed upon Jesus, circumstances are very secondary. He, our Beloved, is our triumph in all, and our victory over all. In Him we can bear, do, or suffer whatever He appoints, and that He may be honored in all, is our highest ambition. Very hard the enemy tries to corrupt me from this simplicity, but my Jesus is stronger than he, and I look to Him for victory; I look that still He may be "all-in-all" to me, nor shall I look in vain: love is my confidence and stronghold; love will not disregard the appeals of love, let the enemy say what he will.

February 9th, Afternoon — I have been just now reviewing a little of my past life; and, oh, of what wonderful mercies and deliverances have I been the subject. I should have ruined myself indeed; but the Lord held me by His right hand, though unseen. I admire the deliverances, but adore and love the dear Deliverer! I praise Him, that He kept me outwardly moral and upright; but I praise Him a thousand times more for that perfection I have in Him, which no acts of mine can ever mar. I wonder at the way in which He has led me, but wonder more at the *end* to which He has brought me, and that is Himself! Yes, He has brought me unto the King with gladness and rejoicing, and I find Him the end of the law, the end of sin, the end of death—eternal life, love, and glory. I do, and must praise Him.

February 15th — Love, Almighty love, is the blissful element in which I still dwell; oh, what soul-dissolvings and heart-ravishings do I there find! I seem all gone, and Christ is "all-in-all."

February 23rd — How is my soul melted this morning, in the feeling of union, eternal union—yea, from everlasting. Thou, Jehovah, hast "been our dwelling-place," and we have had a being in Thee; and now Thou hast given us a conscious being, to know our privilege, and to triumph and glory in Thee.

February 25th — I have had, last evening, a fiery dart from the enemy; but Jesus is my place of refuge. It was a very powerful suggestion of an if, and how has my soul melted to find that my Beloved had felt the *if* before me. "If thou be the Son of God." Oh, my precious Christ, how sweet Thy sympathy, how deep Thy love, to bear the edge and force of all before it comes to me. It is safe to descend with Thee. To Thee afresh I commit myself, and hang on Thee alone. Thy blood, Thy righteousness, Thy love, are all my plea; and, though earth and hell roar against me, here I must be safe.

April 2nd — A dear friend this evening quoted Philippians 4:19; and such a fullness and glory has just beamed on my mind, in the word "according," as I never saw before. "According to His riches in glory by Christ Jesus." Who can get to the top and bottom of that? The Lord be pleased to show me more, for I know but as nothing.

May 4th —
> "Hark! the name of Jesus sounded
> Loud from golden harps above:
> We may blush and be confounded,
> Weak our praises, cold our love."

Thy name, dearest Lord, is as "ointment poured forth" to my soul; it renews the fire of love, and I long to praise Thee as I cannot.

> "Hail! blissful dawn of endless day,
> When sin shall cease, and death shall die;
> And Christ His glory shall display,
> And beam upon my longing eye."

Then shall I praise, and be absorbed in love.

May 15th — I feel powerfully to-day the attraction of love and divine drawings of my best Beloved. My heart rises heavenward and homeward, and anticipates the joy of being unceasingly absorbed in love, praise, and worship. Born of God, my spirit rises to God, and longs to be filled with God, and drink full draughts of bliss from the infinite Source of life, love, and holiness. Dearest Lord, I have so feared lest I have grieved Thee, lest anything should transpire which would cause me to be, in experience, more at a distance from Thee. Oh, let it not be; Thou must keep me close, for Thou art all to me. I ask for nothing earth can give, but I ask Thy constant smile, Thy constant love, Thy constant dear embrace. I ask it in desires of Thine own kindling, and leaving all creatures and circumstances to Thy disposal: my happiness is not in *them*, it is *Thyself* I seek. And here I must be ardent, importunate. Oh, deny me not. While ever I dwell in the body, let me by faith rise much out of it, and be "absent from the body, and present with the Lord." I am too happy, and full of heaven, to work much to-day. I must keep joyful holiday: "The Lord will provide." Christ is my treasure and my "all-in-all." "Bless the Lord, O my soul."

Evening — This has, indeed, been as one of the days of heaven to my soul, a new beaming in of light, love, and glory. What indulgence! How undeserved! Surely, dearest Lord, Thou art proving that Thou art not offended with me, and that Thou wilt not leave me to anything which would, in the leastwise, separate from Thee. Bring me nearer yet, and let more of the fire of love burn in my soul.

May 21st — A sweet portion this morning in family reading. The word was Ezekiel 35:10. I felt the application thus—Though my enemies think to come and possess me, it is in vain, for the Lord is here before them. I am His own, and He will maintain and assert His right, in spite of earth, hell, and self.

May 25th — I desire this evening new givings-up unto the Lord, in all I have and am, that I may be more than heretofore for His glory; which He has afresh shown me is the only real end of my living, and the only right object for my desire and pursuit. I confess, with shame, my shortcomings, and that twice, lately, false and fleshly modesty has prevailed; so that, for fear of seeming too forward, and speaking too much in presence of more aged Christians, I have restrained what I ought to have said in praise of my precious Christ. Oh, pardon me, my Beloved; let me not fear the creature, or mind creature-opinion; but, when others will not speak, make the tongue of Thy stammering one speak out Thy love and glory.

June 1st, Sabbath — How sweet to my soul are these days of rest; they are only too short and too seldom. I would have every day a Sabbath. It is so, in one sense; soon it will be entirely so; one blissful, endless Sabbatism! I have had a sharp internal conflict to-day, but enjoyed the triumph of faith this evening. Many painful things have been presented to my mind, to affright and dismay me; but now my language is—Though "they compassed me about like bees, in the name of the Lord I will destroy them." And, should things so contrary to the flesh await me, I need not be "moved by these afflictions, knowing that we are appointed thereunto"; and, as Christ is my happiness, that will remain the same, let what will be without. Dearest, precious Lord, I am Thine. I have willingly given myself to live only for Thee. I retract not; it is the privilege of love to do as Thou wilt with Thine own. My desire is Thy glory *in* and *by* me. This I ask. Oh, let it be so more and more; reveal Thyself more to me; glorify Thyself more in me; make me clearly understand Thy will and Thy way, and let me triumph in Thee at all times: let nothing hinder, let nothing ever intervene between Thee and me; it were worse than death to be at a distance. Never, oh, never let it be; but in nearest, dearest communion, do hold me amid all the changeful and yet unknown vicissitudes of the wilderness.

June 2nd —
> "Oh, the sweet wonders of that cross,
> Where God my Savior loved and died."

I feel a little of those wonders this morning. My soul melts in the love and blood of my Beloved. By His cross I find death to sin, law, world, and myself. All my black guilt was here removed; "from condemnation I am free." Eternal praises to my dear Deliverer!

June 15th — Another of these dear shadows of eternal

rest, these days which our Father has given to spend with Him; they are dear to my heart, and seem doubly privileged to me, because favored with such quiet and retirement, so that I can enjoy Christ my Lord uninterruptedly. The temptation under which I suffered last week, and for some time past, has been quite broken in its power. To the Lord be the praise! "The Lord is on my side; I will not fear what (flesh) can do unto me."

June 22nd — I have just seen a silly fly, sporting heedlessly close to a spider's web, and most likely it would soon have sported into it, and have become fast entangled in the snare; but I saw a friendly hand sweep away the spider's net-work, and thus remove the danger, while the heedless, helpless fly, was equally unconscious of the danger and the preservation. Ah, then, I thought, perhaps it is thus oft with me. In an unseen snare I had been almost heedlessly caught; but the seeing eye, loving heart, and powerful arm of Jesus are mine. He beholds the intended mischief, defeats the wily worker, sweeps away the entangling thread, and thus preserves my freedom. All praise be Thine, dear Lord, for known and unknown mercies and deliverances. Oh, may I never knowingly sport on the edge of sin, or trifle with temptation. I was much melted in the house of God this evening, by these words, which came with divine power, "He hath made him to be sin for us, who knew no sin." Oh, how great and full did they appear! I am sure there are infinite depths, of which I yet know nothing.

July 10th — I have had a good deal of spiritual indulgence and enjoyment lately. This morning I was mourning the absence of it, when the Lord graciously gave me a renewed insight into the life of faith, showing clearly how it is in Christ, and not in enjoyments; and how that, after great indulgence, it is salutary they should be withholden, to prove whether we are anywise resting therein. Thanks to Him for all the lessons and discipline of love! This evening my soul thirsts and pants after Christ. It seems that one word comprises every desire and petition of my heart, "more of Christ." Oh, my Father, deny me not. Thou hast *given*; do reveal, unfold the gift. Make me, O holy Comforter, to know more of Him, in whom are concentrated all the glories and perfection of Deity and humanity.

July 13th — Oh, my "Abba, Father," I can feelingly say, Thy cabinet is full of jewels, and Thy storehouse full of treasures. Thy beloved Son, my precious Savior, Redeemer, and Surety, is full of radiant glories, ever new. I this day feel Him to be my heaven; let, I pray thee, Thy revealings and unfoldings be so distinct, and in such measure, that I may receive them to profit, and not lose one grain of such gold; for I find the wonders of Immanuel, in union to Him, so to multiply, that, without Thy power to uphold and make definite, my little mind will be fairly overwhelmed in sweets, and retain none, because attracted by so many. Do not stay Thine hand; it is not too much. I want to be absorbed in Him for ever; but oh, enlarge, that what Thou dost bestow may not be in vain, but may render back to Thee a hundredfold again.

August 10th — "With bitter herbs shall ye eat it." Methinks this has been my case to-day. Bitter, indeed, my felt sin and pollution. Precious, most precious, paschal Lamb, who hath removed it from me, so that I am free for ever; and, though feeling and loathing it, yet I trust it with Him, believing Him to be my perfection and purity.

August 16th — Our Friday meeting was last evening precious and powerful. In reading Numbers 19 and Hebrews 13:11-15, my soul was so overcome with the glories and love of Jesus, that I could scarcely find utterance. I have recently seen that there is much glory in His priesthood, and I long to have it more revealed. In truth, I saw Him last night to be such a glorious Priest, such a wondrous sacrifice, that I was lost in wonder. Praise Him, O my soul!

September 7th — Let me note, for the Lord's glory and my future encouragement, that having been for a fortnight under a variety of trying, and seemingly adverse circumstances, my weak heart had somewhat failed and become faint, when last Monday the Lord seemed to say to me, "Thou art mine; I have redeemed thee by My blood; trust thy *flesh* with Me, to do as I like with, and to bring through what I please"; and He gave me ability to give up, and not seek after my own ease and gratification, but be willing for a succession of trials and contradictions, if the Lord should appoint them, embracing Him as my strength to bear them, and seeking only His glory. And I do here record, for His honor and my encouragement, that I find no cause to regret the exercise, or draw back the surrender. All has been well. The Lord will never harm those whom He loves; it is our own folly in having a will, and striving to choose and manage matters, that brings our misery, and not what the Lord lays upon us.

September 20th — "Blessed is the man that endureth temptation." This Scripture is much on my mind, and it is very striking.

September 21st — I feel this morning I must erect an "Ebenezer" to the Lord's praise and glory; not that we are brought *out* of trials, but for support and triumph in Christ, while *in* them. The way, as regards temporals, is quite dark; but I believe the Lord will work for us, though I see not how. All our temporal mercies are only *lent* to us; and, if all are recalled, there will be nothing unkind, it will only be to supply us in another way. I humbly confide in love, and embrace Thee, precious Christ, by faith, that I may trust and triumph in Thee, through all that awaits me. Without Thee I can do nothing.

September 24th — Last evening, Psalm 23:1, was very sweet: "I shall not want," seemed so positive, and also such a necessary consequence of the Lord being my Shepherd, as I never saw before. It seemed like this: To say "the Lord is my Shepherd," and yet to fear, is unpardonable. He will provide all that is really needful. My soul rose in confidence: "I will trust, and not be afraid."

October 7th — Very blessed have been the meditations the Lord has given me lately on the life and triumph of faith, as revealed in the Word—in Abraham, in the children of Israel, in Joshua, David, &c. What a book is the Bible, and what wonders are there revealed, which we find as the Holy Spirit anoints our eyes and opens our understandings. This word was very sweet to me this morning: "What things were gain to me, those I counted loss for Christ." It came in reference to that matter on which I have such conflicts, encouraging me to view that state which I have counted gain, and to which I have most clung, "loss for Christ"; and further, having given up, not to be looking another way, or to another state or circumstance for gain, but still to go on, counting all things, at all times, *loss* for Christ, and take Him as my only gain. The Lord be pleased further to enlarge, explain, and make practical. "I can do all things through Christ which strengtheneth me."

October 19th, Sabbath — Being somewhat shut up in my feelings this morning, the Word came powerfully and sweetly, in Habakkuk 3:17, 18. Here I see the privilege of faith, and how it hinges not on outward things, nor is it dependent even upon our own feelings: they are not the source of its triumph; its Author is its object, and its rejoicing is in the Lord. And, when all the desolation of ourselves is shown to ourselves, faith does not become disconsolate, for the Lord is still the same. Blessed truth! Blessed triumph! Lord, teach me more!

November 16th — It is said of Ruth, my namesake, "She sat beside the reapers"; and I think I do so too; for, indeed, I fare daintily, though, certainly, I seem to have my supply more from the hand of Boaz, than through any instrument; but yet His servants are made a blessing to me, and I give Him all the glory, both of what He *gives* and what He *sends*. Our meeting on Friday evening was most blessed indeed. We all seemed to feel the anointing, which is truth, and teaches all things. My own soul was melted with the wonders of union to Jesus, and free and sweet was my communion with Him. I see more and more how faith looks only forward and upward!

December 1st — I rose this morning very depressed and faint-hearted, but the Lord has strengthened me by Genesis 46:2-4.

December 18th — "I will sing of mercy and judgment: unto Thee, O Lord, will I sing." On Tuesday last, the 16th, we came suddenly into great affliction; my most dear mother being thrown down in the street by a horse and cart. I was not with her, but was told of it. It was a miracle her life was preserved. To the Lord be all glory and praise; and trust Him, O my soul!

December 25th, Christmas Day — My dear mother is better, but still confined to her bed. I know not what is the Lord's purpose, but I think He has brought me to lose my will in His. Yes, dear as my mother is, I do humbly trust my chief desire is the Lord's will, and the Lord's glory. To His praise I must acknowledge that the support and comfort He has given me have been wonderful! When ready to sink from fatigue and anxiety, He has upheld and revived me. When of myself I could not know what to do, He has counselled me. When my heart has been ready to break at the thought of a separation, He has kindly turned my eye to the things unseen and eternal, and restored peace, and kept my mind stayed upon Himself. What cause I have for thanksgiving, and what reason to trust Him still! I am fully engaged in attending upon my dear mother, but yet I had this morning some sweetness and power in connection with the wonder of wonders, "The Word made flesh." I cannot now meditate as closely as formerly, but, when it is good for me, that enjoyment will be restored; at this time more active bodily exertion is needful. For the blessings of this affliction, so far, "Bless the Lord, O my soul"; and that, "unto us a child was born." "Bless the Lord, O my soul!" Welcome to our flesh, Thou Prince of life! All hail, Thou glorious "Second Adam," the Lord from heaven! "Hosannah to the Son of David!"

> "Of all the dear objects belov'd,
> There's none like the Savior to me."

For *such* a Savior, and such a Savior mine, "Bless the Lord, O my soul!"

1846

January 4th, Sabbath — Dear day of sacred rest and heavenly peace. I cannot now go up to the house of the Lord to worship, because my dear mother requires my attendance; but the Lord of the house comes to me, and makes me happy in Himself! Though "He loves the gates of Zion," He neglects not "the dwellings of Jacob"; but sweetly visits His imprisoned ones with His love and favor, which are better than life. I feel most anxious that the new year may be full of Christ to me; that is, that my soul may be more filled with Him, and my life more spent for Him, than it has ever yet been. *How* it shall be accomplished, I leave to Himself. Amen, amen. I almost dreaded entering upon last week; but the Lord has been with me, and, through all, has helped me wonderfully. To His name be glory! I now look especially to Him for the week to come, and desire to cast my whole weight upon Him, doing which, I know I shall be borne up.

February 1st — On reading the memoranda of the last two months, I am much melted to review and remember that, on the 1st of December, my heart was much encouraged from Genesis 46:3, 4. It seemed as if the Lord told me not "to fear to go down into Egypt, for He would be with me." Since then, yea, on the 16th of that month, I did go into Egypt indeed; but my dear Lord has been with me, and now He seems to be bringing me up again, according to His word: but, if it be not so, and heavier trials await me, He still is with me, and it shall be well.

February 22nd, Evening — I have been to the feast. My heart was pressed down with heaviness about my dear mother. "Oh that thou wouldest rend the heavens and come down, and that the mountains might flow down at Thy presence." O Lord, hear me, I beseech Thee: O Lord, hear me, for my heart is sore pained within me, and I am so troubled, I can hardly speak. "I do mourn in my complaint, and make a noise"; O Lord, make haste to hear me, and deliver us. "Make no tarrying, O my God." Oh, let my mother live before Thee.

March 1st, Sabbath — "Bless the Lord, O my soul," that again at our Friday evening meeting much power and blessedness were felt by us. Unworthy I had very strengthening, ravishing views of our "Well-Beloved"; truly and surely Christ was all, and then how little, how verily nothing, am I. It is wonderful that such a worm should be so favored with discoveries of His beauty, who "is fairer than the children of men"; and on whom saints and angels gaze with ineffable delight. And, after all, I know not yet a thousandth part of what He is, and what I have in Him. Oh, for more unfoldings; the door of faith is open; may I enter farther, and yet farther; it is heaven begun, in Jesus to abide; it is as if the pearly portals were thrown back, and open entrance given to one yet dwelling in mortality. Oh, that my lips, my life, and every action, might speak His praise and glorify His name, who is a heaven to me. A most blessed sermon this morning from Psalm 72:17, especially these words, "And men shall be blessed in him"; which "Him" was sweetly and truly applied to a precious Christ. My soul was feasted with marrow and fatness, and I praised the Lord with joyful lips. *Evening* — Another sermon full of Christ. To the

Lord be all the glory! Oh, what a happy, blessed day this has been to my soul; I should like every day a Sabbath. Dear Lord, be with me through the week. Oh, leave me not, I beseech Thee.

March 3rd — How plainly do I see this morning, that as the eye of faith is fixed singly upon Christ, we are ready for anything to which He calls us; but as we are walking by sense, and looking at things "seen," we are fit for nothing; the hands hang down, and the knees are feeble.

March 8th, Evening — A beam of light breaks in upon my soul. One great cause of gloom has been, that I am so much like a drone in the Lord's service, and have done and can do so little. He has now shown me how varied are the different offices and employments of His children. Some have their work outside, much seen and noticed—bringing those in who are afar off by wicked works; others are all within doors, they have a quiet, unobserved path, just amongst the living family, with whom is all their engagement, and about whom is most of their solicitude; "but the Lord has need of them"; and in them, however feeble, He can honor Himself; although often they say, when looking at others, *I* am but a "dry tree." Well, dear Lord, Thou hast untied one hard knot, and I say, content; content, if Thou wilt be honored in me. It is all I want. Anyhow, anywhere that pleaseth Thee, only let me know that I am in Thy service, which is so sweet that I would abide in it fervently to my life's end; even if I knew I should not see Thy face in glory.

> [Reader, this may seem a hard saying, but it contains the very germ of a godly jealousy and divine love. Jehovah's glory—not the creature's happiness—is the great object of faith, next to the person of Christ Himself.]

April 2nd — My ever dear mother has had a whisper from

the Lord this morning, as soon as she awoke; it was this, "Come unto me, all ye that labour and are heavy laden, and I will give you rest," &c. She said, "Oh, it was sweet." Bless the Lord for this gleam of light.

April 12th, Sabbath — My dear mother has been to the sanctuary this morning, perhaps for the last time; for, indeed, I see her growing weaker. May our precious Lord glorify Himself all through the dispensation, and reveal Himself powerfully and graciously to us both; and for the rest, His will be done. He only knows my heart-anguish; He only sees my secret tears of keenest sorrow; but, yet, His will be done. Ten thousand thanks to Him for the sweet feast I have had in His house this morning; the text, Genesis 24:31, 32. The minister spoke of Abraham as a type of the Father; of Isaac, as Christ; of Eliezer, the messenger to Rebekah, as a type of the Spirit, and of Rebekah, as the Church; that is, in this matter. Some might think it strained, but it did not seem so to me; and very sweetly did the truths, and the love of Jesus, flow into my soul, making me forget all my sorrows, and rejoice greatly in Him, my precious Isaac, who loved me before I heard of Him; and who was not only laid on the altar, as Isaac was, but was also really put to death for my sake, and was raised, too, from the dead in my nature, all glorious; a fitting Bridegroom for His Church, glorified in His glory. And the dear Comforter has come, and told me of His love, and lovingkindness, and made me willing to leave all to go to this rich, blessed Isaac; and, surely, we have met, for Christ and I are one; and I know the sweetness and privilege of Isaiah 54:5. Bless the Lord, who hath blessed thee, O my soul.

April 19th — My dear mother seems a little better today. This word exceedingly sweet to my soul: "Ye are not your own." Then whose am I? His who has bought me with the immense, the amazing price of His own precious blood.

My heart bounds with rapture to be His, and not my own; I feel He is my present heaven.

April 24th — Much pressed with anxiety this week; and many fears lest the care which devolves upon me should cause me to be in the leastwise farther from Jesus. Dear Lord, keep me close, very close to Thee. I think we are, as regards my dear mother's soul, like Simeon and Anna, waiting for the "Consolation of Israel."

April 25th, Saturday — My dear mother seems weak. This evening I read John 14, and Mr. S— prayed, during which she evinced unusual fervency. Afterwards, I expressed my hope that the Lord would yet appear; with much energy the loved one replied, "I believe He will, I trust Him for it." This word has been most sweet to me to-day: "When my father and mother forsake me, then the Lord will take me up"; especially this part, "take me up."

April 26th — On reviewing the past month, I fear I have walked too much after the flesh, especially the last fortnight. How has my fond heart clung and turned about to its darling object, now fast withering from my warm embrace. Dear Jesus, pardon all that has been undue sorrow and tenderness; fix my eye singly on Thyself, and in Thee may I triumph even now. And can I triumph? Oh, yes, I can. I shall, if Thou wilt please to make and keep me single-eyed and single-hearted. I am wont, on these days, anew to give up myself, and my all to Thee. I desire to do so now without reserve. What, oh, what will have transpired ere this sacred season returns? May I then have to erect an Ebenezer to the Lord's praise; and may I and my dear mother triumph yet together in Jesus. I desire to rise and shake myself from the dust, to which I have too much cleaved. Oh, precious Well-Beloved, surely I have felt the fibers of Thy love to-day; and my soul says, "Set me as a seal upon thine heart, as a seal upon thine arm: for love is strong as death; jealousy is cruel as the grave." "O Love! O Life Divine! I would be only Thine." Come, with Thy conquering charms, and all absorb this longing soul of mine. Through flood or flame, with Thee it is safe to go. Lead on, O precious One, and be Thyself my courage, and get great glory by all that does befall me. Thou, my Lord, dost seem to strengthen me; and how I long, through the dark scenes approaching, to honor Thee. Do let it be so, my glorious, precious Savior.

May 5th, Tuesday — I have felt last evening and this morning as if I did not half pray, and were not half in earnest. The Lord help me to pray more earnestly. This morning, at family worship, had strong cries for free mercy, free pardon, free grace, free love; all irrespective of the worthiness of the object—all free indeed. My dear mother seemed to weep abundantly, and feel deeply.

May 20th, Thursday Morning, 7 o'clock — What meaneth this? My soul is at the mercy-seat, crying to my Abba, Father, "A shower of blessings, a shower of blessings!" and it is as if the word to me is "Open thy mouth wide, and I will fill it." Oh, is the mercy so long sought at hand? Father, glorify Thy own name.

June 14th, Sabbath — My loved mother rather weaker in body, and much weaker in mind; but, through mercy, collected upon spiritual subjects; and though not more comforted, still deeply anxious. This morning, when taking her medicine, she said,—

> "'When I can read my title clear
> To mansions in the skies—'"

I said, "What then?" She replied,

> "'I'll bid farewell to every fear;
> And wipe my weeping eyes.'"

I said, "Would you wish to fly away and leave me?" She said, feelingly, "Yes." This afternoon, as I sat writing to a dear sister, she spontaneously said, "Oh that the Lord would reveal Himself, and prepare me for heaven!" "Do you long for it?" I said. "Yes, more; yes, more and more." I have to raise a new Ebenezer to the Lord's glory, in that He has helped me triumphantly through a very heavy week, proving that "all things are possible" with Him. Oh, what happiness have I felt in soul, while the body has been greatly weighted. Christ has, indeed, been a glorious all to me.

June 28th — This morning I thought my dearest mother spoke, and, listening on the stairs, I heard her say, feelingly, "Lord Jesus, pardon me. Blessed Jesus, look on me. 'Speak the word only, and I shall be healed'; I shall; only speak. Do, Lord. O Lord, grant it." Yesterday I heard her say, "Have mercy, have mercy." Our dear L— (who has been a faithful watcher in this matter, and with much soul-travail) brought for my dear mother this morning Song 2:11-13; it is sweet. Oh, may it be prophetical of good things about to appear. During the last month the Lord has been very gracious to unworthy me, in upholding under the most painful circumstances; there have been bitters in my cup such as I never expected, but my precious Well-Beloved is still sweetness. Oh, may He be glorified in this dispensation, and may I understand what He intends me to learn in and by it. I have felt very ill during the last week, at times nearly sinking; but I am holden up hitherto, and shall be. It is when sense looks at the waves I feel sinking; thus it was on Thursday evening. Almost more feelingly than ever, I joined Jacob in saying, "All these things are against me." Sorrowful indeed were the tears I shed; but, alas, this was "my infirmity," for good is all the will of the Lord concerning me; and again I will "remember the years of the right-hand of the Most High." Dearest Lord, do keep me from dishonoring Thee, and do yet, somehow, be greatly glorified in what is now befalling us.

July 12th, Sabbath — On Wednesday last, my ever dear mother had an attack most sudden and alarming; and, from its effects, I believe, is sinking into the arms of death, even at this very time. My anguish is very acute; it seems as if the tie that makes us one would not give way, but must be cut to sever us. I try to give her up. I do so and feel so; but when I think her going, the anguish comes again. There is no further manifestation, except a sweet pleading with the Lord, very evident. Twice it has seemed as if death was upon her, and she could not revive; and now she is gradually sinking away, but peace breathes in her chamber. The Son of peace is here, and I trust we shall yet see more of His glory, and praise Him together on earth. Yet His will, not mine, be done.

July 26th — The Lord has indeed "shown us great and sore troubles." It has seemed, at times, as though I could not live under the distressing pressure and peculiar trial; but "hitherto the Lord has helped," and I am sure He is doing all things well. I have this day been led to remember, how at different times I have devoted all I have to the Lord, and no devoted thing is to be redeemed: so now that He is putting everything, almost, into the furnace, I have no right to complain or draw back. I am to live upon the Lord, when all else is withdrawn, and so doing I shall have no lack. The Lord keep me in this fiery trial, and hour of temptation. I am sure His eye is upon us, as the skilful, loving Refiner; and, though my flesh often faints and fails, He is "the strength of my heart, and my portion for ever."

August 30th —
> "As myrrh, new bleeding from the tree,
> Such is a dying Christ to me."

Precious in His blood, precious in His dying, precious in His rising again, is my glorious Lord. This is Sacrament-day; I go not up to the feast, but the great Master has brought me my portion; yea, *Himself my portion is*, and truly "my soul doth magnify the Lord, and my spirit doth rejoice in God my Savior," saying, "God forbid that I should glory, save in the cross of our Lord Jesus Christ." *Evening* — My Christ, my glorious Sun, seems so large and full in my soul, as if I could see no other object; oh, may I study Him more, and be absorbed in and with Him.

September 13th — My dearest mother much the same. My Jesus all and all-sufficient. The past week a heavy one, but brought through it blessedly. In the coming week much labor in prospect; but, "looking unto Jesus," it will only be a new source of triumph to His glory. Still waiting and watching for the Lord in the soul of my loved one—on Him we cannot wait in vain. Much refreshed today by reading a sermon on Hebrews 13:8. Oh how often do we legalize and carnalize; but what unceasing triumph and imperishable blessedness we have in Christ. My heart leaps for joy, though in great outward tribulation (1 Cor. 1:31; Isa. 45:25). Oh, to glory and boast in Him all the day long, and all the night too.

September 27th — Great have been the Lord's mercies to me the last month. My dear mother's many infirmities have much increased; but I cannot resign my post to another. I wish to minister to my dear one to the last. It is not I, but Christ in me, that doeth the works. Praise Him, O my soul! My dearest mother's death appears to be drawing near, but the Lord has not yet spoken peace. I seem to hold Him here in faith and prayer, that He will hold her body in life till the vision has spoken which shall soften the pang of parting, and gain to our dear Lord glorious praise. Oh, that I may yet have this

Ebenezer of Ebenezers to erect to the Lord, on the dark ground of separation. All hail, beloved Savior; Thou hast done wonders. Oh, do yet greater marvels, I beseech Thee. My Christ is my rest and refreshing, in all my weariness: as I lean on Him, I triumph; when I confer with flesh, and look to creatures, I get shame and loss. The unknown future is coming, when I must stand alone in this dark, drear wilderness: but then my Beloved will be all-sufficient, and perhaps He is withholding Mrs. B—, whom I desired in this time of need, that Himself may be all to me.

October 6th, Tuesday — I am watching beside the dying bed of my dearest mother; I think she can hardly live through the day—no word of power in her soul, and her mind quite rambling. I desire to be this day in great stillness from fleshly avocations, and to wait much on the Lord in this chamber of death.

October 7th, Wednesday — My dear mother still lives, but is evidently sinking. The Lord has not spoken, but I hope I am coming to feel completely, "Thy will be done." I have had nothing special from the Lord but this word, "As one whom his mother comforteth, so will thy God comfort thee"; and this has been reiterated in my soul again and again.

> [And what couldst thou want more, dear Ruth? What does not this precious promise comprehend and embrace?]

October 8th, Thursday — The dearest of mothers left this sorrowful world at a quarter-past six this morning.

October 10th — With wonderful cordials, and comforts of love divine, has the Lord supported my aching heart; indeed, He is fulfilling His promise, "As one whom his mother comforteth, so will thy God comfort thee."

October 11th, Sabbath — Still the Lord is wonderful in working, and most tenderly ministers strong consolation to my needy soul. He did not please to speak with power in my dear mother's soul, but He has in mine about her, since her departure; and a sweet assurance I have that she is now in glory; "not lost, but gone before." I am often ready to sink, but the Lord revives and restores me, to my astonishment.

> [Reader, the Lord may not answer His people in their time and in their way, but He does in His own. Ruth expected a word from the Lord before her beloved one's departure. It pleased the Lord, in the exercise of His divine sovereignty, to withhold that word until after her removal; and then gave consolation by a calm, sober assurance centering in and upon Himself, rather than upon a word spoken by Himself. Reader, do you comprehend the distinction? Was it not upon ground the Shunammite exclaimed, "It shall be well"? Had she as yet, or at the time, any direct word from the Lord? We think not. And yet she was not confounded in regard to her simple but blessed venture upon the Lord.]

October 15th, Thursday—Funeral-day — The dear remains conveyed to the tomb, "in sure and certain hope of the joyful resurrection." A day to be remembered. In the waterfloods He is with me.

October 18th, Sabbath — Oh, what multiplied mercies I have to record. While the dear body lay in the house, there was a solemn holy convocation to the Lord, who did graciously minister, and bring out choice and spiced wines for sustaining and reviving. "Devout men," and dear brethren, carried my loved one to her resting-place. They told me there was a peculiar and holy solemnity through the service; and I am sure in this house of mourning, there was a holy calm, and love and peace breathing through each heart. I felt it sweet to belong to the dear living family, and to be in the midst of them. While my dear mother lived, I was once looking forward to the day of her funeral, and the Lord gave me this promise, "When thou passest through the waters, I will be with thee"; and most lovingly and faithfully did He fulfill it. Yesterday my heart was rent and riven in feeling; my loved one gone; it was a heavy day. The Lord lift me out of the flesh! I find over much sorrow brings darkness instead of light.

October 25th — Oh, may Jesus clearly mark my path; already more than one way has presented itself. I wait His guidance. Lord, I beseech Thee, let the pillar of cloud be visible to faith by day, and the pillar of fire by night.

November 22nd, Monday — My poor heart is low indeed this morning. Memory brings back, and affection entwines again around its object; and every word and every look revived, is precious, though piercing. But my spirit strives and longs to look only at Jesus, my Best-Beloved. Oh, to look up instead of back! Mine is indeed a widowed state, for the only one on earth in whom my heart fully confided is gone. Blessed Jesus, take these lingering affections, and cause them to be wholly absorbed in Thyself. Oh, fill up all the void, and consign not this poor, this too fond heart, to any other earthly bosom, as a resting-place for love. How solacing is the use of the pen; it is a luxury indeed, which has often and often soothed my anguished spirit; and, when too full of joy, the overflowings have thus gathered up as a store for future times of scarcity; and both these kinds of musings have had their after-use, as well as present relief. Mine has been the benefit: to my God be all the glory. Last week I had a small house empty, and with no hope of letting it; also, some mischievous persons carried quite away an outer door of a small place on the other side. I expected to have the expense of a fresh one this week; but I told the Lord of it and He has made them bring it back in the night; it was in the night they stole it. Ebenezer. That door will now be of value to me, as a proof of an answer to prayer.

December 6th — I have had great soul exercise about letting my maid go home, and being left alone, night and day; I never had been; and now, in my deep sorrow, and so soon after my great loss, it made me almost tremble; but yet I could not feel at liberty to ask any one to sleep in the house, for fear I should dishonor the Lord. I felt something like Ezra, in Ezra 8:22, and I knew the Lord would be with me. So I did not tell any friend, but the Lord overruled it that M. C—, who had been staying with me (quite casually), overheard us talking about it, and consequently asked me of the matter, feeling grieved to leave me alone; then followed a message from her mother (who knew nothing of this), saying, she did not want her, if well; so altogether it seemed of the Lord's doing that she should stay with me, and His blessing is with us. I take this little matter as a token for good, and believe, that as the Lord has begun to direct manifestly, He will go on to do so in all things. This is my earnest desire. M. C— is gone out to-day; and I am outwardly alone, but not lonely. "Bless the Lord, O my soul!" We both had a message from the Lord, in His house, by His servant, this morning, each according to our case. Mr. B— spoke of the impropriety of growing slack in the Lord's Service, through the pressure of our own personal or relative trials; and oh, what fear I felt, lest the deep I had been feeling should become so absorbing as to weaken my hands in the Lord's cause. May He prevent it. I trust it was a word in season, though somewhat sharply spoken. Oh, it is good to be rebuked by our dear Lord when needful. I desire to cast myself as a "mite" into the Lord's treasury, to be used in His service, for His glory.

December 27th, Sacrament Sabbath — These are my review-days; and I must testify to the Lord's honor that the last has been a month of peculiar mercies; and I do trust my poor heart is somewhat strengthened in the Lord. How much I feel my loss and loneliness, He only knows; but He can make this wilderness and solitary place glad by His presence. He can, for His own glory, make it blossom as the rose. My heart seems anew prompted to seek His glory above everything; and so I yield, by the constraining power of love, myself, my circumstances, my feelings, to the will and wisdom of my almighty Bridegroom, believing His love to unworthy me is a sure guarantee from all harm. I desire that Christ's love may be active, instead of self-love; and Christ-seeking, instead of self-soothing and self-pitying. Dear Lord, renew old lessons with new power, and raise me triumphantly above myself.

December 31st, Thursday Evening — The last day of 1846; a most eventful year, but one of great mercies. And how shall I close it?—with praise. The Lord has brought poor me through wonders. What I have most feared has come upon me, but I have been upholden until now; my loved one, my dearest earthly friend, has left me; but the Lord has comforted me, and, looking up, I still find triumph in Christ. I feel an increase of confidence in the Lord for the future; afresh I commit all my way to Him, and it will not be in vain. The Lord is my helper; He has strengthened me with strength in my soul, and I expect to see more wonders. To God alone be glory! Amen, and amen.

1847

January 1st — The first day of my first year alone. May my heart and life be very full of Christ; and may the Lord be pleased very plainly to show me the way in which I should go; I humbly trust I have had divine renewings in the life of faith this week. How sweet in every state to live on Jesus by simple faith, for the present moment, and leave the rest with Him; looking to Him instead of looking to my dear one gone, the loneliness has been lost. I do think that by Him this "solitary place" is beginning to blossom as the rose; Lord, increase my faith. I give this year and my heart to Thee. Oh, fill them with Thyself!

January 10th, Night — I have committed all my way to Jesus; and I believe His very love and faithfulness ensure me that it will not be in vain. I trust I shall here have to record His mercies, and that He will so plainly show me His way, that I may say, "The thing proceedeth from the Lord; I cannot speak bad or good." My earnest desire is the glory of my most precious Jesus, "who loved me, and gave himself for me"; to minister to His dear saints in soul and body, as He shall give me ability, is my delight. I say, with Abigail, "Let thy handmaid be a servant, to wash the feet of the servants of my Lord." I also have desires for a quiet, secluded life, as hitherto—little with the world, much with Jesus; and I long to do all things spiritual and secular for Christ's sake, not my own, not to the creature. The glories of my Well-Beloved have beamed upon me this evening, so that I longed to be away, fully beholding, and fully enjoying. When will these dusky shades of mortality have fled away, and the presence, love, and glories of my kinsman Redeemer burst upon me in eternal day?

> "Oh, happy souls, that dwell in light,
> And walk with Jesus, clothed in white."

And happy we, who walk by faith in the same perfection, and see through the lattices beams of the same glory. Bless Him, O my soul, who has so much blessed thee— thy God, thy glory. A day to be remembered. May that which has begun in prayer end in praise. "Open thy mouth wide, and I will fill it."

January 12th, Tuesday — I trust I have found solid profit from the exercises of Saturday and Sunday. To the Lord be all the glory! Earnest desire and longings renewed in my soul to "live Christ," and for Him only. This morning I visited the sacred spot where rest in peace the ashes of my dearest mother. My desire was, at that grave, to give myself afresh to the Lord, and seek His guidance. I thought, she is not here, "she is risen." Would I see and commune with my mother, I must look up, and not down. My heart longed to be with Jesus, in the land of perfect love and joy. He it is who attracts my warmest aspirations; but, if He will be honored in me here, will I not gladly stay a little longer? My Lord, Thou knowest all I mean and feel. "Thy will be done." These hands and feet, this heart and tongue, and my whole self, afresh I consecrate to Thee. Wilt Thou deign to accept and use the humble offering of that which is Thine own? Oh, be with me through life, be especially with me in death, and then take me to be with Thee for ever. I am melted by my many outward comforts; "all this, and Christ too!" Why *me* so favored? May my heart and hand be open to the poor and needy. My dear, dear mother, I wish thee joy, and I hail thee blessed. I would not have thee here to sigh and suffer. Thou freed and happy spirit, range over those bright plains of light, gaze on those glories too brilliant for the eyes of mortals, rise higher and higher still in those pure regions, where reigns eternal love; and sing thy anthems, glad and rapturous, in praise of Him who died for thee and me, and soon I shall join thee; till then would I follow on to know the Lord, and, though feebly, praise Him, too, in lip and life.

January 20th — A good deal weighed down yesterday, and many fears about the future, during which I had this word: "They that sow to the flesh shall of the flesh reap corruption"—it was profitable. I saw I was too much seeking fleshly ease; also, a word from my dear sister was very rousing to me; she spoke of those who "live alone, like the snail in its shell; who neither trouble others, nor will be troubled themselves." I felt this was almost what I was wishing for; but it must not be. *Live for myself?* Oh, no, precious Jesus, choose Thou the way, but lead me plainly on, and may I live for Thee, and only Thee. Today this word is sweet, "Take my yoke upon you; for my yoke is easy, and my burden is light."

February 7th — To-morrow it will be four long months since my dear mother was loosed from mortality; how short to thee, my loved one! Thy anthems, thy raptures, are but begun; thou canst not yet have had half thy fill of the beauties of that dear countenance, once "marred more than any man's," now glorious beyond human conception. Gaze on, happy spirit, and praise higher, higher, higher still, Him whom we both adore! With me Time seems to have got his wheels clogged; they have moved heavily since thou hast left me; never did the months seem so long. Oh, when shall I, too, have my fill of love, and my longing soul be satisfied in the very presence and fruition of His glories who, even here in Meshech, is to me so ravishingly dear and delightsome? Stay; the moment is fixed by infinite wisdom. I shall not overpass that bound; till then, whether the space be long or short, may it be filled right full of Christ, and I live for Him only and always. Amen. This first week in this month has been peculiarly favored. How shall I praise? Lord, teach me! Thou deservest nobler songs than I can raise; but let my soul, my lips, my life, let all praise my glorious Lord. Let me have no will, no wish, but Thy glory. But be pleased to let me plainly know Thy mind. I abide in Thee, Jesus, for the answer.

February 15th — Oh, to live Christ only, Christ always, to be ever lost in Him! This is all my happy spirit wants. Sweetest, loveliest Jesus! It cannot be made to appear by pen and ink what glories I have found in Thee. Thou hast brought me hitherto wonderfully. Ebenezer. "The lame take the prey." I still am weak in the flesh, and "halting upon my thigh." I cannot walk another step but in Thy strength. Oh, lead me on; sight forward I have none. Grant me more of the promptings of the sweet Spirit. Be Thou, O my Beloved, my understanding therein, and my willingness and ability to obey: for Thou art all to me.

March 14th — I am perplexed about going to London. Dear Lord, make a plain path for my feet, and let me know it, I beseech Thee. *Evening* — Just now encouraged by Elijah; he seemed to be waiting upon the Lord in prayer, while his servant watched; and, though he sent six times for nothing, on the seventh the answer came. So, although I have been many times looking up for direction about London, and have seen nothing, I desire still to wait and watch, trusting that the Lord will speak.

April 4th—London—Sunday — Arrived in town on Thursday. I had a safe and pleasant journey; all fear of railroad travelling taken away; and I was much blessed and favored of the Lord. Oh, that this day I may be lost in Christ, and Christ found in me.

April 28th, Wednesday — Returned home on Monday, favored with journeying mercies.

June 6th — I feel I am like a wife who has long lived in free and affectionate intercourse with her beloved; but all is now shut up: there is no speaking on one side, and but little on the other. Oh, it is cutting work; and I have this morning said to my dear Lord, "I cannot bear it; I cannot bear it." I know all the fault is mine; may I also know what it is.

June 13th — I trust I have had some sweet renewings in the life of simple faith; and that chiefly from reading former memoranda, as an instrument. The power is from above.

June 26th, Sacrament-day — I desire fresh resignings of my whole self and concerns to the Lord's will. The flesh trembles, unbelief struggles, and carnal reason says, I never can enjoy happiness on earth. Well, if I cannot in the flesh, in social endearments, my happiness in Christ is unbroken. Here may I triumph, when all is drear beside. I have had special mercies this month, and proved it good to give one's self to the Lord in the dark, for His whole will.

> [Reader, remember, it is "in the dark" that faith works, and waits, and watches; here, "in the dark," faith lives, and moves, and has its being.]

July 6th, my Birthday — Some sweet soul-meltings in the morning, in the love of Jesus, and fresh resignings of my whole self to the Lord during the day, that He may be more specially glorified in me.

July 25th — Happy in Jesus! Much blessed in reading a sermon on 1 Corinthians 12:9, 10; it is, indeed, marrow and fatness, just the experience I love: willing to be nothing, that Christ may be all in all. How blessed is my condition! Though so vile a sinner in myself, yet chosen and beloved in Christ from all eternity; every blessing for time, all glory for eternity, secured to me in Him. Himself my blissful portion! Himself my endless treasure! Himself my ocean of love, my God and my glory! "My soul doth magnify the Lord, and my spirit rejoices in God my Savior." Oh, to spend and be spent in service for His glory.

Evening — At the sacrament this evening I was inwardly prompted to give myself peculiarly to the Lord for the coming month. I had heart-tremblings, lest it should be a prelude to some heavy trial; but, whatever may be coming, I am quite sure, that looking unto Jesus, I shall be more than conqueror in all things in Him: because, being one with the conquering Head, I must rise into His victories, and by my very defeats I shall be more abased, and He more exalted. Oh, my sweetest, loveliest Jesus, honor Thyself in me this once again; appear manifestly for me. Oh, let it be seen in me, that it is not in vain to trust alone in Thee! Thou knowest, some friends reproach me that I do not make more effort to find some one to lodge in my house. Plainly, dear Lord, show me what to do; and then show me that I have done all according to Thy Word. Thou knowest, dear Lord, that I eat not the bread of idleness; my hands are daily diligent in labor. I bless Thee for my sanctified employment. Oh, bless the labor of my hands, and in my other matters graciously come forth unto me as the Hearer and Answerer of prayer, that herein I may have to record Thy wonders. Amen.

July 27th — As I have for some time been intensely anxious to know the Lord's will and way about my concerns, and have sometimes felt almost overwhelmed by the delay and suspense, my prayer to-day has been to be humbled into entire submissiveness to the Lord's will; that, however long He may delay the answer, I may not repine; but seek to glorify Him in my present circumstances, and thankfully enjoy my many mercies. It has been a day of deep exercise, but I was blessed this morning from these words, "Regard not your stuff, for the good of all the land of Egypt is before you." Seal home this word, O Lord, and quiet my conflicting bosom. It seems at times as if I must sink under what presses upon me; but anon, my Beloved says, "My grace is sufficient for thee."

August 1st — Outward circumstances not altered, but the burden of them greatly gone. I see faith must go on trusting the Lord. Psalm 37:5; Proverbs 3:6: Himself has brought me to the first part of these words, and will He fail to fulfill the second? Oh, never, never! He will as surely guide me, as He has enabled me to acknowledge Him, and commit all to Him. Our precious Christ is "the Amen, the faithful and true Witness." He is the Amen to every prayer of faith, and, when thus sealed with the King's signet, no man or devil can reverse it; and He is the faithful Witness to see all faith's expectations accomplished, as He saith, "All things whatsoever ye ask in prayer, believing, ye shall receive." How strengthening! What a solid rock it feels to my weary feet. My deep concern has been to know the Lord's will about outward matters. Precious Savior, grant me an answer of peace. Faith looks right on, and wavers not, whoever may oppose.

August 22nd — Many fears to-day, lest I am in anywise sinking into a life of sense. Earnest pleadings to be renewed in a life of *simple faith*. I trust Thee to glorify Thyself in my present circumstances, and not to let a solitary feeling cast me down; also, as the sin of my fallen nature has been active, to my grief, I desire to renew my trust in the sin-atoning sacrifice of a precious Christ. Being Sunday night, I am feeling dreary and lonely; but no, it must not be, it is thus that my foe gains ground. "I will trust and not be afraid" even now. Lord, help, increase faith, and let me not be beaten off this time, but gain an inch or two upon Satan, unbelief, and carnal reason, my close pursuers! I must trust, I will, I do trust to trust more. I have sown in tears to-day; but how strengthening to the soul is trusting; how very weakening is fear, misgiving, and doubt; they not only betoken weakness, but they increase it.

August 27th — Shall Rahab hang out her scarlet line, and, trusting the word of men, whom she never saw before, feel assured of safety, and thus, by faith, perish not? And shall I, with the scarlet blood of Christ upon my conscience, and with my Father's assurance that all such shall be eternally safe, shall I doubt it? Lord forbid! And shall I hang out the appointed token for His direction, which He has promised to regard, even in all my ways acknowledging Him? or shall I fear that He will break His word, and leave me to take my own way, or a wrong one? Ah! never; the Lord forbid!

August 31st — To-day I have been, most unexpectedly, requested to become a visitor at the Refuge; I felt most sensibly my own unfitness, and thought I never could engage in the work; but then I knew, if the Lord called me to it, He would be my ability, and He loves to use things of nought. It is singular, that for a long time, I have yearned towards this institution, and much wished to see it, and have even planned how to do so; but now a message comes beforehand. I think really it is from the Lord, on whom I have long been waiting, to show me how to honor and serve Him. Opened upon Acts 10, at tea-time, and was much melted; it seems something like Cornelius and Peter being prepared for, and sent to, each other. That verse, too, melted me, "Go with them, doubting nothing: for I have sent" thee. If the dear Lord should send me to some one, as He went to the woman of Samaria! It is strange! He sends for one who is holding back; I know another ready, and willing, and more prepared: but, as yet, she is not called. Show me Thy will, and let this be the rule of my decision.

September 5th — Surely few are so favored as unworthy I. The "bottles of heaven," as Toplady calls them, were this morning poured into my willing, wandering soul most blessedly; and, in contemplations of my blessed Lord, for very love, taking my nature to be one with Himself for ever, I could only weep and sing, love and wonder.

September 6th, Night — I have this evening had a short walk, and taken a trifling token of love to a friend; and thus did I ponder, as alone I walked: Suppose two persons had in their gardens choice flowers; one loves to see them flourish, and cannot touch or allow them to be touched by any one; the other loves to pick the very choicest, and gather them, to present to the heart's cherished friend; which has the highest enjoyment? I immediately decided the latter. These were but common thoughts, but immediately it followed: My sweet mother was my heart's loveliest flower; my precious Jesus is my very best, choicest Friend. Would I withhold that flower from Him? Would I rather see it still half bloom in this withering clime, than present it to my dearest Friend, to open out fully in the sunshine-region of His immediate glory? Most adorable Immanuel, Thou knowest I would withhold nothing from Thee. I would find all only in Thee.

> [Reader, shouldst thou have been the subject of bereavement, may the Lord apply this sweet thought of the blessed Ruth's to thy troubled heart.

Think of gifts *to*, as well as *from*, Jesus; and how condescending He, to receive such gifts from the hand of faith. "The Lord *gave*, and the Lord hath *taken away*; blessed be the name of the Lord."]

September 23rd, Thursday — No small tempest has lain upon me for several days, and I have been at times at my wit's end, crying to the Lord to know the right way, but no moving of the cloud. It were comparatively easy to wait, but for the pressing need of money, and none coming. This week is wearing away, and during the next I expect the tax-gatherer; my heart starts, at times, with the thought how near it is; I have read of such straits, but never so closely felt them. Three ways in which I thought supplies might come have been a blank; faith is at times almost failing, unbelief strives hard, and my dear Lord only knows what I suffer. If He will but show me how to be employed, so as to meet my outgoings, I shall be thankful. Much of this day spent in weeping and crying to the Lord, over my needle; this evening I am a little revived. I see I am looking too much at probabilities, as if the Lord were straitened for a means to help me. Lord, I now humbly believe Thou art able to do this, although it seems a hard case, and the sum I need is large. I am encouraged by 2 Kings 7, and also find that in Paul's tempest the ship was wrecked, and themselves cast out the tackling. So may I cast away all human props, and launch out in "venturesome believing." But, oh, the throes of trembling fear, that intermingle!

["Venturesome believing"—the quintessence of faith.]

September 24th, Friday — What further awaits me is unknown; it is a new scene, indeed, but Christ is all in all. It is said of Daniel, "no manner of hurt was found upon him, because he believed in his God"; and I do now believe it will be thus with me; faith revives, though trials abound, and I may yet have to drink deeper of the bitter cup.

September 27th, Monday — I rose this morning with a very heavy heart, and seemed to have this word given me: "Speak unto the children of Israel, that they go forward." I was graciously relieved and blessed at family worship, and, although my flesh has since had a wound, my spirit was helped to yield to the will of almighty Love. No movement in providence yet, but I believe I shall not wait in vain.

September 30th — Much tried in the flesh, much blessed in the spirit. I am afresh in love with the Prince of life and glory. I desire to lie down at His dear feet, and feelingly to say, "Father, glorify Thy name."

October 5th — Still in the same outward perplexities. I seem every day to come to the very sinking-point, and that is the turning-point; but, when overwhelmed, the dear Lord revives and comforts me, by His Word or otherwise, so that I go on again; and, indeed, have most precious visits from my glorious Well-Beloved in this time of trial. His love most sweetly solaces my lonely heart, so that I do praise and adore Him.

October 8th — This day I complete my first year of widowhood, and solemnly commemorate the release of my dear mother from mortality. How tender are the Lord's mercies to unworthy me. This afternoon, when going to my loved one's resting-place, just as I drew near the spot, these words came with power: "The maid is not dead, but sleepeth." My soul was melted and comforted. It was so sweet to be thus reassured, and it was a check to the swellings of grief. The past has been a year of amazing mercies, though one of sharp trial and deep sorrow in the flesh. I am at this time in peculiar straits, but the Lord is with me; and I trust to walk at large with Him, although in the furnace. It is singular, I have to-day had to go to the Refuge for the first time; I trust the Lord was with me.

October 12th — What a feast have I had this evening from these words, "God manifest in the flesh"; or, rather, it is the substance of the mystery which is my joy, and not the words merely. "The Word was made flesh." In my flesh I see God; and here is the spring of my bliss and glory for time and eternity. I feel my heaven begun, and my glad soul would go forth, like Miriam, with the timbrels, in the dance, to the honor and praise of my saving, conquering Lord, who scorned not the lowly door of Mary's womb, that He might afterwards take my flesh, all-glorious, through the heavenly gates and everlasting doors which were lifted up to receive the King of Glory. I wonder, I worship, and think time tardy which keeps me from beholding Him. Hallelujah! Hosanna to the Son of David! Surely some new trouble is at hand, my soul is so blessed and favored with the sweet love of Jesus, in its incomings and overflowings. The Lord be praised! Amen and amen.

> [Reader, in Zion's pathway new distresses in the flesh and fresh discoveries by and in the Spirit, are commonly most closely connected.]

October 17th, Sunday — I have been a good deal instructed lately in reading about Abraham; seeing how, at the Lord's bidding, he went out and went on, not knowing whither he went; and how, though the Lord blessed him greatly, and made him great promises, yet He gave him none inheritance—no, not so much as to set his (fleshly) foot upon. From all which the Lord seems to teach me, that our life in the wilderness must be continually by faith, and not by sight. It seems so very sweet, "not knowing whither he went"; and most truly it is so with me in outward things. I felt it this morning in a new sense, because yesterday and to-day I have been spitting blood continually. I name it to no one but my best Beloved, because I do not like to make much ado about myself. But I feel that it may lead to something serious, and, instead of the Lord opening a new path in the wilderness, He may be opening a door out of it. I have for years felt the dread solemnity of the eternal world, and of entering the unseen state of spirits. Many times the glories of Immanuel and His precious love in my soul have overpowered every other sensation; and, encircled with the beams of His brightness, I have longed intensely to be away in the fullness of His glory, and in the full enjoyment of Himself. This is not looking at death, but at Jesus, "who has abolished death." At other times, when in less enjoyment, I have been subject, not to a fear of my safety, but to a sort of shyness and shrinking from an unknown state of being: something like the thought of appearing at a splendid court without having been initiated into its etiquette, although provided with a court-dress. I have also been subject to an idea that trembling and fearfulness will seize me when mortality is giving way, and eternity close at hand. This morning, however, when I found the symptom before named increasing, and seriously felt it might indicate that soon I should put off mortality, I was surprised at the calm confidence my soul felt. It was very precious, and showed me that Jesus will be all-sufficient when the time of "undressing" comes. And as I sat in the house of God, I kept saying, "Do, Lord, give me a token of what Thou intendest, whether for life or death." Then something seemed to say, "that would be sight"; you must just walk on, believing, like Abraham. Thus walking, it shall be well. Oh, for grace to go on looking only to Jesus, and living only to His glory. He is my heaven here below.

October 21st — This evening Deuteronomy. 8:2, 3, very sweet. I am sure there has been a needs-be for all the rough paths I have been travelling. I might have been much puffed up if all had gone smoothly. By these things I learn, under divine teaching, much that is within; and I also find my heart is much softened thereby, to sympathize with others in their trials. What hath God wrought for me? I believe a complete deliverance out of the "day of trouble," and from the source of fear and conflict, which have continued so long. I have once or twice had relief, and thought the storm was over, but it has again beaten upon me. Now I do think it is a real deliverance. I give the Lord glory, while shame and self-abasement are mine. I see from it that in my fallen nature there is no improvement. I believe, in this mysterious matter, Satan and the flesh have worked with deceivableness of unrighteousness. How do I marvel when I look back; what deep anguish I have gone through; and now I think that some things which I supposed were from above, were not so. I wish to watch closely, to learn profitably, to be humbled exceedingly, and think I must walk softly before the Lord all my days. I wonder if any child of God was the subject of such an exercise. If I knew of such an one, how gladly would I sympathize, and warn them of that soft, and seemingly spiritual voice, which I now believe must have been of the flesh. The Lord pardon me, if wrong, and discover it to me. I bless Him, that He has kept me in fervent cries to Him during the long siege, and thus flesh has not prevailed against me. Surely, now, the walls of this Jericho have fallen. O blessed Jesus, in the tenderness of Thy compassion, pity my infirmity, and, through it all, lead me on to victory.

October 27th — I have been to the House of Refuge to-day. My heart is in that work, and yearns over the souls of those poor girls. Oh, that the Lord may be pleased to bless His Word through such a worm.

October 31st, Sacrament-day — I have not been favored with enjoyment at the Lord's table. I hang solely on a precious Christ, having neither frame or feeling as an accompaniment; but I come, in all need and nothingness, for free-love bestowments, and free-grace communications. I have had much mercy during the month; the sweet love and power of Jesus in my soul has abounded while commemorating the departure of my much-loved mother, this month last year. The Lord has also sent me some relief from pecuniary straits, and has, moreover, delivered me from the source of long, distressing conflict, known only to Himself. For these favors, praise Him, O my soul! Much mystery in the last-named dispensation: "But the woman, knowing what was done in her, fearing and trembling, came and fell down before him, and told him all the truth." This seems just my feeling, that, however great my guilt in this matter, His precious blood is more than a match for it all; and thus He is able to save to the uttermost of my case, and willing, too. Oh, yes; He "will see me again," for I am persuaded that nothing shall be able to separate me from His love. I earnestly desire more light in this matter.

November 3rd, Evening — I have been to hear Mr. C—. His text was Psalm 5:11. I trust I have been much edified, and wish to remember that he said "We should trust the Lord with all He has given us, that is, in prayer give all back to Him, as it were, and trust only in Himself." Then, in quoting Job 22:24, he said: "It may be read, without straining the Scriptures, 'He shall be to thee instead of silver.'" Both these were sweet to me. When speaking of trusting the Lord, he quoted Isaiah 26:3; following which, came in my mind that word in Philippians 4:6, 7.

"Well," thought I, "there must be something wrong in me, for my mind is not kept in that peace, it is full of anguish. So now I pray the Lord to show me where I err. I am much more calm, but am threatened to be invaded again. The Lord subdue unbelief and the flesh, and glorify Himself."

November 18th, Thursday — Christ, the Beloved of my soul, is my perfection, and His blood is my purity, my deliverance, and my preservation from guilt of conscience. This has been like solid rock to my soul these two days. But how are the waves and billows going over my flesh; how is my heart pierced to the quick. Can I ever have an Ebenezer on this dark ground? My Father, I this night ask, in the name of Jesus, that in this "day of trouble," Thy will may be done, however severe to my flesh; Thy name glorified; and my enemies, now clamorous, defeated; and I now erect a thankful Ebenezer on this very place, so dark and drear.

November 19th — A providential mercy; most timely, most wonderful. Is the Lord going to turn my long captivity? I should, indeed, be "like unto them that dream." This passage has been often upon my mind, during the time of trial; but I could not see how it should be fulfilled. Certainly, the supply now so unexpectedly received, is a great present relief, and encourages me to believe that the Lord is not angry with me for waiting to know His will and way. The Lord sanctify the gift, and doubly bless the giver; and keep me "looking unto Jesus."

December 6th, Monday — Much tried by external things. As I mused thereon, something seemed to say, "Leave all these things, and look at the riches and treasures thou hast in Me." "What, leave that which is a pricking thorn?" "Yes, leave all with Me." I felt, after, as if I dare not touch them.

December 18th, Sabbath — Somewhat closely engaged today in seeking the Lord, that I may know His will concerning me; and also, especially, that I may be more taken up with Christ. For, by reason of these peculiar pressures, temporal things seem to have gained too much the ascendancy. Jesus must be all in all.

December 23rd — Christ most precious. He my Ishi; I, His Hephzibah! What love! What wonders, for a worm so vile! But He has borne my vileness away, and is Himself my comeliness! "Praise the Lord, O my soul!"

December 31st — The year 1847 is closing. It has been one of peculiar straits and trials, such as I never passed through before. This evening I have been a little reviewing the path, and find superlative mercies, as well as piercing crosses. My expenses exceed my incomings; though I deny myself in all I can, perhaps too much, yet I cannot make things meet; and cannot feel or see how to move. The Lord has done much; may the coming year be one of enlargement in temporal things, by His taking me to a less expensive home, or giving more means to support this.

1848

January 5th — This word seems very sweet and wonderful to me just now; "When mine enemies and my foes came upon me, to eat up my flesh, they stumbled and fell."

January 13th — Outward things as dark as midnight. I do look up, and at times feel an indescribable confidence that deliverance is not far distant; although, when I judge by sight, it seems impossible; and my flesh would think there is no way for the Lord to help me; faith alone sustains me, and faith in a faithful God will not prove a broken reed.

January 23rd — I know not what the Lord intends to do with me; but, in the midst of present desolation, I desire to go forth in the name of Jesus, which is all-conquering. But all the hardness of my case is nothing with my dear Lord. He is faithful still, and I shall not wait upon Him in vain. Oh, to triumph in Him, all the while the flesh is sinking, and the enemy taunting. Lord, increase my faith; and keep me from dishonoring Thee: although the fig-tree bloom not, and the olive-tree bear not.

January 27th, Thursday — "Do ye not yet understand, neither remember of the five loaves of the five thousand, and how many baskets ye took up? Neither the seven loaves of the four thousand, and how many baskets ye took up?" (Matt. 16:9). Yes, dear Lord, I now remember, and am encouraged. "It is nothing with thee to help by many or few"; "mine eyes are unto thee:" and, though sorely buffeted, faith does at times arise and triumph. I thank Thee, Thou hast said, "According to your faith be it unto you." Not according to unbelief, which so violently struggles, and seems at times to preponderate. That vile abomination sinks like lead in the red sea of a Savior's blood; for though it darkens and distresses, it shall not prevail in those for whom His precious blood was shed.

January 30th, Sacrament-day — I felt at the Lord's table to-day that "His flesh is meat indeed, His blood is drink indeed." Outward things have become darker this last month; but the Lord has been peculiarly with me, and I think faith has more prevailed. It seems to me as if the rod had budded and blossomed; if it be really so from the Lord, fruit will follow, and faith will have fulfillment. I desire to inquire of Him on this matter, as Rebekah did. Lord, bring to perfection Thine own, and crush all the rest while in embryo. Let what is of the flesh never see the light. Oh, be not dishonored in the dearly-bought purchase of Thy precious blood. Fill me with Thyself! Use me for Thyself! Absorb me in Thyself! Sweetly encouraging to my soul is that word, "The way of the Lord is strength to the upright." "He that walketh in the night stumbleth."

February 3rd — In the midst of all, I have an increasing confidence in the Lord; and, at times, a firm belief that there is an order given forth from above, for a blessing for me, though to sense every way seems hedged up; but I thought, yesterday, that the Lord will "open the windows of heaven," rather than that the expectation of faith shall be cut off. To which thought I had afterwards a kind response from the Lord. We had a delightful visit at W—. Saw again the Scripture emblems. Had sweet communion with saints; and heard of one most deeply tried, and most manifestly blessed. This encouraged me, though no one there knew my case.

February 6th, Sabbath — "The way of the Lord is strength to the upright." I feel it so. Christ is the "way" of the Lord, and He is our strength; and, walking uprightly in Him, we walk surely. It is just now a most important crisis with me; but I feel greatly strengthened in the Lord, and a sweet, loving confidence that He will appear for me, and be my guide and my glory. I never was so clearly cut off from outward ways and means. I must, I do, venture my whole weight upon the Lord. Deuteronomy 11:24: "Every place whereon the soles of your feet shall tread shall be yours." I do now believe that wherever true faith treads in expectation at God's command, divine love and power will put in possession in God's time, according to His own promise (Matt. 21:22). As also in the case of Caleb, who followed the Lord wholly: had the promise of the land that his feet trod upon, claimed it in faith, possessed it in power, and gave the Lord the glory of the conquest (Josh. 14).

February 10th — Some close fighting to-day. The enemy very taunting, and my flesh in league with him; but the Lord is on my side, why should I "fear what flesh can do unto me"? I desire to cleave closely to my Captain, and He will overcome. Most blessed Jesus, Thou art on my side; oh, confirm Thy word unto Thine handmaid, upon which Thou hast caused me to hope. Again I cast the burden of all expenses upon Thee; Thou canst sustain them, though they seem unavoidably to increase. If I am right, establish me in Thyself, and in Thy way; if my flesh and foe have beguiled me, discover them, and deliver me, I beseech Thee. Love will not let me cry in vain; my glorious Lord will arise for mine help.

February 13th — Luke 5:5. And what followed this obedience of faith, for it could not be sight? Plenty, instead of poverty. I have been for months toiling, and have not taken what I wanted. I believe it is my dear Lord who has now bid faith let down the net—not on the old, wrong side of creature effort and expectation, but on the right side of the Lord's purpose and power. And here is the gleaner, just happy in the Lord, waiting His will; and, though often taunted by the enemy with the thought that He has not spoken, yet, believing that He has, she is saying, "Behold the handmaid of the Lord, be it unto me according to thy word." Surely the net is let down. I would bless my precious Jesus. Oh, what a present heaven do I find in Him! No tongue can half His beauties and His sweetness tell! Oh, to live ever by simple faith upon Him, till called up to live in open vision with Him. Flesh gets most complete starvation, when Christ is all in all!

February 15th — "My fruit is better than gold, yea, than fine gold; and my revenue than choice silver." Thus speaks Jesus, the true, eternal wisdom; and sweet are His words to my soul this evening.

February 18th, Friday — To my astonishment, the Lord sent an answer to the faith He had given about temporal things. It is the Lord's doing, and it is marvellous in mine eyes. Thus has He fulfilled those words He gave me on this matter: on October 9th, Isaiah 54:17; and on January 9th, Exodus 14:13. I am surprised and thankful, but fear to look too much at the gifts. I desire to have a single and loving eye upon the Giver, who directed how the net should be let down. I believe the Lord will employ and provide for unworthy me, without engrossing me in worldly cares, for which I have no spirit left in me, by reason of the love and loveliness of Jesus, whom alone I desire to serve. This word has been powerful the last day or two, "If thou canst believe; all things are possible to Him that believeth"; "Power belongeth unto God." To the Lord be glory! Amen.

February 20th, Sabbath — The Lord was very gracious to me at the Refuge on Friday. I had a melting-time; I thought of that precious Jesus, who wept over Jerusalem; and my heart and my eyes wept, too, over those poor girls. Surely, there are among them vessels of mercy; they are most attentive, and some of them weep under the Word. I have to go twice this week, if the Lord permit. I tremble, but my "sufficiency is of God."

February 26th — I have been to the Refuge. I know not whether any of it is natural feeling, but my very heart seems to yearn over those girls. More of them were present to-day, and there seemed real feeling. Dear Lord, do seal home Thy Word upon some of their hearts, and give a token where Thou art working. Make us faithful; and may they fall down wounded under the arrows of King Jesus.

February 27th, Sacrament Sabbath — A memorable day. My soul has *bathed in bliss*. At our little meeting on Friday evening, I was led solemnly to renew my vow before the Lord, to live for Him alone; and, laying down enjoyments and delights at His feet, to seek His glory only, and by what means He should see best. On retiring to rest, I joyfully felt that "the vows of God were upon me"; and was privileged with heavenly and ineffable delights; in the midst of which was great yearning over the souls of the poor girls in the Refuge, for whom I seem to "travail in birth till Christ be formed" in them; and also to believe that all will not be in vain in the Lord. This morning I was mourning the loss of dear Mrs. A—, because she only and M— know fully what it is to lose self and be absorbed in Jesus. And then, on my knees, I besought the Lord for such a companion. It was very striking, that before I had risen from my knees, a letter came from A—, to say how the Beloved had just revealed Himself to her soul, as her blessed Bridegroom; and she used love's own language; and my soul was as *liquid love* while I read and wondered. I must wait the Lord's further mind. This has been a blessed month, indeed. At its commencement I thought the rod had bloomed and blossomed; it has since borne fruit. I am astonished at the Lord's love and lovingkindness. What will heaven be, where, without interruption or intermission, we shall love, adore, and praise?

> "Oh, for a thousand tongues to tell
> My dear Redeemer's worth."

I long that my dying lips might sound His praise, and tell His love, who will be my life in death. But He knows best. Friends do not think it will be so, because I enjoy so much now; and I have thought so, too, and trembled; but "All things are possible to him that believeth." Yes, my blessed Jesus, a happy life, and a happy death, are in Thy power to give; for Thou hast made an end of sin, and conquered death; Thou hast also drunk up all my hell. What can I render? Only my *whole self,* with all I have and am. It is not worth Thy picking up; but love puts a value upon its object. My Lord, my life, my happiness, my heaven, my all! Thou hast loved and chosen me; Thou wilt not turn away; but, filling me with Thyself, Thou wilt use me for Thyself, and Thou shalt have all the praise! I would now go forth in Jesus, and all will be well.

March 5th — Oh, keep me believing, and let not mine enemies prevail to set me reasoning. I was lately thinking of my temporal matters, when something within seemed to say, "You must not sit still, and expect the food to drop into your mouth." And directly, with power and sweetness, came this in answer, "Open thy mouth wide, and I will fill it." It has melted me to tears more than once since. He has filled, and will fill, I believe, in spite of my taunting foes. Oh, sweet and happy life of faith! May I know more of its privilege and power.

March 12th — This afternoon I opened upon 1 Samuel 8:5, from whence I read forward, and can truly say, "Thy words were found, and I did eat them," and they are refreshment to my spirit. How plainly I see Saul, a man in the flesh, continually acting from fleshly expediency, thereby dishonoring and displeasing God. And as I read, it made me tremble, lest I should, under my present straits, turn again to folly. And now I have just come to David, and my soul is melted where he says, "I cannot go in these, for I have not proved them." They seem to me like creature ways and means, as if they were not to be my ways; for, like David, I can tell my experience of the Lord's wonders by the hand of faith, when He delivered me out of the paw of the lion and the bear. I see that, as is the man, so is his strength; if he be a man in the flesh, his strength will be in ways, and means, and fleshly contrivances; if he be a man in Christ, his strength will be in the Lord his God.

March 14th — Much shut up in spiritual feelings, striving to pray, but seeming only to "chatter like a crane or a swallow"; to "mourn in my complaint, and to make a noise." While reading the cruel treatment of our gracious Lord, when He was "made sin," I was grieved that my heart did not melt; but I thought that sensation might be withholden, that I might be taken up with Christ and His sufferings, and not with my own feelings. Then I longed for Christ to be all, and was enabled to come before God with Jesus only, just pleading Christ. In this way I found my soul strengthened; afterwards, our Friday evening meeting was sweet and powerful. So this day of storm closes in peace, and I am anew in love with my *new creation,* in Christ Jesus, longing to know more of it.

March 19th, Sabbath Evening — I trust I have this evening heard to edification a sermon from Psalm 37:4, in which the Person of Christ was set forth. This is savory meat, such as my soul loveth. Although I know, to my shame, that I have been often unfaithful to my glorious Husband, yet my heart yearns for full restoration to its whole privileges; and I think my Beloved has this evening whispered, "I will restore thee." Oh, wondrous, matchless love! "He hateth putting away." "To her was granted that she should be arrayed in fine linen, clean and white." Away with every idol; may Christ be all in all!

March 26th, Sabbath — I am going to the Lord's supper, it being "our solemn feast day." Oh, that I may have the privilege to appear before the Lord, and *present some bills of promise at heaven's bank,* and either get present payment, or renewal of faith on my part, and acknowledgment on that of the King's. And, if they be not His own, but the inventions of Satan, may the King tear such forgeries in pieces, and burn them, that I may never see them again. Thus may I either get confirmation or confutation; and do real business with heaven, in the name of Jesus. Amen.

> [Blessed and profitable trading this, reader! Do *you* know what it is thus to be engaged?]

April 2nd — The times look threatening. Great commotions abroad! Sovereigns dethroned! The reins of government seized by the people; and mighty overturnings going on. At home, a great moving in the minds of men towards a republican form of government; and an apparent effort to bring it about. Many hearts are failing for fear; many are agitated and perplexed; and a remnant is crying to the Lord in secret, and rejoicing that He is reigning in the midst of all. For myself, though alone and unprotected, my confidence is in the Lord Almighty; and if I dare record anything of my soul estate, it is, that He is strengthening my faith in Himself; and I do indeed feel Him to be a rock—yea, the rock of my heart, and my portion for ever. Oh, for more faith.

April 9th — We have had A— here. And sweet it is to hear her speak of the secrets of love, and the mysteries of the kingdom. Political events assume a portentous aspect. The disaffected are very threatening, and the civil and military powers are making preparations for the defensive. This very week is the time expected to be eventful. My felt security and peace is in the thought that the Lord Jehovah reigns. Last Sabbath evening, I was seized with a very nervous panic during the service, thinking I heard the noise of a mob; I have since been kept in solid peace, with a sweet inward assurance of safety. This word is very powerful: "Whoso putteth his trust in the Lord shall be safe." And, although I have no human protector, I feel the power of Omnipotence around me for defense. It is sweet; to the Lord be all the glory. In pleading for my own country, I blush to lift up my face to heaven, on account of our great sins; but I beg deliverance for the sake of the remnant that is left therein. May the salt be full of savor, and preserve this corrupt land from complete corruption.

April 23rd — Through mercy, the country has been kept in peace; and, during the time of threatening, the Lord has made me happy in Himself, although I have no human defender.

May 7th — In reading a sermon of Mr. T — 's to-day, in which he quoted, "He was manifested to take away our sins," that word "away" had particular power, and I saw how free I am from a thing that is taken away. It remains in the flesh; but I am to walk in the Spirit, reckoning the "old man" dead, being crucified with Christ; in which mystery I wish to be renewed. Sin can never attach to me, as a new creature in Christ Jesus; then, indeed, would God's creation be marred, of which Christ is the beginning (Rev. 3:14). Then I saw how free I am from sin, in union to my Beloved; "because He was made sin" for me, and then put to death (1 Pet. 3:18). Now, if my sin was put to death, what remains but eternal triumph in Him, who rose again without sin? I rose with Him, and He is my resurrection and my life; and in that resurrection-life sin never was, sin never shall be. It is almost too much for me while I write and feel it. So real, so true, so rich, so full of marrow and fatness.

May 14th, Sabbath — "Our Father, which art in heaven," I beseech and entreat renewing in the "mystery of Christ." In Him may I abide; thus will much fruit be brought forth, and I not filled with *it*, but with Him. O Holy Father, Holy Son, Holy Ghost, Israel's one Lord, renew faithless me in the simplicity that is in Christ. I am perplexed by creatures; clear teaching comes from Thee alone and is by "that anointing which teacheth all things, and is truth, and is no lie"; for this I humbly ask, in Jesu's name. I feel unfit for the world, and unlike everybody else; weak, ignorant, and stupid. Of whatever use I am, it is only "Christ in me" not I at all. Oh, for more of Him, in heart, lip, and life!

May 18th — Sighs and tears are my daily portion. "Help, Lord, for vain is the help of man." The enemy rageth, my heart sinketh, and my spirits are truly borne down. Lord, renew my faith, I earnestly beseech Thee, and do plainly appear for me. I am ashamed of my anguish, but cannot help it. Surely it is sharp work to live so closely, incurring expenses beforehand, and not daring to stir, for fear of doing wrong. My dear Lord, Thou hast not in Thy family such a poor creature as I.

Oh, do tell me what I must do! Do not let me dishonor Thee, nor let mine enemy triumph. I am thine own. Oh, save me, for I sink in the mire! This has been a heavy week; but I do not forget Thy mercy of the five pounds. Thou hearest my heavy groaning. I want again to be filled with Christ; and this sore pecuniary pressure seems to hold me down. O Lord, my Lord, Thou must help. I am sure I cannot exist thus. Thou wilt not look on indifferently. "Lord, I believe; help Thou mine unbelief."

May 1st, Monday Night — Mr. D— expounded this evening 2 Samuel 23:1-5, and preached from Psalm 89:34. My soul has, indeed, had a rich, large blessing under his preaching. I have fed and feasted on royal dainties. Bless, O my soul, the living Lord. He spoke of the 39th and the following verses—His covenant, His hedges, His stronghold, His glory, &c., as being not the Lord's covenant, but David's, so ours also; the covenant we cleave so fast to, that we should be something, do something, improve something; but the Lord breaks it all up, and plunges us in the ditch, so that our own clothes abhor us; and He says, "my covenant will I not break, nor alter the thing that has gone out of my lips." Mr. D— said, it is good to remind the Lord of what He has said; not that He forgets, but He loves us to plead it with Him. "Put me in remembrance; let us plead together." He has "cast our sins behind His back," and says, "He will remember them no more"; so, if the devil likes to remember them, he may go behind, and feed upon them. We love to sit down before the Lord, and feast with Him. My soul was full to overflowing. He did speak so gloriously of our precious Jesus, and of our privileges in Him. The word came into my soul in the power of the Holy Ghost, and I can say, "How beautiful upon the mountains are the feet of him that bringeth good tidings, that publisheth peace." Surely, I am too happy, and shall either have some great trouble, or I shall soon be taken home. The feeling of my soul has been to-day—

> "To Thy glory take me in,
> For there I long to be."

The overflowings of heavenly joy and glory unfit one for earth, except for Christ's sake, that He may be glorified in us.

May 24th — I rather expect to go to the Refuge to-morrow. Oh, that I might be a guide-post, pointing to Christ, and saying, "Refuge, refuge!"

May 25th, Friday — I have been wonderfully helped at the Refuge. The Word flowed freely and very solemnly, showing the only refuge for guilty sinners; the awful consequences of sin to those out of Christ; and the dreadful "for ever" of fiery wrath which awaits them dying thus. O Lord, acknowledge Thine own word. I go, because Thou didst send me. Oh, I beseech Thee for souls, as my hire; not in way of payment, but of free grace bestowment. I believe the feeblest worm in Thy family will not go on that errand in vain. I was mourning last week, that I do not know that one soul was ever awakened from a death in sin, by a message through me. But the Lord has His chosen instruments for all His work; and afresh, this night, I cast my whole unworthy self into His service, as He deigns to use me.

May 27th, Sacrament Sabbath — A day of jubilee. Enjoying rest and peace in Jesus. I tremble; every day thinking that some terrible trial will follow this holy baptism of love and joy.

July 23rd — For some weeks I have been much straitened in spirit. No felt access in prayer; often much wandering. No power in reading or hearing; and many jealousies, because of the seeming stillness of my Beloved. He has kindly given me needful supply for special seasons, with others; but then afterwards no spending money: I mean, no sweet indulgences in that intimate intercourse I am wont to enjoy. Oh, it has been trying work.

July 30th, Sacrament Sabbath — Still in much debility, and my flesh wasting. The Lord renew the "inner man." I have not had enjoyment in public ordinances to-day. Instead of feasting, faith was constrained to be embracing Christ as my victory, in felt conflict; and that exercise shall not be in vain. I long for renewal in the mystery of Christ; and feel at times that anything and everything must go, that I may be absorbed in Christ. Love in my soul says, "Let Him kiss me with the kisses of His mouth; for His love is better than wine." Faith in my soul says, let Him do with me as He sees best, so that He may be glorified.

August 27th, Sabbath — I did not hear with any power this morning; but much refreshed at the Lord's Supper, I trust from faith in a precious Savior. I took Him for my all for this month. Something whispered, "You only do it in the hope of gain." Still my soul would not be hindered, but, pressing forward, I gave all my things to Him to manage, desiring not to touch them, but press after Himself. O Thou all-lovely source of my delights, Thou overfillest and over-matchest this poor soul of mine. And now, my Beloved, let me ask Thee for souls at the Refuge. I look at those who have begun to weep. Oh, may I prove them to be Thine, and others too. Let there be joy in heaven and joy on earth over repenting sinners. Precious Lord, my love, my life, my Christ, deny me not. Oh, use me in Thy Church, unworthy to keep the door, or wash the feet of Thy saints. But, in Thine own dear bosom, perfume me with Thine own fragrance; then cast me among Thy loved ones, to be to them of Thee a pleasant savor.

September 17th, Sabbath — On Friday went to the Refuge. The matron told me that of the inmates, one whom she had thought most under soul concern, was not so much so this week. She has wished me to speak to each of the three alone. I so fear to touch the Lord's work with a fleshly finger; and this has kept me back at present. I feel considerable anxiety, and am looking to the Lord. O Lord, I beseech Thee for souls in that place. At our evening meeting, I had rich experience of the love of God shed abroad in my heart by the Holy Ghost.

September 19th — I have for some days been attending the death-bed of a poor blind pilgrim, to whom I generally read on a Saturday; in doing which we both have had sweet refreshment. A week ago, she said, "I would not be without my Saturday mornings for all the world." She is dying, and unable to speak; while she could do so, she said she had no fear, and was sure the Lord would receive her to Himself. Such scenes are profitable.

September 20th — The aged pilgrim departed at three o'clock this morning.

September 21st — One Friday I went to the Refuge, and spoke separately to one girl, whose heart we hope the Lord has touched. Oh, that it may prove a work of grace indeed! I was much blessed at our evening meeting. I saw transcendent glories in the incarnation of our blessed Lord.

October 6th, Friday — Went to the Refuge trembling; but Jesus was very precious, and many tears were shed. Oh, that impressions may not pass away like early dew. Dear

Lord, quicken those souls into spiritual life. This word sweetly applied to-day, "Thy maker is thy husband; the Lord of hosts is his name."

October 24th — A case is pending. Friends think this house is too much for me, and that I ought to lessen my expenses. I am willing, but want the word of the Lord; feeling a belief that He holds me here, and has promised to bless in temporal things. Well, the rent is now due for half a year. I have not enough in hand. To sense, this seems against me; but mine eyes are "up unto the Lord." And I beseech Thee, Lord, who hast been my Helper, either to supply my present real need, and send sufficiency for what is now pressing, or to let Thy withholding it be a sure token that I am wrong, and thus show me what is the right way. Though driven very near to the time, I believe the answer will come, and will not be too late. I have fears of presuming; but, dearest Lord, to whom can I go? Thy mind I want, even more than the supply I so much need. I must trust Thee, and thus test Thee. Oh, pardon me, I pray. I wait, I hope, I believe, and still tremble. No creature knows my strait or present conflict. Creature friends would help, but that will not do. My Husband, my Banker, alone, I must draw upon; and from Him learn whether I overdraw. It is a crisis! Oh, for more faith, to get it put right clearly into the hands of my dear Lord. If the Lord pay my rent without my borrowing, it is a token for me to stay here.

> ["No creature knows my strait or present conflict." So writes this beloved one, and it is a most remarkable feature in her character, proving in itself the simplicity and the ardor of her faith, that those who were most intimate with her, and loved her for both her natural and spiritual worth, had not the very slightest conception of her straitened circumstances. She had many who deeply valued her

friendship, and who would have felt it the richest privilege to have ministered to her necessities; but her extreme modesty as to anything that related to herself, led her most scrupulously to avoid the subject. Now that she is gone, and these facts have become known to those whose privilege it has been to read these sacred records, there has been much weeping of heart, that they had not been permitted to know somewhat of the unbosoming of her sorrows, and to aid her in regard to them. But most evident it is, that Jesus, her best Beloved, had reserved this unbosoming to, and for Himself, in order that He, personally and sovereignly, might Himself bestow the succor of which she thus stood in need.]

October 25th — An evening all alone, producing much calmness. The word to-day has been, "Believest thou that I am able to do this?" Yes, Lord, indeed I do. Carnal reason and unbelief assail me sorely at times, as to whether Thou wilt, and whether I am not presumptuous in expecting it. But this word comes ever and anon, "Fear not, O land; the Lord will do great things." Something very much amiss in this poor tabernacle this last week or more. Prepare me for life or death; and do Thou, dear Lord, be honored in both. "Hallelujah to him that sitteth upon the throne, and to the Lamb"; and so shall we sing, without tiring, for ever and ever. Amen.

October 29th, Sacrament-day — I have feasted at the King's table with delight. Heavily pressed in the night, and before service this morning; because the very crisis concerning my rent is come, and no supply to meet it. Mine eyes and my cries are up unto the Lord. Satan, the flesh, and unbelief thrust sore. Faith pleads hard, and the Lord will arise, I believe, though I can see nothing; and I tremble while I write it. At the Lord's supper I had the substance of the feast, my very Christ; who is more precious than words can tell. His obedience delights me; His blood over-matches my heart; His love overwhelms my soul; but Himself is the glory of it all: and I feel that His Person is mine. Oh, bliss inexpressible! Of Christ, Jehovah, Immanuel, I can sing with a good conscience and warm heart, "My beloved is mine, and I am his"—unworthy I; but so it is, Heaven's own signet has made it sure upon my heart, and that pledge of eternal love I shall wear for ever. Precious, over-matching, all-lovely Jesus! Thou hast made me full with the blessing of the Lord; and I would bless, and adore, and praise the great Three-One in Thee. Happy Sabbath-day! Sweet antepast of everlasting bliss. At the table of my glorious Well-Beloved, I did pledge myself to Him afresh, in the bread and in the cup, to be His, in weal or woe, in His giving or withholding, in sickness or health, in life or death. I did give my whole self to Him in love, for what He wills, only claiming that He will guide me aright about this house, rent, expenses, and everything. But, precious Lord, give me a true token. My soul is so happy in the Lord, I think some great trial must be coming. He may test my pledge as I little expect; but, blessed Jesus, I must be all Thine own.

> "Oh, happy day, that fixed my choice
> On Thee, my Savior and my God!"

Great mercies during the past month; Jesus more solidly sought after. In a great strait now, but I believe I shall have to record a deliverance; and yet it seems almost like presumption to say so.* Lord, I look to Thee to do great things. "Bless the Lord, O my soul," for the favors of this day, but most for my precious Jesus Himself, who will be the same, and the same to me, when my

---

* Indorsed with these words: "Sacrament-day, November — It is now proved faith, not presumption."

feelings are at low-water mark. Again, Hallelujah, and praise from the heart, to my covenant God. Thy kingdom come, O Thou Most High. "Take to Thyself Thy great power, and reign" manifestly, and amongst Thy people gloriously. We long for Thy kingdom, where all is holiness and love. This is an uncongenial clime. Dear Lord, "Thy kingdom come." Come, Jesus, blessed Lord Jesus, quickly come! Thy bride, in love, says, "Come"!

October 31st, Tuesday — No supply yet. A sharp struggle between flesh and faith. To sense, it is vain and presumptuous to trust now; but faith struggles through all, and, taking hold of the promise, says, "Thou saidst, I will do thee good." Lord, I renew my trust; oh, increase my faith!

November 2nd, Thursday — While at my lonely breakfast, I read about David and Goliath; and how did it fire my soul to hear the stripling defy the giant, who had defied Israel and reviled Israel's God. I saw quite plainly, that I was taking side with the enemies of my God, when giving way to distrust. My faith arose, my soul triumphed, and I did in spirit praise God for the deliverance He would bring, though yet unseen. I did believe I should yet pay my rent with joy. Oh, yes, the Lord will appear! Has He said, and will He not do it? He will, He will. And, moreover, after reading the chapter, it seemed to me, that as David went forth with such unlikely things as five smooth stones, so I, in faith, went forth to pay my rent, not really in the act, but solidly in confidence, while, as yet, I had not the means to do it.*

November 4th — Yesterday, while looking at the Word, in much heaviness, it met my eye that one of the kings of

---

* Indorsed, "*November 16th* — I have now paid my rent, with joy indeed. Ebenezer!"

Judah "proclaimed a fast." The words, "proclaimed a fast," struck me at once as if for me; and I wish to taste nothing till tea-time to-morrow, in token of humiliation before the Lord in my present circumstances, and for close waiting upon Him for manifest guidance, which I so much feel to need. As I so stand in the court of the King's house, may I find favor in His eyes, and be granted an audience, with an answer also to my urgent request. My case is pressing but not hopeless. *Evening, 10 o'clock* — Some entrance with my petition to-night. My heart just melted and encouraged, in remembering how many of the Lord's servants are spoken of in His Word, as fasting and praying when in great trouble and perplexity; and I do not call to mind one who had not an answer. Oh, it will be a wonderful deliverance, indeed, if the Lord condescends to arise for my help now, makes a plain path for my feet. No creature knows my exercise; I desire to wait on the Lord alone. Thanks and praise for some liberty already, in spreading out my case.

November 5th, Sabbath morning — When going to bed last night, I remembered that David did fast and pray about his child, and did not obtain his request. But, however, there are so many on record who did succeed, that I must wait on, in hope of an answer of peace. My requests are, that the Lord will pay my rent and expenses; that He will please thus to grant me a sure token of the way He would have me take; that He will appear for —; that He will grant me anointings of the Spirit, renewing me for His service, especially in the Refuge. *Afternoon, 4 o'clock* — I believe the Lord will answer. It is believing, not seeing; though faith in the Lord is no delusion. I cannot let Thee go without the blessing, though Thou shouldst seem to hold back or deny. I desire a clear token of the Lord's mind, whether I stay in this house, giving myself up to do so, if His will; or to go into ever such a little one, if He will open the way; to let lodgings if it please Him, or to live alone, if He wills it, and will provide; anything, so that the will of the Lord be done, and I kept from distraction about money. Great things I do not want, but desire greatly to live within my means. Much pleading, also, for my friends. At times, heaviness of heart, with weeping, and my sorrows turned upon me. But, for the most part, both last night and this morning, great encouragement in pleading for Christ's sake, and a real believing in so doing that the answer will come, though to sense very unlikely. Upon the whole, a most profitable exercise, and very close dealing with God. My flesh always does dread and dislike fasting, but I find it so good, I wonder I do not practice it more; and, really, to-day I have been kept, in a great measure, from my usual bodily sinkings, although on my knees five hours or more, having since twelve last night, never moistened my lips until half-past four. Oh, for more self-denial. I hate my self-love. I find how the Lord can keep the soul in vigor without food, through the power of Christ, and remember how He fasted forty days and forty nights for me, and was in sore temptations, too. But how stinted am I in all spiritual service. How far short of Him do I come, and how I must turn away from exercise, and look afresh to Jesus, my only perfection! I was kept so alive in prayer last night, that I afterwards felt condemned, that I did not sit up all night, or, at least, till the weariness came; but flesh is always ready to say, "it is enough." Last Sabbath was a high day in feasting, this a blessed day in fasting—both in nearness to my covenant God. I wait His answer, in answer to my requests. "Praise the Lord, O my soul"!

> [It is next to impossible to read the foregoing without deep, deep humiliation and self-abasement! To think of one with so weak a frame, and yet upon her "knees for five hours or more." This is in very

deed *faith* triumphing over *flesh!* What cannot a precious Christ effect *in*, as well as *for*, His people?]

November 6th, Monday — Very weak and feeble to-day; also thrust at by the enemy. O Lord, establish my goings in Thy paths; and my heart in Thy faith and fear. Make me aware of the enemy, and not so easily moved. Give me patience to wait all Thy time, and to be satisfied with all Thy will. Thou hearest every sigh, and seest every fear; "All my desire is before thee, and my groaning is not hid from thee." Often I believe firmly, that deliverance will come; then, again, it looks like fancy and delusion; but, in all, to Thee do I cry, "O thou that dwellest in the heavens"!

November 7th, Tuesday — A very dark cloud. My dear sister has been to London; she has just returned, and brings me very bad tidings about the house, and no money. O my Lord, what will be the end of these wonders? My heart is truly overwhelmed, but longs to trust, and not dishonor, my dear Lord, who is, I am sure, doing all things well, though roughly. "Lord, help me!" Oh, that I did but know what way to take. Surely I have been deceived, and what I thought to be faith was but fancy; and what I thought a word from the Lord was only the imagining of my flesh. Dear Lord, discern for me, for I am distressed and confused. *Night* — Have been to the house of God this evening. A most suitable hymn was sung; also, this word mentioned, which was sweet to my soul: Isaiah 50:10. My heart kept crying unto the Lord, and I felt that I would and must plead on, even if the Lord would not speak to me, and only seemed to deny me. Once, just before service, I thought things never looked so discouraging; but still I found that praying breath was not extinct, for my heart would talk to the Lord. Since then I have received intimation of a handsome present of coals. This will not pay my rent, but it is a welcome hint that the Lord does remember me. Ebenezer, in a dark place!

November 8th, Wednesday — My soul much revived while busy this morning. I was looking at my ease, and crying to the Lord, when the thought came that I must not be cast down, because all likely means dry up, and my set time is past. This is just like the Israelites, when they had no water. They were weary and thirsty, and there seemed to be no way of supply; but the Lord could smite a rock, and made the welcome streams flow out plentifully. I thought, there seems no way for my supply; but the Lord can smite a rock for me. It is not for me to find ways and means for His wonders, but to trust Him wholly, though seeing nothing but discouragement; and I really felt I could do so, and was refreshed. Something says, "All this is fleshly fancy, not faith." The event will decide.

November 9th, Thursday — A day of bitterness and of conflict. The Lord grant me some real benefit from this fiery trial. I have opened two or three times at Daniel 10:12.

November 10th, Friday — I have been to the Refuge, and not in vain, I trust. I was led to speak very solemnly to those who had once felt convictions, and seemed in real earnest about their souls. No. 7 was overwhelmed, and her eyes were as a flood of tears. Poor girl, my heart yearns over her. I remember, some time ago, how she seemed to cry for mercy, while I was in prayer. The Lord renew power, and seal her heart for His own.

November 11th, Saturday Night — May the Lord be pleased to pardon me, in that I desire to wait before Him in prayer with fasting, in my poor little way, until teatime tomorrow; and this because my case is urgent, and the answer yet delayed. Dear Lord, I beseech Thee, take not Thy Holy Spirit from me, but enable me further to plead with Thee. Oh, wherefore the delay? Why tarriest Thou, O my God? Do arise, that my enemies may be scattered. Do make me know Thy mind concerning me; reveal Thy will, and take mine away. I fear to offend Thee by being importunate, and repeating this exercise. Oh, do not be angry. I am much distracted by uncertainty, as to whether I am in the right way in outward things. O Lord, decide in my heart, and give the token in my conscience, I beseech Thee. "Lord, help me"!

November 12th, Sabbath Morning — This is a peculiar time of trial. I have had some fears, lest I should offend the Lord by fasting before Him again, as it seems too importunate. But oh, what can I do? My case is pressing, and the vision tarries. Appearances grow darker; "Mine eyes fail with looking upward: O Lord, I am oppressed; undertake for me," and pardon this renewal of humiliation and pleading before Thee. I tremble lest I should fall into weariness of the flesh, and so lose my aim. *Afternoon, 4 o'clock* — "Bless the Lord, O my soul"! I wonder at the Lord's great mercies to unworthy me, in that my body has been kept vigorous nearly all the day, though without rest, till one this morning, and not feeling nearly so well as last week. I trust the wrestler will be the prevailer, through divine power. *Evening* — I must again testify that the exercise of fasting, with supplication, is most truly profitable to the soul; and I wonder it is so cast out of the Church in the present day. It is good to spend the time set apart for fasting in close dealing with God, in prayer, confession, praise, reading the Scriptures, and, as much as possible, on the knees. If there is an interval of public worship, I find it helpful. From bodily weakness I trembled this day, but it ends with a Hallelujah! The spirit has gained more than the body has suffered. My petitions have been the same as last Sabbath. The King permitted me to press my suit both last night and this morning (for I like to begin the exercise the night before), and He did not seem offended. It was suggested this morning that I was like Saul, whom the Lord would answer no more. This was bitter; but I felt, in a little while, that I was not so, for I have the love of God revealed in my soul. And I firmly believe that the Lord is lovingly withholding, to try faith, but not to deny. I think, upon the whole, I have not felt so much confidence in expecting an answer from the Lord; but I desire to have the eye quite single, and to trust, praising Him, and seeking to lay on the top of all my petitions, "Thy will be done." This exercise has closed with seeking, that after these sowing days, I might have reaping ones, and a glorious "harvest home," with thank-offerings to the Lord. I have sown in tears. May this memorandum be stirring, if ever I got too slothful and fleshly for fasting. It is not in vain. May Ezra 8:23, be my experience.

November 14th, Tuesday Morning — Wonderful! The giving is more wonderful than the withholding. My greatest joy is, that it was faith, and not fancy, that was working in my heart. I have been walking in converse with God, and not in my own imaginings. The sweet words and breathing of encouragement which I heard in my soul, were from Himself! This is even more to me than the deliverance, though that is almost the greatest I ever had. I have just received the half of a ten-pound note from Mr. F—, for rent of the London house. "Bless the Lord, O my soul"! I can hardly believe it.

November 16th — Yesterday I felt very ill. I think the sore conflict, and then the great joy, were too much for this feeble body. This morning I received the other half of the note. I have, indeed, paid my rent with joy, in accordance with the faith given me on the second of this month. I have, also, thank-offerings to lay upon the Lord's altar, which I do with gladness. Truly, the Lord's dealings are marvellous in my eyes; and, although the exercise has been deep and dark, I believe it was very profitable.

November 17th — Having obtained my temporal token and mercy; the question now is—How can I return according to the benefits done unto me?—how can I spend and be spent for the Lord? And the plea is for the fresh spiritual anointing which I have sought.

November 18th, Saturday Night — Here ends this blessed, wonderful week, to the Lord's praise, who has performed all things for me. I have very peculiar feelings, as though I were in the middle, and not at the end, of this dispensation. And this word keeps coming, "What is thy petition? and it shall be granted thee; and what is thy request? [further] it shall be performed." Dear Lord, I fear to presume upon Thy mercy in asking for the flesh. Thou knowest there is a stone for my dear mother's grave, and the five pounds I borrowed in my straits last year. Thou hast enabled me to pay the interest with joy; and the sum itself Thou canst easily give. These things I submit to Thee; if of faith, answer; if of the flesh, pardon. "Is anything too hard for the Lord?" "Thou shalt see greater things than these." Is this faith, or fancy, which works within my breast? Lord, Thou knowest.

November 19th, Sunday Morning — "Behold the handmaid of the Lord; be it unto me according to thy word." *Afternoon* — Psalm 103:2. I thank and praise Thee, O my God, that I can now go about this dear house, and sit down in it without feeling that I am intruding, which I have constantly feared, for it seemed too good for me. Two long years have I watched and waited, with prayers and tears, to have my way made plain. I dared not stir without a token from the Lord: yet I stood still with the greatest trembling, lest I should be wrong; and had the most cruel taunts from the enemy, because I did not make some effort to improve my case, he showing me that everybody could do better than I. But rather would I die from the bitter anguish these suggestions cause me, than move an inch contrary to the Lord's will, or take a step in the flesh. Now, I find it is good to be thus obstinate in waiting only on the Lord. Now I have got my token, and can hardly believe, for joy. "Blessed be the Lord, who daily loadeth me with benefits." And yet, ever and anon, it rings in my heart, "Thou shalt see greater things than these." Dear Lord, support me, for I tremble under the weight of these words, and Thy great mercy. I know Thou canst easily double the benefits, and perfect the miracle, though it seemed already most complete in my eyes, till this new feeling came. The other ten pounds are not so much to Thee as ten farthings are to me. And I remember that I did, in my pleading, mention before Thee, O my God, that twenty pounds would clear all, cover my dear mother's grave, and leave me some for present daily expenses. And I remember, after I got this ten pounds, Thou didst gently say in my soul, "Didst thou not mention twenty?" and I said, "Yea, Lord"; and then, again and again, it sounded softly within, "Didst not thou say twenty?" and I just answered, "Yes, Lord." And now, while I am writing, a belief will come that Thou wilt make it twenty, that I may be out of debt, though I cannot see the way. Pardon me, blessed Jesus! Thou art so very kind, I tremble to presume; and my tears flow, yet I cannot help it. It seems so great a favor for such an insignificant worm as I to expect; but I expect it upon the ground of Thy largeness, love, and liberality, which can easily come over my insignificance. What can all this mean? Is the Lord again drawing me out in faith? Is it the shadow of another ten pounds from Him, to stop all mouths that have questioned whether I was right? Pardon, pardon, gracious Lord. Establish Thine own word, and take mine out of my mouth, and heart too. My flesh fears to go into such another conflict directly; it seems as if this frail body must sink under it; but Thou canst sustain, and Thou wilt, if Thou callest me to it. Hallelujah! Oh, praise the Lord my God. Yes; and I praise Thee for the other ten pounds; for I believe it will come, and I cannot help it, though trembling all the while.

November 20th, Monday — In very deed, I am not worthy of the least of all the mercies of the Lord our God. And yet hath He done me this great favor, to show me He is with me in the way that I go, and that I am where and as He pleases. I wish to praise Him all this day; I cannot praise Him half enough.

November 21st, Tuesday — Arose this morning under much heaviness of spirit, or rather dulness; and was greatly afraid, lest divine breathings should be withholden; but I cried unto the Lord for new quickenings; for, in very truth, no outward relief will satisfy the soul. I want close walking with my God in Christ. *Night* — I have been favored, I trust, with much of the Spirit to-day. As it is now just a week since my mercy, I have sought that I may keep another seven days with gladness.

November 26th, Sacrament-day—Noon — My heart seems to be urgently taking hold of my dear Lord Jesus, saying, "I cannot let Thee go"; and, like the disciples at Emmaus, would constrain Him to abide with me. Having Thy leave and approval, O Beloved, to stay in this house of my dear parents, and of my childhood, I now beseech Thee to dwell with me in increased power. I tremble much, lest being a little more at ease, I should slip, and not walk closely with Thee. I ask importunately for more grace, and to know how to glorify Thee; and that Thou wilt outwardly "perfect that which concerneth me," and fulfill "the word upon which thou hast caused me to hope." Oh, what cause have I for thankfulness! "What can I render to the Lord for all His benefits?" *Evening* — I have partaken of the Lord's supper, not with so much delight as last time; but earnestly desiring to discern the Lord's body, with thanksgiving for the past. This has been a month long to be remembered. The trials so great; the petitions so pressing; the answers so striking. Yea, it has included an answer to the anxious cries of two long years of suspense. "Bless the Lord, O my soul!" I am so surprised, because this house looks too large for me. I have been looking for pulling down and breaking up. Lord, sanctify this mercy, I beseech Thee; and prepare me for the greater things of which Thou hast spoken. I look at every room, and everything in this house, with wonder. Do teach me how to use them all for Thee. I heartily desire more grace for the Refuge, and souls to be born there. I have, dear Lord, these two years sought Thee about this house. Thou hast given many sweet hints and encouragements; but never a positive token, until this crisis about my rent, when it was put into my heart to ask that Thou wouldst pay my rent without borrowing; and, if Thou didst not, it should be an assurance to me that I must make some change. But Thou hast bountifully overpaid the demand. So now, the case is decided in the highest court, and there must be no more appeal about it, but a going on in faith.

December 2nd — I was graciously helped yesterday at the Refuge. Three of the girls wept much, and another, who has been less hopeful, has shed some tears. I do really believe I shall meet some of them in glory. O my Lord, come in great power, and work very manifestly. Enlarge unworthy me in Thy precious gospel. I do not yet half speak its freeness and fullness. Do Thou Thyself give the certain, effectual sound, and make it reach their hearts.

December 6th — Nehemiah 4:9. This I desire to do at this time. O glorious Holy One of Israel! Thou must conquer; Thou must reign alone in me. What is of Thee, Thou must confirm and accomplish; what is not, Thou must break to pieces. Love holds Thee fast by Thine own sweet power working within.

December 15th, Friday — My heart and my mouth blessedly open at the Refuge. The Lord bless and save. My soul is happy in Jesus this night, and so filled with praise, that no words seem full enough. Much flowing of love toward my Beloved—

> "If such the sweetness of the stream,
> What must the fountain be."

December 24th, Sabbath — A week full of mercies, and much up-bearing under outward pressure and great bodily weakness; with abounding joy also in the Lord, which has made me feel that I may soon sleep with my dearest mother in the dust. Oh that my lamp may burn clearly and brightly at the last, to the glory of Him who lighted it! Greatly blessed at the Refuge on Friday. The matron has complained of some who are careless in their work, and of others who are deceitful; so I have been led to search for, and read to them passages of Scripture under different heads, as idleness, lying lips, deceitful tongue, dishonesty, and many others; together with passages showing God's strict justice, and how He is closely observing all the actions of men, as in Job 34:11, 12, 21, 22. I desired, by the Word, to find out each of their prevailing faults, and to show their hatefulness in God's sight; with also the evil effects which must accrue to them as they pass through life: and then to encourage them by Scripture in seeking to strive against them. Afterwards, in case all were not found out, and perhaps some of them might be saying, I am not guilty of any of these, and feeling proud of their outward propriety, I turned them to Mark 10:18-21, showing they had one thing wanting, viz., to forsake all this, as nothing before God but filthy rags, and as vile sinners to follow Jesus only. I then told them I should take my stand with the worst and vilest; and both *with* them and *for* them at the mercy-seat. I do trust it was of the Lord, and that His word will not return void. Several wept; No. 13 sobbed aloud. The Lord break the heart!

December 25th, Christmas Day — "Unto us a child is born, unto us a son is given." Hosannah to the Prince of Peace! Welcome into our flesh, Thou glorious Prince of Life!

December 31st — Oh, what a year has the past been! What a cup full of mercies I have had; and the bitter part how salutary! My soul, praise thou the Lord! I desire fresh devotedness, in the Lord's own strength, to His service, if spared.

1849

January 1st — Affliction holds my body with a strong hand; but the silken cords of divine love hold my soul still firmer; and sweet indeed are those bands. I seem to lie in the embrace of love, so as to feel no bitterness in what the flesh suffers. It is perfect peace, a quiet calm pervading the inner man. What is pending I know not. If deeper afflictions or a speedy coming forth, may the Lord therein be glorified, in life and death. This is the center wish of the heart. My Father's will is love. Oh, for more submission to it, however strange it may seem to the flesh. Precious Jesus, "Abba, Father," tender Comforter, the holy, holy, holy Lord God of Israel, Thy consolations do delight my soul this night. Thou glorious Well-Beloved, how doubly lovely and precious art Thou, as Thou art more revealed. Happy, happy sinner saved, am I; to my God be all the glory!

January 3rd — A most wonderful Ebenezer, in that the Lord has this day sent, to my astonishment, five pounds of the ten which He promised. I muse and marvel, and am sure the other five will come; though I have still a sort of trembling while I write it. But this is in the flesh; the spirit is sealed in assurance on this matter. Very ill all day, but happy in the Lord. I am astonished at the perfect peace I enjoy. To the Lord be praise. Ebenezer!

January 12th, Friday — Glorious times in the "happy valley," where I now am. Only my dear sister in the Lord and myself at our meeting this evening; but such a blessing as set our souls on fire. I thought surely we were like the two lepers, who ventured out and found great spoil (2 Kings 7:3-8). Truly the glory of the Lord filled the room where we were. To Him alone be glory!

January 14th, Sabbath — I call my illness a "dinner of herbs" in the "happy valley." Oh, what cause I have to praise my blessed Lord, who is so good to me. At times I feel very ill; still I believe, on the whole, I am getting better. I have to-day felt more desire "to depart and be with Christ, which is far better." I seem not to like coming into the world again; but it shall be well. I have had blessed dissolving into the Lord's will, and trust it will be continued.

January 15th — I cannot speak half enough of the Lord's great goodness to unworthy me, I am so much blessed. It is indeed heaven begun below. No one knows how I have dreaded being quite ill, without a dear mother to soothe and cheer me. The Lord has unexpectedly brought me into it, and by His own sweet presence and love He has taken all the bitter away. Oh, that I could praise Him suitably, and live to His glory. It is quite plain that for every circumstance He is all-sufficient; and that according to our day shall be our strength and supply. I had very great power in prayer last night in bed; and, this morning, such blissful communion, that I lay weeping most joyful tears: praising, blessing, loving—wondering at such mercies to one so vile. "Bless the Lord, O my soul." Spiritual Ebenezer!

January 21st, Sabbath — I much desired to go up to the house of God to-day, but I am not able. All "my times are in thy hands." They cannot be in a better place. Flesh and strength are still wasting; but I am kept in peace, and surrounded with lovingkindness and tender mercies. Oh, that I could praise my gracious God! Oh, that my heart were as a ten-stringed instrument, and my tongue as a well-tuned harp, to sound His praise! Tune and touch, most gracious Comforter, that melody may be made unto the Lord, who is so good to me.

February 4th, Sabbath — I have had a week of amazing mercies. I am overwhelmed at the Lord's goodness to me. Sometimes I fear I am too happy; the sweet peace I enjoy is very great. It has quite seemed to me this week that Home is near, and that is pleasant. I love my dear, kind friends very much; but to behold Him who is dearer than all, and to be absorbed in untiring, unceasing worship; yea, to live and breathe in the pure element of holiness and love, will, indeed, be delightful. O Lord, I pray for such an issue out of this affliction as shall be most glorifying to Thee; and, if it please Thee, sanctify me for Thy service below or above.

February 6th, Tuesday — Last week I was led in spirit to give up all to the Lord afresh, and I found it sweet. Well, yesterday He put me to the test: for my most kind friends proposed that I should go away for change of air. I, who have not been from home for years, to go now in sickness, and that to a strange place. But I have vowed to the Lord, and dare not hold back; He must do as He will with His own; so I gave myself up to the leading of His Spirit in providence. May He choose the place where I am to rest for a season. Bodily weakness is fast increasing, I think. My cup abounds with mercies, and my heart this evening was overwhelmed in reading Luke 22:37-44. Oh, those drops of blood, more precious than mines of gold! My heart dissolved in love and wonder; surely heaven is indeed begun below; and what a miracle, to think that my joy should come through such a channel!

February 10th — Though in excessive weakness, I must record the lovingkindness of my covenant-keeping God. Yesterday He sent me the other five pounds, making the twenty, together with that mentioned November 19th; so now my dear mother's grave has a stone upon it; and I have also paid this night the five pounds I borrowed. Thus has the Lord fulfilled every word. He spoke to me on the subject, and proved to me that those peculiar emotions in my soul were of the Spirit, though I tremble at their greatness. He teaches, also, that secular things become spiritual, as we undertake them in the name of Jesus, and seek His glory by them. My mercies are so great, I can hardly believe in their reality. Who should trust so much, or sing so loud, as I? Surely these great wonders should encourage me in the severe trial just at hand, of leaving my home, and going among strangers, with an almost dying body. This is Saturday, and on Monday we depart, if the Lord permit; my kind friends are to take us. My Savior, into Thy loving arms I cast myself for life or death, at home or abroad. May Thy precious name be glorified, and Thy saints be edified; then all will be well. The memorandum of October 12th encourages my trembling heart, for when my dear friend was gone, my Beloved looked in upon me, and filled my soul with joy; so, perhaps, when I have really left all, at His bidding, He will come to me with new sweetness. "I will trust, and not be afraid." Hallelujah to the Lamb! If I never write again, I testify that my God is faithful, and worthy to be trusted in life or death. Praise Him, O my soul. Amen.

March 9th — Ockbrook — Chamber of peace. It is three full weeks this day since I left my home and friends, to come to a place I knew not, but which the Lord had provided for me. The journey of twelve or fourteen miles laid me very low, and for some time I was fed by the hands of others. My dear friend was most watchful and tender through my extremity; and all are unceasingly kind. The Lord repay them! There has been, indeed, but a step between me and death; but that step was so guarded that I could not take it; and here am I, still fettered in clay, and my soul still encaged in the wires of mortality; but through them beams the glory of the better country, and the loveliness of my Beloved. And though yet in my cage, I can sing His matchless love and worthy praise, for the dear Comforter has tuned my heart. How to recount the Lord's mercies I know not, they have been so beautifully unfolded in this affliction. My strength is somewhat returning. I sat up four hours yesterday—longer than I have done since I came here.

> ["Fettered in clay," "encaged in the wires of mortality; but through them beams the glory of the better country." Such expressions show at once the character of the writer's mind, and the heavenly mindedness that pervaded her Christ-aspiring soul. Emphatically it may be said of her, that she was "blessed with all spiritual blessings in heavenly places in Christ Jesus."]

March 18th, Sabbath — Still suffering from great bodily weakness; but the consolation and glory far exceed the pain; such visits as I have had to Gethsemane, such meltings at Calvary, and such beamings of the glories of a risen Redeemer! Being much alone to-day, I feel drawn out to take hold of the Lord afresh, in order to the further development of this beautiful affliction, that His glory may be manifested, and His dear saints be by any means refreshed. To be willing to come back to the wilderness again costs a struggle. It seems so like leaving this celestial valley, with the glory sometimes full in view, to climb a dark, black hill; but yet I really think the Lord has breathed into my soul sweetly, several times, Isaiah

55:12, 13, on this matter; and if it be so, it will be wonderful indeed. My heart is ready to say, "I will trust, and not be afraid."

> [Reader, do observe the sweets of either mental care or bodily affliction, when the Lord condescendingly and sovereignly moistens it and mellows it by His sweet presence and blessed power! Oh, how highly favored was the privileged Ruth in these respects. How did the Lord make Himself known to her in the depths of human sorrow, and how did He enrich her with Himself, and with durable riches and righteousness, whilst at the same time she was the creature of want and necessity, in regard to time-things.]

March 20th — The Lord's leadings and teachings are so wonderful, that I call this "Ockbrook School."

March 21st — Quite ill again to-day; unable to leave my bed. Still holding fast by that which holds me—"the name of the Lord." This morning I thought of Hezekiah—"He turned his face to the wall": so I turn away from all, to trust in the Lord alone; and feel like her of old who would not take a denial. But if the Lord seem (by allowing me to grow worse) to refuse me, in love I would press all my suit upon Him, feeling sure that He will, from the same love in His heart, return with a blessing. This word seemed sweet, "For my own name's sake I will do it."

March 22nd — Acts 3:16, was brought home with power to me this morning. And I saw, in verse 6, that it was in the name of Jesus the healing was done: so I have got the right end in taking hold of "the name of the Lord." But, like Daniel (chap. 1:12, 13), I desire to be proved awhile, waiting only on the Lord: "He that believeth shall not make haste."

March 25th, Sabbath — I am here in a strange place, and have not one true kindred spirit to commune with in rapturous heights of love divine; but I have heavenly company, and often feel,

> "The saints above, and saints below,
> But one communion make."

March 28th — I have had a blessed, soul-melting view of my precious Lord in His temptation in the wilderness. Every repulse He gave the prince of darkness was a triumph for me; and, as my faith is enabled to lay hold thereof, Satan can make no way. My heart and eyes have overflowed in the sweetness I have found; and Jesus is again more precious than words can tell. Blessed Comforter, lead me more into the deep, sweet mystery of Christ, my Lord. Eternal praises to the great Three-One!

April 1st, Palm Sunday — Since I have felt a little stronger in body, I have much desired to go up to the Lord's house before going out to breathe the fresh air. When I heard what day this was, I longed to go and bear my feeble branch before the Lord, in acknowledgment of His great mercies. There was only the Moravian Chapel; but there I went, in the name of the Lord. I was mercifully helped, but found myself much weaker than I expected; and, on my return, thought it impossible I could ever again engage in the activities of life.

April 15th — "And they sung, as it were, a new song before the throne." Oh, it is ever new! I seem often in spirit to join them; and, when so enabled, I always find a freshness in the theme. Oh, that precious blood, how words fail to express the immense value and efficacy of it! Praise Him, my saved soul!

April 29th, Sabbath — Some heavy tossings in mind. No savor in the preaching; but, this afternoon, sweet meditations upon our great High Priest entering the true Holy Place with His own blood, and of our having boldness to enter there by the same precious blood. The minister, this morning, quoted Hebrews 6:1, 2, about first principles; and, on turning to it when I got home, I read forward, and also found Hebrews 6:12, very animating; not viewing it as referring to departed saints, but to those who, in experience, have already crossed the Jordan, and are living joyfully in Christ, who is the good land, flowing with milk and honey; thus, through faith and patience, inheriting the promises; for the Lord does, as Job says, "Appoint us a set time, and remember us." Being thus brought in, I desire to follow those who have been walking the land, in the length and in the breadth of it (Gen. 13:17; Rev. 21:7). And here I would erect an altar, as Abraham did, in remembrance of all the mercies which I have received in this place, where I am a stranger. And now, my glorious Lord, I yield myself afresh to Thee, for new fillings of the Spirit, and for more communion with Thyself, Thy Father, and my Father. And oh, my God, I humbly say, for outward things, "Thy will be done." And now unto the glorious Three-One Jehovah, incomprehensible to sense, but blessedly revealed to faith, to the God of Abraham, Isaac, and Jacob, Israel's one Lord, be glory in the Church by Christ Jesus, both now and throughout all ages, world without end. Amen.

May 5th, Saturday — Again has the Lord, this morning, seemed to say in my soul, "Be thou faithful unto death, and I will give thee a crown of life"; not the death of the body, but the death of self, in all its willing and wishing; and this must be the death of the cross! The Head humbled Himself unto it, and the members must be conformed thereunto; and that experimentally, or they cannot come to resurrection glory, or wear the crown of resurrection life. The Lord has shown me, this morning, that He will not crown my flesh; therefore the sooner it is yielded to the death, the better.

May 13th —
"How rich, how sweet, how full, how free,
O Jesus, are Thy grace and Thee!"

I received most blessed bedewings of the Spirit, and opening thereby of the wondrous efficacy of the death of my precious Lord. This life of faith is all of Him, by Him, in Him, and for Him; and it shuts out the creature more than anything beside: it is most blessed, and nothing exceeds it but the life of glory.

May 20th — I cannot half speak of the fresh glories and beauties I have lately seen in my blessed Jesus, my all-lovely Immanuel! Oh, indeed, I know but a mere nothing. It is marvellous that Thy glorious, holy salvation, should enclose unworthy me; but so it is. The Lord has shut me in; yes, I am brought by Jehovah's own power into holiness, happiness, and everlasting bliss; and who shall pluck me thence? I have them in Himself: and He holds me fast—oh, so fast! Blessed security! Law, justice, holiness, all on my side; because I am one with Jesus, who has met them all with infinite satisfaction. I do love a salvation which can look at law and justice with an open face. No other will satisfy a Spirit-awakened conscience. And with such a great salvation am I saved. Happy I, with such a glorious Jesus; happy, happy, saved sinner!

> [Reader, in sweet accordance with the foregoing testimony, "a salvation which can look at law and justice with an open face," some poet has said, most blessedly—
>
> "Here's an amazing change indeed!
> Justice is now for me."
>
> A Spirit-quickened soul would not be saved at the expense of divine justice; the ground of his rejoicing

is that Jehovah can be "just, and yet the Justifier of him who believeth on Jesus." It is at Calvary, "Mercy and truth have met together, righteousness and peace have kissed each other." Reader, may the Lord mercifully lead thee into a personal knowledge and glorious faith's apprehension of these things, for they are most Christ-exalting and God-glorifying.]

May 31st — My dear — has just left me, after spending two days here. The water of life has flowed refreshingly from on high; and I surely hope she has not been in vain. It is marvellous that I should have such enjoyments: this quiet retreat, this most beautiful country air and scenery, everything I need, provided without cost to me, and the kindest attentions from dear friends! It is wonderful, for I never looked for anything like prosperity on earth till the Lord so strangely whispered to me in December last. I wait Thy will. I do enjoy Thy mercies, and Thy beautiful creation, now in the freshness of spring. But Thyself art the sweetness of all.

June 21st — Surely I must again record, with thankfulness, the Lord's great mercies to one of the unworthiest of His creatures. Health really seems returning. It has cost a painful struggle to be willing to live longer in Meshech, and to return thither from the gates of glory. But the last day or two I have felt the Lord's power in my soul, conquering all, and causing me thankfully—yea, joyfully, to receive returning health. I am daily giving myself and the future to the Lord; praying Him to manage all, and to be glorified therein. I feel most unfit for any usefulness: my hope is in the Lord alone. He has most kindly gratified one ardent wish, in opening a way for me to help a friend here to work for the poor. This has, indeed, been to me a sacred place—"the house of God and gate of heaven"—my soul being often filled to overflowing with the love and glories of Jesus. I felt a peculiar longing for the quickening of dead souls, and for the enlivening of living ones. Oh that the blessed gospel and so great salvation were more fully preached. "Lord, revive Thy work," and send forth more faithful laborers into Thy vineyard. How often does my heart turn to the Refuge at N—. May the Lord clothe the Word with power!

June 25th — Yesterday I was feeling deeply my ignorance, when the Lord seemed to say, "I shall never make thee wise, *I* will be thy wisdom; I am killing *thee*." I was inquiring why I am so often depressed, and have thus far got an answer: "When thine eye is single, thy whole body shall be full of light." Surely I would wait further at Wisdom's gate.

June 26th — From circumstances which have occurred today, I have been thinking how we each have a distinctiveness of character, and our heavenly Father has a different work for each: so that while seeing the excellence of others, and being humbled, let me see to it that my own little measure of ability be not unimproved. This thought has much relieved and encouraged me; and I do afresh, my Lord, consecrate my one talent to Thee, for increase and use to Thy glory.

July 23rd — I received part of my rent this morning, and, when going to take a tenth for the Lord, I felt an incitement to give it all; and was reminded of David, who would not drink the water brought to him at the risk of life, but poured it out before the Lord. Knowing what great straits I had been in before my illness, I waited a day or two to prove if it was from the Lord: the impression continued, and I dare not touch the money for my own use. I had some more to receive, and almost thought I might have *that*; but these words stopped me, "he kept back part of the price"; so I put all into my charity purse, asking pardon of the Lord for not doing it more heartily, and yet having some fear that I might come to want it. Oh, for a more clear understanding of the intimations of the Spirit! Today I most unexpectedly received five pounds from town, for rent. Surely this says I was right in giving the other. I am indeed astonished at the Lord's mercies. I am most unworthy of the least, but it is all for Jesus' sake. I trust Thee to guide me aright. Thou knowest my deep conflicts, but with thanksgiving I renew my trust, and yield myself afresh to Thee; from which Satan and the flesh have tried to hinder, urging that I only bring myself into fresh suffering and fiery trials. May the Lord pardon me for being beguiled by it for one moment; bring me to new and full surrender of heart—not courting affliction, yet not withholding myself from my Lord to escape it.

July 29th, Sacrament-day — I have not the outward privilege of the Lord's table, but much desire to remember His dying love. Trials have arisen; and Satan's power was terrible; but the Lord is above him, and He has graciously supported and delivered me. A family from town have been staying in this house for twelve weeks; they are quite worldly, and the gentleman delicate. I have had great wrestlings of spirit for them, but could not speak. Just before they left, it was strongly laid upon my mind to write to the lady, expressing my concern for their souls. After much heart-exercise, I wrote, and put it into her hand as she was leaving the house. Oh that the Lord may bless that or some other means. I can hardly expect so great a favor as to see the fruit; but "power belongeth unto God." I have now earnest desires for new closing with a precious Christ, as my all in all; that the shadowy things of time may less cumber me, however contrary to flesh, and to live Christ be my one concern. I also cry to Thee, my conquering Captain, against the power of Satan over me, either by depression, or anxious care, or in any other way he *has* worked or *may* work. I pray against him, and embrace Thee by faith as my power to resist him. I fear I have been ignorant of his devices, and sunk under what I ought to have stood against; but now I yield up all to Thee, and myself to follow afresh hard after Thee, and afresh to "count all things but loss" for Thy sake. Oh, my beloved, my all-lovely Savior, Thou art gain, and gain enough. Something whispers that trouble is near. I commit to Thee whatever is approaching: keep me in Thee abiding, and all shall be well.

August 8th — Again I am renewed in earnest pleadings, and taking hold of the Lord for a token, about my future home. My Father, to Thee I cry, in the name of Jesus. My precious Jesus, Thy company and communion—yea, fellowship with a Triune Jehovah, is what I seek; and for it give up as nought what mortals so pursue—riches, honor, appearance, fleshly indulgence. I ask, my Father, at Thy hands, for Thy glory, a home within the means Thou hast given, that I may minister to Thy saints, and that my soul may be free for fullness of Thyself. O Lord, hear. I have great hope that Thou wilt, though the enemy hath well-nigh smitten my life down to the ground with fear and terror.

August 12th — Much harassed lately about writing so much in my diary; but it is such a blessed help to me on the pilgrim-road, I cannot refrain. I seem to see with fresh light, that it is vain to expect to come to a certain state, when we shall act grace constantly and spontaneously. The desirable position is, to live in felt dependence and emptiness, seeking constant renewings of the Holy Ghost, to live by simple faith on Jesus: therefore, if I receive ever such large and fresh inflowings of grace today, I must not think *that* a stock for to-morrow; or think then to act by this day's power, or walk by this day's light. I have at times had a word of power brought home to my soul, which has been like light, and food, and strength, and all I could need; and by faith it has been used with wondrous profit, and I have felt now that I had only to go on using this glorious word, certain of success; and so I have done, until it has seemed dry and powerless, and my soul was defeated and disappointed. I think the Lord now shows me this was wrong, and that it is in constant renewings and fresh power that the work of the Lord must go on; this is living by faith, the other by sense; this is more emptying, humbling, and abasing; the other more independent and exalting. Another Ockbrook lesson. *Five o'clock* — I feel most thankful that the Lord has graciously kindled in my soul the desire again to follow hard after Him. I fear that the pressure of outward things upon my spirit since the loss of my dearest mother, has been a great hindrance to me. I have used my feet too much, my wings too little; I have lingered on earth, instead of forestalling heaven. Dear Lord, renew in the fervor of holiness and love, which will abound in me as I abide in Him. *Ten at night* —

> "Oh, glorious hour! oh, blest abode!
> I shall be near and like my God;
> And sense and sin no more control
> The glowing pleasures of my soul."

Even so, come, Lord Jesus!

August 16th — Psalm 27:4. More and more anxious to be delivered from worldly care. Oh, I must not be buried in the stuff of Egypt, and have the health of my soul eaten away by corroding cares for this world's gain. I have thought that, as I am waiting for a token of my future way, and know not whether it will come by the Word or by providence, I will, by the Lord's help, when I am alone, take my dear Bible, and on my knees before God, looking to Him, see whether He will give the token there. I began this morning, and opened strikingly upon 1 Chronicles 4:10, the prayer of Jabez, which is, to the letter, what I want; and the last clause is, "and God granted him that which he requested." I wondered with great admiration; my soul was melted and humbled: "Lord, do as thou hast said." I wait for Thy salvation with trembling confidence. Lord, guide plainly, and give me as much of Thyself as possible in this mortal body. My purpose is to wait on the Lord, in and with the Word, directly after breakfast each morning, till deliverance come. I think much, with encouragement, of Abraham's servant (Gen. 24:13-15). I do not want a creature-companion, as he did for Isaac, but I want to be as clearly guided about a home where I may enjoy my best Beloved. "Is anything too hard (or too large, or too small) for the Lord?" I trow not.

August 19th, Sabbath — I leave my temporal requests today, and sum all up in seeking Christ, whom I desire to seek more earnestly and exclusively. Renew me, O most Holy Comforter, that I may make diligent search for Christ in every thing, pleasing or painful, He being the very kernel of all. The Lord has been very gracious to me the past week; to His name be the glory.

August 24th — Most exceedingly blessed this morning in family prayer, wherein it came suddenly to my mind what instances we have of answers to prayer in the Word, and how God will even turn the course of nature at His people's cry. He bade the sun and the moon stand still a whole day, and the world was wondering what was the matter, while only a sinful man (but a redeemed man) was praying. At another time, at the voice of prayer, the Lord shut up the heavens from giving rain, three years and six months, and the whole land was parched with barrenness and thirst, because of His people's sin: and again He opened heaven, and gave abundance of rain, when His servant prayed for it. Peter, too, when bound fast with chains, between two soldiers, and secured with bolts and bars besides, could not be held, for "prayer was made without ceasing of the Church unto God for him." Jacob prayed, and wept, and prevailed; and the promise is, "I will make thee a new sharp threshing instrument, having teeth; and thou shalt thresh the mountains." Surely, this is the prayer of faith. Truly, the whole Bible seemed opened to me, as full of answers to prayer; and this did much encourage and fire my soul to pray—yea, to pray on. The Lord increase faith and prayer.

August 26th, Evening, Sacrament-day — It has pleased my gracious Lord again to weaken my body; but all is well, though in very deed it is like a dying life. The Lord has been near and precious in the affliction. A month of love and mercy has just closed. I have had the blessed benefit of more realization of the love of my Beloved: I have at times been absorbed in the dear element of love divine, which is the home of my soul. I have not to-day had the sensible communion which I sought; but my condescending Lord will not be waited on in vain. He has some reason for tarrying out of my sight, and will come again with His overmatching love, of which mine is but the effect. But, however, while He seems absent, I would engage in recording His praise. Praise Him, O my soul. And now afresh I give myself to Thee, my blessed Jesus, to look at Thee, and only Thee; all else is confusing. I must erect an Ebenezer to the honor of my gracious Lord, who has been above my foes, above my fears, and immeasurably above my deserts.

August 27th — I do not know anything about being at sea, literally; but am just taught in spiritual matters, when the wind blows hard against us, it is best to hold firm at anchor: since striving then to get forward is wasting strength in vain. I think I must always be thus engaged on Monday morning, which is generally stormy, and the wind contrary. My blessed Rock, keep me from getting one inch further from Thee.

September 8th — I have again to record lovingkindness and tender mercies. Still waiting upon the Lord in the morning about going to my little Bethel home. I think Genesis 35:3, and the last clause of Genesis 32:9, are words upon which I am caused to hope. Also one morning it was rather opened to me that I had been, like Hezekiah and Judah (2 Kings 19), standing a long siege of the enemy, and hearing the dreadful threatening, but still, by divine power, kept trusting in the Lord; and that, like them, I should be fully delivered from the straitness and scarceness. I was mercifully blessed last evening in a poor cottage, which I have weekly visited for some time. It is sweet to find some poor who love to hear of Jesus. Dearest Lord, use me where and how Thou wilt; but let me be a savor of Thee, and let souls be benefited.

September 13th — The occurrence of this morning seems remarkable. Some weeks ago I met with a poor girl in the fields reading her Bible. I spoke to her, and found she really seemed to be a lamb of Christ's flock, who had felt both sin and salvation. I have since seen her, but have never had much liberty in speaking to her. I have made inquiries, and find she has a mother of bad character, which makes one feel for her. This morning, to my great surprise, she came to beg from me, and though I could not relieve her, yet my mouth was opened to speak solemnly to her of her state as a sinner, and of the awful consequences if she died in sin. Words flowed freely indeed, and she wept abundantly. I prayed with her, wondering at the courage and power I felt. Oh that this sinner might be turned from darkness to light, it would indeed be worth coming back from the gates of glory. "Power belongeth unto God." Oh that she may be slain, and then the Holy Ghost breathe upon her, that she may live. A light springs up, showing me that my forte is not to dispute against false doctrine, but to warn poor sinners, and to seek to comfort and establish saints. This somewhat relieves my mind, which has been much harassed about the former.

September 16th, Sabbath — I expect this will be the last at Ockbrook, and on Tuesday I shall journey home. My precious Lord has afresh ravished my soul with His love. I humbly desire that my spared life may be for His glory, and my return to N— for His people's good; for which I must look to Him alone. He has graciously granted me some sweet communion with Mrs. B— this last few days. I do think Satan has striven hard to hinder it.

September 18th, Tuesday Morning — I am preparing to depart hence this evening. My heart this morning has said, "Who hath believed our report? and to whom hath the arm of the Lord been revealed?" But, though I see no signs, "the day will declare it." And now an Ebenezer in remembrance of all the spiritual and temporal mercies received in this place. To the Lord be glory in the highest.

September 22nd — What a death is put upon my return home, in the excessive bodily weakness I feel. Lord, what can it mean? "Thy will be done!"

September 23rd — When wondering, with much perplexity, I thought there was whispered, "Stand still, and see the salvation of God"; and this morning, "They that sow in tears shall reap in joy"; and, "Weeping may endure for a night, but joy cometh in the morning"; and this evening, "Cast thy burden upon the Lord, and He shall sustain thee." I have, in answer, cast it all upon Thee, my Lord. Oh, increase my faith; and make me willing to endure as well as to enjoy: and let me not live to dishonor Thee, or be a cumberer of the ground.

> "Once they were mourning here below,
>   And wet their couch with tears;
> They wrestled hard, as I do now,
>   With sins, and foes, and fears."

Yes, there are dear ones before the throne, who once in this very cottage groaned and prayed, as their poor child does now. But they had "victory through the blood of the Lamb"; and so shall I, though now sore buffeted in the place of dragons.

September 25th, Tuesday — A day set apart in Nottingham, by the suspension of business and observance of public worship, to acknowledge the Lord's hand in the cholera, which is devastating our country; and to call upon Him, as a God of mercy and judgment, praising Him for a plentiful harvest, and for sparing our town from the pestilence, and praying Him to stay it where it is raging. I feel it very solemn and blessed too. *Night* — I have attended the three services. It was an extra effort to this poor body; but I felt it so good to be there, and so precious to hear the breathings of the dear saints: their songs of praise did thrill through my soul, and indeed I am glad to be again among my own beloved people. May the Lord hear, and be gracious to the pleadings of His children for our guilty country! The cholera has been within four or five miles of Nottingham.

September 30th, Sacrament-day — I see He did not send to the poor widow some sacks of meal and a large quantity of oil; then her faith might have had a holiday. But

He just kept the little in the barrel, and the cruse from wasting, and so faith had exercise every time she had a renewal of need. Oh, I must, I must believe, and not want an independent stock.

October 1st, Monday — Oh, what depths and darkness I have gone through this day, as regards temporal and spiritual matters—feeling ill in body, and unable to bear such roughs, and the harrowing suggestion within; and bewildered, too, and beclouded, as if I could not tell right from wrong, and enjoying no sweet communion with my Beloved, and no power in prayer. I told Him I would pray, and spread out my case before Him, but could not; so I must kneel in silence, and He would know what it meant; and when I did pray, it was just like "the chattering of a crane or a swallow." Oh, I do know what that means, and felt I could only make a noise while mourning in my complaint. It has been a day of night. I felt, as I was reading Psalm 23:4, that I was passing through the "valley of the shadow of death," as regards the Lord's promises, without the sensible enjoyment of His presence. And then it was as though He said, "I am with thee; trust me in the dark." My very soul was bowed down with tears of anguish flowing, and I thought, "Thou shalt hear the voice of my weeping." And, in the middle of this day of night, I thought how silly I was to write what I did last night about faith and this house; it looked to me like nonsense, and I thought I would not write again for a long, long time, as only worse seemed to follow. But just now this word has melted my heart, "At midnight Paul and Silas sang praises, and the prisoners heard them." It is just like me, midnight enough, in stocks fast enough; but I too, in my poor way, will praise my God. I can only take the three last Psalms of David to express His worthy praise; and I find there that "all deeps" are called upon to praise the Lord; and why should not mine? They are deep enough and dark enough to sense; but praise Him they must, and I sing in the stocks to the praise of Jehovah. I praise Him, indeed, for His longsuffering and forbearance with me, whom Satan has so sorely provoked to murmur; and I praise Him more for His precious, most precious Son, my glorious Well-Beloved.

> "Jesus, the gift of gifts, appears,
> To show that God is love."

My soul, praise thou the Lord! Hallelujah! For, notwithstanding all seeming contrarieties, "the Lord God Omnipotent reigneth."

October 3rd — Very peculiarly has my Beloved been to me to-day the suffering Lord of glory. Oh, what blood was that, what rich, rich drops flowed for vile, unworthy me; I wonder, and adore! "He shall see of the travail of His soul, and shall be satisfied." And His spouse shall see somewhat of His soul-travail for her, and be satisfied with His love and favor. And that Thou, immaculate Lamb, shouldst be bruised and wounded for our sakes, is overwhelming indeed!

> "I long to see Thee as Thou art,
> With eyes made strong to bear the sight."

I long to fall at Thy dear feet, and, before all the glorious company, confess myself a trophy of redeeming love, a miracle of Thy saving grace and cleansing blood. I long to be with Thee; but Thou hast sent me back, to confess first on earth and before men, what Thou hast done for my soul. Thy will, not mine, be done. Speak Thou through me, and that to win souls.

October 14th — I find my blessed Lord is calling me to walk by faith—believing against appearances; and I am sure it is well. I love sensible delights; but through divine power, my soul is being taught to walk confidingly in the dark, trusting to my Beloved to keep me from going astray, though no guide-posts appear. My heart says to Him this evening, "Behold, [I] am in thine hand; as it seemeth good and right unto thee to do unto us, do" (Josh. 9:25). Luke 4:4: I remember that during great straits, many blessed words of God have come to me, and thus my faith has been greatly strengthened; but because deliverance did not come immediately, I have sunk lower than ever: and on that account I have almost shrunk from being so revived, lest disappointment should follow. But now I stand thankfully reproved, inasmuch as I was thinking that I could only live by the bread of deliverance, whereas I am to live also by every word of God which I have received with power.

November 5th — My case is very pressing; I must be importunate. My heart cries unto the Lord. Oh, it will be great grace if He does now rise for my help! Lord, help me, and be glorified in me; and let Thy dear saints have some benefit by me. Abraham's servant did not pray in vain; Hannah, when provoked sorely, did not pour out her soul before the Lord in vain; David, when harassed and hunted like a partridge upon the mountains, did not ask counsel at the mouth of his God in vain; the poor woman of Canaan did not press her suit in vain; and unworthiest Ruth will not sigh and cry in vain; she will be heard and answered, though she dare hardly believe it. Surely a cheerful hope beams in upon my heart. "My soul, wait thou only upon God; for my expectation is from Him." Dear Lord, all hearts are in Thy hand; the silver, and the gold, and the blessing are Thine. I must follow Thee, with importunate prayer, until Thou arise and help me.

November 8th — I received tidings from dear Mrs. F— of a trying nature, respecting the rent of the house in London, but the love of my crucified Lord sweetened it all; however, I was enabled most feelingly to bless the Lord for my temporal mercies, and still more for my cross-sweetening Savior. I cannot see the least token of deliverance; but

> "God is His own Interpreter,
> And He will make it plain."

My heart, in the midst of all adversity, adores, confides, and loves. "My soul waiteth for the Lord, more than they that watch for the morning."

November 9th — How sweet is the precious Bible to me this morning; and such a melted heart, that I think perhaps more trouble is at hand: the will of the Lord be done. Isaiah 25:9, very sweet; and also these words, "Thy God reigneth."

November 10th, Saturday Night — I have taken counsel again in my heart, to humble myself before the Lord tomorrow, with fasting. I felt some trembling in so doing, somewhat like Esther, who thought it was a venture to go into the royal presence with her petition; but my case, in some respects, grows very urgent; and, like her, I say, "If I perish, I perish." What I seek is like asking for a miracle; but that does not prevent my plea, for the Lord has wrought many, and He can again. Oh that I may have audience, with power to plead!

November 11th, Sabbath Morning — The Lord has never stood aloof in the day of my calamity, and, although I am not yet delivered, He has already given me cause to say, "It was good for me that I was afflicted." I humbly desire to seek heart-holiness, and life-holiness, through union to Jesus, and faith in Him; also close walking with God, and the fullest enjoyment of Christ and salvation—present salvation, that can be had in the body; also devotedness to the Lord's service. *Night* — I seem to have been praying through a dense cloud to-day, without the sensible power I desired; but was kept crying on, assured the Lord did hear, although He saw fit not to speak; and, by my want of felt power, I was driven to lay firmer hold of that dear name, in which alone we can prevail. I now feel it has been a profitable exercise: the issue is with the Lord. And now, my Lord, I wait, expecting Thou wilt answer: how I know not; but it is Thy great love which makes me bold to believe, and sink deeper into the depths of that love. I yet know nothing, comparatively, of that love which "passeth knowledge." Oh, to be filled with the fullness of God. Surely this my cross has become a budding cross; and I humbly hope it will be a fruitful cross, to the glory of Thy name.

November 15th — This day is set apart, by our sovereign and rulers, for public worship and thanksgiving; in that the Lord has been pleased graciously to subdue the fearful pestilence of cholera, which has cut off 13,000 in the metropolis, besides its ravages in other parts of our land. His people cried, and He has answered them: now we return to render Him the praise. The latter part of yesterday I was in much heaviness, and feared that my songs would be choked with sighs. But I cried to the Lord for a praising spirit, and in great mercy He has vouchsafed it. Bless, O my soul, thy faithful God. This has been a favored day; I should like two Sabbaths every week. My own mind, also, has been much relieved to-day, without the least change in outward things; but it has seemed to me like this word, "We walk by faith, and not by sight."

November 17th — Yesterday and to-day I have been suffering under the deepest depression, almost past endurance: "Surely an enemy hath done this." I sent this evening to ask my friend A—, whom I observed last night to be under a heavy trial, to come and unite in prayer, as

I thought we might present both our cases to the Lord; she did so, after which came these words to my mind—

> "And Satan trembles, when he sees
> The weakest saint upon his knees,"

and also Christian's weapon of "all prayer." Oh, what a solemn season I had in wrestling with the Angel of the covenant; beseeching Him for strength against our spiritual foe, and for enjoyment of the fullness of redemption, and that we might be filled with all the fullness of God. In doing this I so lost sight of my temporal case, that when I would, I could not remember one outward thing I wanted; so I finished without naming my temporal wants; it was truly a blessed season, and Christ all in all.

November 23rd — This evening I opened upon Job 7, and felt the truth of verse 20, "I am a burden to myself"; but then with what sweet power did it follow in my soul, "I am not a burden to Thee, my Lord"; for Thou dost lovingly bear with all. Oh, what condescension, what unutterable love! My soul wonders and adores!

November 25th, Sacrament-day — I was much blessed this morning, in hearing a sermon from Deuteronomy 32:4. It was a time of love and power. Surely the Lord has come into my heart, as His guest-chamber; but it is not I who entertain Him; He entertains me, and most blessedly too. Surely, He is fulfilling the word He gave me on Friday (Isa. 44:3). I have again taken the emblems of the broken body and shed blood of my precious Lord. It was a solemn season; I did surely eat and drink in remembrance of my Beloved, and gave myself to Him afresh for all His holy will. And, under a sense of His majesty, even in His humiliation, I was constrained to kneel before the crucified one, and to worship Him as my God and Savior. The last month has been peculiar. Many teachings and sweet inlets of love and communion, but no outward opening or apparent answer to my cry. Still, all is love. I desire to go forth only in Thy name, and for Thy glory.

November 28th — Yesterday I received a request to go to the House of Refuge, on Friday; and this morning my soul is humbled in reading Ephesians 3:8. How did the apostle seem to marvel at the great privilege of telling poor sinners of Jesus; and how am I melted at the thought, that unto me, "who am less than the least of all saints," should this grace be given, to taste of salvation, and then to tell fellow-sinners what a Savior I have found. I am astonished at the mercy, and weighed down under the sense of my insufficiency; but my insufficiency for all shall be of God alone.

December 2nd, Sabbath — On Friday I went to the Refuge. The dear Lord made good His promise, given me two days since. His grace was sufficient for me. I do earnestly long and cry that souls may be quickened into spiritual life. *9 o'clock* — I trust my desire has been granted. It has been a time of privilege, I think both in reviewing and renewing; and again I give myself up to live on, and for Christ alone. "There is a time to embrace, and a time to refrain from embracing," so the Scriptures declare; and surely this is my time for renewed faith-embracements of my Beloved, whom I have afresh turned to for all I need; and I trust it is by the power of the Holy Ghost. "My meditation of Him hath been sweet." Oh, what fullness of grace and glory is there in Him! Under divine anointings, I will be glad in Him. Ah! and seek for gladness in nothing else. This is the secret of peace. O God the Holy Ghost, renew in living Christ; I have *lived myself* too much. Ye happy hours of this favored Sabbath, adieu! Ye are fled, but ye have been to me a breathing of Sabbatic rest; and I hope my soul is fresh energized in the way of faith. Surely, no one is so much indebted to the Lord as unworthy I. Even now that He is keeping me shut up in outward things, He sweetly blesses me with the flowing of the "upper springs." These words have been sweet to me to-day, "He shall be to thee instead of silver." Mr. C— once said, Job 22:25, might be so read; and now I feel it verified in myself; and, as the next verse says, "For then shalt thou have thy delight in the Almighty, and shalt lift up thy face unto God." "Accepted in the Beloved," my soul blesses the Lord!

December 5th — I have received no money yet, but all is well. I feel, that when I was first put into the furnace, I fell down bound; but that now I am loosed, and my precious Beloved is sweetly with me, and I walk with Him unharmed amidst the flames. I praise and adore!

December 14th — I have been to the Refuge, to me a solemn, sacred place. I was favored to see — overwhelmed in tears, in repeating that verse—

> "I would, but can't, repent,
> Though I endeavor oft."

It seemed to be the very feeling of her soul, and I do trust she is a repenting sinner, though she feels her heart is so hard. I had hopes of her before my illness. The Lord be very gracious unto her at the voice of her cry; and when He hears it, may He answer. — says she has found pardon and peace since I saw them. May the work be real, and that which will stand the test of fire.

December 26th — Heard Mr. H—, from Psalm 39:7, 8, with power. I did earnestly cry, this morning, that the grace of the gospel might flow into my soul, as well as that the words of the gospel might sound in my ears; and I humbly trust it proved so under the sermon. The minister said, "The living soul waits for answers to prayer, for mercy, for salvation, for the presence of God, and the revelation of the Person of Christ. To have the husband's inheritance will not alone satisfy the bride: if she has affection, she must have personal communion with the bridegroom; so, all spiritual blessings will not satisfy the Church, without the Person of Christ. The soul also waits for particular deliverances in trials and perplexities, and sometimes has to wait long; and also waits and longs to be gathered home, to be with the Lord for ever and ever. For this she hopes. Hope is called the anchor, but there must be anchorage as well as an anchor. And so hope takes hold of the everlasting love of God; the 'everlasting covenant, ordered in all things and sure'; the Person and finished work of Christ; the Word of God; the promises, as spoken to the soul by the Holy Ghost; and the power and faithfulness of God." Oh, my precious Jesus, my heavenly Bridegroom, I commit the events of this evening to Thee. Be Thou to me as Genesis 20:16. Oh yes, be Thou to me a covering for the eyes. Keep me for Thyself, till Thou shalt call me home.

The last Sabbath in 1849 — What a peculiar year! How rich in mercy, high in joy, deep in conflict, sweet in love;—the love of my precious Beloved, the love of my covenant God. I think I never endured such anguish as at times during this year, from the deep feeling of bereavement, and also from pressing contrarieties and fears, lest I should not be in the right outward path. But love has softened and sweetened all the trial; and here I am, a monument of love's upholding power, feeling sweetly assured that the Lord has heard my prayers, seen my tears, and is with me in this way which I go. Oh, yes; all shall be well; and this deep and dark dispensation shall end in songs of praise. "He knoweth the way that I take," and though, to the flesh, it is like a long dark avenue, with only occasional rays of brightness, yet, "my soul, wait thou only upon God," and wait for Him still; it will not be in vain. He will either release from this fettering clay, or He will carry triumphantly on; and all shall redound to His praise who lived and died for me—my Lord, my life, my all. Praise for the past, trust for the future, becomes Thy favored worm, O Lord. My blessed Lord, on Thee Thy poor Hannah does call, provoked sorely to fret. I do afresh embrace Thee by faith, as better to me than ten sons, as my joy, my treasure, and my absorbing all. I fall heavily into Thine arms, with all my weights. Thou wilt sustain; Thou wilt still further bless me in Thy love, and use me for Thy glory, in life or death, as seems Thee best. Amen.

1850

January 1st — "I am thy shield, and thy exceeding great reward." "Walk before me, and be thou perfect." "Unto Hannah He gave a worthy portion"; and He said unto her, "Am not I better to thee than ten sons?" And so my glorious Beloved is Himself the worthiest part of my portion. Lamentations 3:24: Yea, I will triumph in Him, too, as the summer of my year, the sun of my day, the glory of my life. These are the thoughts of this New Year's morning: "When thine eye is single, thy whole body also is full of light."

January 6th, Sabbath — "Looking unto Jesus" has been the prevailing position of my soul during the last week, and I long for continual renewings therein by the Holy Ghost. Surely, when looking by faith away from all to Jesus only, He does become, in soul experience, "all in all." I cannot describe in words how earthly cares and interest have melted away before this glorious Sun of Righteousness, who is "all my salvation and all my desire." This word has just struck me, "In the way of thy judgments have we waited for thee, O God"; and I seem to see that when we are brought to walk in the way of the Lord's judgments, we are sometimes looking more for the deliverance we hope the Lord will work, than for Himself. I fear it has been so with me in my present straitness. Just as the lame man looked at Peter and John, expecting an alms, so I have looked at my dear Lord for the wonders of His hand in making a plain path for my feet. But He has royally outdone me, in giving me Himself in new revealings, with which my heart is satisfied, and my mouth stopped, and I leave all outside things to His will. Oh, to look on, to look ever, and to look nowhere else, though Satan and the flesh fight against it mightily.

January 13th, Sabbath — Peculiarly held down in spirit, the last week. Just now, while wondering how it was, Psalm 62:4, came to my mind with power; and methinks it may be that Satan, who does delight in lies, is stirring up carnal reasonings, to cast me down from my high privileges in Christ; and, though the words spoken seem fair to the flesh, they are, indeed, but a curse within. Yesterday and to-day these words have been often sounding in my ears, "Open thy mouth wide, and I will fill it."

January 21st — This morning I opened upon Numbers 22:7, 8; and then it followed me, "Lay up the rods before the Lord"; and I said, "I lay up myself and my circumstances before the Lord"; and I besought that, though so dry, they might be made fruitful.

January 28th — Surely, my exercise this evening is just renouncing self entirely—good self, bad self; self pleased, self displeased; self in its complainings, beseechings, enticings, desirings; self entirely. Oh that it may be once and for ever! And my all-lovely, soul-satisfying Christ do I embrace instead of myself. Blissful exchange! Perfect purity and beauty for ugliness and vileness.

January 29th — I have thought I have surely been as happy this evening as I could be in mortality; such blissful rest in my glorious Well-Beloved, and nearness to a Triune Jehovah in Him. Praise Him, ye hosts above! Praise Him, ye saints below! Ye heavens, praise Him!

Earth, praise Him! All animate creation, praise Him, and the inanimate works of His hands, re-echo the sound of His well-deserved praise; while worthless I, in happy nothingness and sweet absorption, listen with glad delight, and lisp the lovely name of Him whom my soul adores, my God, my glory! Bless, O my happy soul, the God of love; and in the love of God for ever dwell. Yea, dwell in God, for "God is love"; and they who dwell in love divine, do dwell in Him. O my glorious Lord, I wonder at my mercy, and at Thy great condescension; and tremble extremely, lest I should lose, by any means, the precious treasure of Thy manifested self. Oh, stay with me. In Thee I find treasures of holiness, happiness, and love, past all description. O Holy Spirit, enable me ever to renounce flesh, forsake creatures, and embrace Jesus.

February 3rd — I have this week been somewhat tossed in mind to find Christians of many years' standing very jealous of any one having too much enjoyment. This very thing has grieved me ever since I was brought out of bondage. It seems marvellous; for if I am saved, and positively know it, how can I but be joyful, and sing aloud of His righteousness who was "made sin for me"? My sorrow is, that I do not rejoice more. Lord, what is for Thy glory, increase; what is of the flesh, take away. Creature opinions confuse me, but Thy teachings my soul understands. I do marvel to hear so little of Thee, and Thy finished salvation, from believers of forty years' standing. "Lord, increase our faith," and simplicity.

February 7th — "And they sung as it were a new song before the throne"; and my soul longs to join them, being this morning filled with His praise, who alone is worthy, and whose mercies are ever new.

> "If but the Spirit touch my soul,
>   And grace her mean abode,

Oh, with what peace, and joy, and love,
She communes with her God."

February 10th — May not my shallow entrance into the blessed mystery of the Holy Trinity be owing to my expecting to receive it with my natural powers of intellect? And just now it seemed to be whispered, "Be still, and know that I am God"; be still in thyself, to know me in Christ, the only way of beholding and receiving unfoldings of ineffable Deity. In Christ alone, the Holy Ones, the Three who bear record in heaven, are revealed. Thou, O Beloved, art my nearness; quiet Thou my creature-powers, that I may receive in Thee, and be filled with all the fullness of God.

February 18th — This evening Mr. S— preached much about a precious Jesus as a tried stone, and after saying who tried Him in various ways, he said, "God the Father tried Him." "Then," thought I, "if He tried the *Living Stone*, which is the foundation, He will also try the *lively* stones, which are laid upon it; so I need not wonder at the unlooked-for ways in which He tries me"; and my mind is much relieved. It is better to be tried now than rejected and destroyed hereafter. The will of the Lord be done. Surely I have often said Psalm 139:23, 24. And surely the Lord does sometimes to His lively stones as 2 Chronicles 32:31; Deuteronomy 8:2, 3; Psalm 105:19; 1 Peter 4:12, 13.

February 24th, Sacrament-day — A blessed month has passed away. I must write upon it, Ebenezer, for surely "the Lord has triumphed gloriously"! In Him "have I righteousness and strength," and His service is "perfect freedom." May I go into it heartily and cheerfully, in His name. Unexpected trials have arisen; but they have been the Lord's opportunity, and hitherto He has graciously helped. Oh, my precious Christ! Thou art my life—I was Thy death; may I weep, love, and praise Thee evermore.

March 17th — Surely Jehovah-Jesus is my gold, and He will be unto me instead of silver. By His help I will look away from all which has entangled and bewildered me, unto Himself alone, to which trust I feel renewings by the power of the Holy Ghost in my soul this night. Oh, my precious, all-loving Savior! There is in Thee such an infinitude of blessedness as will fill and delight my perfected capabilities through all eternity. Oh, why do I ever wander, ever look away from Thee? Thou wilt overrule and manage my mean affairs; and I may safely be absorbed in Thee. Oh, grant it even now, amongst threatening straits. Thou lovely, glorious Immanuel, my soul burns with new ardor in intense longings after Thee; all else sinks into nothingness. Thee, and none but Thee Thyself, does my soul desire.

March 24th — Our dear brother in Christ, Mr. Harvey,* is just waiting at the portals of celestial bliss; perhaps, ere another morning dawns upon the earth, he will have made his glad escape from the fetters of clay. I have had much sweetness of spirit in bearing him before the Lord. It seems he is entering glory very triumphantly, and in the very article of death testifying that it is but a shadow. Bless the Lord for leaving testimony with dying breath. This is proof positive that Jesus has "abolished death," and left it stingless and harmless for the redeemed; He having gone before, and made way for them to pass safely over. My soul, praise Thou the Lord. Dear brother, I could envy thee; the conflict seems over, and already thy victory begun; the cloud of mortality will not long intervene between thee and Thy Lord, but soon Thou wilt

---

* Author of the little work entitled "The Sherwood Gipsy."

behold Him face to face. Oh, that Thou couldst come and tell me of the glory, and chant me one note or two in pure celestial harmony, to cheer my longing soul, which has been spoiled for earth by little foretastes of the eternal weight of glory. Dear brother, I have not known thee much, but deeply feel thy removal; thy life was useful, and much desired, and thy death is blessed indeed. I trust I have had some reproof, instruction, and encouragement this week about my outward path. Reproof, Isaiah 48:18; instruction, James 1:5; and encouragement to go forward in faith.

March 26th — Mr. Harvey was received into the presence-chamber this morning, at nine o'clock. I have not yet heard full particulars, but it seems his departure was most triumphant, and that rays of glory were visible on his dying countenance. I think dear friends must look at poor me, and wonder why I should be spared, while such a saint, and one so useful, is taken away, of whom it may be said, "For my name's sake he has labored, and has not fainted." Truly I blush, and am ashamed to lift up my head.

March 31st, Sacrament-day — I have this afternoon attended the feast, but I "sought Him, and found Him not," and returned home sad and sorrowful. But surely, "though He slay me, yet will I trust Him." I seem to see nought but gloom in outward things, but feel sweetness in confiding. The trial of faith grows very sharp, and I greatly fear dishonoring my Lord. Oh, strengthen Thy poorest child, or grant some relief! Help, Lord, lest the enemy triumph. I feel a vile, unworthy, unholy being. I loathe myself beyond expression; but the blood and righteousness of Jehovah-Jesus is my confidence, and here I have a place of refuge. I give myself to Thee, for the unknown events of the coming month; Thy will be done. This frail tabernacle suffers much, but I would wait only on Thee. Oh, increase faith! My poor heart trembles, and seems at the sinking-point. Oh, let me not listen to carnal reason, and dishonor Thee. "Save, Lord, for the waters are come into my soul." I do not fear sinking into hell, Thy love prevents that; but I fear sinking into a life of sight and sense, and thus judging Thy providential dealings after the flesh. Lord, prevent it, and be better to me than all my fears. My Savior, I call upon Thee amidst the water-floods; I hear Thee not, but Thou art precious in presence, and in absence too.

> "Why, then, my soul, these sad complaints,
>   Since Christ and thou art one?
> Thy God is faithful to His saints,
>   Is faithful to His Son.
>
> Beneath His smiles my heart has lived,
>   And part of heaven possessed:
> Then praise His name for grace received,
>   And trust Him for the rest."

April 16th — Wonderful! Again privileged to behold the Lord's wonders, as a Hearer and Answerer of prayer. Two or three months ago, an aged female, who has been very respectable, but is now in very reduced circumstances, applied to me to intercede for an almshouse. I feared to do this, but I could plead in the Highest Court, and I did; for, though this person was quite a stranger to me, I felt much interested in her cause; and I have seen her several times since. She had applied before, and has been waiting two years. Well, the Lord has worked, and given me the privilege to look on. A vacancy occurring, she obtained an interview with Mr. S— which she never could get before. The Lord touched his heart. He thought she was the right person, and to-day I had the pleasure of going, with a friend, to present it to the poor woman, who was overjoyed. "It is the Lord's doing, and marvellous in our eyes." Oh, for many such blessed errands; it is the delight of my life. What encouragement to go to the Lord about everything, and still wait, though He tarry long. Ebenezer!

April 21st, Sabbath — Heard Mr. C—. He advanced some weighty and solemn things, which I was glad to hear, and to be searched by. I trust I was edified with what he said about the Person of Christ, and also about the Lord's choice of His people, on which my mind has been much exercised lately. But on one point I differed with him. He seemed to speak against full assurance. Now, I find it in the Scriptures, and the Lord has put it into my soul. He also maintains it there by the renewings or witnessings of the Holy Ghost. *Night* — I have not been out this evening. My Beloved has surprised me with a visit, and "or ever I was aware, my soul made me like the chariots of Amminadib." How has the precious gospel flowed, like oil and wine, into my soul!

April 28th, Sacrament-day — I humbly trust the Lord is deepening His work in my poor soul, and renewing me in faith. But it is wonderful how He works by contraries; and I seem just now to see, that where a thing is evidently set for me with a cross in it, I may safely take it up, expecting a blessing. I am not a Romanist, I do not mean a literal mark of the cross; but I mean something which crosses, and is contrary to, my fleshly will, choice, ease, or gratification. Dear Lord, help me! It is a hard lesson to flesh and sense; but light and glory now beam upon it. How I must have loved self and its ease, for it to be yet so hard to welcome its crucifixion!

May 3rd — "But He answered her not a word." These words very sweet and encouraging this morning; for, on one pressing point, my gracious Lord answers me not. But

I am sweetly enabled to wait still upon Him, and feel an assurance in His love, that to me also He will vouchsafe an answer, in the right time, as well as to the poor woman mentioned above. My soul glows with desire to praise and trust my faithful God, though my way be dark.

May 12th — The trial of faith sharp the last fortnight. I often groan before the Lord, and feel overweighted; but there are two staffs in His Word, on which at times I am brought to lean, and then get rested. They are these: "Father, glorify thy name"; "Thy will be done." I long for a more single eye, and more triumph in Christ, amidst many perplexities.

May 23rd — Psalm 45:11. What words are these, and how sweetly did they smile upon me, above all the rest in the Psalm, "So shall the King greatly desire thy beauty." How? In thy forgetfulness of all but Himself; for when we are experimentally, with single eye, beholding Him, then is His glory visibly reflected in us; we are beautiful in His beauty; but it is like an eclipse, when we get taken up with self and creatures. Oh, for this happy forgetfulness! My glorious Well-Beloved, my soul desires Thy beauty, with intense longing. Thou hast ravished my heart; none of the sons of men can fill the place Thou hast occupied. Oh, come and bless me again with Thy overwhelming love and loveliness! The Spirit in me says, "Come"; Thy poor gleaner says, "Come"; yes, "Come, Lord Jesus, come quickly." Thou still dost closely hedge me up in outward circumstances; and this, with other pressures, has entangled and turned my heart from Thee. But I come, I return by Thine own sweet drawings in my soul. I desire Thee; I invite Thee. I would forget all I inherit in the first Adam; I would resign myself and my circumstances to Thy will; and by faith embrace Thyself, and, in Thy glorious Person, find everlasting bliss! Alas, those wondrous wounds! Have they left immortal scars? Wilt Thou, through all eternity, wear those marks of Thy matchless love? And wilt Thou, in those blissful realms, dissolve our souls in holy rapture and adoring love, by saying, "Behold my hands and my feet, that it is I myself"? Surely, if aught could add beauty to that glorious form, it would be, in the eyes of love, those deep engravings, "I have graven thee upon the palms of my hands." And surely Thou, O Beloved, art engraven on the table of this longing heart. Set, oh, "set me as a seal upon Thine heart, as a seal upon Thine arm," too. Oh, grant another glimpse of Thy surpassing charms! Let me—

"Behold the God who died for man;
And praise Thee more than angels can."

Thou didst not take their nature into union with Thyself, but mine, for evermore: amazing mystery! Oh, give me deeper entrance into, sweeter experience of, my oneness with Thee, Thou lovely Immanuel! Give me to abide in my perfection and completeness in Thee; so wilt Thou greatly desire Thine own beauty in me! While I would sink into the arms, and recline on the bosom of love. "He is thy Lord," O my soul; "worship thou Him."

May 26th, Sacrament-day — I am again almost overcome with love, my Beloved is so precious. And this is quite old-fashioned; for when the spouse, in the banqueting-house, embraced by her Beloved, cried, "Stay me with flagons, comfort me with apples, for I am sick of love," she was not sick with longing, because her Beloved was absent, as in Song 5:8, but with enjoyment; that is, right down overwhelmed with the amazing love and loveliness of Immanuel; and such is somewhat my happy case. Oh, I long to be away in the land of spices, to see Him as He is:

> "Nought but the Fountain Head above
> Can satisfy the thirst of love."

I can find few kindred spirits; all seem afraid of being too warm, and dare not quite forget, their "own people," and their first "father's house," for Christ's sake.

June 14th — "How unsearchable are Thy judgments, O Lord; and Thy ways past finding out." I have been advised to sink most of my ready money for a life annuity. This might make me a comfortable income, but I cannot do it with a good conscience. It seems taking my affairs out of the hands of the Lord, and preferring human security to divine. And, looking at it in a more natural light, it seems selfish; for then all would die with me. Thus feeling, I have concluded to take money from the stock, when I cannot get on, and trust the Lord for the future.

June 23rd — My health indifferent again, on which account it was suggested, yesterday, that I should go to Matlock for a fortnight, at the expense of some friends, who paid all for me at Ockbrook. I feel utterly unworthy of these great favors, but I commit it to the Lord, and wait now for a heavenly gale in my soul, which has somewhat been becalmed. And, oh, what a solid Rock have I felt Him to be in my soul!

June 28th — "In the light of the King's countenance is life; and His favor is as a cloud of the latter rain." So my soul findeth it this evening. Our little Friday evening meeting has been very refreshing. My mind was in much confusion, but the Lord has allayed it. This word is very sweet, "There the glorious Lord will be unto us a place of broad rivers and streams."

June 30th, Sacrament-day — Not favored with sensible enjoyment, but for past mercies I would give thanks; and the heart longs to go forth afresh in His name, who loved me, and gave Himself for vile, unworthy me, all holy, and all lovely as He was.

> "Oh, for this love, let rocks and hills
>   Their lasting silence break;
> And all redeemed human tongues
>   The Savior's praises speak."

Oh, Thou glorious Well-Beloved, reveal Thyself afresh, and eclipse all other objects. If I am to behold the works of Thy hands in creation as I never saw them before, let me feel the love of Thy heart as I never before did. Let me not turn away from high or low, where I may speak of Thee for the good of souls; and, oh, grant that unfolding of Thy glorious Person for which this spirit pants.

July 1st — Surely the language of my soul this Monday morning is, with felt humble solemnity, Psalm 123:2. Watching Thine eye to guide me, and Thine hand to provide for my need.

July 6th — It is late, and I am weary; but I cannot let this day pass away without some little memorial of the Lord's goodness to unworthiest me. The past has been a year of much trial; but often have I worn the crown of lovingkindness, and tender mercy, and often testified, "He doeth all things well." Forty-five years have I now spent in this great and terrible wilderness, and "hitherto the Lord hath [wonderfully] helped me." "Praise Him, O my soul, and forget not all His benefits"; and trust Him still—trust Him with all.

July 7th —
> "My soul, repeat His praise,
> Whose mercies are so great."

And record it, too, that again thou mayest look to the hill Mizar on some future day, and remember thy God from thence. The heavenly dew fell upon my weary soul very refreshingly this morning in the house of the Lord. Before the service began, Habakkuk 3:17, 18, 19 seemed suitable to my outward state. How encouraging that it is lawful to rejoice in the Lord, even when His providences wear a stern aspect towards us. Truly it was rejoicing and reproving, for how have I failed; how have I hardly dared to trust at times, because of the dark cloud which has kept thickening around me, until I seemed enveloped in mists of perplexity; and how have my praises been choked with anxiety. Pardon me, O Lord, and renew me by Thy Spirit. They sang, "God moves in a mysterious way," &c., and my own verse, "Ye fearful saints," &c. Oh, that the Matlock clouds may break in blessings: they have often looked very dark. "Lord, if thy presence go not with me, carry me not up hence." I commit all to Thee, and beg Thee to bless us and make us a blessing. I hope to journey hence in the morning; the Lord preserve our going out and coming in, and be glorified in all.

July 8th — Matlock Bath — Through the tender mercy of our Lord, we arrived here safely last evening. I never saw anything so enchanting as the view from our windows. The thought that the Lord specially guided me here, makes me glad; and then to look constantly at the majestic works of creation, elevated my heart very much. Bless the Lord, O my soul, for His wonders to such a worm.

July 13th, Saturday — We have been seeing some of the wonders of nature—such wild, romantic scenery. Wood, hill, and water, ever varying, enrich the lovely scene. I have much enjoyed it, but want more Christian communion, to hear more of the love of Jesus.

July 27th — We all returned home yesterday. Through mercy, we travelled safely, and the Lord did sweetly presence Himself as we passed through the long, dark tunnels. His Word was a light and a comfort: I trust and believe it was ministered to my soul by the Holy Spirit. The first portion was Micah 7:8; the second was Psalm 139:8. I desired to come home with my eyes shut—that is, the eyes of flesh, sense, and carnal reason; just to walk through the dark, and the difficult, and the pleasing also, looking only to Jesus, and trusting only in the Lord.

August 18th, Sabbath — A rich feast this evening in hearing Mr. —. He preached Christ, the Christ of God, not in the letter, but in the Spirit; not in the history, but in the mystery of godliness, and under that anointing by which alone He is revealed. He preached Christ up and me down; seemed to batter me into happy nothingness, so that afresh I lost all identity out of Him, and came home, feeling myself the happy bride, and gladly finding that I could afford to lose self and creatures for, and in, so rich a Husband.

August 30th, Friday — The Lord has been very gracious to unworthy me to-day, in taking me to the Refuge. I had much trembling about it yesterday, but I have been mercifully helped. I felt much power, and there seemed much melting among the girls. Oh, that it may not be like "the morning cloud," which soon passes away. May the Holy Spirit deepen conviction, and seal impressions. Ah, indeed, what is of Him shall endure, for He will have respect to the work of His own hands, and make it prosper.

September 6th, Friday — Yesterday, as I was walking, the thought came to me, Why do those who have been brought to count all things loss for Christ, find a double desolation in turning back again to any sort of beggarly elements, to anything but Christ, for satisfaction? Blessed be the Lord that it is so, though keen be the smart. Afterwards, as I came home, another "blink" was let into my soul, teaching me that I had been too much living upon feelings, and less than formerly upon Christ by faith; with this word, "His paths drop fatness," showing me it was my own paths which were so dry.

September 19th — I have had sharp exercises this week, concerning what many would think a trifle. On Monday, a tenant gave me half-a-sovereign, which was lost I know not how. It appeared most mysterious, for I much needed it. My soul sank within me, because I feared my Father must be angry, or He would not so constantly smite me in providential matters. It seemed as if my Lord would speak there would be a calm; and I know He will, although I cannot see how He can be glorified in this thing. I felt much encouraged by reading "Burroughs on Contentment." It is to encourage dependence on the Lord when ways and means seem most shut up. He quotes 2 Kings 3:17: "Ye shall not see wind, neither shall ye see rain; yet that valley shall be filled with water." I never saw the passage in this light before. My God, Thou art able. My soul was afresh encouraged to supplicate, notwithstanding long delays and straitenings.

September 24th — I have been much harassed on account of my temporal affairs, but in the conflict have been brought to close dealing with the Lord; faith has afresh taken hold of His faithfulness; to fulfill His promises. Psalm 37:5, and Proverbs 3:6. I have been enabled to "commit my way unto the Lord"; and, after strong crying and tears, have at length found peace and calmness in what I call my little corner; "Thy will be done." *Evening* — A large demand for half-a-year's poor-rate has drawn the providential knot still tighter. Through divine mercy and power, I am enabled to bless the Lord, assured He does all things well!

September 25th — Yesterday came tax for highway rate, which, with the other, only left me a few shillings in my purse. I cried to the Lord to have pity, and before noon was sent £1 2s., which was owing for needlework that I have done. How timely! How merciful! What a ray across my dark path. It is like a gift from the Lord. Thanks and praise be to the Lord for this great mercy. He is dealing wondrously with me for some wise purpose.

September 29th, Sacrament day — I have felt great jealousy lately, lest, being alone in the wilderness, I should, by the pressure of time and things upon me, get one inch further from my God. God forbid! My Father prevent, by Thy own almighty power. Draw me nearer, much nearer. I cannot endure the thought of "following afar off." Lord, draw me, and keep me very close to Thee. *Evening* — I have not had the sensible presence of my Beloved at His table, as I expected, but have felt some earnest seeking there, that I may have as much of Him as can be had in mortality. Glorious Redeemer, come to me in further and fuller developments of Thy personal glories; and, in the warmth of Thy love, make me a live coal to many hearts, for nought have I here but to live for Thee and Thine. Let me see Thy heart laid open by the sword of justice, and read there the deep inscription of almighty love. I have presented a check to Thee, as my banker, for a certain sum of money. I have asked the Father in Thy name. I wait the reply. If it be of the flesh, Thy name will be as a knife to cut up, or a fire to burn up my check; but, if it be for the divine glory, Thy name will secure the bestowment. Thou knowest all the secret. Help me to wait, and patiently hope for Thy salvation. In the meantime breathe, sacred Spirit, into this heart, quickening there desires more ardent after Jesus.

October 1st — Sweet breathings and bedewings of the Spirit in my soul last evening and to-day, bringing sweet odors of my precious Jesus, after whom my soul has been eagerly pursuing for some time. Outward straits continue, but it is as if the Beloved were between them and me just now, seeming to say, "Am not I enough?" and my heart answers, "Yes, Lord, Thou art, without anything else." I just present my check day after day, not knowing yet whether it was drawn up under promptings of the flesh, or anointings of the Spirit. But this I know, my Jesus is sweetly all to me, unworthy though I be. I long to walk more erect in Christ. Blessed are they who dwell in Him by faith. "They will be still praising thee." There are few rejoicing souls now; it is thought dangerous. I want more of it day by day. Our Head has "the Spirit without measure"; He has "the oil of gladness above [His] fellows"; but He can bestow upon them a large measure, for in Him is no straitness or scarceness of either gift or grace. Lord, overrule all, and, when Thou hast tried me sufficiently, bring me forth like gold purified. But must I wait till then to praise Thee? Paul and Silas sang Thy praises in the stocks, and we read of "being joyful in tribulation." My God, my flesh writhes under Thy present circumstantial dealings; but my spirit longs to praise Thee, and walk closely with thee, even when Thou walkest contrary to me in outward things.

November 3rd — Earnest longings for more of Christ, and pleadings to be renewed in the "simplicity which is in Him"; unbelief struggles; faith wrestles. O Lord, increase my faith. Thou art the land of plenty, where we eat bread without scarceness, and have no lack of anything. Oh renew, restore my longing soul, which this night "counts all things loss" for Thee, and feels, if Thou gavest a mountain of gold, it would turn from it, or clamber over it, to get at Thy precious self, if it could not find Thee in it.

November 12th — A morning stormy indeed. The poor heart aching because needed relief comes not, and fearing there must be something wrong and displeasing to the Lord; also fearing to dishonor Him by tears and anguish, and struggling to look to Jesus above it all. *Noon* — A mercy-drop, in a small sum for work done, with one shilling and sixpence over pay. *Evening* — Just a gleam in hearing Mr. D. F— speaking of the resurrection of Jesus as a pledge of ours. And, thought I, "Shall I trust Him with this body, to raise it up at the last day, and not trust Him with time things, with my present debt and difficulty?" My heart seemed to melt into trust, and I could only say, "Precious Jesus."

November 16th — On Wednesday evening I heard Mr. D. F—. He spoke much of love to the saints, and of doing them good, to our inconvenience. I had a clear sight why I had not had so much bright shining lately, and what I should be without Jesus, by whom all the fruits of righteousness come. I saw also what a vile wretch He had loved; and how did this melt my soul, and enhance His matchless love. I could only bless Him for the very withholding, which had been so painful, but laid me low at His feet. I should remember, that on Friday I thought I should never have another temporal Ebenezer to raise, but soon after came a ton of coals as a present. I was astonished. It seems the Lord will supply the house, though so much trying me about the rent. May He pardon all my mistrust.

November 21st — I have decided to sell sufficient stock to pay my rent, feeling it will be better to be reduced, and have Jesus, than to keep stock in hand, without His company. Dear Lord, Thou must come in, if all else goes out. I do love Thee, and long for Thee, Thou knowest.

November 22nd — I have been to the Refuge this afternoon—a hallowed place to me. I was peculiarly blessed in prayer. The Word also appeared to open in reading, and there was some deep feeling in the girls. Lord, breathe upon the dry bones, or all the prophesying will be in vain. "Can these bones live?" "O Lord God, Thou knowest." The change in my spiritual feelings is great indeed; the mountains seem removed; and now that I am come cheerfully to lessen my earthly store, my heavenly one is more freely and fully opened: my blessed Jesus seems more free of access; and nought on earth, or in heaven, is like communion with Him. I am longing exceedingly for souls to be quickened, or liberated. Oh, to know that I am of use to one soul, would be to me more than a mountain of wealth.

November 24th, Sacrament-day — The Israelites came to the impassable place, and the enemy behind kept them from turning back; they must go forward; but the sea is there, and no bridge; and, when the strange command is given by their leader, the waters shall wonderfully withdraw to either side, and between the liquid walls they shall safely pass over, to the honor of their God. This seems like me. I have come to the place of hedging up. I have looked all ways for an outlet, and cried to the Lord for it, but in vain. I find deliverance *in* the trial, not *out* of it; and now, while going through the deeps, my sighs are changed for songs.

December 16th — Rich, full, glorious Christ, how near hast Thou come; how precious hast Thou been to this poor heart to-night; and now the desire is, "I beseech Thee, show me Thy glory": let it shine through surrounding gloom. Now, in these eventful times, when Popery is putting forth a fresh horn of power, be the wall of fire round about Thy Church, and the glory in the midst of her. Shine in us, shine on us, shine through us; and be Thou glorified, and gloriously revealed.

December 22nd, Sabbath — The Lord very gracious. Ten thousand thanks, dear Lord, for all Thy mercies. I only want more revelation of the personal glories of Jesus, and more power to speak of Him to fellow-saints and fellow-sinners. Surely with joy I have payed that I have vowed, and triumphantly sing, "Salvation is of the Lord."

December 29th — Our little church is sending a petition to our dear Sovereign, against Popery. Every one may sign it; and surely with heart and hand I subscribe for Christ against Antichrist.

December 31st — Psalm 26:8. At our prayer meeting today, my soul cried to the Lord for a blessing upon the coming year, with some poor praise for the past. Whilst there, these words seemed sweetly given me for 1851: "Ye are not your own"; and "Thou art mine." Dear Lord, "Thou art mine, and I am Thine." This is my glory and joy.

1851

January 12th, Sabbath — "Bless the Lord, O my soul," for more mercies in the wilderness, for another sip of the brook by the way. We have heard Mr. R— this morning. The text was, "Casting all your care upon him, for he careth for you." The word itself was suitable to my outward case; for there have been many burglaries in the town of late, especially during the Sabbath services. Having always left my house in the morning, I have gone out as usual, just committing all to the Lord, who once told me, "No man shall desire thy land when thou goest up to worship the Lord"; and who has lately often said, "According to thy faith, be it unto thee." I cried to the Lord to know the right way. It was a trial of faith, and a sharp struggle. I thought the enemy was consulting to cast me down from the simplicity of faith in Christ. I was encouraged by "Whoso putteth his trust in the Lord, shall be safe." I concluded to go, telling the Lord, if this trusting in Him were presumption, I was willing to know it; and if it were true, living faith, I should have the token of a safe house; and so has it come to pass, to my furtherance and great joy of faith. Wherefore, I testify to all whom it may concern, that it is "better to trust in the Lord, than to put any confidence in man."

January 14th — "I will cause them that love me to inherit substance; and I will fill their treasures." Most precious

Lord Jesus, this soul does inherit substance in possessing and enjoying Thee, who art substantial.

"O! to grace how great a debtor!"

February 1st, Saturday — Isaiah 12:1. "My cup runneth over; I am full with the blessing of the Lord." It seems as though the Lord would again turn my captivity, and a second time restore unto me the years the locusts, the cankerworm, and the caterpillar had eaten, renewing the blessedness of 1839. "I am a wonder to myself"; few conceive the happiness I enjoy. My soul, praise thou the Lord.

February 13th — My soul has been clouded for a day or two. This morning I was desiring communion with the Holy Trinity, when my precious Immanuel shone forth as the Morning Star to me. He seemed the coming forth of Jehovah from behind the cloud. Oh, for more of the glory shining in my soul, in the Person of Jesus Christ!

February 17th — I have again been exercised about writing so many letters, thinking it was "labor in vain, and wasting my strength for nought."* But the Lord has graciously, this week, sent me two messages to the contrary. Blessed Jesus! I only live for Thee and Thine. Thou dost pour into my heart what is poured out by my pen. All the goodness is Thine, bless it; all the badness is mine, forgive it.

February 23rd — My life seems all miracle and mercy. I am a miracle of mercy, and a vessel of mercy! The Lord's goings are very stately, and His ways very majestic to His unworthy worm. It is wonderful how He answers me in little things, proving my "desire is before Him, and my

---

* Many of these letters have been collected, and are so valuable, that it is hoped in due time they may be published.

groaning not hid from Him." It does truly look as though my temporal straitness was passing away. Lord, keep me from evil this month, and from any snare that may be laid for me.

February 26th — I plainly see that neither my old man nor my new man can be mended: the one is too bad, the other too good. There is no patching or painting the old man to advantage; it will still be "corrupt, according to its deceitful lusts"; and the new man wants neither patching nor painting, for it is "created in righteousness and true holiness" (Eph. 4:24). There is nothing for the old man but the cross, and for the new, but to "grow up into Christ in all things." Most Holy Comforter, exercise my spiritual senses to discern between good and evil, not seeking to confound or blend them, but understanding that what "is born of the flesh is flesh," and will act after its nature; and "what is born of the Spirit is spirit," and will aspire to its source!

March 17th — Precious Jesus! I embrace Thee as all-sufficient for me, and as all I need for work and welfare. Thou art the Rock of my heart; I feel Thee to be so. My hopes rest in Thee; my faith centers in Thee; my love has its repose in Thee, and by Thee goes forth to the Father. From my sins Thou art the Deliverer; under my trials Thou art my support; and of my joys the sweetness and crown! I long for dear saints to know Thee more, enjoy Thee more, and have less to do with self, which is all loss and misery.

April 1st — A sweet outflowing of the Spirit of adoption, in bed; so that I could sweetly say, "Abba, Father."

April 2nd — I have just been to the Refuge, and found it a privilege. I had a very wrestling spirit in prayer, much longing for some soul to be benefited, though feeling I am truly an unprofitable servant! But work Thou, dear Lord, for Thy great name's sake. Oh, "wake, arm of the Lord!" Christ of God, come forth, as in former days. We have felt power, even in that place, and have had seasons never to be forgotten. Do renew former mercies. "Revive Thy work," where begun, and quicken Thy dead, who have never felt before. My soul is afresh enkindled with desires for these young women.

April 3rd — I have this evening heard Mr. C—, with much unction and sweetness, from Isaiah 61:10. It was a time of sweet refreshing to my soul, and Jesus was all in all. Oh for renewings in the "simplicity which is in Christ"! Mr. C— is a father in Christ, and seems almost ripe for glory. He spoke sweetly on the fitness, beauty, and fullness of Christ—fullness of grace, and fullness of glory. And he spoke of the joy, the clothing, and of the ornaments of the Church—"the things which accompany salvation," a meek and quiet spirit. And I now see, as I never saw before, how many think it will do to be clothed, and through soul-sloth neglect the ornaments, which are to the Lord's glory. Lord, quicken me, I pray, and give soul-diligence; and "let the beauty of the Lord my God be upon me."

April 6th — I have had great profit from Mr. C—. Jesus is very precious; and a life of faith in Him, by the power of the Holy Ghost, is very blessed, world-conquering, Satan-overcoming, and sin-subduing. But surely, "My feet had almost gone, my steps had well nigh slipped." Almost all around are so engrossed with the workings of self, that I was almost beguiled to turn away from the holy commandment delivered unto me, and look there too. But for this "there has been deep searchings of the heart." I was many years sinking into the pit of corruption, and passing through the valley of the shadow of death; but the

Lord has brought me out; and why should I wish to return? I would not palm my experience upon any one; nor will I, by God's help, try to conform to theirs; but leave myself in the molding hand of my God, who hath called me into liberty. "Where the Spirit of the Lord is, there is liberty"; whom the Son makes free, are free indeed; I feel it, let who will gainsay it. "Jehovah hath triumphed"; His prisoner is "free." Precious Jesus, keep me from entanglement in any yoke of bondage (Job 17:9)!

April 8th — Some dear friends kindly propose that I should go from home again. I feel abased and ashamed. The Lord reward them; and lay and keep me low. Malvern is the place thought of: I suppose it is very lovely. I committed it all to the Lord.

April 17th, Thursday — O my Savior, my soul melts this morning in remembrance of Thee, and of Thy sufferings; ten thousand thanks for Thine amazing love! We are busy cleaning this house; but Thou must cleanse this heart; we use water and much soap for the house; but only blood, Thine own precious blood, will avail for the heart. Grant a fresh sense of its efficacy; and let my meditations of Thee be sweet this day. I do, in love, commemorate the death of our great High Priest, my Brother and my Friend.

April 20th, Sabbath — Through a very fatiguing week, the Lord has graciously brought me, by divine power; granting sweet bedewings of His Spirit, in the midst of domestic engagements. I am trusting that the Lord will clear my way as regards expense of house cleaning, begun in faith. While thinking over this matter and my London house rent, which is due, this word came to me: "They shall not be ashamed that wait for me"; and has been a stay to my soul. In the evening I went to pay for the painting, &c., of my house, when I found a kind friend had already done it for me. Here was an unexpected token; to the Lord be the glory! Surely, He is "with me in the way that I go."

April 29th — A morning of gloominess. Dear Lord, "I am oppressed: undertake for me." Thou didst provide a piece of money for the tribute; oh, send the needed sum for my rent, which the event of this morning has so pressed upon me afresh. If I am right, grant me again this token, and defeat unbelief and Satan. "Thou hast known my soul in adversities"; "Thou hast been my help"; therefore, I come again to Thee in the day of trial. Oh, hear and help me, my Lord and my God!

May 3rd — The Lord has heard and answered, by sending rent from town: so I have this day paid my rent here. Ebenezer.

May 4th, Sacrament Sabbath — I have partaken of the Lord's Supper, in loving remembrance of Him whose mortal "vesture was dipped in blood." Surely He hath kissed me with the kisses of His mouth: His love is most sweet. The fire of jealousy hath been kindled in my soul this week, for want of personal communion with my Beloved. And, since He has heard the cry of my distress, and sent me some outward help, and thus given me another token about this house, I began to fear, lest He would withdraw still further, as some say He has done, when their trials have been lessened, and the outward path made smoother. But I could not bear it; and I told Him yesterday that I could walk cheerfully in the path of trial with Him, but not in the path of prosperity without Him. He did give us a good unctuous season on Friday evening; but then yesterday He was gone again; but today He has been known, in the breaking of bread. Most precious Savior, I would hold Thee, and not let Thee go. What in heart, or lip, or life, or friends, offends Thee, discover to me, for Thee I must have: Thou art essential to my life, my peace, my happiness, my holiness, my usefulness; all are bound up in Thee. Thou knowest this is the true confession of my heart. I give myself to Thee, my best Beloved, for the events—it may be important events—of the coming month. "If Thy presence go not with me, carry me not up hence." Keep this Bethel safe in Thy absence, or let me not leave it. Amen.

May 18th — The past week has been one of much fatigue, sharp conflict, trial and much mercy. I feel to-day faint and low; but the Lord can revive me. My heart sinks at going from this quiet home: we expect to go to-morrow morning, if the Lord will. May He preserve us, and bring us back in peace, to erect another pillar in His name, to His praise. I was encouraged this morning from Jeremiah 24:5, 6. I again commend myself and friends to Thy care. Most glorious Three-One Jehovah! Thou wilt be faithful still, I humbly believe. I again record Thy praise.

May 20th — *Great Malvern* — Through mercy, we arrived safely at this place last evening. The Lord's mercy was very manifest while travelling.

May 20th — The loveliness and beauty of this place quite exceeds my expectation. Its majestic hills, and extensive scenery around, are very striking, and delight me much. This morning I had a very early visitor. Mr. Godlyfear knocked loudly at my heart before I was up: instituting inquiry, and commanding a watch, lest, having more society, and so much change of scene, a trifling spirit should unawares intrude. Lord, prevent it, and keep me in Thy fear all the day long.

June 8th — Surely it becomes me to record the mercies of

my covenant God, to a most unworthy creature. On Friday, June 6th, we journeyed safely home, preserved by Israel's God and Guide. I found this Bethel-home quite safe, which is another proof that it is good "to trust in the Lord." The ministry of Mr. — very savory to my soul; and I had some precious visits from my dear Lord. The beauties of His creation delighted me; but the love of His heart was the crown of the whole; and to feel that I am enclosed in His everlasting covenant of peace, fills me with wonder and delight.

July 6th — "And thou shalt remember all the way which the Lord thy God led thee these forty years in the wilderness, to humble thee, and to prove thee, to know what was in thine heart, whether thou wouldst keep his commandments, or no" (Deut. 8:2). So I would do this day, which is my birthday. "Marvellous are thy works, O Lord; and that my soul knoweth right well." In Thy great mercy Thou hast led me hitherto, and none seem to have so much cause to praise Thee. The past year has been rich in bestowment; and, to my surprise, I find myself much relieved from the so long distressing outward straitness. "I have waited for thy salvation, O Lord," and I have not waited in vain. How I would encourage all tried souls to wait on the Lord, and wait for Him, though He tarry long, and not turn to carnal means for relief; but wait for His bidding, though in the most trying circumstances. "The way of the Lord is strength to the upright." The enlargement of my spirit, in this respect, has been very striking. What can I render? My whole self, a living sacrifice for the Lord's glory. For the coming year I humbly ask, in the name of Jesus, spiritual increase and enlargement, and that prayer, the Bible, and ordinances may be more blessed to my soul; my friends more blessed to me, and I to them; and Jesus more glorified in all.

[Reader, how sweet, and full, and comprehensive,

this prayer! Is it in thine heart to plead the same? How comforting the thought, then, that thou canst and dost appeal to the self-same gracious Listener!]

July 20th — I heard Mr. J— this morning from John 5:4. Oh, mighty, matchless Jesus, Thou angel of the everlasting covenant, my earnest cry is unto Thee, to "trouble the waters," and put virtue into them. Trouble the waters of instruction at the Refuge; trouble also the waters of ordinances, the waters of adversity, and the waters of friendship. Oh, come in all, to put power into them, for Thy glory and our profit.

July 22nd — "My soul is satisfied as with marrow and fatness; and my mouth doth praise Thee with joyful lips." I can feelingly say, "Worthy is the Lamb"; He is my worthiness: praise Him, O my soul.

July 28th, Monday — The Lord, I humbly trust, gave me two portions yesterday: Philippians 4:19, and Hosea 6:1, 2. They were reviving; but the heart continues heavy. "They feared as they entered the cloud"; and my soul trembles at the return of former straitness. "Lord, help me"!

July 30th — "The Lord has put a new song in my mouth" to-day: Habakkuk 3:17, 18. I have often sung it before, but it is new every time the Spirit's power is in it, and especially under fresh trial.

August 3rd, Sacrament-day — I had some soul exercise and sweetness at the Lord's table; but I want more unfolding of the "unspeakable gift." My circumstantial calm was short. A letter brought heavy tidings, which makes the future look dark. I commit all, with myself, to Him who ruleth the winds: and, when the waves are high, He stilleth them. Lord, I wait for Thy salvation; but more for Thyself, in manifested love. Oh, come, my glorious Redeemer, skipping over the mountains of difficulty, and over the worse mountains of my sins. The moments of Thy absence are as days of tedious gloom. Shame upon me, that my trust is not always triumph; for whether Thou smite or smile, whether Thou come with sword or with the horn of plenty, Thou art my Savior still, and my portion.

August 25th — Much pain of body, but my soul strengthened afresh to trust my glorious Lord, and venture upon Him for time and eternity. My outward things are a cloud of perplexity to me, but not to my God. He sees the end from the beginning, and He will clear my way.

August 27th — I am far from well. The winter of last week's buffeting is over and gone, and the voice of the turtle is heard in my soul, proclaiming the love of the Holy Ones. Ezekiel 1:28, very sweet. The glory of the Lord is, indeed, in my soul, "as the appearance of the bow in the cloud in the day of rain"; it looks peace, and betokens safety. Also Lamentations 3:22, and Isaiah 54:8, 9, have smiled upon me. I could only weep tears of love and praise before my God. I could not ask anything, nor promise anything; but seemed a happy nothing in the glorious river of life, having nothing to do but to be absorbed in the wonders done for me by the great Three-One—the salvation planned, accomplished, and applied to my soul.

August 29th — I had a tooth extracted last evening. It was rather severe; but the strong cordial of divine love was a preparative. "Bless the Lord, O my soul"!

September 5th — How unexpected the events of this week! My kind friends, seeing me so much out of health, propose to take me with them to the sea-side next Monday. This great kindness has quite overcome me. I have committed it to the Lord.

September 7th, Sabbath — I am ready to depart on the morrow. "Not knowing what shall befall me there," I commit all to my covenant God and covenant Head, in whom I am chosen unto life and salvation, knowing all will be well. I have felt my thread of life may be short. Well, to depart and be with Jesus will be "far better."

September 10th — Bridlington Quay — Arrived here quite safely, through divine mercy. The God of Bethel had made provision.

September 14th — The Lord is truly gracious. He has met me here over and over again, and blessed me. He is the God of our Bethels, and of our Peniels; and we come to these places when we so little expect it. Truly, Thou art a God doing wonders.

October 12th — We arrived home safely on Friday, the 10th, with abundant cause for thanksgiving, on my part, to the God of my mercies.

October 25th, Saturday — In the past week I have had much spiritual darkness; and felt this evening that I was, as it were, in "the lion's den," and in the "mountain of leopards," through the felt evils of my fallen nature. When the Lord makes it night, all the beasts of the forest do creep forth; but, when the blessed Sun of Righteousness rises again, they creep into their dens, and hide themselves. How evil things do dislike the light.

October 26th, Sacrament Sabbath — Again have I sat at the Lord's table with mine own people. I can only plead the blood and righteousness of my Surety, and, by faith, cast all my debts upon Him. Most Holy Spirit, by Thy anointings, renew me in the simplicity which is in Christ. I wait for fresh power from on high. Much mercy since my last communion season. I want more melting of soul under what I receive. Lord, be pleased to guide my future path. Keep me from creature-snares of all sorts.

> "Weaker than a bruised reed,
> Help I every moment need."

Lord, renew faith, to live in emptiness upon Thy fullness; and oh, my precious Beloved, be revealed again in power as my all in all.

October 30th — I was much blessed to-night, in reading "Letters, &c., of Oliver Cromwell." "He, being dead, yet speaketh" to my heart, showing me how Christ must be all in all. He was but a man, and therefore not perfect; but evidently, to the spiritual mind, he was a "man in Christ," and hence the sweet savor that breathed in much that he said and wrote. This must be discernible to all who are in the secret of the Lord.

December 6th — I am much pleased with Ephesians 1:3, which is very full and precious to my soul. Blessed and praised indeed be our Father for such a store, and for such a store-house, and most of all for experience therein, or enjoyment thereof, under the anointings of the Holy Ghost.

December 14th — A few days ago, I discovered in this frail tabernacle a new sentence of death, the symptoms of which have, for the last few years, been lulled to sleep. Under these circumstances, I desire to give myself into Thy loving hands, my best Beloved, for all Thy will. To leave this sinful body is joyous, not grievous. But, oh, I feel piercing pain, that Thou hast been so little glorified in me. I fall blushingly at Thy dear feet, and loathe myself for my many abominations and shortcomings. And yet my heart seems to trust Thee, without fear, in the fearful disease which threatens me. I wonder at what I feel; but it is Thy perfect love which casts out tormenting fear. For life Thou art mine! For death Thou art mine! For eternity Thou art mine! Though I tremble at the article of death, Thou wilt order all about it, and will not fail or forsake me at the time of undressing. Oh, grant me renewings of faith by the Holy Ghost. Exceeding praise to Thee, my covenant God, for the great relief in my mind about temporal things; so that I can use what Thou hast provided, and leave the future to Thee. Thou broughtest me to this before I knew of this mortal disease. Oh, that I could praise Thee. Further, my gracious Lord, there seemed in Thy house, this morning, a sentence upon my soul-case, that I should now have to walk in darkness and felt distance. I ask if it was from Thee? If so, get glory to Thyself in the change. If it was not, I beseech Thee to "turn the counsel of Ahithophel into foolishness." Let my sentence come forth from Thy mouth. "I appeal unto Caesar"; I mean unto Thee, my God, the highest authority.

December 21st — This afternoon I have been reading a translation of the Psalms, by Romaine, which is very cordial-like to my soul, because therein my glorious Lord has so sweetly the pre-eminence. I do praise my God and King, who condescended to be born in the city of David, in the Church, His spiritual Zion. Most glorious One, I love Thee with Thine own love, the fire of which Thou hast kindled in my new heart. Thou, the First-born, art formed in the heart of all Thy younger children. "Christ in us the hope of glory." Because I feel this, I welcome Thee into this world of woe, into this flesh and blood (Heb. 2:14); and rejoice that "all my springs are in thee," "the word made flesh," in whom "all fullness dwells." "Crown Him Lord of all."

Christmas-day — Surely this is the happiest Christmas-day I ever had, though there is a thorn in my flesh.

December 28th, Sacrament-day — A softened spirit and melted heart at the Lord's table. My tears freely flowed under a sense of my unfaithfulness; but I trust my Lord's fruit was "sweet to my taste." Dearest Jesus! I find the leprosy in every part of my house, and therefore I desire to dwell in Thee, the House of the Lord, every day. Some high mountains are before me; but before thee, O Zerubbabel, they shall have become a plain: "not by might, nor by power, but by [Thy] Spirit, O Lord of hosts." For the mercies lately received, and that the dark sentence in my experience is not come to pass at present, I must erect a thankful Ebenezer! How do I long to be more fruitful to the praise of my redeeming Lord. Matthew 15:30 was very sweet last night. There are many spiritual cases I would thus bring by faith, and lay before my all-healing Savior.

December 31st — Another year is closing. To Thee, my God, be praise for all the peculiar mercies of 1851. But, oh, I want a touch of divine power to put my heart in tune!

> "Come, Holy Spirit, heavenly Dove,
> With all Thy quick'ning powers."

Set my mercies in a bright light before me, that my heart may dissolve in love and thankfulness. None can have greater cause than I to praise my gracious God; but yet my spirit is a little drooping, not for want of anything on earth, but I want a fresh blessed anointing from the Holy One, our sacred High Priest, from whose head it descends to me, the lowest of His members. Oh, adorable Lord, do anoint Thy worm with "fresh oil." May the beauty of the Lord our God be upon His Church. "Peace be within thy walls, and prosperity within thy [living] palaces. For my brethren and companions' sakes, I will now say, Peace be within thee."

1852

January 6th — I have had a rich feast this evening in hearing Mr. S—, from Song 4. Gladly would I have returned to earth no more. My soul did glow as he described the glory of my beloved Lord; and did swell with rapture while he described the harmony above echoing and re-echoing, "Worthy is the Lamb! Worthy is the Lamb!" Again I feel the blessedness of union, and that I dwell in the married land: "Thy Maker is thine Husband; the Lord of Hosts is His name."

January 18th, Sabbath — On Friday evening I was informed that the French were likely to invade our dear country. My heart was much moved at the thought of a Popish power, or, perhaps, an infidel one, I knew not which. Our little evening meeting was solemn. We pleaded with the Lord that He would be on our side. But oh, how I felt our guiltiness, in giving liberty to Papists in the midst of us. For this I "blush to lift up my face to thee, my God." We do deserve judgment, but ask for mercy, in the name of Jesus.

February 1st — My heart much comforted concerning the threatened invasion of our country. My eyes are up to the Lord; and, if He be for us, it will not matter what thousands are against us. "Whoso putteth his trust in the Lord shall be safe." I trust the peace of God is caused to rule in my heart through Christ Jesus.

March 7th, Sabbath — My soul has been convicted by my Lord of heart-wanderings. He used Ezekiel 16, turning me to it again and again. I pleaded guilty, but was not broken down until this morning, when my soul was melted, and humbled, and ashamed beyond expression. Oh, to dishonor such love, or ever turn from such a Savior! Glorious Lord, pardon and restore vile, vile me! I know Thou changest not, and I fall into Thy arms of injured love, to accept whatever punishment Thou shalt appoint.

March 8th — Noah, and those with him, entered into the Ark, because of the waters of the flood; and so I desire by faith to go into Christ, because of the waters of temptation which now assail me.

March 21st, Sabbath — My mind has been much exercised this last week by a remark about the liberty of soul which I enjoy. What anguish has this caused, with "strong crying and tears" to the Lord, not to condemn me to experimental banishment from His presence. I may deserve it; but I plead for Jesus' sake. Surely there is grace and liberty enough in Jesus. Dear Lord, save me from what I fear. Outward things I leave with Thee, only asking that situation and those circumstances in which I can have most of Thee. Oh, pardon what is wrong! I do not covet trials; but I do covet Thy sweet, blessed company. I have had some words of encouragement; one, Romans 14:4, last part. O Lord, to Thee have I revealed my cause.

March 25th — I have been walking in much heaviness from the remark made, which has entered like iron into my soul. But I was comforted this morning from Psalm 81:9, 10, 15, 16; Isaiah 58:17, 18. Attended a prayer-meeting, last evening, at —, for one who is near death, and in great distress of soul. The brethren pleaded very sweetly. I think the power of the Lord was present. May the bound one be loosed.

March 28th, Sacrament-day — A day of conflict; but my precious Jesus is the same in the battle as at the banquet. In Jesus I may triumph, though my enemy thrust sore at me. Reading the "Letters of Anne Dutton" has been very confirming to me. She was taught the way of faith, which the Lord alone taught me. I want renewing in it, by the power of the Holy Ghost. I have been sorely harassed by wandering thoughts, so that I could get no fixedness of meditation. At the table of the Lord I cast myself upon Jesus for deliverance. He performeth all things for me. If He put me in the furnace, there is a needs be; it will be all love, and I may safely welcome it; and, if He slay me, safely trust Him still. The enemy suggests, "But perhaps it is for sin." Well, if it is for sin, still I must trust Him, who alone can remove it. Sin must not make me hide myself and my case from the Sin-Bearer. That were the way to let sin grow strong, and give Satan an advantage. I must walk openly with my Beloved, in my worst moments as well as in my best. The dying person is brought again into joy and peace by the faithful God. When I heard it, these words came with power, "Not for your sakes do I this." Ah, no; it is for His holy name's sake. How this does lay all creatures in the dust. The painful words to which I have referred are still like a barbed arrow in my heart. Only Jesus, my sweet Savior, can extract it, and heal the wound. Mr. B— departed this life at a quarter to seven this evening. Thus one pilgrim after another lays the staff and sandals by, to sleep quietly in their bed of dust till the morning without clouds, when they shall awake up with His likeness, and be satisfied.

March 31st, Evening — Much trial of soul these three days. Wind and tide contrary. Much crying to the Lord about the remark of my friend. How could I live if banished from Christ? Same melting this morning from 2 Kings 8, concerning the Shunammite, who hath her land restored;

verses 5 and 6. Jesus is my land, and I am crying for full restoration to Him. My glorious Redeemer, I cannot believe Thou wilt condemn me to absence and gloom, when my whole soul, and every particle of happiness, is bound up in Thee. I do deserve the worst Thou canst inflict; but, oh, for love's sake, let me see Thy loving frown, and feel Thy loving stripe, but not find Thee gone. Thy absence is hell to the heart that has seen Thy glorious charms, and felt Thy matchless love. Oh, do not, do not leave me; and do not let me leave Thee!

April 3rd, Saturday — I have been much edified by again reading "Anne Dutton"; and, though still much in the dark, I have great longings for the activity and strengthening of faith. I feel as if the Lord dare not trust me with much manifestation at present; but my soul has been arrested by Luke 23:17. I thought, to-morrow is the gospel feast. Oh, for the release of the prisoner! I then saw who was released; not the holy, immaculate Jesus, but the guilty Barabbas. Ah, and it is guilty I who wants to be released from felt-bonds, on the very ground that the guiltless Savior suffered in my stead. Pilate might strive to release Him, because of His personal innocence; but He stood under responsibilities which neither Pilate nor the Jews knew anything about. He was Surety for debts; and now was the time of payment—the price His precious blood and His precious life.

> "What wondrous love—what mysteries,
>   In this appointment shine:
> My breaches of the law are His,
>   And His obedience mine!"

April 4th, Sabbath — My soul laid in the dust this morning. I went to the house of the Lord, saying, "I am the guilty Barabbas"; and, feeling as vile as he, I could not plead for sweet indulgences of divine favor, fearing I should misuse them; but my heart just felt, "Thy will be done." I heard Mr. J— this morning, from John 15:1, 2, with profit. He spoke of the need of pruning the branches and I felt it very good.

April 8th —
   "When on the cross my Lord I see,
   Bleeding to death for wretched me,
   Satan and sin no longer move,
   For I am all transfixed with love."

March 9th, Good Friday Morning — I have tender remembrances of Thee, O holy Redeemer, my suffering, atoning Lord. May I be closeted with Thee this day, and learn more of Thy matchless love, in Thy bitter agonies for my vile sin. *Afternoon* — A few mornings since I awoke with Hosea 2:15; and this morning Mr. — pleaded it in his prayer. My soul has a hope that the conflict, tears, and prayers, which have been caused by the late painful trial, may issue thus. I think there has been profit therefrom. Dear Lord, Thou readest all my heart; pity, compassionate, and renew in me a life of faith.

April 14th — A day of conflict. Some one says, "Walking beside a smooth stream, on a bright day, we may see the sun clearly reflected; but throw a stone into the water, and it will no longer faithfully reflect the image of the sun." It is thus when temptations or trials suddenly disturb the soul. This heart has felt the truth of it. But Jesus remains unchanged, however our views and thoughts of Him may be obscured.

April 18th, Sabbath — I went to the house of God in much fear of being turned from faith to sense by the ministry I expected. I was led to plead two words which the Lord gave me years ago on this subject. One was Ruth

2:9: the young men are the reapers, answerable to ministers; the other word was 2 Samuel 9:7. How earnestly did my soul desire the dear Lord to remember these words, "upon which He caused me to hope," and to which He has indeed been faithful. When there, I opened upon Isaiah 54, and found power in the four last verses as an answer to my cry. I am sure the Lord has brought me into liberty; and, although it be a bondage-day, my soul pants and longs to be kept from entanglement. Those who are in Egypt, or in the wilderness experience, are not under the same rule as those that have crossed the Jordan, and are dwelling in Christ by faith. Wherefore, let us not judge one another; but "whereto we have already attained, let us walk by the same rule," living in love, and pressing after the things which are before. *Night* — I have had much close waiting upon the Lord for my own soul-case. Psalm 81:10, seems to have been given several times. Thus have I encouragement to faith, though not the response of love from my Beloved. Lord, enlarge me to open my mouth wider.

April 19th — This word very sweet this afternoon: "I will make the dry tree to flourish." It just fits me; but this morning, at family prayer, a blessed gleam came, turning my soul to Christ, and showing that He is to be the plea, not my emptiness and need. This evening these words very sweet: "And the tabernacle shall be sanctified by my glory." The glory of Jesus sparkling in all its vessels, sacrifices, and services; He being the fullness of all. "Moses wrote of me."

April 22nd — I heard Mr. C— this evening, from Proverbs 22:20, 21. How very precious was the word to my soul. The redeemed earth did "drink water of the rain of heaven." Mr. C— does not turn us back into our own feelings for comfort, but leads straight out, and straight on, to the Person and work of Jesus. The other day, when reading Luke 24:31, where I always regret that Jesus should depart the moment His disciples knew Him, a sweet beam shone into my soul, showing that His departure was to teach them that they were not to live by sight now, but by faith, and that manifestations were to be short and occasional; but that faith was to continue, being constantly renewed by the Holy Ghost. He came, that they might see and be comforted; then went, that they might believe and be established.

April 25th, Sacrament-day — I heard Mr. P— this evening, from Isaiah 22:20. He spoke of Zion in the sufferings and death of her King; in the call, work, and soul-travail of her ministers, and in the heart-experience of her children. Then of the "quiet habitation," peace in the soul with God, through the blood of the Lamb. Then the tabernacle, which, he said, was the humanity of Jesus. Our tabernacle will be taken down, but that will remain for ever. 2 Corinthians 5:1 was quoted. He also spoke of the stakes as believers, and of the cords as the love of the Triune Jehovah. This I blessedly feel. Oh, make mine eye single, that my whole body may be full of light. Make me follow Thee wholly, that I may "not walk in darkness, but have the light of life." Sanctify the pain and weakness I constantly feel in my body; let all that befalls me glorify Thee. Oh, reveal Thyself; for this I long, more than words can express. Thy rising glories in Bethlehem, the bright glories of Thy holy life, Thy setting glory in Gethsemane and Calvary. Oh, how I long to re-visit the sacred scenes under divine anointings! Oh, bow the heavens, and rend all that is a cloud between me and Thee. I ask it for Thy great name and love's sake.

April 27th — I again feel the sentence of death in my body, as on December 14th. Let it be a medium of communion with Thee and my soul, and be Thou magnified in my body, by life or death.

May 9th — I have been much longing to lean on Jesus' bosom experimentally, as John did literally. Divine love is the very element of my soul.

May 12th — Some kind friends propose a journey to Beaumaris. The Lord reward them, and show us the right way.

May 23rd — It just beams powerfully upon my mind, that the more we live upon things seen, the more we shall be filled with worldliness; the more we live upon self, the more we shall be perplexed with its workings; the more we live upon Christ, the more we shall be filled with Christ, and the two former will be subdued. The Lord has ordained laws, as in natural so in spiritual life. He has appointed that food shall be received to strengthen the body, and Christ to strengthen the soul that has been quickened into life by the Spirit. All our victory over the first Adam nature is in the second. Therefore, no health or vigor of soul, excepting as faith has much to do with Him! Faith is certainly not in the power of the creature; but He who gives spiritual life, gives power also to perform the functions of that life: as in eating, John 6:53, 56; looking, Hebrews 12:2; working, John 6:29, Ephesians 2:10; walking, Colossians 2:6; fighting, Ephesians 6:11, 12, &c.; in all of which exercises, the Scriptures show the activity of faith on and upon a precious Jesus. It is true, indeed, the babe in Christ cannot eat, walk, &c.; therefore, for them, is gospel milk of precious promises, and the "breasts of her consolation"; and when the enjoyment for a time of these is withholden, there is much fretting; knowing only the life of spiritual sense at present; but, as there is growth into Christ (Eph. 4:15), He increasing, we decreasing, we come to live, not merely upon manifestation, but upon Christ Himself, by the faith of Him, under the renewings of the Holy Ghost. And, though our fallen flesh, like the city of Jericho, is under the curse, yet Christ is like the salt cast into the spring, to bring forth health and fruitfulness, by subduing the works of the flesh, and bringing forth the fruits of the Spirit (Phil. 1:11).

Friday, May 28th — Matthew 28:7 and 10 were specially applied, in reference to our journey. Lord, "do as thou hast said." Meet us in that strange place, and let us see Thee there, to the joy of our hearts.

May 30th — I am encouraged in the love of a Triune Jehovah: the Father giving the Son, and bruising Him; the Son giving Himself to the bruising; and the Holy Spirit testifying of Him, and applying His merits and blood. Here my soul feeds in green pastures with thanksgiving and praise. Lord, enlarge poor Japheth further to dwell in the tents of this glorious Shem. Let who will condemn, the Lord has taught me the privilege and victory of living out of self by faith, and by faith living in Christ, the good Land. Ready to depart on the morrow for Wales. I would lovingly go forth in the name and strength of my glorious Husband, and seek that He would be "a covering of the eyes to me," to those with me, and to all others I may meet. Thus veiled, I would go forth to know nothing but my glorious Christ, and Him crucified for me.

Beaumaris, June 1st — Last evening we arrived safely, through the tender mercies of our covenant God. The first word that was given me here was, "He hath been mindful of us: He will bless us." Lord, "do as thou hast said."

June 6th, Afternoon — We cannot hear the sound of the gospel this day, for all the preaching is in Welsh; but the Lord has made it a blessed day. I had deep soul exercise in the night, and much humbling work, under which I pleaded guilty; and this morning have felt sweetly how the Lord does dwell in the broken and contrite heart, and how He alone can give the brokenness. As I gazed upon the mountains just opposite our window, I had sweet musings upon a precious Christ, whose immaculate feet trod the mountains of Judea. I was favored with nearness and communion, and realized the fulfillment of the Lord's promise, given the Friday before we came. Matthew 28:7, 10. This word was sweet this morning, "The Lord thy God turned the curse into a blessing"; and, "He that hath the bride is the bridegroom." How thankful I am to meet my Beloved in this strange place.

June 18th — In great mercy we were safely brought home yesterday. Oh, for more gratitude and power to praise!

June 23rd — "And now, Lord, what wait I for? my hope is in thee." Returned home in peace, I now want fresh anointings of the Spirit for work or warfare, as Thou shalt appoint. I am a poor creature. Oh, keep me looking to Jesus, and following closely after Him!

June 27th, Sabbath Morning — "The diligent soul shall be made fat"; "They that seek me early shall find me." Dear Lord, please to give me the grace of diligence, and of early seeking Thee. *Five o'clock* — It is Sacrament-day. I have had some dear remembrance of a crucified Savior. "My body broken for you"; "My blood shed for you." Here is personality. Much savor in Ruth 4:10. Jesus, the heavenly Boaz, and I the gift of His Father, the purchase of His blood, and the conquest of His love.

July 25th, Sacrament-day — A day of humiliation before the Lord, and deep abasement on account of sin. I fly to Thy blood, and cleave to the crucified One. Union remains unaltered; but, indeed, I abhor myself, in dust and ashes, for "I have fallen by mine iniquity." Some close soul exercise at the table. Only in Thy sight have I committed evil; oh, make me to hear the forgiving word, and give me to receive instruction by this thing. Much blessing during the past month: to the Lord be praise: "shame and confusion of face" belong to unworthy me.

July 30th, Friday — Isaiah 26:3. I have been to the Refuge; and oh, what a pleading spirit was given me with those girls: "my mouth was filled with arguments." Since I was last there, one girl has been removed by death, of whose safety the matron had no doubt; she had been in the house about two years, and was quite dark, spiritually, when she came in. "Is not this a brand plucked out of the fire?" To the Lord be the praise!

August 15th — Yesterday I was much cast down in not hearing any tidings of dear C—, who has been paying me a nice visit. He had gone away by a fresh railway, and I feared all was not right; but, after looking up to the Lord, there was sealed upon my heart a sweet assurance that all was well, and this morning I have a letter to say all is well. I call it only an echo of the Lord's message, for He brought the tidings first, and set my heart at rest. This is a dreary land, and I a trembling traveller; but the Lord is very gracious to His "sparrow alone." I want supporting, like the ivy which clings round the oak. Lord, lead me, but do not leave me.

September 5th, Sabbath Morning — I have been much tried lately how to know and do the Lord's will in little things. As, for instance, when a friend wants me to go anywhere, and I feel pre-occupied. Must I consider my own convenience, or must I quite give it up, and take every invitation, or wish of others, as from the Lord? Or how must I discern? I earnestly desire to walk with God, but seem to make many mistakes. While waiting before the Lord just now, these words came with sweetness, "Commit thy way unto the Lord, and he shall bring it to pass." Also Psalm 55:22, Proverbs 10:29, and Psalm 56:13, which were very applicable. I wait for further light.

September 12th — A friend was conversing with me last evening, and spoke of the many different denominations of Christians in this day. Soon after came to my mind, with guiding power, "God hath in these last days spoken unto us by his Son." It was timely and sweet, showing I must cleave closely to Jesus, and leave outward forms alone. By Him my Father hath spoken to me, and said in my soul, "Hear ye him." Lord, keep me from every strange voice.

September 26th — I have been suffering in a very unusual way from headache, and am quite unable to grasp a subject, or meditate with clearness. It has distressed me, but "I know whom I have believed"; and however, through infirmity I may not be able to apprehend Him, He apprehends me still, in love and power, for salvation; and is able and willing to "keep that which I have committed unto him until that day" when He will "present me faultless in the presence of His glory, with exceeding joy." Trust Him, O my soul!

October 6th — I have been praising the Lord for tribulation. I do feel it good, though not pleasant to the flesh. But how Revelation 7:14, reconciles to John 16:33! I am earnestly longing for more outgoings of faith upon Jesus by the power of the Spirit.

October 31st — On Friday evening we had a choice meeting. Isaiah 55 was read, and ver. 13 sweetly sealed upon my heart as my portion; that, through union to Him, Jesus will bring the evergreens, instead of the thorns, which have lately distressed me so much. Satan fights hard against me, to turn my eye from Jesus. It is a sore struggle, but the Lord is on my side, and He will prevail. He has often, the last week, made my cup run over with spiritual joy—still keeping me empty in myself, and glorying only in Him.

November 14th — Surely I know something of recumbency in divine love. I am "dead to the law, by the body of Christ"; "Sin is not imputed where there is no law"; "He that is dead is freed from sin." Here is the blessedness of one "to whom the Lord will not impute sin"; "ye are complete in Him." Can anything be added to such comeliness? Here is ugliness gone, and beauty come, through union to the Lamb. My feelings are indescribable; such stillness pervades the soul in finding all in Christ.

November 24th — No rent yet. I am still kept in suspense about it; every post-time seems a fresh disappointment; and this morning it has been sharp, and my heart sinks anew. I cried to be kept from a murmuring feeling, knowing all is right. And, surely, my soul has been brought to kiss the hand that holds the rod, and cleave closer to Him who is thus trying me.

November 26th — I saw a dying saint yesterday, lingering on the banks of Jordan; but, though in a painful state of body, she is kept very peaceful. She said, "I have been thinking, 'the lines are fallen unto me in pleasant places; yea, I have a goodly heritage.'" My own temporal case is still pending; my eyes are up unto the Lord; the vision tarries long; things are very pressing. Dearest Lord, be pleased to make Thy meaning plain in the present trial; and make my heart perfect with Thee through all wilderness discipline.

November 30th — The Lord is faithful; and what He promised that He does perform; nor can all our fears and faintings hinder it. This day the rent has come from town, and I have paid mine here: to the Lord be all the glory! It is not in vain to wait for Him; but, oh, how hard to flesh and blood. Ebenezer! And now, my dear Lord, I crave more revealings of Thy precious, glorious Person. I find to-day a fresh sentence of death in my mortal frame. I consecrate this threatening malady to Thee; let it be Thy chariot, in which Thou wilt come to me, and I to Thee; let it be—

"An opening door; and let me fly,
And build my happy nest on high."

December 15th — Yesterday I saw the dying sister; she was sensible, but breathing painfully, and could not speak. I left her about half-past three; and, between six and seven, her spirit was released.

December 16th — Dear departed one, how little can we conceive thy joy. "Present with the Lord." Probably, I too, before very long, shall cross the Jordan: my Savior, come then, or how shall I do in the swellings thereof? Jesus is felt to be very precious in believing this week: no praise to me. The actings of a living faith are by divine power; be it mine to entreat for them: all the glory, Lord, be thine. Mr. H— has again put a letter of mine into the "Gospel Magazine," without my knowing. A sharp cross to my flesh is this, but I dare not draw back; having done so in 1842, in the same thing, to my cost. Dear Lord, it seems impossible Thou canst speak through me to any profit. But here I am, Thy very own; if Thou please to bring me forth only to abase me, it shall be well, if Thou wilt be glorified.

Christmas-day — I have had sweetness in Acts 2:38; and much in Isaiah 60:19, 20. Oh, what a narrow path I have to walk in: Lord, hold Thou me up, and I shall be safe; let me not fear to acknowledge what Thou hast done for me.

> "Behold! my soul at freedom set:
> My surety paid the dreadful debt."

December 26th, Sacrament-day — I heard Mr. H— most preciously this morning, from these words, "Jesus only" (Matt. 17:8). Surely, I could experimentally subscribe to all he said; my soul was satisfied with marrow and fatness. This afternoon I had a good time at the Lord's table; and do desire to go forth with "Jesus only." It is safe and blessed, although many who admit it in their judgment that He is all in salvation, do, in experience, seem to put it away as a thing not to be known here below. Well, my blessed Lord, the secret is between my soul and Thee. It was Thyself taught me this privilege of love; and afresh I give myself to Thee, that the last little inch of my life may be "Jesus only." What glory I see herein! I do experimentally find that nothing is so subduing, humbling, and emptying to me, as going on with Jesus all, and "Jesus only." I have had great mercies the past month. The painful have been profitable; and for many things mortifying to the flesh I have feelingly thanked the Lord. Am I coming to Marah? Blessed Spirit, cast into the bitter waters a branch of the "tree of life," and I shall then drink with praise. Christ in the affliction will be a blessing.

1853

January 1st, New Year's Morning — Oh, my Father, bless me, and make me a blessing this year. I ask, in the name of Jesus, for more unctuous entrance into Thy Scriptures, more anointing of the Spirit, more communion with a Tri-une Jehovah, in union to Immanuel. *Night, 11 o'clock* — Though weak and weary, I must record a sweet new year's visit from my Lord this evening, at the family altar, wherein again I feel His exceeding preciousness, and can feelingly say, "Thou art altogether lovely." Thus have I already got a new song this year.

January 16th — I have been depressed, because I see not my tokens. It seems as if I lived a useless, profitless life. I was much blessed this afternoon in Genesis 15:17. It seemed to me that the smoking furnace was a type of the iron furnace of Egypt, where Abraham's seed were in cruel bondage; the burning lamp a type of the divine guidance they should have out of Egypt, and thence to Canaan. These two passed through the pieces, which was a token of the covenant, and seemed to show that all the circumstances of Egyptian bondage, wilderness travel, and divine teaching, were ordered in the covenant, and so covenant blessings. This, spiritualized as to the children of promise, was very sweet. Then I sought something touching my own present soul-case, and it seemed powerfully given in these words, "This also we wish, even your perfection." Here Christ was afresh set before me as my perfection in doctrine, experience, and practice; He as the fullness of it all, and, as brought by the Spirit to apprehend Him by faith, it will make me neither barren nor unfruitful in the work of the Lord.

January 18th — Oh, how has my soul sunk within me in fear and trembling, lest, in the midst of all my varied occupations, I should lose "the piece" of silver—the assurance of faith; lest I should have to say, "While I was busy here and there, He was gone." My Savior withdraw to a distance? Oh, I cannot bear the thought! Seclusion, poverty, anything with Jesus; but life is death without Him.

January 29th, Sacrament-day — "I will sing unto the Lord"; for that which hath been set upon His table is full of fatness. Mr. S— preached this morning from Deuteronomy 33:8. He took the text spiritually, in reference to our glorious Christ; and, in explaining the name of Levi, which means joined, he said many things which had been opened to my soul some months since, from Malachi 2:4, 5, causing me to rejoice greatly in this "Joined One," who is one with His Father, and one with His Church. When Mr. S— was concluding his sermon this morning, it occurred to me, sweetly, that the Lord's people were a tribe of Levis; every believer is a joined one, for "He that is joined to the Lord is one spirit"; and "we are members of His body, of His flesh, and of His bones." I was blessed in hearing, but still wrestling with the Lord for more; it was not a cup running over. Sensible enjoyments have run in a lower channel for the most part lately, which exciteth longing and jealousy. My Beloved has seemed "behind the wall," and only looked through the lattice, instead of full, personal communion. I was blessed at the Lord's table more than for some time past. The dignity of that precious Sufferer, and His mightiness to endure, were a little set forth in my soul. He was a royal person, even when made a curse; and the "mighty God" when He stooped to the dust of death, or He never could have taken its sting away.

March 6th, Sacrament-day — I have had my mind much distressed in hearing of the apparent dishonesty of one whom I thought a brother in Christ; "Lord, what is man that Thou art mindful of Him?" What an impure mass is the whole human race as found in the fallen head—evil, and only evil. My heart saddens continually at the sin and sorrow I hear of, which makes me groan in my secret places, and long to be away from the body of sin, and the world of guilt and woe. Lord, if this man be Thy child, send an arrow of conviction into his soul, humble him in the dust, and restore him to the good and right way. If he be a hypocrite in Sion, let fearfulness surprise him, the mask fall off, and salvation yet reach him, if Thy holy will. Lord, keep the feet of Thy saints from the paths of the destroyer! Oh, hold us in Thy ways, order our footsteps in Thy word, and "let not any iniquity have dominion over us."

March 8th — Surely unfixedness of thought has been like a "fiery furnace" to me for some months. Perhaps this thing has come upon me in reproof for some unknown sin—perhaps some lightness of spirit, or something else. I remember the calf which was ground to powder by Moses, for the children of Israel to drink. I have formerly known this bitter experience, when the sin I had trifled with became my daily and sorrowful portion, nor could I rid myself of it. Oh, this is sore work. "Lord, help me," though I feel I am not worthy of the crumbs which fall from Thy table!

March 10th — I have taken counsel in my heart to fast till tea-time to-morrow—fasting before the Lord, and waiting upon Him to find favor in His sight, and an answer of peace on several pressing accounts, and my own soul-case of unfixedness of thought, which distresses me so much. Oh, my precious Savior! I want Thee to have all my heart, and all my thoughts; do take what is Thine own. Also, I want to plead that my dear Lord will be specially present and precious in the bodily affliction which seems to threaten me; also for our country, and for Thy Church; for an outpouring of the Spirit, and for some hard cases which are on my mind. I have much fear lest weariness of the flesh, and languor of spirit, should prevent close dealing with the Lord. I feel to-night like a broken vessel. May the Holy Spirit help my infirmities, and plead in me. While thinking of the matter, a suggestion came, how vain it would be to put aside my work, and be thus occupied; but this word followed, "Them that honor me I will honor." Lord, cause me to honor Thee in my fasts and my feasts. Lord, give me power to plead with Thee. I would wait like Esther; like her, may I be called to touch the sceptre, and gain my request. I do feel helpless: may it be "out of weakness made strong." Amen. In the midst of my fears, I must confess, to the Lord's praise, that hitherto He has always helped me; and that it will be the first time if He now stands "aloof from my sore." *Half-past Ten* — "The valley of Achor shall be a place for the herds to lie down in"; and, "The valley of Achor for a door of hope."

March 11th, Morning —
> "Lord, I come before Thee now,
> At Thy feet I humbly bow;
> Lord, do not my suit disdain,
> Nor let me seek Thy face in vain."

Our God is very gracious—yea, and very merciful; and I feel it, in that I am not straitened or bound in approaching Him, but have permission to speak, who am but dust and ashes. Lord, hear and answer, for Thine own name's sake. I want more power and deeper humiliation in my feelings. *After Tea* — I have great cause to praise the Lord for upholding me during my exercise before Him. About three o'clock I was sorely cast down, thinking all was in vain, because I did not feel a sensible answer in my soul. For a short time my grief was very great, but "when the enemy came in like a flood, the Spirit of the Lord did lift up a standard (of the Word) against him" in this sweet portion, "As the Father hath loved me, even so have I loved you: continue ye in my love." It was like oil upon the waves of my troubled soul, producing a great calm. And to the love of Jesus I did commit my petition—pleading for many others and for myself; desiring that His blood might be upon all. Blessed be the Lord, who hath not turned away my petitions, or His mercy from me. Dear Lord, send answers of peace and power. While before the Lord, I thought of the precious Savior, when He fasted forty days and forty nights, and fought that fierce but bloodless battle, with our great foe; and it seemed to the spiritual eye as if the wilderness was strewed over with the broken shafts of hell, and arrows of the mighty, which had been hurled at our great Champion, and by Him repelled and broken. Every weapon that hell could devise was tried, but all were in vain; and now there are no new ones to bring against the Church. Satan can only assail her with those which her Lord has already blunted and spoiled—yea, written "conquered" upon them all. Dear, redeeming Lord, this view encourages this trembling heart in this time of conflict.

March 20th, Sabbath — Again the Lord has graciously come forth as the answerer of prayer, to the joy of many. This morning it was announced, that those persecuted believers in Tuscany—the Madiai—are set at liberty from prison, and we are to have a thanksgiving meeting on Thursday. Much prayer has been made for them, and it is indeed new encouragement to pour out our heart before the Lord, however hard and difficult the case may appear. Ebenezer! *Night* — Before service this evening, I was musing on the Lord's mercy in answering prayer about the Madiai, when there came a sweet encouragement to my soul, that He would also graciously answer about my —, for whose salvation I have prayed, and groaned, and travailed heavily for years. Lord, do as Thou hast said. Mr. T— preached from Acts 13:38, in which I feel a sweetness I never did before. Through the heart of this precious Man—Christ Jesus—comes every covenant blessing to unworthy me.

March 22nd — Much enlarged into Christ in writing to Mr. T— to-day. How often has that correspondence been a blessing to my soul. I have felt somewhat of the blessedness of dwelling upon Mount Hermon, "where God commands the blessing—even life for evermore." I have seen, that, though for some time "the iniquity of my heels" has compassed me about, in those wandering thoughts which have so distressed me, yet I am safe from condemnation, because that very iniquity compassed my precious Jesus about first, when He felt the substance of those words which were prophetically spoken of Him (Ps. 40:12). He called His people's sin His own, because He had taken their place in law, and "the Lord laid upon him the iniquity of us all." Thus I am free from sin in Christ, and I have afresh blessedly felt this freedom; and, though I dwell in dust, have afresh been made to rise and sing unto the Lord, for mercy and judgment—judgment to Jesus, and mercy to me—to the glory of a Triune Jehovah. Oh, it is wonderful! Blessed are they to whom "the Lord will not impute sin." Dear Lord, let me into the sweet secret of which I have tasted a little, and find such celestial flavor, debasing the creature and exalting a glorious Christ.

March 25th, Good Friday — I love to meditate upon what this day commemorates, for the Lord does at times make the keeping of it a door of communion to my soul. It is now between one and two, and the sun is shining beautifully; but, on that solemn day when Jesus suffered, it withdrew its beams from this guilty earth, refusing to enliven that scene so shrouded in gloom, so darkened with sin, curse, wrath, and suffering, when the Lamb without blemish, the Antitype of the Paschal, was offered "once for all," and by that one offering entirely put away sin from His Church. Oh, the agonies He endured when His righteous soul was made sin; when "He was bruised for our iniquities." I would now, in spirit, sit at the foot of that cross, and learn more and more deeply and experimentally the mysteries thereof. Only those who eat the Paschal supper here with bitter herbs shall sit down at the Marriage-supper with everlasting joy. This word is sweet to me, "He turneth the shadow of death into the morning." Our blessed Surety had the substance and sting of death; and what He so endured is turned into a spiritual morning to us, because by it our deliverance comes.

March 27th, Sacrament-day — "Peninnah had children, but Hannah had no children." How this word has sounded in my heart this morning. It is just like — and me, spiritually; she is made useful to souls, and I am a poor barren thing, not knowing that one has been called through me. It says that Elkanah gave to Hannah "a worthy portion," and this is spiritually true of me. "The Lord is my portion, saith my soul." I do rejoice in Him, though the least and most insignificant of His members. I was much blessed the other day in seeing Psalm 89:32, fully applicable to Christ, as shown out in 1 Peter 2:24. He was the Surety, and He had the stripes; and coming to realize this in faith, heals sin's malady in its guilt and power more than anything else, because it is God's own way. O

"Abba Father," I humbly beg for the spirit of wisdom and revelation in the knowledge of Jesus, and of Thee in Him.

> "Prove His wounds each day more healing,
> And Himself more deeply know."

The threatening symptoms of disease have seemed to abate. I have no liberty to speak of the matter, excepting to my dear Lord. I have no wish He should remove it, but that He would come in it, and sanctify it, and glorify Himself. I commit it all to my precious Savior, who "Himself took our infirmities, and carried our sicknesses."

April 17th — From weak nerves and unfixedness of thought I am unable to meditate closely, but I am sure my soul is fixed all the while on my covenant God, and my precious Savior. This want of power to think is mine infirmity, Thou, Lord, knowest. My heart says, "Whom have I in heaven but thee? and there is none upon earth I desire beside thee." Amidst all I am suffering, the Lord seems strongly confirming me in the doctrines of grace. Exceeding light and power keep breaking in upon my soul upon the divine sovereignty, and the majestic holiness, love, and glory of Jehovah, are increasingly revealed. Thus, though tempest-tossed, I am safe; and I think I shall soon be at home—in the haven of rest.

April 24th — I have been unexpectedly called to visit Miss G—, in consumption. I saw her on Friday; she was in great distress, fearing she had been deceived. During conversation she said, "I fear I do not feel sin enough; that it is only from a dread of punishment. I cannot pray; I can't believe." I saw her again yesterday; she was more comfortable. I read Zechariah 3, in which she seemed deeply interested.

April 27th — I had a nice time again, with Miss G—; she is rather better. I trust it was profitable. I read Mark 5. In speaking I referred to Isaiah 13:2; in reading which I was struck with verse 3, and told her of some different explanations I had heard. When I had finished, Miss G— said, "How singular you should speak of that verse; we were so wondering what it meant."

May 27th — When thinking of a proposed journey to Scotland, I had much trembling about travelling by the express train, but last evening the Lord gave me a sweet assurance of safety, and this morning Psalm 139. We are not going to "the uttermost parts of the earth," but we are going far away; yet, even there Thy right hand shall keep, and guide, and hold me up, O my God.

Edinburgh, May 31st — Ebenezer! Through divine mercy, we find ourselves located, for a short time, in this great city, to which we were safely brought last evening, about half-past eight. Great was the Lord's mercy in protecting, and He kindly communed with me in the night-watches, so that I did sing, and weep, and bless my loving Lord. Oh, for faith to live in all the fullness of Jesus.

June 8th — The first minister I heard here was on Thursday evening, Mr. M. S—. A word in season to my soul, from Ephesians 1:11. He was speaking much on the subjugation of the will in us, which was just what the Lord was instructing me about on Monday night. Oh, to learn the lesson! There is one dear saint in this house, and we have together been holding intercourse with the King, while all the rest were in bed.

June 20th — I "am ready to depart on the morrow." The Lord has been bountiful and gracious to my soul in this place. I have been favored with the communion of saints, with the King of saints. I have had some severe exercise also, according to that saying, "Day and night shall not cease"; it is also written, "Because they have no changes, therefore they fear not God"; but, indeed—

> "My soul through many changes goes,
> His love no variation knows,"

And "Now, Lord, what wait I for?" "My eyes are up unto thee," for a parting blessing, and for journeying mercies on the coming day.

June 23rd — Ebenezer! I was favored with a safe journey; and my dear Lord did let me feel His presence by the way, and spoke to me by His holy Scriptures: praise Him, O my soul! I felt peace of soul on arriving at my sweet little home. I am *in Jesus* as safe as I can be, and very happy: a sinner saved by grace; free grace and free love is all my theme.

June 26th — Scotland was a place of royal dainties to my soul: may the Lord pour out His Spirit upon His people there. He is still fulfilling to me Isaiah 43:16; and I desire to be still learning His will to the subduing of my own.

July 3rd — I have been to see Miss G— for the first time since my return. I think her not so well. My spirit feels refreshed with a comfortable hope that she is a vessel of mercy.

July 10th — Again I find a blessing in taking up the cross. I sought deliverance *from* it; but I find the Lord had placed deliverance *in* it; praised be His name for not letting me escape, and turn away from the blessing.

August 15th — "The earth is the Lord's, and the fullness thereof"; why, then, are so many of His people poor? To draw out their faith upon Him; to show forth His marvellous works; and because this world is neither their home nor their portion. It is all right, and I feel it so. We need not be in abject poverty to be in pecuniary straits, as those who have small incomes well know; for they often "see the works of the Lord, and His wonders in the deep." A life of faith is a life of miracles, temporal and spiritual.

September 3rd — "Out of the depths have I cried unto Thee, O Lord." In addition to outward trial, there is deep inward conflict. Under an agonizing sense of unprofitableness, there seems to come a blight upon everything I touch: oh, it is bitter! I have not a doubt of my precious Savior's love, but I feel as if all else is torn from me; and I am covered with shame because I make Him such poor returns. Dear Lord, enable me to endure all Thou seest needful. I am sure it is well, though I feel something like David, in Psalm 66:12; but I deserve a thousand times worse. "Father, Thy will be done."

September 11th, Sabbath evening — In the past week I have had deep conflict, many storms, but sweet interminglings of mercy. I feel weak and faint, as if the journey were too great for me; but my dear Lord will sustain me. I am the poorest worm, and must let fall my whole weight upon Thee, my precious Savior. Lord, help me on, and help me home. Isaiah 43 is very sweet to-day; I am much pleased with the expression, "dragons and owls honoring the Lord" (verse 20; Job 30:29).

September 18th — I bring a hard case to Thee, my Lord; some of Thy dear children think I am in a wrong position, and would delight to have me again in the depths of my own corruption. My heart is deeply wounded: I commit it to Thee. If constantly looking at what I am in the first Adam will most honor Thee, I resign myself to it; if looking to my dear Lord, and learning what I have and am in Him, is most God-glorifying, I pray for it, whoever may fight against it. I do marvel that some of the living family should so seek to take off my eye from Jesus. O Lord, undertake for me, and judge between us! Make me know the right; confirm what is Thine; deliver from what is mine, or any other creature's.

October 30th, Sacrament-day — The past week one of trial, and I have not had such near communion with my Lord as formerly; many sweet visits from Him, but not that constant abiding with me, and I with Him, as once. I received great blessing at the Lord's table this afternoon; surely the King was held in the galleries. My heart-backslidings reprove me; all withholdings, all trials are deserved. I do *not* deserve that my dear Lord should ever speak in love to me again on this side Jordan; but I must cling to Him. He is my Sun, though he forbear to shine:—

> "Though for a moment He depart,
> I dwell for ever on His heart,
> For ever He on mine."

November 24th — "Blessed be the Lord God, the God of Israel, who only doeth wondrous things. And blessed be his glorious name for ever: and let the whole earth be filled with his glory. Amen and Amen" (Ps. 72:18, 19). Fill, O Lord, my body, which is Thy *earth*, with Thy glory, by using all its powers in Thy service. This I have long asked; but I feel so unprofitable that I have lately come into despair about it, and thought that I must just be useless in the bosom of divine love. I have had some blessed hours with a poor tempted and distressed soul, with whom I have been often of late. Her trouble comes from the death of a brother, whom she dearly loved. Her body is weak, her nerves shattered, and evidences all clouded; at times she seems almost distracted. She sent for me this afternoon. I went; and oh, what a season we had in mutual prayer and reading of the Scriptures. It was indeed a pouring out of the Spirit. Our mouths were filled with arguments, and my soul with power. No creature effort, no fleshly excitement; all was calm and quiet, but very powerful; it was a hallowed season, "a shadow of good things to come." The dear soul was encouraged. Satan and her trouble may return, but deliverance is sure to this daughter of Abraham; either below or above, she shall surely sing the praises of our covenant God. Shall the typical David slay the lion and the bear, and rescue the lamb they had taken out of the flock, and shall not the spiritual David, our Good Shepherd, rescue this torn sheep from the roaring lion? He will; He will.

December 18th — On Friday this word was sweet to me, "In the days of famine they shall be satisfied." I felt satisfied with Christ, although I had not a shilling in the house to call my own, and money is wanted for many things. My dear friends would help me if they knew of this trial; but I could not thus go *before* the Lord, and lose the blessing which is in it. "My soul, wait thou only upon God; for my expectation is from Him." Philippians 4:19 was very sweet an hour ago. I saw more largeness and richness than ever in those words, "According to his riches in glory by Christ Jesus." What a rule to be supplied by! It is like an infinite investment on our behalf, from which shall flow all we need for the wilderness journey. "Lord, increase my faith." "O God, command deliverances for Jacob."

December 31st — The last evening of 1853. Truly the past year has had deep trial to me; I think more so in experience than ever since I came into liberty. It is worth anything to have my dear Lord's presence, and fixedness of mind. But oh, what a blessed mingling of mercy in my cup during the past year. Lord, increase my gratitude and my praise.

> "Here I raise my Ebenezer;
> Hither by Thine help I'm come;
> And I hope, by Thy good pleasure,
> Shortly to arrive at home."

This has been my word to-day: "As dying, and behold we live!" Ebenezer!

1854

New Year's Day — "Jesus Christ the same yesterday, today, and for ever." "Looking unto Jesus."

January 8th — The Lord has helped me in outward things; it is a chastened benefit; I feel abased in my own eyes. I am very unworthy; but I must, I do, praise the Lord that He hath not shut up His tender mercies from me.

January 22nd — "The way of the Lord is strength to the upright." This word has again been somewhat speaking in my experience. And what is the *way* of the Lord? None other than a precious Christ. Surely, "the Lord God is my strength; and He will make my feet like hinds' feet"; to tread lightly upon earth, to go safely over the mountains of difficulty and tribulation; and to have my footsteps ordered, and my goings established upon the rock of Christ. A good deal raised above outward trials, and Jesus precious the last week.

January 28th — On Thursday evening I had deep soul-abasement and wrestlings with the Lord, on account of spiritual unfaithfulness to my heavenly Bridegroom. Oh, I was caused to hold Him by faith, and say, "I will not let Thee go"; frown, reprove, smite, wound, anything Thou pleasest; but I *must* have Thee. In Leviticus 26, at our family reading, I saw my own case, and that of the living Church in this day. How was my soul humbled and broken under a sense of our declension and departures from our blessed Jesus. Jeremiah 9:1. Oh, He did lead me, "with weeping and supplication," desiring His holy presence to destroy all in me that offended Him, as the Ark, His ancient symbol, destroyed Dagon. Words cannot express what I find in Him. Oh, indeed there is a heaven of love and holiness in my glorious Christ. Abiding in Him is "as the days of heaven upon earth" (Deut. 11:21).

February 5th — I was sorely distressed last night about dear Miss G—'s state. I have had great fear lest she should not be the Lord's; but this morning, in the house of God, her safety was sweetly sealed upon my heart. I believe she is amongst the redeemed. My soul rejoices over her salvation next to my own, and adores my God that through eternity I shall join her in praising Him for this wonder.

> "Oh, for this love, let rocks and hills
>   Their lasting silence break;
> And this poor softened, gladdened heart,
>   My Savior's praises speak."

February 12th — I heard Mr. F. this evening, with much soul profit, from Song 4:8, 9. He said that the Hebrew word there rendered "ravished," is not used in all the Scripture beside; and it might be rendered, "Thou hast taken possession of my heart for Thyself," or, "Thou hast *unhearted* us"; as if the Holy Trinity were absorbed in delighting in the Church. Lord, enlarge my heart. I come with Thee, adorable Redeemer, to look away from all besides.

February 16th — Revelation 7:13, 14. This passage has come before me again to-day beside the dying couch of a stranger whom I have been asked to visit. I went with trembling, fearing to find her in nature's darkness; but I believe she is one of the hidden jewels of Zion's casket—a gem to shine for ever in the crown of the King of Glory.

March 8th — For the immense favors in my unworthy soul I must raise an Ebenezer. When I speak of what I have been passing through these last few months, none but the Lord can understand me. Oh, what I have suffered in wandering thoughts; and, though having often sweet messages and communion with my Lord, it seems as if I got but a *side* view of Him, and not that open gaze and unreserved intercourse as before: whatever degree of communion we have been brought to, nothing less can satisfy us. I now feel all still in my soul, lest I should lose that sweet embrace of love divine which begins my heaven.

Good Friday — That lovely countenance of the suffering Savior! How it is marred more than any man's; but faith and love see beauty still. *There* is love's climax! The Bridegroom enduring for the Bride, and leaving her only a cup of blessing, although she, as well as He, must be a sufferer.

> "Here it is I find my heaven,
> While upon the cross I gaze:
> Love I much? I've much forgiven;
> I'm a miracle of grace!"

I would love to sit in this hallowed seclusion all day; but I must leave it. Sweet Savior, enfold me again in Thy bleeding embrace; let me into the secrets of Thy love and union; oh, absorb me for ever in Thyself, my God, my glory!

April 26th — A day of national humiliation and prayer. The Lord hear, and send peace to the kingdoms of the earth. But, oh, my soul says, "*Thy* kingdom come."

May 13th — I was richly blessed last evening from Isaiah 50; Romans 8:33, 34. The justified Head and the justified members both say, "Who is he that condemneth?" My dear Lord opened the door of my heart by that 50th of Isaiah, and revealed Himself gloriously: all praise to the Lamb!

June 15th — Home. Peculiarly blessed in soul and strengthened in faith, during a recent visit to Brighton.

June 25th — Since my return home I have found indescribable blessedness and fullness in Jesus. I cannot express what my soul finds in the realization that I am in Him. It is rest indeed; although blight has followed blight in outward things. But the rod of Jesse blooms in my experience; and "His fruit is sweet to my taste." The government also is upon His shoulders: so all will be well, however contrary to the flesh. Being in Christ, all is mercy. How marvellous, that there is so little praise in the living Church! We lie too much "among the pots."

July 6th, my Birthday — Here I desire to give glory to God in the highest, that I was born in union with the Lamb. And because of this, I was, at the appointed time, quickened into spiritual life; and shall live through death, because united to Him, our living Head, who has for us "destroyed him that had the power of death, that is, the devil."

> [Believing reader, mark the glorious mystery, "We shall live through death." Why? Because we have a life in Him who is the Resurrection and the Life which death can never touch. It is in Him, and of Him, and through Him: hence, every soul in union with Christ may triumphantly say, "O death, where is thy sting? O grave, where is thy victory? The sting of death is sin; and the strength of sin is the law. But thanks be to God, which giveth us the victory through our Lord Jesus Christ."]

Thou knowest my request is this day for a closer walk with Thee, and deliverance from wandering thoughts; for more of the activity of that faith which purifies the heart; for the Spirit to be as springs of water in my soul; and for more realization of that perfection and glory which the Church had in Christ, before she fell in the first Adam. May I behold the Three divine Persons therein, with Their distinct love-acts; and thus live much more above the fogs of earth and vapors of fallen flesh. I also long for an open heart to speak of the mysteries of Christ to some dear saints, by word of mouth, as well as by letter; that the well-spring of wisdom may be a flowing brook between us, and He a sweet savor through me, and to me, in life and in death. O Lord, these are my requests, with thanksgiving for all that Thou hast done; to Thee be glory and everlasting praise. Let all my powers be Thine; and this affliction consecrated to Thee; so that, instead of an ill savor, there may be a sweet fragrance of Thyself! Ebenezer!

August 5th — This week I have suffered great pain and weakness of body; but have most fully experienced that "Himself took our infirmities, and bare our sicknesses." Most sweetly have I felt the suffering lightened, as if my dear Lord did bear the heavy part for me. Sweetly solemnized this morning by 1 Kings 8:5, where it speaks of sacrifices which could not be told or numbered for multitude. The glory and majesty of the holy Jehovah were there, and Solomon felt the need of blood, yea, an ocean of blood, as it were, to enter upon the worship of so holy, holy, holy a being. The ark was placed in the holiest place, in thick darkness, showing that Jehovah can only be seen in His own light. All light of nature must be shut out, for *it* only causes confusion in the things of God. This evening, again instructed in 2 Samuel 6:1-8. Much zeal and praise are mentioned, but no blood; and it ends in death and condemnation. For (verse 13) the ark was only taken six paces when oxen and fatlings were sacrificed; so that blood was mingled with the praise, and the end was life and peace. There is no right prayer or praise on earth without blood. And what is it above? Oh, there the song of the redeemed is of blood, and praise to Him who shed it. Revelation 1:5: "Unto him that loved us, and washed us from our sins in his own blood." This is most sweet to my soul.

August 6th, Sacrament-day — I longed for my heart to be as a ten-stringed instrument, and every string swept into harmony by the touch of the Spirit, in praise of Him, my Beloved, whose heart was laid open for me. Oh, that I could praise Him, and cleave to Him with full purpose of heart. My soul afresh would "make her boast in the Lord." "Who is he that condemneth? It is Christ who died." A Person so holy, so majestic, so glorious in Himself, though humbled to the death of the cross. It is He that died and is risen again. Here rests my soul; here hangs my salvation.

August 13th, Sabbath — This morning I had a word in season. Mr. H— spoke from Psalm 104:21, 22, 23. Speaking of faith, he said, "One work of faith is to lay hold of the Lord Jesus, to lay hold of eternal life, another is to hold Him fast. Hold that fast which thou hast, that no man take Thy crown. Not the crown of *life*, for none can take that; but the crown of *rejoicing*, which we have when we lay hold of Christ; and, while so doing, none can take it from us."

September 3rd, Sacrament-day — I have much enjoyed Psalm 126. The Spirit opened it to me about Christ and His Church. Surely they *both* "sow in tears and reap in joy." How bitter the cup He drank when the Lord was doing "great things for us," by laying upon Him "the iniquities of us all."

September 10th, Sabbath — My heart cried to the Lord to keep me following on. In the midst of outward trial I have considerable inward peace and rest in the Lord, to my own astonishment; so that while flesh trembles at the little store wasting so fast, the inner man reposes in the Lord, and feels sure that in plenty or in straits He will be the same—a sufficient portion.

September 19th — I have been in the deep to-day. The enemy and carnal reason strong, and my soul much distressed, I was greatly relieved by faith being again renewed. This evening we have had an exposition of Psalm 23, which was quite a word in season.

September 24th — "Thanks be unto God for his unspeakable gift." The love of God, and God of love! Here be my resting-place; this be my theme. How I wonder at the stupendous love. Not one drop of mercy to the suffering Redeemer, in His own precious body and soul, that He might receive all the mercy in His mystic members. No pity shown to *Him*, that the Lord might be very pitiful to *us*. No comforts to the Bridegroom, as He says in Psalm 69:20, that the Bride might receive the Comforter (John 15:26); yea, and Himself come, and comfort her too (John 14:18). Oh, the depth of infinite love laid up in the heart of Jehovah! I cannot fathom it, but would continually sink deeper and deeper into that bottomless abyss. "Keep yourselves in the love of God." "Continue ye in my love."

October 1st — This is a thanksgiving-day for the plentiful harvest, and that the Lord has, in some measure, stayed the dreadful pestilence which has been raging in many parts of our land, though Nottingham has been mercifully preserved. The Lord give us humbled, grateful hearts, and accept in Jesus our poor thanks. *Evening* — Dearest Lord, what means this note of gladness in my heart? Is this Thy voice, which speaks of brighter things approaching? O my Lord, Thou knowest all things: do not let me be deceived by the flesh, or the devil. Most lovely Savior, Thou art enough to fill the soul with rejoicing, whatever may be my outward state. I long more for the heaven of Thy love, and the beamings in of Thy glory and beauty. Oh, come to this longing heart, and let it be all taken up with Thee. Thou wilt: this is Thy love burning in my bosom, and Thou wilt "rest in Thy love."

October 20th — Richly blessed yesterday in hearing dear Mr. H—, and have had as one of the days of the Son of man in my soul to-day. It is a most timely blessing, for my heart is peculiarly exercised. It has been singing with the thorn at my breast, and the cross on my back; but the presence of my precious Jesus makes me sing, *anywhere* and *anyhow*. Oh, dearest Lord, do stay with me; do separate me from everything that grieves Thee; and do grant me the "Spirit of wisdom and revelation in the knowledge" of Jesus Christ.

October 23rd — "Behold my hands and feet, that it is I myself." "My soul doth magnify the Lord, and my spirit doth rejoice in God my Savior." A faith's view of Jesus doth make the heart rejoice. Oh, open my understanding in the Scriptures, that I may see Jesus in every part. Oh, for much heart-burning, through His talking "with us by the way."

October 29th — I thirst and long to be absorbed in Thee, and used for Thee, and must sing to Thy praise of—

> "Sovereign grace o'er sin abounding."

Blessed Spirit, ever give me lively actings of faith upon the glorious Person and finished work of this Immaculate Lamb. Feeding upon Him, I shall grow more and more out of love with self, and all that is not of the Father. And now I go forth "up and down in the name of the Lord," by the anointing of the Spirit of truth.

November 5th — Ebenezer! "He giveth meat in due season." He toucheth the upper springs, and the heart runneth over; He toucheth the nether springs, and the cup runneth over. "He hath remembered (me) in my low estate: for His mercy endureth for ever." He first delivered me *in* the trouble by His own love and presence, and then delivered me in a measure *out* of the trouble, that is, as to present straitness. I *must* sing of the mercies of the Lord, which are for ever and ever. Precious Lord, Thou hast revealed Thyself in me, the last few weeks, and taken away all strangeness. Oh, stay, ever stay, and keep me from dishonoring Thee in any way.

November 12th — My heart mourns for my country. It is a time of war, and hundreds of our fellow-countrymen are slain. O Lord, if Thou art on our side, give success to our armies, and end the bloody strife.

November 19th — Romaine says, "The way to live *for* Jesus is to live *on* Him." This is a true witness, and is what I seek.

November 26th, Sacrament-day — I am much abased in my own sight, because of sin. "O Lord, thou knowest my foolishness, and my sins are not hidden from thee." I know that the precious blood of my Surety has atoned for them all; but I loathe the evil working of my nature. Dearest Lord, hear the cry of my heart, which cannot be put in words, and with precious blood purge my conscience, and fully restore my soul to the simplicity which is in Thee. Thou alone didst teach me the life of faith. Oh, renew that teaching amidst all discouragements! Work for thine own glory. Lord, hear the groaning for our country and soldiers. Lord, pardon, spare, save, and restore peace. Lord, humble us as a nation before Thee.

December 10th — For a week after the above "I sunk in the mire where there was no standing." My case grew very heavy. Then came Psalm 126:5, with a little power and sweetness; and Jesus whispered in my heart the precious words, "Child, thy sins are forgiven thee." Thus hath the Lord brought me up out of the depths by little and little, feeding me with spiritual "food convenient for me." Ever praised be Thy holy name, whose right hand and holy arm hath gotten the victory over all my foes.

December 16th — Last evening Isaiah 25:5, came to my mind very sweetly: "The noise of strangers," that tumult of thoughts within, which hinders quiet meditation and communion. But it says here, the Lord will bring it down, "like the heat in a dry place." Lord, "do as Thou hast said," Let it be so experimentally in my soul. Let strangers' voices by Thee be silenced,

>"And Thou be only heard to speak,
>And Jesus reign alone."

December 24th — Happy Christmas-eve! Welcome, thrice welcome, into our flesh, Thou glorious Prince of Peace. What a moist root Thou art in our dry ground: what a bright Sun in our shadow of death, which Thou hast, indeed, turned into the morning. Oh, for privilege to come by faith to Bethlehem, and afresh to see Thee arise upon our dark world: to see Thee coming from the virgin's womb, as a bridegroom coming from his chamber, to claim for himself his betrothed bride. For this Thou didst come from the heaven of heavens to Bethlehem's manger—made royal by Thy presence. Thou wast born to die! Thou didst die to redeem; Thou didst redeem to possess and to enjoy. I, worthless as I am, am part of Thy purchase, "to make mention of Thy righteousness, even of Thine only," for "it is finished" and complete; it is like a "garment of fringes." So I henceforth would cease from my own broken works, and by faith be searching into these unsearchable riches of Thee, my glorious Christ.

Oh, Thou blessed Jesus, deign to spend Christmas with me. Come, and make the feast. I am sure we follow Thee too far off. Draw us to Thy feet, to Thy bosom. Bless and comfort each precious son and daughter in Zion who may be in affliction or perplexity. Make this night bright with Thy presence.

Christmas-day — Was not well enough to go to W—. The tabernacle shakes, but I have "a building of God, a house not made with hands, eternal in the heavens." Precious Jesus, again I rejoice in Thy lowly birth, which was the first step to Thy wondrous death. Oh, come nearer; be more and more fully revealed in this heart, which longs to be filled with the fullness of Thee. Order every step in the wilderness; cause me to speak of Thee in life and in death. Oh, demonstrate to the living in Jerusalem that a life of faith in Thee *is* to Thy praise. Embalm me for the death and burial of the body; or rather, perfume me, that I may be a sweet savor of Thee, as Thou art to me.

December 26th — It has been a great trial to me for my complaint to be known; but my health has so failed, that I have thought it necessary, and the Lord has truly blessed me in the deed, as He said, "When thou passest through the waters, I will be with thee." Again I beg Thee to consecrate this affliction all to Thyself, and grant a rich blessing to all concerned in it, that Thy joy may swallow up creature-sorrow. Be Thou seen, heard, felt; be Thou praised and crowned by me, and my companions, in drinking Marah's stream.

December 27th — I am very happy in my precious Lord. If Thou wilt be glorified through this trial, I will, for Thy sake, forget the shame, and "rather glory in my infirmities, that the power of Christ may rest upon me." I did not expect such rich cordials, after all my unfaithfulness to

Thee. Surely Thou hast "kept the best wine until now." Oh, grant that my beloved friends and I may drink together of the spiced wine of Thy love. I do sing with love and wonder, "Grace, grace unto it!"

December 31st, Sacrament-day — My glorious Lord, Thou hast crowned this year with Thy lovingkindness to my soul. My remaining steps may be few. The sentence of death is openly declared in my leprous house. I humbly and confidingly embrace Thee as my life, and peace, and pardon; my purity, my joy, and my all. May I ask to be led by the blessed Spirit afresh into the love scenes of solemn Gethsemane and Calvary? May I see Thee baptized in suffering for me; and may I, by Thy Spirit, be baptized into Thy death, as my only victory over self. Thou hast gone through the dark river when its waters were at their highest. Lord, comfort me when I follow Thee there; and may the blessed Spirit write the last pages of my life with Christ in Thy own living characters, that He may be exalted and honored, and I lost sight of in Him.

1855

January 10th — A week ago dear Mr. H— called for a few minutes, and, in speaking of Psalm 23:4, he said, "Because Christ had the sting of death for His people, it is, therefore, only a shadow to them, which is elsewhere called a sleep." Last evening I was telling this to Miss W—, and we conversed upon the subject of death; and in the night-watches I was thinking that if death came from union with the first Adam, it must be as a penal punishment, because part of the curse. Then was sweetly opened to me 1 Corinthians 3:22, 23, in which everything is included; and, besides, death is especially mentioned there as ours, because we are Christ's; therefore it comes to be so in union to Him. In the first Adam we were death's prey; in the second, death is the gate through which we must pass to obtain the perfect likeness of our Lord. In the first Adam death was a conqueror; in the second, "death is swallowed up in victory" (1 Tim. 1). These meditations were most sweet to my soul, making me at midnight to sing aloud songs of praises unto the Lord.

January 14th — I heard Mr. S— this morning from Psalm 1:3. This afternoon greatly blessed in meditating upon the first verse, and seeing Christ and the Church therein. Mr. S— spoke of this, but not in the fullness and glory the Spirit showed it to me. Christ is "the blessed Man," as the federal Head of His Church; and the description of Him is quite in accordance with 1 Peter 2:22, 23; Hebrews 7:26.

He is the Man, who, doing these things of the law, does live in them (Rom. 10:5). His righteousness is of works, and He is blessed in His deeds. His reward is of debt. He owes nothing now; but the Father owes Him the acceptance and glorification of all His seed. Law and justice have payment beforehand, and now owe Him the indemnification and justification of all His people, in their individual experience. He is the blessed Man, and His bride inherits the blessing in Him. She is blessed as Eve was (Gen. 1:27, 28). Eve was not brought out of her husband, when it said, "God blessed them." So it is with us. We are blessed in Christ (Ps. 72:17; Eph. 1:3; Eph. 10), and thus dwell in those mountains where God hath commanded the blessing (Ps. 133.); yea, upon Mount Gerizim, where all the blessings of full obedience are promised. See Song 4:7; Ezekiel 16:14. To talk of the Church being blessed or beautiful, except in the obedience and beauty of her Husband, is strange language to me. Whatever good works or fruits are seen in her, they are His fruit and flowering through her. They do not procure the blessing, but are the effects of it. He is the tree of life by the waters, and we, receiving His fruit, are made fruitful.

January 16th — I have been much exercised by my friends wishing me to have further advice for my malady. My soul was greatly bowed down, fearing to dishonor my precious Lord, and yet sorry to grieve kind friends. I desired that this day of quiet my soul might be closely engaged with the Lord about it. All I want is the Lord's will and the Lord's glory. This evening these Scriptures have been applied: Psalm 50:15; Psalm 32:8; Micah 2:7. I trust this is the blooming of the rod, and that it will also blossom and bring forth fruit; for which purpose I lay it up still before the Lord.

January 21st, Sabbath — There is much snow on the ground this morning, and my Lord melted my heart with

Isaiah 1:18, and this because of 2 Corinthians 5:21. Before divine service that word came sweetly, Song 7:13; which the Lord fulfilled to me, showing me from His Word how, for His own good pleasure, *He* had long led me in the way of faith, and had been to me, instead of human advisers, medical, legal, and spiritual. Often has He also turned about the cloud to guide and instruct me. I am fully satisfied to be in His loving hands. May He cause my dear friends to know that I do these things by His Word. "Them that honor me I will honor." *Evening* — I venture upon Thee, Lord, as my way. Answer—"The way of the Lord is strength to the upright." I venture upon Thee as my wisdom. Answer—"The Lord giveth wisdom; out of his mouth cometh understanding."

January 22nd — "The preparations of the heart in man, and the answer of the tongue, is from the Lord." He seems to be giving me the first part, and I trust the rest will follow, that I may give an answer to my kind friends.

January 23rd — I am almost too ill to write to-night; but I must, for further profit, note down that from reading 2 Chronicles 16 the Lord has brought me (contrary to the judgment of the flesh) to the decision not to go to Oakham for human medicine, but to commit myself wholly to Him, in whose hands I feel safe and happy. Jeremiah 42:15, 16, and Hosea 5:13, have seemed weighty.

January 24th — With the heart we believe, and then with the tongue we make confession. Praise to Thee, my Lord, for Thy kind answer to my poor cries in the hour of trial, when waiting to know Thy mind. "Was I ever a barren wilderness to Thee?" Answer—Never, never, my dearest Lord; it is I who am the barren wilderness; but Thou makest the wilderness to bloom, and rejoice with joy and singing. "Ye are my witnesses, saith the Lord."

January 30th — Isaiah 33:24, is just as I feel. Though afflicted in body, yet I am dwelling in Christ by faith. In my precious Jesus I enjoy experimentally forgiveness and healing. I could not have thought to have seen such good days. I have often prayed to possess the west and the south together. The west—the setting sun, the evening of life; the south—warm, bright, and cheering. And if this disease is taking down my tabernacle, it surely is with me as with Naphtali: "Satisfied with favor, full with the blessing of the Lord"; yet all I enjoy is free and sovereign, "without money and without price."

February 1st — O Lord, give me a thankful heart. Answer—Dost thou want one to feed upon? Feed upon Me, and then a thankful heart will not be wanting.

February 18th — I felt this morning rather weary, and, like Jacob, "would needs be gone," because my soul longed sore for my Father's house above. I had afterwards a refreshing time in the sanctuary. Mr. D. F— preached from "Having nothing, and yet possessing all things." During service the Lord sweetly renewed in my soul two formerly given portions, in Isaiah 35:10, John 14:3; which came home to my case of affliction, and I felt they were a pearl dropped for me, which I must put amongst my treasures for this last stage of the journey.

February 20th — Mr. T. S— kindly called upon me to-day. In conversing upon death, he said he had been thinking that Naaman the Syrian had to go into the waters of Jordan before he could get rid of his leprosy; and so the believer goes through the Jordan of death to get rid of the spiritual leprosy. This was very sweet to me. It is at death we drop the image of our fallen head, by whom we received the dreadful disease.

February 22nd — "We which have believed, do enter into rest." Surely this is known by me this night, after enduring much temptation. Oh, the excellent overcoming life of faith; how it strengthens grace, and is the beginning of glory.

> "Believing, we rejoice
> To see the curse remove;
> We bless the Lamb with cheerful voice,
> And sing His bleeding love."

March 4th — What must I do with these books of my heart's journey through the wilderness? How I shrink from leaving them behind for other eyes than my own to see. Oh, it seems impossible! And yet this word has come, which has made me to pause, "Destroy it not, for a blessing is in it." O Lord, I commit them to Thee. Thy will be done. I cannot be too much abased. Oh, set Thy foot on me, if thereby thou mayest be more seen, and exalted, and enjoyed by any of Thy redeemed.

March 9th — For two days I have been asking that I might come more into the light of eternity, which the Lord has graciously answered; for this afternoon, while at the divine footstool, I was favored with a little revelation of *absorption in bliss* in the fullness of Jesus. It was a little in comparison to the consummation; but yet, there was that in it, which earth's language cannot express, opening sweetly to me the thought that eternity is, with Jehovah, one "eternal now"; and how there is no night there, no weariness—an everlasting glory, uninterrupted by the revolvings of time. I realized a little of what it is to be unshackled, not only from earth, but from time. But words fail to describe that fullness of glory, activity of worship, and perfection of rest.

March 18th — I have felt great blessedness this morning, and as if every cloud of guilt and trouble were under my feet, in union with Christ. He has also given me another comfortable whisper about dying, "If thou abidest in me, thou shalt not feel it." What a passage! It never seemed so full before. Dear Lord, fulfill every good word "on which Thou hast caused me to hope." I am pleased to find that while I was so much blessed on Friday, a dear brother was pleading for me, and enjoying much blessed freedom with the Lord, and union with my spirit. This is "communion of saints." Oh, for more walking in the Spirit! It is He who reveals spiritual secrets, and opens love's stores, such as 1 Corinthians 2:9, as I am a happy witness. Ebenezer!

March 21st — Day of national fast and humiliation, on account of the dreadful war. O Lord, hear Thy people's cries, and spare our beloved, but guilty land. I have long blushed before Thee, because of our favoring Popery. O Lord, open the eyes of our Sovereign and rulers, that this sin may be put away, and Thy just judgments be removed from us.

March 22nd — "Thy will be done," has been the peculiar feeling of my soul to-day, and for some time previous. The Spirit has kept me bowing to meet every fresh wave as it comes; for, oh, this is a stormy world. But the true feeling, "Thy will be done," is like oil upon every wave, *so* calming the soul that there is no contrary current. The Spirit bends us, the wave passes over us, and we say, "It is well!"

April 2nd — Precious Jesus, I am glad Thou bringest out good wine at last. I need a strong cordial. Oh, renew the miracle of Cana of Galilee! I know six of Thy vessels which are filled with the waters of temptation or tribulation, and Thy power is the same as ever. Let us all feel it; and let this very water be turned into the wine of the kingdom. How sweet and strong has this word been to me to-night, "He is able." Also Zechariah 10:1, and Ephesians 1:19, 20, &c. Oh, that mighty power! Lord, give me faith to take hold of it, in my present state.

April 3rd — This is called "Passion-week." I feel it precious to have the companionship of a once-suffering Savior, who was "a Man of sorrows." He drank of every bitter cup, that He might feel with and succor us. The times and seasons are in the Father's power, not in the hands of men. But I am glad, if through these times of commemoration, I can get a view of my Lord in His humiliation or exaltation. Dear, precious Lord, I afresh crave fellowship in Thy sufferings.

April 6th, Good Friday — I have been looking much at the last hours of my precious Lord, this morning. This afternoon I have been somewhat beholding the precious Sufferer on that middle cross. Both the thieves railed on Him, but one, by the Spirit, was brought to confess his own sinfulness, and by the same Spirit to call Jesus "Lord." Then how sweet was the answer of peace, "Today thou shalt be with me in paradise." Thus did redeeming love break forth in a refreshing stream from that suffering heart and those parched lips, to give drink to that other sufferer, who was, indeed, "ready to perish." After this, came the cry of agony, "My God, my God, why hast thou forsaken me?" Oh, that was the climax of woe! And then those mysterious words, "I thirst." Mere bodily suffering was not all which was couched in these words; but that righteous One was dwelling with the devouring fire, and enduring what would have been to us "everlasting burnings." The wrath of the Lawgiver was going forth upon the sin which was found upon *Him*. He thirsted, as in hell, that He might "lead us to fountains of living waters" in heaven. And those tender looks and words to His mother and His beloved John, do indeed show out a heart without an atom of that selfishness which we inherit by the fall. Truly, I have almost seemed to stand beside His cross, and gather up these precious fragments with wondering love, and mingled joy and grief. How I wonder, whether, in the multitude of those gazers, any one in that hour beheld the "Fountain opened to the house of David, and to the inhabitants of Jerusalem." We know that, afterwards, some were washed therein, as St. Peter testifies, in Acts 23, 36: "Whom ye with wicked hands have crucified and slain"; at which time they were pricked in their hearts, and brought to look by faith "upon Him whom they had pierced; and by His stripes they were healed." Then came the end, when, after receiving the vinegar, Jesus said, "It is finished," and gave up the ghost. What amazing weight and fullness is in those three words, "It is finished"; and finished for me, the vilest of the vile, whom Thou hast privileged to stand, with dear Mary Magdalene, at the foot of Thy cross, and listen to Thy dear lips, which, even there, do drop as the honeycomb. If these sips in grace are so sweet, what will those draughts in glory be? Ah, when I have received the vinegar, I shall follow Him. Hasten on the happy day! Oh, bless all my loved ones with like sweets from Thy bitter cup.

April 8th — My precious Lord, I long for entrance to-day into the glories of Thy resurrection by the power of the Spirit. Oh, come and show Thyself to me, as Thou didst to Mary Magdalene. I seem to have got to Thy feet for a moment, as my risen Lord, and Thou hast sweetly repeated in my heart, that "where I am, there shall ye be also"; above sin, the world, and death. But, dear Lord, I want a fuller revelation of Thyself, as it is written in John 16:1. Come, and do the same to me. On Friday Thou didst give me a place with Mary Magdalene at Thy cross, where, as chief sinners, we loved and wept to Thy praise.

Oh, now give me her privilege in the garden—to see Thee risen; and do show me, as Thou didst those other disciples, Thy hands and Thy feet; and let me hear Thee say, "Behold my hands and my feet, that it is I myself"!

May 6th — I have been in the deep of soul-exercise and anguish, five days in this week, but have since enjoyed a Bethel visit, when meeting with two dear saints. It was a time long to be remembered. My soul's sins seemed to be lost in Jesus, and for some moments I enjoyed heaven beyond expression, in all the stillness of love. Oh, did dear saints speak more of Him, they would have more heart-warming seasons. My heart gladly sings, "Hosannah to the Son of David"; for though I go down to the deeps, His love is under all, and when I get above earth, self, and creatures, His love is above all, whether I apprehend it or not. Praise to my covenant God for ever. My outward things are rough, but it brings my Beloved nearer, and that is more than all. Oh, that I could praise and honor Him more, and win His loved ones and mine to walk closer with their God, by abiding in Him. Oh, Thou precious Christ, eclipse all besides, by revealing Thyself more fully.

May 13th — I heard the sermon with a blessing this morning, from Habakkuk 3:18. The minister remarked, that where it says, in verse 17, "Though the fig-tree shall not blossom," it intimates, not only dearth at the present, but also a prospect of it for the future; for, if there is no blossom, there will be no fruit; yet would the prophet "rejoice in the God of his salvation." In this thought there is something solemn as well as sweet. When present trials are heavy, flesh would take shelter in hope; but when there is no blossom, and therefore no fruit, faith only can rejoice here. Jesus is the object of faith, and He is "the same yesterday, and to-day, and for ever."

May 14th — I have this day learned a lesson, never to do anything when feeling very impetuous. Then should we wait, and waiting is the work of faith, which is no easy matter at such a time. Dear Savior, seal home this lesson to my heart.

May 27th, Sacrament-day — The past month has been a stormy one with me, but I have had great joy in the Lord. I think I shall never have much ease in the flesh, because I am so very covetous of the Lord's choice spiced wines, and they are chiefly found in trials and adversity.

July 6th — Jubilee. My birthday. I had scarcely thought to see another, but hoped I was almost at home. Disease has made decided progress, and I have suffered much, but in the furnace of affliction many bands have been burnt off, and I certainly now walk more at large with my Lord. I am this day fifty years old, therefore it is the time of Jubilee; and surely, during some past months, a blessed return has been proclaimed in my soul. I had been suffering much for a year or two, from want of that close sweet contemplation enjoyed before. In this affliction it has been restored—all glory to the Lord. Another peculiarity has been, that when very ill I saw such folly, extreme folly, in my anxious care about outward things, because the Lord knew He would soon take me home, and that little would do. Oh, I felt ashamed of my perplexities and want of trust!

> "I find myself a learner yet,
> Unskillful, weak, and apt to slide."

I am much abased in mine own eyes, and truly dependent on the Lord for faith and everything else. I have had a quick succession of trying events this year, but much spiced wine of my Lord's love. Oh, what cause I see to praise Him, for He has indeed done great things for unworthiest me; and yet I am desiring more. With thanksgiving I further seek enlargement into a glorious Christ, and abiding in Him by faith, that His fruits may more abundantly flow out in my life and conversation to His glory. Anew, my precious Lord, have I this day sought that all I have, and am, should be consecrated to Thee, and Thou much honored in all that shall befall me. Oh, guide me with Thine eye, make Thy way plain before my face. If I live, may I live unto the Lord; if I die, may I die unto the Lord; may Jesus be more revealed *to* me and *through* me; may His savor and perfumes be breathed to living souls. Oh, bless all my dear friends abundantly, and may we all be full of Him. Grant still more, a south land, and springs of water also. Amen, and amen. Ten thousand thanks for all Thy matchless favors, in the sunshine and in the storm. I dare not look forward with the eye of sense, but would go forth by faith, with Jesus only. Lord, give the single eye. A poor, weak, lonely creature, leans all her weight on Thee—and shall be blessed and shall bless Thee, for Thou hast blessed, and none shall reverse it.

Praise. Ebenezer! Praise. Jubilee!
Thine eyes shall see the King in His beauty.
The voice of my Beloved. Behold, He cometh.

July 8th — Surely some of the silvery tones of the Jubilee trumpet are sounding in my soul, in which I discern liberty, return, rest. Oh, my precious Lord, thoroughly fulfill these in my experience while I sojourn below. In Leviticus 25:13, it is said, "In the year of this Jubilee ye shall return every man to his possession." I much enjoy this in connection with Numbers 18:20, where the Lord says, "I am thy part and thy inheritance among the children of Israel." This includes just the very thing I want, which is, fully to leave all trials and perplexities, and dwell in Christ as my possession and experience. Leviticus 25:19: "And the land shall yield her fruit, and ye shall eat your fill, and dwell therein in safety." I do not mean any outward improvement, but to dwell in Christ by faith, feeding upon His fruits, and to receive all outward things for His sake, seeking only His glory; and so to welcome them, whether pleasing or painful. This is walking uprightly in union-privilege. To have this fully, I humbly seek as my Jubilee, in connection with experience of Romans 6. Oh, my precious near Kinsman, Thou hast redeemed me: and, in right of Thy redemption, I seek these things. I, a poor, enthralled, sin-bound worm, could have had no Jubilee but for Thy redemption. Thou hast bought me with Thy blood, I am Thy land, and I must return unto Thee: love brings me. Oh, possess me fully in every power and faculty; dwell in Thy poor land, and be its riches; dwell in Thy poor garden, and be its fruitfulness, and then eat Thy pleasant fruits. Oh, come, for it is Jubilee; and Thy land cries unto Thee to come, that she may enjoy her Sabbath, and be refreshed by resting in Thee. And then also Thou, Thine own self, art my Land, for we are married; "my Beloved is mine, and I am His." Oh, delight of delights! And Thou possessing me, I shall possess Thee; and this makes my heavenly Jubilee my foretaste of the fullness of joy.

July 24th — The following portions, as heavenly manna with dew, have come into my soul to-day: "Ye are complete in him," which was repeated in my heart when feeling the abominations there; and then Song 4:8, Look "*from* the lion's den, and from the mountains of the leopards" (our own corruptions), *to* Jesus to subdue; then Psalm 110:3, these words, "Thy people shall be willing in the day of thy power," willing "in the beauties of holiness." Here was the power at this time—Christ "the beauties of holiness"; even amidst all we feel within, He is our comeliness—and the Spirit does strengthen faith to be willing to glory in Him alone. This is a mystery, and a mighty triumph of faith, but not too hard for the Lord; and, moreover, faith is enabled to embrace Jesus as its victory over the very evils which the soul may be feeling and loathing. The "beauties of holiness." How that word has sparkled as a description of my Lord. "Wilt thou go with this Christ?" Ah, willing, most willing, indeed, am I to leave all, and follow Him whithersoever He goeth. I had also much sweetness in Genesis 22, especially verse 8. Our Father has provided Himself a Lamb. He has looked into Himself for it. He spared not His own Son—His beloved Son: He delivered Him up to bear all that sin deserved. Here is the sufficient sacrifice for all the abominations which are my plague. Hence it is they are not my destruction; the guilt of them has been atoned for; and, therefore, it is not presumption to have rich consolation in Christ, and to rejoice that I am complete in Him, even while feeling that in my flesh dwelleth every evil thing, and groaning under it, too. Adored and adorable Lord, seal Thy lessons with power on my soul: let my meditations of Thee be increasingly sweet; make me glad in Thee, the Lord—the Lord my Righteousness.

July 25th — I was much profited last evening in hearing a sermon at St. Paul's Church from Psalm 119:75. It was very simple, but many remarks were suitable for those in tribulation, and I have since had great profit from the text itself. It has been most searching in my soul. In my bodily affliction all seems right, but in those providential trials which have so continually come upon me, am I in them thoroughly reconciled to the Lord's will? Do I realize that it is all love? Have I not often been kicking against the pricks? Have I not at times thought it hard? Have I not listened to carnal reason instead of walking by faith? And thus this text has, by the blessed Spirit, searched me as with a candle. Oh, gracious Lord, bring me fully to the experience of it in all things. This word has been sweet to-day, "I have refined thee, but not with silver, I have chosen thee in the furnace of affliction." Ah, indeed, I seem to see that I must not pray to come out of the furnace; I am not half broken and humbled. Do, dear Lord, bring Thy glory, and my soul health, out of those things so bitter to the flesh. I render praise that I heard that text and sermon.

July 29th, Sacrament-day — This morning I heard a sermon from Hebrews 4:14, in which Isaiah 53:6 was quoted, and never did I see so much in the last half of it—"The Lord hath laid upon him the iniquity of us all." I seemed to realize the weight of sin and guilt so ponderous that none but Jehovah could have laid it upon the Surety, and none but such a Surety could have borne it. My soul was humbled and melted. I did not enjoy the Communion as sometimes, but faith and love were stretching after a dear crucified Savior in all His solemn glories, where it is said, "His soul was made an offering for sin," by which "one offering he hath perfected for ever them that are sanctified," whereof the Holy Ghost also is a witness to us; and also, "he that believeth hath the witness in himself," the Spirit bearing witness to our spirits that we are the children of God. That is a wonderful word, *perfected* by His one offering: may the Spirit seal it with instruction in my heart, that I may feed and grow thereby. Oh, glorious King, come and sit at Thy table: and, while faith is feeding upon Thee, my spikenard will send forth the smell thereof, which can be nothing else but the graces of the Spirit. Oh, do bid the north and south wind blow upon my soul, that the spices may flow out, and Thou mayest be regaled with Thine own—for from Thee is all my fruit and spice found. I offer Thee warm thanks for all Thy mercies during the past month; indeed Thou hast not been a barren wilderness to me.

Though in tribulation, Thou hast been with me, and Thy paths drop spiritual fatness upon the pastures of the wilderness. I praise Thee, and would praise Thee more, and rejoice that Thy "mercy endureth for ever," and that Thy will runs as a straight line through all the crooked things of this time-state. Oh, reveal Thyself to me in more fullness; let the shadows of temporal things shorten, and the substance of eternal things brighten and deepen in my soul; let me live *above* while I walk below. I am not refined, but refining: sustain me under the more fire that may be needful. Many clouds are around me, but this word is on my mind, "The way of the righteous shall be made plain." I can only be righteous in Thee, "the Lord *my righteousness*." I had a very sweet view of death while in God's house this morning. I saw that this mortal flesh is like a veil upon my spirit, and it was as if my Beloved said, "At death I shall only come to turn the veil aside, because I want to see thee face to face." Oh, this was precious, for surely I do want to see Him face to face; and, if disease should remove the veil of this flesh with a rough hand, my dear Lord will sustain me, and one view of Him will swallow up all remembrance of self-suffering.

August 19th — I was much blessed this morning under the word preached from Colossians 3:1, "Risen with Christ." Oh, what volumes of blessedness are in it! I see it in three parts—virtually, vitally, and experimentally. The sermon was very strengthening. Oh, to live constantly in this privilege by the renewing of the Holy Ghost! Much glory beams on my soul in seeing how we are risen with Christ, which must be in His perfection and purity. This is the fact of the case, and it is establishing to search into and meditate on facts, and not be circumscribed merely within our feeling of them; though where faith realizes the former, the latter will not be predominantly at low tide. I have been feasting on, "Where no law is, there is no transgression"; "We are dead to the law by the body of Christ"; hence He can say, "There is no spot in thee," no transgression. "He hath borne our sins in his own body on the tree." Law and justice took hold on *Him*, and therefore they let *us* go—they cannot hold both; as the sin He died, and as His members, we died with Him; and as we abide in Him do we enjoy the freedom, for "he that abideth in Him sinneth not." This is the true gospel way of having the power of sin broken. Oh, what glories do we inherit in union to the Lamb. We lose our own impurities, and are ever beheld, in the divine eye, in His perfect holiness. Precious Beloved of my soul, bring me by the Spirit to live in Thee, walk in Thee, and never wander more.

August 26th, Sacrament-day — How very wondrous did it appear to see the King of Glory crowned with the curse—showing, as one has said, that He has conquered it for His people. Oh, for more revelations of Christ crucified—this is the way to enjoy Christ glorified.

August 31st, Thursday — To-day I have enjoyed Him as the smitten Rock. I see how all grace-fullness was stored up in Him for His needy members; but He must be smitten, that they might honorably receive of it. Moses smote the rock—the law smote Christ, because His people had broken it; and thus streams of grace flow out to them, their conscience being smitten by the same law with conviction of sin, which makes them thirst for this suitable supply; and this dear Savior says, "If any man thirst, let Him come unto me and drink." Precious Jesus! Thou hast refreshed me with this living water; keep me coming, keep me believing, for Thou hast said, "He that cometh to me shall never hunger, he that believeth on me shall never thirst."

September 2nd, Sabbath — I came home on Friday, and the dew of divine blessing has richly rested in my soul since. Dearest Lord, Thou hast been most kind to provide this little rivulet of love in such a dry and thirsty land.

September 7th — Very refreshing gales from the everlasting hills have revived my soul this week, and cheered me on in the pilgrim way, drawing out my heart afresh in faith upon Jesus; and the two past nights, in the silent watches, my dear Lord has given instruction—the first night upon union with Himself, and last night showing most plainly that it is not feeling and knowing *corruption* is salvation, but knowing the Deliverer and deliverance by Him.

September 16th — I have had a sweet meditation on the miracles of our Lord. I saw how in the first Adam every part and power were broken by the fall—and this is shown by the blind eyes, deaf ears, lame feet, withered hand, palsied limbs, maddened brain, leprous flesh, &c., which were brought to the second Adam; "and he healed them all," for He was in all senses the Restorer of the breach, and was manifested in flesh for this very purpose, to destroy the works of the devil. These diseases of the different parts of the body which He healed, seem to show what I feel spiritually—even so maimed and broken, that I cannot use this body for His service as I would; and I feel sweetly encouraged to bring each diseased part (every one is diseased) to Him, that, having quickened me from the dead, He would so dwell in me that my members shall be instruments of righteousness, and by His own healing power overcome the dry and barren land; that while sin dwells within, it may in no part reign over me; and that while in each member I feel, "without Thee I can do *nothing*," I may, by the Spirit's enabling, come to Him by faith, and find also, "I can do *all things* through Christ, which strengtheneth me." I have heard it said, that our dear Lord living so many years in seclusion, shows the hidden life of the believer.

This is very sweet to me, and I see that those works which are manifest must, if they are worth anything, flow from that hidden life, and the power of God therein.

September 22nd — A few mornings ago these words were sweetly opened in my soul—"The just shall live by faith"; and the subject has continually returned since, showing the Lord's way of working, in giving a promise and faith to receive and enjoy it—at times so fully, that the soul feels it to be almost like the possession of the blessing included in the promise, according to that word, "faith is the substance of things hoped for"; which substance is for the time so satisfactory, that no further trial is expected. Frequently, however, the Lord permits contrary winds to blow after this, which make the soul to stagger. In such seasons we can only "live by faith"; and, if the blessed Spirit keep faith in exercise, there will be a steady going on through these dark shades of death, saying, "I will fear no evil, for thou art with me." Usually, every child of promise has to be offered up in sacrifice at the word of the Lord, for these are deaths which the redeemed family are continually called to pass through, because, being "children of the resurrection," their blessings shall have a death put upon them, that flesh may be kept down, and they enjoy all, within and without, in resurrection power. Here the "just shall live by faith." The Lord is showing me how these things apply to my own providential matters, as regards the rejoicing confidence given me in the winter; and feeling the folly of anxious care, as noticed July 6th, and also the unlooked-for trials which have come since. I now see the latter are only to try the faith of the former; and the fears and tremblings I have at times felt, prove how much sense there was mixed therewith. Inasmuch as faith prevails, I do experimentally live in the trial, and look for resurrection life out of seeming death. "Lord, increase my faith." How plainly does each living soul discern *His* coming and going, that is, in manifestation. On Tuesday I was much favored with the liberty of the Spirit. Yesterday more bound, but in the afternoon Judges 6:38, seemed powerful; and this morning the word in Exodus 16 has been sweetly fulfilled in my soul, about the dew, and the manna, &c. Oh, how full of instruction and refreshment has that chapter been. "Bless the Lord, O my soul."

September 30th, Sacrament-day — A blessed month has passed away, "full with the blessing of the Lord." My heart would praise Thee. Oh, tune it, touch it, that there may be spiritual melody unto Thee. Much blessed in hearing this morning from John 17:24. What a glorious view I had of my precious Lord having finished perfectly the work of obedience *unto* sufferings and death, for through them He must enter into His glory. It seemed as if He had said, "I have finished Thy work, now smite me. I have loved Thee, served Thee, never transgressed at any time Thy commandment: now bruise me, and call for the sword of justice to awake against me." But why smite, if thus perfect in His work? It was for the sins of His bride. He had worked for her, and He would now suffer for her; for when He added, "Now, O Father, glorify me," &c., He knew that He stood as Surety for His Church, and that neither He nor she could be glorified till He had drained the fiery cup of indignation—and again said, "It is finished." He was perfect in His Person, and perfect in His work: thus He stood now before the Father, as a lamb without blemish, to be offered for the transgressors, and as a fatted calf, ready to be slain for the prodigals. My soul melted in this view of Him, and on Him by faith I sweetly fed. At the Lord's table, too, this afternoon, I was again refreshed with "living bread," which words were read, and seemed fuller than ever. A precious Christ is living manna, rained down from heaven for those who are written among the living in Jerusalem. His body was broken, but not His bones, which represent His members; these He preserved by yielding up Himself to the stroke—"If ye seek me, let these go their way." Precious Jesus! I would now thank Thee for every wound and every sorrow Thou didst endure; for "Thy bloody sweat," caused by agony of soul. It was all in payment of my debt, all was atonement for my guilt. It was the dignity of Thy Person made every stroke and stripe of worth indeed. My poor body is worn and weary, but I would fain go on; for the Rock pours me out rivers of oil, and my happy soul longs still to pour it out, as I have been trying to do before, to one dear to Thee and me. Oh, what will it be to see Thee face to face? If streams are so sweet, what must the Fountain be? I long to be there; till then, oh, do renew living faith in lively actings upon Thy precious Person, and work continually by the operation of Thy blessed Spirit; do use me for Thy glory and for the profit of my loved ones. I am fit for nothing; but Thou art the Worker, and the *fitness*, in all things.

October 8th — Praise! It is nine years to-day since my dearest mother was taken to the bosom of Jesus. I never felt so much longing to gird up the loins of my mind and look up, and look on, but not look back. This heart would swell, and this breast would heave at times to-day; but then did I struggle towards my Savior, desiring to leave the dead for the living, sweetly feeling that in our living Redeemer we are still and for ever one; and that to look at her, my loved one, with fleshly regrets, is to dishonor Him, and darken my own soul. To Thee I come, my glorious Beloved. Oh, take and use me for Thy glory, and make my remaining *inch* of life below show forth Thy praise. I thank Thee for my revered parents, and for all blessings by them: I thank Thee they are safely housed—

"Far from this world of noise and sin,
With God eternally shut in."

October 28th, Sacrament-day — I have the last three weeks had deep soul exercise, with many tears, about allowing my letters to be published in the "Gospel Magazine"; but, when covered with shame and grief before the Lord, He seemed to say, "For your shame ye shall have double," and Exodus 2:3, 4, has come with power. When he (Moses) could no longer be hid, then his mother in faith laid him in an ark at the river's brink; it looked like giving him up to the Lord at a venture, and so I must do, hiding what He has done no longer. This word has come to me with power, "Go, borrow vessels of thy neighbors, even empty vessels; borrow not a few"; also (though I do not know that it is Scripture), "like oil from vessel to vessel." Oh, it is most blessed to be under divine teaching! Dear Lord, I wonder and adore. Oh, pardon the vilest of all Thy children. If Thou wilt take just the fag end of my days, and honor Thyself therein, it will be another of Thy wondrous *stoops*. Behold the handmaid of the Lord; "be it unto me according to thy word" and Thy will. I am ashamed of the past, and my tears will often flow on reviewing it. I had a blessed season at the Lord's table: I went to sacrifice freely unto the Lord in the above matter. Oh, my precious Beloved, if this thing is of Thee, let the yoke of my timidity be destroyed by the anointing. Lay Thy cause, truth, and people closer upon my heart, and, at whatever cost to my flesh, be Thou honored through me. Oh, can it be? It can; "nothing is too hard for the Lord."

November 26th, Sacrament-day, Morning — Ebenezer! O my God, my soul has been cast down in me; but now Thou comfortest me before any outward deliverance comes, and art filling me with Thy hid treasures of spiritual wine and oil, in Ezekiel 44, where, O blessed Spirit,

Thou dost richly preach Christ unto me. Oh, how blessedly does that 27th verse show how we are to go to the Lord's table, even with Christ as our sin-offering; and especially how we who feel our own unholiness may come near to a holy God, and worship Him within the veil which has been rent in twain. The outward rite of this is fully shown in Leviticus 16, and the spiritual secret in 2 Corinthians 5:21, where we find our sin-offering, which God first found for us—which our High Priest hath offered (Heb. 9:14, 7:27)—and which God hath accepted. We who are thus made priests unto God are to bring the same offering by faith under the anointing of the eternal Spirit, and that, not only when we first believe and know that this precious Jesus was made sin for us individually, but also in all our after approaches to the mercy-seat. Now those who would come near to God, must do so with a true heart and a single eye to Christ (Heb. 10:22). There is no other way of approach. Then verse 26 of Ezekiel 44 points to Christ again: "They shall eat the meat-offering and the sin-offering"; explained by "Take, eat, this is my body"; also, John 6:53, is another exercise of faith-feeding on Christ. But verse 28 is most blessed, alluding to the sin-offering: "It shall be unto them for an inheritance"; not a thing enjoyed and done with, but that which is to continue a blessing and benefit. Then follows, "I am their inheritance." How striking, for surely here shines out that He is our sin-offering, since both the sin-offering and Himself are our inheritance, and we, as His priests, are to have no other; also, Numbers 18:20. He gave to Abraham, in the promised land, none inheritance; no, not so much as to set his foot on. He dwelt there a stranger and sojourner, and yet he lacked no good thing, but had a goodly portion; for the Lord said unto him, "I am thy shield, and thy exceeding great reward." So, in all things here below, we too are but strangers and sojourners, but our Christ is our inheritance; and we find in Him all that a holy God requires—even precious blood without taint, and a sacrifice fat with perfect obedience to the law. "The fat and the blood are the Lord's" (Lev. 3:16, 17, and verse 15, of this 44th chapter), but we partake with Him, for "He has made a feast of fat things full of marrow, and wines on the lees well refined," which is spoken of in John 6:55. Our God has, indeed, "prepared of His goodness for the poor," and with Him we feed on His own chosen Lamb, in whom He is for ever delighting. The 5th verse strikes me very solemnly. I look not at any of the literal meanings of the prophecy, but at those which are experimental. The entering in is by Christ, and the going forth is by self. Mark it well, O my soul, for indeed thus thou hast found it. When Christ is all, and thine eye single, there is blessed entering into holy nearness with God. When self is set up, there is a going forth from that near approach. Verse 4 says, "the glory of the Lord filled the house." Christ is that glory, "whose house are we," and when our hearts are full of Him, and fixed on Him, then self falls, and our spirit worships in Christ, who is "the beauties of holiness" (ver. 17, 18). Those who entered the inner court were to wear nothing that "causeth sweat," as sweat was connected with the curse: "In the sweat of thy brow thou shalt eat bread." But when Jesus took away the curse from His people, He sweat *for them* great drops of blood, that they might enter into rest by believing, and worship in quietness and peace, not in the warmth or effort of fleshly feeling and excitement. They must have on the fine linen, even "the righteousness of the saints," being clothed upon, with His obedience, who is the "Lord our Righteousness."

December 3rd — I had a rich feast yesterday in Lamentations 3, where Christ did have the pre-eminence as the Prince of sufferers. On Friday evening those words were most powerful, as the language of Jesus (Lam. 1:12), and I saw how much His own children pass Him by—how much I pass Him by. O precious Lord, how canst Thou bear with me so?

December 9th — This morning Job 38:4 was opened to me. God asks, "Where wast thou when I laid the foundations of the earth? declare, if thou hast understanding." In Proverbs 8, Jesus, under the name of Wisdom, says, "I am understanding"; and it is in Him we find the answer. The Church was in God from everlasting (Ps. 90:1); but she was left to fall from her creature perfection in the first Adam into the mire of actual transgression; yet hath He devised means whereby His banished ones should not be expelled from Him (1 Sam. 14:14). The Church is of God; there is her divine origin; but also in Christ Jesus (1 Cor. 1:30); for "the Father gave her to His Son, and Christ betrothed her for His own." Then comes Hebrews 2:14. The elder Brother taking flesh and blood is the devised means to bring back the younger children—His banished, saying, "Return, ye children of men" (but children of God also). Now we could not return where we never had been before. Here, therefore, is plainly shown that eternal truth (which I never could receive till God Himself revealed it in my soul)—eternal *union* as well as eternal *choice*. In the resurrection, this "purchased possession" shall awake from the dust, incorruptible, and return "to Zion with songs and everlasting joy." The first return is experimental, when quickened, or rather new born; and these privileges are opened by the Spirit as the new man grows. But the fuller, and more glorious return will be in the resurrection. Truly, the Lord fed my soul with the fatness of His spiritual house. I had been much awake in the night, and was earnestly longing to apprehend Jesus by faith, as the death of my old man, and the life of my new. "They shall not be ashamed which wait for me." Blessed are all they that by the Spirit wait for Him. That I should be one—oh, what a marvel! Grace, grace unto it.

December 23rd — I have been much desiring the grace of the coming season (Christmas), to commemorate the incarnation of our Lord. He can make it as a lattice, through which He will show Himself to His believing people, and often has He done so to my soul. Never did I need it more than now. This very morning a trifle seized my fleshly mind, and stirred up its vanity and folly, by which my thoughts were for a time brought into captivity. How abominable and filthy is my natural heart, drinking down any iniquity or foolishness like water. Truly, raven-like it is, for it feedeth upon corruption, which bringeth the Dove, or new nature, into true mourning. Thus am I now. Behold, I am vile. Woe is me, that such a mere *feather* weight of temptation, finding me off the watch, should carry me away into lightness of spirit, with vanity of mind, &c. My precious Savior, I fly to Thee by faith. Only Thou canst give me rest and peace, by Thy blood and in Thy love. *Evening* — Let me remember the sweet sacred power with which the following thoughts have just melted my soul, while crying to the Lord for instruction in the way of wisdom, and for faith to apprehend afresh the atoning efficacy of the death of Jesus as regards my present feeling of sin. First, I was much arrested with Exodus 30:1-3, &c. The altar of incense, made of shittim wood and of gold, on which sweet spices were daily burned. Here my precious Jesus beamed upon me, to the reviving of my soul; and methinks I did by faith take hold of the horns of that altar while waiting for a word from the Lord with much desire. After that came to my mind, "The just [or justified] shall live by faith"; "There is not a just man upon earth that doeth good and sinneth not"; "He that abideth in him sinneth not." When the Spirit brings the sentence of justification into the conscience, through the blood and righteousness of the Surety, thenceforward the justified one lives in the blessedness and grace of justification before God; but we have *experimental access* and *continuance* in it by faith alone. There is not a justified person on earth who so constantly lives by faith as always to realize experimentally that he is, before God, as one that sinneth not, because of union to Him who was made sin for him, and bore it all away. "He that abideth in him sinneth not." It is not that he sinneth less, or sinneth unwillingly, or hates it while he does it. All this is true, but more also. In a law sense, he sinneth not. He is one to whom God will not impute sin, because his Surety has stood in his law place, and has had it all imputed to Him. This is a *sinning not* which will stand the strict scrutiny of a holy God, for it is the way of His own devising and accomplishing. So to live by faith, looking only to Jesus and His blood and righteousness, is blessed indeed! Alas, however, guile comes in, and, by giving a side-look at self, we go down again into the ditch of our sin; for if we will, through legality, touch our own responsibility, we must fall and sink under the weight of our guilt. If we, in our own personality, say we have no sin, "we lie, and do not the truth"; for the mystery of iniquity is all within, and we shall feel it. It is only in *union-privilege* we sin not; the Husband standing, in law, responsible for the wife. It is not that she contracts no debts, but all is in His name; so it is as if He contracted them, and not His bride. Thus the law and the divine Lawgiver look at it. But, woe is me, I fail in faith, and turn to sense, and bow down under my sin; yet rich have been those words to me: "If any man sin, we have an Advocate with the Father, Jesus Christ the righteous: who is the propitiation for our sins"; and afresh we do realize, that though sin worketh in us, yet we are "complete in Him"; which humbles and melts more than anything else, as my heart does this evening prove. All my feeling of sin and shame this day has not softened my heart so much as a sense of non-condemnation through non-imputation. Words cannot express the rich healing grace that flows in. I wonder and adore, and long to live by faith to honor my glorious Lord, who has justified me from all things, and for ever. The poor dove has got back to the ark, and the raven may starve. Never does the old man get so little food as when we are truly living and walking by the faith of the Son of God. Thou precious near Kinsman and Redeemer, Thou hast taken my responsibilities and liabilities. Oh, give me faith to live in this blessed freedom—loathing sin, renouncing self, exalting Christ, "made wise unto salvation." All praise to a Triune Jehovah, from a chief sinner saved. Surely such an one should be a chief *singer* upon the stringed instrument of the new heart. "Unto Him that loved us and washed us from our sins in His own blood, be glory and dominion for ever and ever."

December 24th, Christmas-eve — Praise! Ebenezer! The well of Bethlehem opened.

> "A debtor to mercy alone,
> Of covenant mercy I sing."

Through a covenant Savior, yea, through His very heart and veins so precious, which were pierced that there might be an outflow of the living stream to the covenant family, and that we might know how deep was His love, which thought not such a cost too much for His bride the Church. And am I a covenant child? Am I one of that happy number? Can such a vile worm be of the Royal family? Even so: all praise to my covenant God. I am alone in the house; but while at tea, my royal Lord came, to the joy of my heart, and over my lonely meal He caused me to sing with heart and voice, "Crown Him Lord of all," while joyful tears flowed in love and wonder at His great kindness to His "sparrow alone." Through free grace, I experience Isaiah 45:24, 25. How I am thinking of the shepherds and the angel's message: "Unto you is born this day in the city of David a Savior which is Christ" Jehovah. And now we can take up the song in nearer interest, "Unto *us* a child is born; unto *us* a Son is given." Oh, it is "an unspeakable gift," a precious gift. I feel it to be so, and long ardently that all my loved ones might share my full cup of joy and gladness. Precious, precious Jesus, visit them all, and then they will, they must, sing unto Thee, and will not condemn me for being too happy in Thee. O Father, do pour out Thy Spirit more copiously upon Thy redeemed, to raise them more above flesh and sense, that they may sit in heavenly places. Oh, that they sought it more, for Thou art a liberal Giver. Yet for all these things will I be inquired of by the house of Israel, saith the Lord. That was a blissful day when, in the stable, the Lord of glory came forth in the prepared body—an Infant of days, and yet the Father of eternity. Profound mystery, in contemplation of which I am happily lost, but find Him whom my soul loveth, and in His praise would join that most wonderful concert, when a multitude of the heavenly host sang His entrance into the Church *by the door;* for He was the good Shepherd, and did not climb up some other way. And now He is to me an open door, a gate of praise, a way of life, my glorious all in all. "Glory to God in the highest."

December 25th, Christmas-day — I had not thought to be yet in these *lowlands*. Last Christmas-day I seemed getting near home, but my disease has been rebuked; its progress is now slow; and I may still have long to wait in this leprous house. Dear Lord, let it be all to Thy glory, and it shall be well. My cup of joy has not been so full today as last evening, but my fountain is still the same, and in Him I do rejoice. I welcome Him into my nature as "the branch of the Lord," beautiful and glorious. Now do I long for more unfolding of the glories of His Person. These words have been rich in my soul to-day: "Ye are complete in him." There is a wonderful mine of tried gold in them, which just suits my poverty.

December 30th, Sacrament-day Morning — What, think you He will not come to the feast? Do come, precious Jesus, and meet me there, and renew my faith in lively actings upon Thy Person and works, love, and blood, and righteousness. These are the green pastures of Thine own providing. Oh, lead me afresh therein. May I journey to-day from Bethlehem to Gethsemane and Calvary, and find Thee in them all—the Man who hath "stood in the gap" for me, in contrast with Ezekiel 22:30, 31, and hath borne on Thine own holy devoted Person those vials of wrath which were justly my due. During the night-watches I had a solemn view of the exceeding vileness of my past life. I am sure I am the worst of all.

> "My faith would lay her hand,
> On that dear head of Thine"

as my "sin-offering," and there confess it all. Blessed Spirit, grant me solid soul-exercise this last Sabbath in another year. There cannot be a thorough faith-view of Jesus, and entrance into His finished work, if we fear to see the worst of ourselves which He is pleased to show us. The whole we can never know. But oh, what an abasing sight it is. I seem to myself a monster of iniquity.

December 31st, Monday Night — An eventful year is just closing; for it heights and for its depths I have cause to praise the Lord. Oh, my heavenly Boaz, Thy unworthy gleaner gives Thee praise for all Thy covenant handfuls of spiritual favor, but most for Thyself, my boundless, endless treasure; my everlasting all. It was wonderful to let me into Thy field; more so to invite me to Thy meal; but most wonderful of all to take me for Thine own, and give Thyself to me in everlasting bonds. Oh, that I could praise Thee. Time cannot attain to suitable strains; and oh, eternity will be too short to utter the half of what Thou art worthy to receive. Renew faith in lively actings upon Thyself; then wilt Thou be more known, more loved and honored. Ebenezer!

1856

January 1st — Precious Jesus, be manifestly with me in each flood and fire of tribulation, and in the swellings of Jordan. Oh, ripen me to be gathered in. Do sanctify all present and future trials. I do not mellow and mature under Thy *much* discipline as I desire. I see others so much more profiting by it than I. Blessed Spirit, exercise me thereby, and cause the peaceable fruits of righteousness to be yielded. I have been thinking of the prayer of Jabez. Dear Lord, so let it be; and on Mount Gerizim be my dwelling-place. Amen. Amen.

January 27th, Sacrament-day — A season of peculiar temptation. James 1:12. Oh, for grace to endure; and to have the blessing. Sweet are the thoughts of a once-tempted Savior. He will not leave me in the enemy's hands. Oh, no, my Lord; Thou wilt conquer *in* me as Thou hast *for* me. Oh, strengthen my faith to cleave to Thee through all, and to cleave to Thy will, however contrary to my own sense and reason.

February 6th — The first chapter of "Thoughts in Suffering" has proved quite a balm to my wearied soul this evening. To the Lord be the praise for this streamlet in my wilderness! I do love anything that tends to encourage faith, and to discover any corner of unbelief in which I am hiding. That which maketh manifest is light.

February 24th, Sacrament-day — Afresh have I presented a hard case to the King at His table to-day, and watch for an answer of peace. I do long to be all-absorbed in love divine. This is my own dear element, where only my soul can thrive and be happy. Praise and thanksgiving for the mercies and teachings of the past month. Oh, to spend this one in Gethsemane and Calvary. An Ebenezer for our dear country, in that our rulers have prevented the desecration of the Sabbath which some desired to bring about; in vain the heathen rage, when the Lord is on our side.

March 14th — "Do you see yonder shining light?" said Evangelist to Christian. "I think I do," said the other. "Then towards it you must run." And surely this morning the shining light of glory beams in the distance; and, through the crevices of this decaying body, I behold it, and towards it I must run, leaving my mortal interests behind. "To depart to be with Christ" is far better; and these gleams are tokens to me of that joy's approach.

March 16th — Very feeble, but happy in Jesus, the blessed "Sun of Righteousness," who is chasing away some mists that have for some time in a measure bedimmed my soul. Oh, how glorious, how loving He is. I do wonder dear saints do not talk with more ardor about Him who has, in love to our souls, brought them up from the pit of corruption; but oh, what it cost Him. Price beyond all computing. Heaven's richest treasure paid for worms of earth! Precious Lord, Thy dealings in providence the last year have been mysterious, but all blessed. Thou hast dried up streams to bring me nearer to Thee, the Fountain. I have formerly been too anxious, and Thy way of lessening the care is just leaving me less of earth's store to be anxious about. Beautiful and wonderful is Thy working. Blessed be Thou!

March 21st, Good Friday — I went to the house of God this morning. It is said of our dear Lord's crucifixion, that "there were women beholding afar off." I have today been like one of these as to feeling, for I have been looking after a crucified Savior, and the scene of His sufferings; but have not been standing at His cross, and hearing His precious words, as I did last Good Friday. My blessed Lord, "Thy will be done."

March 27th — O Lord, Thou hast this morning fully proved that Thou knowest the thoughts of the heart, and hast kindly answered the little weak faith which went out upon Thy all-fullness. Oh, the wonders and blessedness of union to such a *rich* Husband, who thought not His own precious blood too much for my ransom. Eternal praises to the worthy Lamb.

March 28th — I praise Thee and bless Thee, O Lord God of my Father, and my God in covenant for ever and ever. I humbly and heartily thank Thee that Thou hast heard my voice out of the depths, and this day hast granted me relief. I must still lift up mine eyes unto Thee, for Thou the Father, Son, and Holy Ghost, art "the everlasting hills" from whence cometh my help.

March 30th, Morning — Acts 9:6 was shown to me spiritually and experimentally last evening, as referring to Jesus. He is my city "of refuge," "of habitation," "of defense"; and, entering into Him by faith, and there abiding, I shall be told by the Lord what He will have me do for His glory. Oh, it is in the city, even in Jesus, that we hear the King's voice, and see the King's face. Afterwards, in Isaiah 66:13, I saw the *city* again. Jerusalem was the city of the great King; it was the place of worship, and of sacrifice; and in the holy life, sufferings, and death of Jesus is *our* city and temple; in Him we find most acceptable sacrifice! (Ps. 40:8; Luke 22:42; Heb. 9:14.) Also, as brought experimentally into Him, we get the sacrifice of a broken heart; Psalm 51:17; Matthew 21:44; and of a resigned will, which is one part of true spiritual worship, besides the sacrifices of praise and thanksgiving; Psalm 22:22; 84:4; and the power to do good and to communicate, with which sacrifices God is well pleased. Oh, what a city of store and blessing is our precious Jesus. Dwelling in Him, the "lofty city" of self is brought down and laid low. Isaiah 25:12. He maketh us poor in spirit, and then causeth the feet of the poor to tread it down. Isaiah 26: Oh, to dwell by faith in the spiritual Jerusalem in daily self-sacrifice. My very soul says, "One thing have I desired of the Lord, that will I seek after," &c. Psalm 27:4. What a wonderful book is God's Bible, as opened to the heart by the Spirit; and Christ is the key that fits every ward, both in the book and in the heart. My soul is satisfied with marrow and fatness. How I long to open to other dear ones the secret of joy in the Lord; but they are affrighted at the rough way to it, for we must "pass through the valley of the shadow of death," yea, self must be crucified with Christ; and they are afraid to die, and "venture to be nought." But oh, the eternal sweets which open in resurrection glory, when the lofty city *is* laid in the dust, when He liveth in me, and I in Him.

April 20th — I have had much conflict the past week; sorely cast down, on account of my useless, unprofitable life. This morning was favored again to go up to the Lord's house, and I trust the sermon was edifying and humbling; there was much to suit my case; text, 2 Peter 3:18. Blessed Lord, I fear I am not growing in grace. Oh, search and see my case, and minister thereto for Thine own glory. I do seem to see to-day that Satan has been consulting to cast me down from Christ my excellency. I cry to Thee, my Lord, against him! Oh, renew my faith.

April 27th, Sacrament-day — I am too weak to write much. I have been to the table spread for the poor, and have given myself afresh to the Lord, with earnest desires to be nothing at all. The last month full of mercy, but shaded as to actual communion. For this to be restored, I do, my dear Lord, anxiously plead; nothing can compensate for it. Oh, hear and answer, to the joy of my heart and the glory of Thy name. For the love, blood, sufferings, and death of my Savior, eternal thanks to my covenant God. I fall my whole weight on Thee, my precious Jesus.

May 4th, Sabbath — Dear A— and I have had letters of perplexity. We spread them together before the King, and found Him come as the dew upon our souls. It was a time of refreshing.

May 8th — Surely I ought to record as a waymark that this passage, "He that shall endure to the end, the same shall be saved," has been verified the last few weeks, upon the matter for which they were given, April 15th, 1855. To the Lord be all the praise! He only can enable us to endure, and He must bring the salvation.

May 10th — "O give thanks unto the Lord; for he is good; for his mercy endureth for ever." This morning favored to hear the Word preached with profit to my soul; text, Romans 2:21, 22. Bless the Lord for such a joyful sound! The righteousness of God for poor sinners like me, whom the law has killed, and Christ has made alive, by the power of His resurrection. I had a blessed time on Friday evening. I was panting and pining for Jesus, and how welcome was His dear presence to my heart, which again He condescended to make His guest-chamber. Oh, come dearest Lord, and dwell for ever there. Thou alone must be my companion and solace, and Thou must be my veil and covering from all besides. Strange and mysterious is my path. Afresh my heart has said, "None but Jesus!"

May 13th — Local rejoicings on account of peace restored. The God of peace be praised for this great blessing to the nations of the earth. He surely has heard the cry of His own elect. The 53rd of Isaiah has been sweet to me. I can just see that there are great glories within it, and I am knocking for opening into them. Oh, I must follow hard after Him who is "our peace." My soul pants to be all-absorbed in that once-suffering, now-glorified Savior. I have seen much in these two passages, Psalm 45:2; and Isaiah 52:14. Love unutterable! Wonders inconceivable! From all the sights and sounds of earth I gladly turn, to seek for new beholdings of this wonder "done under the sun." Oh, my Father, grant me the spirit of wisdom and revelation in the knowledge of Thy beloved Son, in whose face Thou dost give us the knowledge of Thy glory. Oh, bless all my loved ones with like favor. "How greatly I long after [them all] in the bowels of Jesus Christ." Oh, draw us, quicken us, call us onward; for how slowly and feebly do we press after the prize. Thanks and praise for this day of peace in Jesus, with some "joy in the Lord." This is a drop; but oh, there is an ocean-fullness yet to be enjoyed. Oh, pour out Thy Spirit. Ebenezer!

May 18th, Sacrament-day — I have had a blessed communion season, and have seen afresh what a glorious shelter and hiding-place is our precious Christ; how the vials of wraths must have long since been poured on a guilty world, but for His covenant undertakings and accomplishments. I have felt much glory in these words, "Your life is hid with Christ in God." The enemy aims at this precious life, but he can never touch it. This is a cordial to my soul. I do enjoy this sacred ordinance. It is to me one of those gates at which many pleasant fruits have been laid up by my Beloved, and all flowing through His bleeding heart. The well of Bethlehem was opened on Calvary for thirsty souls:

> "There Jesu's blood in rivers flowed,
> For love of worthless me."

Eternal praises to the Lamb which was slain. Oh, what a banquet we shall have above! Even here we have precious sips from the streams of salvation; but *there* will be an eternal draught of the river of life. The poorest of all Thy living creatures humbly sues for more outflowing of faith, and inflowing of Thy love this month in near communion, making me much less, and exalting Thee more and more. And oh, my precious Lord, while touching the sceptre, I beg to plead for my loved ones who are sick, tried, or tempted, and for those dead ones for whom I travail in birth. Oh, quicken them, and increase soul-communion with saints in Thee (Ps. 71:16).

June 1st, Sabbath — I have been thinking how natural things are types of spiritual. When we are moving towards the sun before noon, our black shadow is seen in front of us. When the sun is vertical, there is no shadow. And, after noon, it is cast behind us. So before Christ, our Sun of Righteousness, was fully revealed in my soul, though walking towards Him, sin and self were ever before me (Ps. 51:3). When He was revealed in His glory, sin and self disappeared, and all was love, joy, and peace. Now, in the afternoon of my experience, they are in measure cast behind me; they are not between me and my Beloved, for I have "set the Lord always before me"; and, looking unto Him by faith, I am lightened. The dark shadow or old man is behind, though still it follows closely; and, alas, at times, I turn to it from my glorious Sun, and then all is gloom indeed.

June 5th — Have I sinned, O Lord? If so, pardon me, I humbly beseech Thee, and bring Thy glory out of all that concerns me, while I in the dust am lower and lower laid. I do commit all to Thee, who judgest righteously and triest the reins and the heart. Help me to endure, and let precious blood cleanse away what is wrong in this matter.

June 6th — I have spoken unadvisedly with my lips, and fly to the blood of atonement. Oh, that I could have endured all meekly and silently! Let Thy multiplied pardons be felt in all my transgressions. Through rich mercy my heart has just been melted, at the thought of Peter wanting to make tabernacles on the mount for Moses and Elias with Jesus; but no, *they* must pass away—type, shadow, prophecy, and law service must give place to the substance. And oh, how favored to be found with "Jesus only," yet we fear to enter into the cloud of separation through which we arrive at it. I see more than I can express in the withdrawing of Moses and Elias. Things which have been highly prized and made real blessings must give place to Jesus. "Hear ye him."

June 16th — Very full blessings hath the Lord vouchsafed to me during the past week, and my glorious Christ hath been to me "a place of broad rivers and streams" in this dry and thirsty land. He has sweetly manifested Himself to me on Mount Ebal, in reading Deuteronomy 27. The blessed Spirit seemed to show me that Calvary was Mount Ebal to me, where I sit in the dust at the foot of the cross, hearing the solemn thunderings of the law, "Cursed, cursed, cursed," which I have thoroughly deserved; but beholding them fall short of *me*, and rest upon my adorable Surety, the suffering Lamb sacrificed for us. Oh, what blessedness flowed into my soul! It seemed as if Mount Ebal were become Mount Gerizim. My precious Bridegroom was made a curse for me, and every open vein seemed as a mouth proclaiming to me "Blessed, blessed,

blessed," in time and eternity. Then did I feelingly understand how on Mount Ebal we eat and drink by faith the flesh and blood of our Paschal Lamb, and rejoice before the Lord, and find the peace-offering in the place of curses (ver. 6, 7), which is just where we need it. Truly, here our Father supplies our need "according to His riches in glory by Christ Jesus." I have also been richly enjoying those two expressive words, "in Him." Throughout eternity, we shall never fathom the depth or reach the height of that blessedness. O Lord, grant me further entrance into it now. Exercise me in the written Word by the Spirit, showing me therein the Incarnate Word. Adorable Immanuel, Moses wrote of Thee, the Psalms and prophets speak of Thee. Open my dull understanding to discern Thee through the type and through the cloud. Show Thyself through these lattices, and open Thou my heart to receive Thee experimentally in all, and my mouth to show forth Thy praise everywhere. Bodily strength increases, I do long to devote it to Thee. "Eternity will be too short to utter half Thy praise." Oh, cause me to lisp it more constantly and feelingly in the low notes of the wilderness!

July 6th, Sabbath — Heard dear Mr. H— most blessedly from Proverbs 12:9. The saints, the despised—Christ their Servant. Oh, the wonder of wonders, that such a worm as I should have such a Royal Servant! It was a time of love and praise!

July 13th — Received much blessing in hearing Mr. G— from Psalm 119:41. I felt I was under the *wing*, under the *skirt*, and under the *arm* of my Beloved. The wing to heal and nourish (Mal. 4:2); the skirt of righteousness to cover (Ezek. 16:8); and the arm to protect—and that arm looked so strong that it would ward off anything. It was a blessed season in a time of trial. He may try sharply, but I believe He will preserve and bless. He never will put faith to shame. Mine is very weak; but oh, I cannot tell what sweet assurances the Lord puts into my heart; and, while some dear saints condemn me because I speak so little of corruptions, and am ready to think I have no exercises, the Lord is exercising me touchingly in His own way. Oh, my blessed Lord, I praise Thee for Thy sweet supporting and delivering mercies, which come even unto me.

"Guide me, O Thou great Jehovah."

July 22nd, Tuesday — "Mary sat still in the house"; but when she heard that Jesus was come, and called for her, "she arose quickly, and came unto Him." I am sorely distressed about doing so little for the Lord; but this morning He has graciously opened to me the Word in Jeremiah 35:7. There I saw how the Rechabites were unlike all the rest of the Israelites, just as I feel unlike the Lord's people around me; yet they had a blessing in obeying their father. Afterwards, He showed me the Martha and the Mary character, both in the living family, but so opposite. I saw there must always be Marys at the feet of Jesus, and that *there* was *my* place, and when I stray from it, I mar my usefulness instead of increasing it; for I am just to be a savor of Him to the two or three He may send, and to be much in supplications for many. Oh, this teaching did take a weight from my heart, whereby I believe Satan was consulting to cast me down from my excellency; and through this lattice my precious Lord revealed Himself a little to this longing heart.

July 26th, Sacrament-day — I have had some blessing in the Lord's house to-day, some divine dew at the King's table; and liberty to present petitions, and to confess my sins upon the head of the precious Scapegoat. O Lord, I cast myself and weights upon Thee. Oh, rebuke Satan, where he has been so oppressing me. Make me look unto Jesus more singly and simply, then would Satan be oftener defeated. And now, my blessed Lord, manifest

Thy precious Self to Thy poor weary pilgrim, for Thou art my rest and my refreshing.

August 3rd, Sabbath-morning — "Yea, though I walk through the valley of the shadow of death, I will fear no evil, for thou art with me." I have just found some support in the above words as regards my experimental case, which is like "the valley of the shadow of death"; but my precious Lord is with me, though unseen.

August 13th — Last evening I was favored to hear with power a sermon from these words, "Yet hath He devised means that His banished should not be expelled from Him." The subject was handled in a threefold way—the banished by the fall brought back in regeneration; the banished by backsliding brought back by healing them; and the body banished in the grave brought back at the resurrection.

August 15th — "Lord, I am not worthy that thou shouldest come under my roof," has truly been my feeling this morning. Yesterday I was much tried, and longed for the sensible presence of my Beloved; but this morning I feel more like Peter, when he said, "Depart from me, for I am a sinful man, O Lord." Nothing but Jesus can satisfy me, and without Him all is dreary; but to lie with my mouth in the dust seems more fitting for me than to banquet with the King. Oh, my Lord, do "lay me low, and keep me there." Thou knowest my abasings. I desire to serve Thee, but cannot attain to it.

August 16th — I am experimentally passing over a boggy place, where continually I sink into some evil of my fallen nature—into sins and evil propensities which seemed crucified, but now come forth again very boldly. It is most trying, and deeply abasing. I can only cleave to my crucified Surety, who has borne all my "sins in His own body on the tree," and whose precious blood cleanses from it all. Blessed Lord, Thou knowest all I suffer, and how I loathe the evil. Let it be for Thine exaltation, a fresh crowning Thee Lord of all, while I lie low in the dust at Thy dear pierced feet. I have had some melting of heart about the "bitter herbs" of sin, of which my precious Jesus partook. If He had not, there would have been no Paschal Lamb for me; but now, even *I* eat that wondrous food, though most truly proving that, "with bitter herbs shall ye eat it."

August 31st, Sacrament-day — I had a refreshing communion season to-day, but not a full banquet, and was brought to resign frames and feelings to my precious Lord, to give me what will most honor Him, and to

> "Keep me still in faith abiding—
> Life deriving from His death."

I "bless God for Jesus Christ," and long for more revealings of His glorious Person and matchless love. My mind is perplexed about going to Filey. Lord, make Thy way plain before my face.

September 3rd — Many sweet words have been given me about going to Filey (Isa. 65:8; Exod. 33:15; Ps. 121:8); but there are mountains of difficulty. Father, accomplish Thy will, and glorify Thy Name.

September 7th — The past week has been one of mountains and mercies. O my Lord, I cannot praise Thee enough, for Thou hast done wonderful things. Thou hast put it into the heart of kind friends to take me to the sea, having Thyself provided for it. Oh, do get glory out of it, for Thou hast turned my captivity and blessed my soul, since I was made willing to go.

September 14th — "He blessed him there," is written of Jacob, and so it may be truly said of us at Filey. Oh, what blessed heavenly lessons have we had from the Spirit, and how have our hearts burned within us in fresh enjoyment of a precious Jesus, and His all-fullness! Oh that my mouth may be opened to testify of Him to the profit of some redeemed soul!

September 17th, Wednesday — Filey is to us, indeed, in difficulties and deliverances, "a land of hills and valleys," and truly it drinketh water of the rain of heaven, for here our precious Lord has come down as the rain upon our souls.

September 25th — Yesterday we went to see what is called the Bridge, but it is more like a natural pier. It is composed of immense rough pieces of rock, jutting far out into the sea, which dashes its waves on and over it, so that at high-water much of it is covered. In one place there is a mass of huge stones, over which we have to scramble. While looking at one of these with a rough surface, like a large honeycomb, in the cavities of which water was standing, and at another next to it quite smooth, I thought they were an emblem of two believers, one constantly tried with waters of a fall cup wrung out to him, the other less exercised, but both placed by covenant love upon the same Rock. I enjoyed this; but, while walking back again, the rough stone was strikingly placed before my mind, with these words, "His visage was marred more than any man's." Here I saw my blessed Jesus having the preeminence in suffering. The waters came in unto His soul. "All thy waves and thy billows" went over Him. Hence the Church is, in comparison with Him, like the smooth stone, for all *her* sorrows are lightened and sweetened by His having gone before in the tribulated path, and taken away all the curse. My soul melted under this teaching. This morning I have had fresh honey from the Rock in several passages of the word (John 15:5, last clause; Heb. 7:25; Acts 2:18). Truly this Filey journey is a wonderful dispensation. It has been to me both a place of straits and of deliverances.

October 15th — It is ten years to-day since my dear mother's sleeping dust was committed to the tomb, and there it rests, part of the dust of the spiritual Zion to which Jehovah has an eternal favor; and He has set a time when He will visit it again, and raise it up in the incorruptible image and perfect likeness of the glory-Man, the precious second Adam, who will awaken His sleeping bride to be with Him for ever. My dear mother, these are thy prospects and mine, through free grace and everlasting love. I sorrow not as those without hope, but while lovingly remembering thee, I look soon to be where thou art, not to gaze upon *thee*, but upon *Jesus* for ever and ever.

October 19th — Very great blessedness do I find in a life of faith. I quite marvel at what my dear Lord does for unworthy me in each new dispensation of Providence. My precious Jesus is just what suits me in every case and every place. Oh, what a gift has my Father bestowed! Never, in all eternity, shall we fully learn His glories, beauty, and love. He will be ever revealing Himself more and more, and filling all our enlarging powers with bliss ineffable and now inconceivable. How I long that dear saints were more completely enamored and taken up with Him. Oh, beloved Bridegroom, take us wholly and absorb us with Thyself, and use us for Thy glory. Thou hast lived, died, and risen again for us. Thou hast bought us with Thy precious blood, and we are altogether Thine own. To the glorious Triune Jehovah be endless, boundless praise!

October 26th, Sacrament-day — "Iron sharpeneth iron; so a man sharpeneth the countenance of his friend." The blessed "Man Christ Jesus," seen by faith in the sanctuary or elsewhere, does so enliven his poor sinner friend. "It is good for me to draw near to God," entering "into his gates with thanksgiving, and into his courts with praise." I seem to have more cause for praise than anything else. I cannot recount a tithe of the blessedness enjoyed. It is not that all is smooth to flesh and blood, but it is abiding in Jesus, instead of conferring therewith. It is not that flesh grows more holy, but it is apprehending Christ as my holiness, and in His death finding its crucifixion. Oh, the life of faith is wonderful. Blessed Spirit, lead me on in this path of life, so hidden that nature's keen eye never saw it, but "the new man" joyfully walks in it while "the old man" is crucified with Christ. All praise to my Lord that I know the experience of this new-covenant secret. Hold Thou up my steps in this "highway of holiness," until I leave the body and mortality. My natural health improves by sea-air, but the disease slowly progresses. My precious Lord seemed to-day to ask me if I could accept longer life cheerfully for His sake. I hesitated, longing to take anything He pleases, but wishing also to be absent from this leprous house of clay, and present with the Lord. I have felt afraid because I could not joyfully take the cup of life, but am now comforted by the words of Paul (Phil. 1:23). Dear, precious Lord, I am willing to tarry Thy time, if to me to live may be Christ, and all my powers of mind and body be filled with Him and used for Him. Oh, the superabounding mercies which have been mine for the last two months, the last ten years, yea, during my whole life. Dark things and light, painful and pleasing, have been made to "work together for good" by my gracious God. I marvel and adore. Oh, why am I in the covenant of life and peace? Why am I in Christ, chosen to salvation and brought to sanctification of the Spirit, and saving belief of the truth? Why am I shut in and not shut *out*? "Even so, Father; for so it seemeth good in thy sight." Oh, let me be a ten-stringed instrument, tuned and touched by the Spirit to praise Thee below and above.

November 9th, Sabbath —
> "What is this absorbs me quite?
> Steals my senses [from earth],
> Shuts my sight [on creatures],
> Drowns my spirits [in love],
> Draws my breath [in adoration and praise]?
> Tell me, my soul, can this be death?"

Yes: crucifixion with Jesus, which kills to all but Himself, and through which His resurrection glories beam upon me in love and loveliness, taking my heart away. Such were my thoughts and feelings while sitting in the house of God this morning. I had also some little beam of the glories of the divine Trinity. Jehovah, as a Spirit, did break through the crust of flesh into "the new man." I long for further revelation therein, but it is sovereignly bestowed, and quite out of the reach of human intellect. My glorious Jesus is to me a land of delights. I have this day had experience of those words, "I bare you on eagle's wings, and brought you unto myself."

December 7th, Sacrament-day — At His holy table to-day, my faith seemed fed and strengthened by the precious flesh and blood of Jesus. How did I realize His finished work, sin made an end of, and righteousness brought in. The way of faith seemed opened afresh. I could only weep at His dear feet who was pierced for me. He is my own vine and fig-tree, and, sitting under His shadow, none can make me afraid. Dear Lord, keep me there.

> "Bruised Bridegroom, take me wholly,
> Take and make me what Thou wilt."

December 14th — "Clean provender, which hath been winnowed with the shovel and with the fan": these words have been a good deal on my mind lately, and to-day I see that the Lord gave the desire, and is fulfilling it, by sending me the teaching and preaching of Christ, "with the Holy Ghost sent down from heaven." Ten thousand thanks be unto Thee, my blessed Lord; this is the instruction which is food to my soul. Oh, continue it to us, that "we may grow up into him [our living Head], in all things." Lord, pour out Thy Spirit largely upon my dear people. Oh, grant us a blessed personal revival.

December 18th — The Spirit leads into all truth (John 15:13, 14) and makes us to know the things which are freely given to us of God (1 Cor. 2:10, 12); therefore, when we are rejoicing in the truth, and walking in it, delighting in Christ and His benefits, which are the things freely given to us of God, then are we walking in the Spirit who hath made them known unto us. *Self-Examination*—when the leper first discovers his miserable malady, he will be examining himself and his symptoms continually; but when cured, the command is, "Go, show thyself to the priest," and from thenceforward his health will be most promoted by examining the wonders of his cure, and the person and work of his healing Savior. Jesus is our life, health, and strength, and when He is revealed in the soul, then begins a life of faith, not in the miseries of self, but in Him. *Acceptance in Christ* — This is a fact or blessing sure to all the seed, from eternity—the sense or enjoyment of it is brought into the soul when the blessed Spirit makes the fact known, and brings home the blessing; but when the sense of it is gone for a time, then is faith to go out upon the *fact*, which remains still the same; faith has to do with fact: sense cannot go beyond feeling. There is much contrariety of opinion working at this time in some whom I know on these subjects; they are contending that faith is only passive, and can only act when the soul is enjoying sensible manifestation: while a few believe that where Christ is revealed, the soul is to abide in Him by faith, and that so abiding, the Spirit is plentifully enjoyed, and thereby faith goes out upon Jesus amidst all the changes in self and feeling.

December 21st — Romans 12:1, with Judges 6:20, 26. Psalm 20:3. Christ is our Rock; on Him we must present our bodies a living sacrifice. And this fire will consume the power of the flesh in its carnal workings; sin shall not have dominion over us. Oh, precious Jesus, I see more and more the great blessedness of *abiding* in Thee and *walking* in Thee, then do we abundantly realize the privileges of union, and that all our weights are even Thine (we twain being one). I praise Thee for fresh opening in the blissful secrets of union. Thou hast seen my anguish for want of it. Thou hast seen some beguiling from the simplicity which is in Thee, through some aged and experienced ones of Thy children urging me to look into self, although Thou hast taught me the contrary. I was somewhat turning back to this folly, through a feeling of their superiority, and fearing to be too bold. Oh, pardon Thy vilest worm, and fully restore me to the dear *losing place* where self is forsaken, and Thou art all in all. The last three or four months Thou hast been graciously working towards this end, giving me much wrestling and travail of soul for it, with increasing blessedness in Thee. I cannot be thankful enough, and would still press on towards the mark. As the Eolian harp vibrates to the wind, so may every chord in my soul vibrate to the breath of the Spirit who testifies of Jesus; and as Echo repeats the sound given, so may my inmost soul receive and reverberate the Spirit's testimony of my Beloved; and Father, Son, and Holy Ghost, shall be honored in me. My temporal strait continues, but Thou, my precious Lord, art so precious, that I seem as if I must abide in Thee, and lovingly wait Thy will.

December 25th, Christmas-day, Morning — I have had a restless night—my soul seeking earnestly to praise my precious Savior, and Satan at my right hand to resist me. Oh, what an awful fiery dart did he cast against my God about permitting sin to need such cost for its remission. Oh, it was fearful. I could only keep saying, "I will ascribe righteousness to my Maker," and "Jesus Christ is come in the flesh." *Afternoon* — Heard Mr. H— this morning from Matthew 21:5. Many things suitable to me, especially James 1:12, which he quoted. My precious Lord will rebuke Satan, and in Him I shall be more than conqueror. It has been sharp work to-day—songs and sighs mingling with my prayers. When Mr. H— said "Christ came to do the Father's will," great glory beamed in my soul, in seeing how the image of God in our nature was lost, when the first Adam acted in his own will contrary to the revealed will of God, "Thou shalt not eat of it." Then how the Word "was made flesh"; how He passed by the nature of angels, and took hold of our nature to do therein the will of His Father, and restore the image of God, but much more gloriously than it was possessed by the first man, even in his innocence, and I saw that He must do the will of God *in* us as He has done it *for* us. Adam had the image of God *passively*, if I may so speak; but when that image had to be carried out *actively* in doing His will, so that every action should be a reflection of God's glory, herein he failed, preferring the image of himself, even his wife and her will, to the image and will of God. He sought his meat in doing the will of the creature, but it proved deceitful meat; so that instead of being "as Gods" they became as devils, thenceforward having a disposition to do Satan's works rather than the works of God. Thus was human nature in the first Adam spoiled to good and prone to evil, and in this state it has been communicated from the parents to the children ever since; so that "we are all as an unclean thing, and all our righteousness as filthy rags." But oh, how precious it is to my heart to see the second Adam, who is the image of God again in human flesh, taking up our nature by a conception immediately of God, thereby showing that HE can be clean who is born of woman, because HE is not the seed of fallen man, but of God alone. Into that stable at Bethlehem He comes, even through the lowly door of the virgin's womb, "made under the law." Under it He was to work, and walk, and think, and speak. In His circumcision He acknowledged Himself a debtor to keep the whole law, and that not in a compulsory but in a voluntary way. So that if He had failed in one point, His Church, for whom He stood, must have been lost for ever. One feeling or thought of sin would have brought condemnation to Bridegroom and bride, for He had so married her and her interests, that they must stand or fall together. He must be justified by the Lawgiver *for* her. "He is near that justifieth me," was His language, and "in the Lord shall all the seed of Israel be justified, and shall glory." Oh, what a burden did He take on His shoulders, what a work in His hands, when He came, as the second man, not to destroy the law but to fulfill it! Oh, wondrous birthday this which we commemorate, when God Himself came down to do the will of God in human flesh, and thus to raise to His Throne the objects of His choice, for whom He thus a Servant would become. I marvel and adore; and oh, my Lord, I lovingly beg for deeper entrance into this deep "mystery of godliness." Blessed Spirit, lead me on in meditation, while Thou dost testify of Christ Jesus, for only in union to Him can I live in the divine will, doing that will from the heart in my life below. Another beam of glory I see in that as He, the Head and Husband, was born of God and of His will; so also are all His members (which are His bride), "born not of blood, nor of the will of the flesh, nor of the will of man, but of God." Nothing is a greater hindrance than the creature-will; for whatever (in this sense) "is born of the flesh, is flesh." Hence the apostle denounces all "will-worship"; and the more we are enabled by the Spirit to walk in Him who did the will of God perfectly, the more clearly shall we discover what is the working of the creature-will, and the more hateful will it be. We shall then see how many strange children it hath begotten us, which were not fruit unto God, and we shall cry, "Rid me and deliver me from the hand of strange children" &c. (Ps. 144:11). Oh, I see there is no self-glorying here; but as the First-begotten of God sought not His own glory, but His Father's, so His seed in us will do the same, and the more so, the more it thrives and grows. I can heartily join one who has said something like this, "I would that Thy love in me should judge and consume all that is not of Thee." I see what creature-will has done for me to Thy dishonor. Oh, turn me fully, wholly to Thyself, my most precious Immanuel! Words cannot express the heavenly lessons of these silent hours with Thee. Wherein mine enemies have dealt proudly, Thou hast been above them, and spread me a royal table in their presence. To Father, Son, and Holy Ghost be endless praises!

December 28th, Sacrament-day — It is a time of storms, but oh, what mercies! Help me to trust Thee in the dark, and in Thine own time open to me the treasures of this darkness, and the hidden riches of Thy "secret places." I believe Thou art with me, my most glorious and precious Lord, though Thou dost not fully show Thyself. I am in the valley, but I desire to be sowing there in faith and prayer by the power of the Spirit, and I believe Thou wilt make "the fruits of the valley" to flourish, though now Thou willest me to follow Thee "in a land not sown." Amen.

1857

February 10th — Richly blessed in the 20th of John. Oh, how it shines and warms me, because so full of Him who is the Heaven of heavens to me. When the blessed Spirit opens the Word, and shows Christ in it, it is indeed "a feast of fat things," full of marrow. Oh, my precious Jesus, how fair and how full art Thou, and how pleasant for delights! Again hast Thou proved the enemy a liar, by putting him to silence, and turning my prayer into praise. Blessed Father, Son, and Holy Ghost! Blessed Three-One Jehovah, who art my God in covenant; I praise and love Thee, so gloriously revealed to me in the Person of my adorable Immanuel. Blessed be Thou, Lord God of Israel; yea, blessed Thou art, from everlasting to everlasting. Amen and Amen.

February 16th — My soul much dissolved at the footstool of mercy this morning, under "the love of the Spirit." Oh, it is such condescending, tender, noble love; for He shall not speak of Himself, but He shall take of Mine, and show it unto you, said our precious Christ; and so He does. First, He comes as a Convincer, showing *self* to ourselves, to prepare the way of the Lord before Him; and when He has thus wounded and killed, He begins to speak of precious blood, and of Him who shed it in love to us; and thus He woos and wins the heart to Jesus, and not to Himself. Eternal praise and thanks to Thee, O heavenly Dove, who art so kind and *comfortful* to us, poor worms.

February 19th — My soul was much melted this morning over Zechariah 11:12, 13, where our dear Lord speaks of being valued at thirty pieces of silver, and says it was a goodly price. Ah, an unworthy one indeed for Him whose price is above rubies; "no mention shall be made of coral or of pearls"; "the gold and the crystal cannot equal" Him; yet for only thirty pieces of silver was He sold—His love calling it a goodly price, because the redemption of His Church beamed through it. If a female were to be redeemed, thirty pieces of silver was the price (Lev. 27:4). His bride did indeed need redeeming, and He scorned not to be, for her sake, valued at the price of a female and a slave. I worship and adore, and would joyfully sink into Love's unfathomable abyss, where sins and self are lost.

February 22nd, Sacrament-day — Very memorable. Before going out this morning my heart was dissolved in the loves of Immanuel. Boaz reached Ruth parched corn. Our precious Christ, the true corn, was parched, indeed, in the fires of wrath and justice; and dipping our morsel in the vinegar seems like fellowship of His sufferings. I went to the Lord's house under the sweet bedewing, and did, indeed, banquet there with the King, sitting under the droppings of the sanctuary with great delight.

February 23rd — Mr. W— preached this evening from Song 4:7, and in speaking of the *fairness* of the Church, he mentioned her as often *feeling* so vile and guilty, and said it was because she has the two natures. This painful *feeling* of sin is fellowship with "the sufferings of Christ." The thought came with living power to my heart, and did seem a blessed and divine opening up of the subject. How are the sufferings of the dear Redeemer, under the sins of His people, expressed in the Psalms, and how do those Psalms express also the very heart-beating of His people. There is one heart in Christ and His Church.

February 24th, Morning — I have had a most blessed night. Whenever I was awake the Spirit was enabling me to feed upon the kernel of that nut which was cracked for me in the house of God last night, namely, "the fellowship of his sufferings"; and Scriptures were unfolded to me, setting forth the oneness of Christ and His Church, till I was constrained to sing aloud upon my bed the high praises of my God and King. This morning, before I rose, I had a most melting view of the Father giving the Church to Christ in eternity past, and that in perfect beauty and glory, "without spot, or wrinkle, or any such thing." How Jesus accepted her in love, and engaged to bring her back to the Father in the same beauty and glory, knowing that the Adam-fall would come between, and that she would be involved in it; and fully viewing all the degradation it would bring her into, and all the mighty cost it would be to Him to fetch her out, and raise her up. But He loved, and so loved that all these waters could not quench it. He seemed to delight thus to show it forth, for in the sight of all this, His "*delights* were with the sons of men." Oh, how safe we all are in His blessed hands. Our Bridegroom is risen and crowned, and ere long shall His bride stand on His right hand, "all glorious within," her raiment being of wrought gold. Oh, how the threefold love of a Triune Jehovah beams in it all, and warms my soul with gladness!

March 6th — When Amalek came out against Israel, Moses went up to the hill with the rod of God in his hand. I think that rod was a type of Christ: as *it* was held up, Israel prevailed, when it was let down Amalek prevailed. My position to-night seems to be that of Moses on the mount, faith holding up Christ as the only victory against the Amalek which is come out against me. O Lord, let not flesh prevail, and let it not be permitted to mar the exceeding glory which continues to open to my soul in Thyself. I long to pour into other hearts the rich blessedness I enjoy; but so many are afraid of it, and think they are safer in looking at self than in looking at Jesus; but oh, indeed, when their heart "shall turn to the Lord, [then] the veil shall be taken away." Then will His perfect love cast out the fear of looking, or leaning upon, or making too much use of Him, which we can never do. All praise to the matchless, worthy Lamb!

March 9th — Exceedingly blessed in my precious Lord yesterday and to-day. I have the last fortnight had a clearer revelation of the Person of Christ than I ever had before; and herein my heavenly Father has centered all my blessings, even in *His* Beloved and *mine*. "Sing, O heavens! and be astonished, O earth!" that such a vile worm should be so sweetly blessed and absorbed in the ocean of love, without bottom or shore; but it is all according to the eternal plan and purpose for the divine glory. Blessed by the great sacred Three in the two eternities, the little isthmus of time between them must partake of the blessing, too. I marvel exceedingly, but find the blessing flow in my soul by night and by day.

"Jesus is mine, and I am His."

I seem like the four poor perishing lepers, who found such great spoil (2 Kings 7). I want to share it with others. Blessed Lord, pour out Thy Spirit abundantly on all my precious friends in Jesus. Oh, bring them into that secret of loves and blessedness—the Person of Christ, and experimental union with Him. I feel at times too much blessed to live long.

March 14th — The short period of the year already past has been an eventful one. I am astonished at the superabounding blessedness which has been poured into my soul: truly I have had a foretaste of heaven, some draughts of the river of His pleasures who is my all in all, which make the great things of earth seem contemptible, and this lowly Bethel to be as the gate of heaven. To-day I have had a most unexpected and timely flowing from the "nether springs." For this unlooked-for temporal favor, ten thousand thanks to my covenant God. Praise! Ebenezer! Praise! Jehovah-Jireh!

March 20th — The Lord was graciously pleased to grant me a most blessed glimpse of Gethsemane this morning. The Spirit did, indeed, open the wonders of that sacred scene, and my Lord Jesus did manifest Himself through the lattice. "His sweat was as it were great drops of blood falling down to the ground." Here I saw that the ground was cursed for man's sake; but His redeeming blood fell to the ground, and took away the curse on behalf of His people; so, that though they must feel the briers and thorns (Judges 8:16), there is no curse in them. Yet Jesus will *by* them teach His children to profit, and, when they are smarting, His precious blood will heal every wound. In Gethsemane I saw the bread-corn bruised to make food for *bruised* souls; the ripe grape was pressed into the family cup, that there might be "strong drink" for those who are "ready to perish," and wine for the heavy in heart. Oh, the agony of that bitter hour, when our precious Surety said, "Father, if it be possible, let this cup pass from me." My soul was melted in the contemplation. Blessed Savior, lead me on farther into these mighty depths of "love and blood," where self and sin are drowned.

March 26th — Oh, the sweet wonders of a life of faith: deep conflicts and glorious deliverances, both causing us to praise Him.

March 27th, Friday Night — We have had a Bethel season this evening. I am overcome by the goodness of the Lord—feeling in my soul that some dear absent ones were present in spirit. How sweet to my heart is communion with saints, and with the King of saints!

March 29th — Adorable Immanuel, I give myself up to Thee afresh, that in endeared experimental union Thou mayest be all, and I joyfully nothing; just lost in Thee, which I find the best preparation for doing and suffering Thy righteous will. "Abba, Father"! In Jesus I have sweet nearness and fellowship with Thee, for in Him Thou art always well pleased. Ever praised be the covenant God of Israel.

March 31st, Morning — Yesterday afternoon I was severely tried in mind, unable to realize the presence of my Beloved; but He has "shewed Himself again" to me, as it says in John 21:14. I saw how I, like Peter, in verse 3, had gone after something of the creature; and consequently had "toiled all night, and caught nothing." But now Jesus was come, leading me from poverty in the creature to plenty in Himself; "cast the net on the right side of the ship, and ye shall find"; "the Lord is at my right hand."

April 10th, Good Friday — I have been favored to sit under the shadow of my suffering Savior with great delight, and His fruit has been sweet to my taste. Much blessed in Psalm 22. I never before so fully realized how our precious Lord felt the anguish of unanswered prayer. He seems to have gone before us in every sorrowful step, and most precious is He to the sin-burdened or sorrowful soul, when revealed by the Spirit as bearing all for them. Love and blood. Ebenezer!

April 13th — "The fire shall ever be burning on the altar; it shall never go out." Hence the unsatisfactory nature of the sacrifices under the law: however many, however costly, the fire was still waiting for more: showing that justice was yet demanding payment, and only taking these as shadows of good things to come. That ever-burning fire seems now to me like "sacrifice and offering Thou wouldest not: in burnt offerings for sin Thou hast had no pleasure." Then said I, "Lo, I come to do Thy will, O God." Behold the sins of my Church upon me; *there* let the consuming fire kindle. And there it did kindle, and expend itself as regards His Church. There justice was satisfied; and though the Father had no pleasure in those former sacrifices, it pleased Him to bruise His precious Son. In *this* He had pleasure, because every stripe brought satisfaction or payment; the sufferings were expiatory, the fire devoured till it had enough. Well might the fire on the Jewish altar then expire, and thence be kindled from heaven no more. May the flame of love and praise daily burn brighter in the hearts of the justified. I have also been seeing a little of the wonder of our dear Lord during the "pains of hell," how it would be double and treble to Him, coming as He did from heaven—from the ineffable delights which He had in the bosom of the Father—to endure His frown, His forsaking, and His curse. This was love, indeed!

April 20th — "In His hand are the deep places of the earth." Through some of these deep places have I been passing, but all in union to Him, and therefore safe, though this sensitive heart has smarted keenly. Mental suffering has abounded, but consolation by Christ has superabounded.

April 25th — Much depressed. O Lord, command deliverances for Thy worm Jacob, and fulfill that good word upon which Thou hast caused me to hope: "Thine enemies shall be found liars unto thee, and thou shalt tread upon their high places" (Deut. 33:29).

April 26th, Sacrament-day — I was not favored to feed by

faith on Jesus, as at times I have been privileged to do. Oh, my Beloved, do use me for Thy glory, not as a piece of scaffolding, to be cast away when done with—but as the purchase of Thine own blood, in which Thou wilt dwell and delight for ever, while I ever rejoice with Thee. I bring Thee my present hard cases. Oh, work all according to Thy will. Oh, my Father, I humbly beg for further revelations of Christ in me. Do lead me on in those dear secrets which are hidden from the wisdom of the flesh, and revealed unto babes and simple ones.

May 3rd, Sabbath — For the last few days my soul has been most earnestly pressing after fuller revelation of a precious Jesus, and in holy sovereignty He has sent me help that way, in a letter from a friend. Oh, my blessed Lord, do bring me right out of self, to dwell in Thee as some of Thy dear ones do. I must press after Thee for this. I do see there is such glory to Thee in it, and that thus self, sin, Satan, and the world are most truly overcome. Oh, bless the dear friend whom Thou hast made a help to me. Amen. *Afternoon* — To the praise of my prayer-hearing Lord I must note, that, in answer to my poor, but wrestling cry, He has caused Christ to be preciously preached this morning, and distilled the Word in my soul. The text was Psalm 116:13.

May 13th — Isaac went out at eventide to meditate. And whom did Isaac meet when he went out into the field? His bride, Rebekah, whom He took to himself and loved. So, when we go *out of self into* Christ, "the field which the Lord hath blessed," we find Him as our Bridegroom, and our meditation of Him is sweet, and we are glad in the Lord. So am I this evening, to the praise of my Beloved. This has been one of "the days of the Son of Man" to my soul.

May 31st, Sacrament-day — A feast for the poor and needy. There is nothing to pay, and they have nothing to pay with; so the feast and the guests go well together—in truth, they were prepared for each other. I long and pant for more revealing of the *incarnate* Word in the *written* Word. O blessed Spirit, testify of Him to my soul in the Scriptures. Abba Father, reveal Thy precious Son more fully in me; and Thou, my Beloved, make Thyself known to me more than ever. How much I thirst for Thee, Thou knowest. Thou art most kind, but more unfoldings of Thyself I still desire.

June 3rd — I seem to have been following my Beloved in "a land not sown" the last two days, but am more and more convinced that it is good to follow on to know Him, however low feeling may be; and also that it is one part of the "work of faith" so to do. Oh, what substantial blessings and strengthening food we have in Him whose "flesh is meat indeed," and His "blood drink indeed."

June 7th — Though in much circumstantial straitness, my heart is greatly wondering at my temporal mercies, which seem too great and good for unworthy me. I am most earnestly longing for more knowledge of Him, and more revelation of Him in the blessed Scriptures, and humbly believe I shall have it, for His glory who inspires these desires. Oh, make me diligent in seeking, as well as earnest in desiring; for "the soul of the sluggard desireth, and hath nothing: but the soul of the diligent shall be made fat."

June 14th — Psalm 103:1. I have been thinking of Esther, how she stood in the court for audience with the king. First, he accepted her person; she found favor in his sight. Then he granted her request. My glorious Lord, Thou hast accepted me in love, in the royal apparel of Thine own righteousness, and I wait Thine answers to my petitions.

June 26th — Much encouraged this morning in reading, that after Moses went up into the mount, he waited six days before the Lord spoke to him (Exod. 24:16). Therefore I must wait on, for that fuller revelation of Christ after which I pant. It will not be in vain, for He has said it, and He is faithful. It is said of Moses, that "on the seventh day the Lord spoke to him out of the midst of the cloud." Here is much encouragement to wait, even though a cloud hang over us, for there may be a voice of instruction out of that cloud by-and-by.

July 5th — I have this morning heard a sermon from Isaiah 33:17, and, since my return, the text itself has been brought with much sweetness into my soul. Beautiful, indeed, is our King upon His holy hill, in His Person and work—beautiful is He in His authority and rule. Oh, His is a reign of love! Glorious King, my soul adores Thee, and it is in Thy beauty Thou beholdest me, and Thy desire is towards me. To-morrow will be my birthday. Oh, show Thyself to me then in Thy love and loveliness, and give me a *birthday kiss*—"let him kiss me with the kisses of his mouth"—and a birthday blessing. *Thou* art the "blessing of the Lord, which maketh rich," and addest no sorrow with the riches; while they who will be rich in this world's things, pierce themselves through with many sorrows.

July 6th, my Birthday — I have felt rather pensive today, but must praise my precious Lord, if it be in pensive strains, who has opened a spring in a desert place, to supply the need of His poorest worm. "Whoso is wise, and will observe these things, even they shall understand the lovingkindness of the Lord." Warm praises to Thy most excellent Majesty, oh, our Jehovah-Jireh. Thou canst always find a rock to smite for Thy poor and needy ones. My precious Beloved, Thou art come in to me this evening, now I am all alone. Oh, abide with me all the night—

> "And in the morning, when I wake,
> Me, in Thy arms, dear Jesus, take."

Thou dost concentrate my heart's love and desires on Thy one dear glorious Person. Oh, satisfy me early with Thy love, which is wonderful to me, surpassing all the love of women. Happy, happy R. B—, when Thou art here; but when not sensibly enjoyed, still "Thou art my Elkanah and I Thy Hannah." "Thou art fairer than the children of men. Grace is poured into Thy lips," and Thou dost pour it out. Thy "mouth is most sweet." Thy lips drop as the honeycomb. Oh, what a heaven begun have I in the revelation of Thee. Pages and volumes could not tell it out. I do banquet with Thee, my King. "Thy love is better than wine." Oh, I feared Thou wouldst not come to manifest Thyself, and thereby to brighten my birthday; but Thou *art* come. I was born for Thee, and Thou for me. Oh, what joy now, and what glory afterwards, when in Thy blissful presence I shall be absorbed in Thy loves and beauties for ever, with no more cloud or veil, or glass between. Oh, bring our loved ones to dwell in Thee by faith. Here they will learn how Father, Son, and Holy Ghost, do always love them, and delight in them, in Christ. Thou art the blissful "secret of the Lord," in whom dwelling, we are overshadowed by the Almighty, Psalm 91. Oh, draw me, precious Lord, into Thyself. "The enlarging of the house is still upward." Teach me how to tell it to the King's house *within*, that they also may share the precious spoil my hungry soul finds in Thee. Oh, why should kings' sons and daughters go lean from day to day (2 Sam. 4)? True, these heavenly viands do spoil one for earth-born cares, but then much less of earth's good things suffice, when we thus live in and upon a glorious Christ. Oh, come, ye loved ones, Spirit-born and heaven-bound, why linger ye so about the stuff? Why cling to the *dunghill?* Ye are princes: this becomes you not. There are such loves, and glories, and wonders in Jehovah-Jesus to be enjoyed even below, as yet we little think of. Oh, come, let us

> "Arise, and after Jesus go."

Jesus, our divine Magnet, attract us to Thy dear Self, no more to be "twain, but one flesh." One with Thee, as Thou art one with the Father, and one with Him in Thee.

> "Earth has no dainties half so sweet
> As my Redeemer brings."

And these streams are all to end in the ocean of glory! Perhaps I shall soon be there. I often think so, when these full tides of love roll into my soul; but I am still confined in this cottage of clay, through the crevices of which the beams of glory burst, and make my poor heart very glad in the Lord. "Choose Thou the way, but do lead on." Happy, happy banquet with the King!

July 20th — My soul has just been melted in reading that the tabernacle was to have one of its coverings made of goats' hair. Herein the love and humiliation of my precious Lord beamed upon my soul anew, for the goats typify the lost—the cursed ones (Matt. 25:33, 41). The judgment of the sheep took place in the fullness of time, when the great Shepherd was made sin for them (Isa. 53:6), and sentence was passed upon *their* sin whilst judgment was executed upon *Him*. He was dealt with as a goat, and, in that awful hour, placed at the left hand, under His Father's frown, and under the hidings of His love. Oh, what anguish was that to His holy and loving heart! Well may the goats' hair be introduced, to remind us at what a mighty cost to Himself He became a covering and hiding-place *for us*. Precious Jesus! Thou lowly Lamb, I hail and adore Thee in the depths, when Thou wast numbered with the transgressors, and dealt with as a goat, for my sake. I also see that the goats' hair reminds us that we "were by nature children of wrath, even as others." But over the goats' hair was the covering of rams' skins, dyed red, showing the precious blood by which we were cleansed from our filthiness, as it is written, 1 Corinthians 6:11. Thus "the mountain of our guilt, falling into the sea of His blood, cometh to nought, for when sought for it shall not be found, and the rock is moved out of its place" (Job 14:18); for He taketh away the heart of stone, and giveth a heart of flesh, which feels His love, and the flowings of His blood.

July 22nd, Monday Evening — I have had much mental suffering the last two days. This evening a beam of heavenly light illumines my tried soul, by which I seem to see that there has been a mighty struggle between it and the prince of darkness, who has harassed me severely. Dear Lord, make me like the deaf adder to his suggestions, but very watchful for Thy word. Keep me close to it, in word and deed.

July 27th, Communion-day — I have had a feast of love at the Lord's table.

> "As myrrh new bleeding from the tree,
> Such is the dying Christ to me."

I have been sweetly absorbed in Himself and His precious love, and longed to fly away to behold His unveiled glories. But still He says, "Return to thine own house, and tell how great things the Lord hath done for thee, and hath had compassion on thee." So

> "Would I tell to sinners round,
>   What a dear Savior I have found;
> Would point to His redeeming blood—and say,
>   Behold the way to God!"

Blessed Lord, subdue my will, and make me live in Thine. The past month has been sharp in conflict, but very rich in blessing, through the love of a Triune Jehovah and the blood of my precious Surety. Oh, that blood, it does dissolve the heart—it is wonderful! Our glorious Immanuel is always as a Lamb newly slain: the efficacy and sweet savor of His sacrifice is ever new, when brought home by the eternal Spirit. Eternal praises be to my gracious, glorious, covenant God. Precious Savior, do quite hide *me*, and do Thou be seen and heard through me.

August 13th — A day of awful storms—thunder, lightning, and torrents of rain; just like Numbers 24:7: "He shall pour the water out of His buckets."

August 16th, Sabbath Morning — This is Thy *rising* day and my *resting* day. Oh, my precious Savior! Thou hast ascended up on high in my nature, and for me "hast led captivity captive." Blessed be my conquering, crowned Head, in whom I find Heaven begun below. Let my soul still abide in Him, through all the aboundings of joy and sorrow, both of which are alternately strong in my breast. But, oh, the large happiness I find in my Beloved words cannot fully express. I am much puzzled by some dear ministers and saints, who seem jealous of enjoyed blessedness in Christ. They are always saying we must not have two heavens; and, if we are so happy below, we shall have no desire to depart. In very truth, I find it just the opposite; for the more happiness I enjoy in Christ, the more ardently I long to be with Him. How is it that I am so much alone in these things? How is it there is so little joy in the Lord? The ocean of love is full and free to all the house of David; and a tried path is not the hindrance, for I am seldom long without some source of pain and perplexity. Oh, dearest Lord, be more revealed in Thy bride, and remove whatever hinders that joy which is our strength. The past week has been wonderful to me. Thou hast gone with me to the poor, and Thou hast spoken through such a stammering worm. Thou art my rest in weariness, my ease in pain, my strength in weakness.

The week began in confusion and heaviness, and has ended in peace and praise. Bless Thy ministering servants to-day who preach "Jesus only." Thou heavenly, precious Boaz, be pleased to be seen and heard in Thy field, and bless all Thine own reapers and gleaners with that "one rich blessing—Love." Praise! Ebenezer! Is anything too *hard* for the Lord? Is anything too *small* for the Lord? Is anything too great or heavy for the Lord? No.

September 2nd — Filey — Praise! Ebenezer! We were brought here yesterday in safety by our gracious Lord. Oh, make this a consecrated spot by Thy presence. My spirit desires the glory of Thy name, and profit to our souls and others by this journey (Micah 5:5).

September 11th — This morning I was struck by these words, "Behold the Bridegroom cometh: go ye out to meet Him." They came first to me literally, but afterwards I was melted by the thought that my heavenly Bridegroom might be coming to me in fresh revelation; and truly this evening He has marvelously done so, in a sermon by Mr. G—, from 2 Corinthians 3:18, which seemed to turn me *inside out*. I longed to hide myself, and wanted a place wherein to weep; while my Bridegroom's beauty and my own deformity were revealed. The effect in my soul was humiliation before the Lord, crying to Him in brokenness of spirit (Ps. 139:23, 24). Behold I am vile. "Thou art all fair, my Beloved." Oh, I do feel it, and long to put off this tabernacle, that I may never see evil more. I cannot describe the joy and sorrow, love and grief, which work in my soul this night—this memorable night. I hope to sleep under the shadow of the cross.

October 4th, Sabbath — Lord, blot all sin out of my conscience, with that precious blood which blotted it out of Thy book.

October 7th, High Pavement — We arrived safely at home last night, through the tender mercy of our God (Praise! Ebenezer!), who did graciously talk to me by the way, melting my heart with His goodness. It was as if He had said to me, "Linger not in any creature; arise, and depart to your rest in Jesus; and the peace of God, which passeth all understanding, shall keep your heart and mind through Christ Jesus." My soul answered, "Blessed Lord, do continue Thy instructions." Then followed, with Proverbs 8:10, Jeremiah 10:23. "Hide thy diminished head in My bosom, and seek not to see any object but Me." Wilt thou be at home to receive Me? I have been in new scenes, and have proved myself wayward. Then Isaiah 48:8. "But how have I forsaken Thee?" "I will draw Thee again *unto*, and *into*, myself." So be it, dear Lord, and shut me in experimentally for ever. The second time He said, "Choose my instructions rather than silver, for the Lord shall be Thy gold, and He shall be to thee instead of silver." "O Naphtali, satisfied with favor, and full with the blessing of the Lord: possess thou the west and the south." "It is finished"! Here are green pastures, even pardon, peace, and rest. Everything *you* do is defiled: everything *I* do is perfect. Thus did my dear Savior instruct and comfort me. This is a day of general humiliation and fasting, on account of the dreadful war in India. May the Lord hear His people's prayers, and be favorable to our land. May the Lord draw me near to confess and to plead, for we are "a people laden with iniquity." Blessed Spirit, come and make intercession *in* us, while our ever-adorable Advocate makes intercession *for* us.

October 11th — I desire to bless the Lord at all times, and that His praise should continually be in my heart and mouth. Blessed Lord, Thou hast indeed been "wonderful in counsel," "mighty in working," and loving in blessing, since I have been a "sparrow alone." Although the enemy thrust sore at me, that I might fall, the Lord has helped me; and though my foolish heart died within me, in seeing others around blessed with a home for their affections, yet the Lord did lift me up again into His own dear bosom, and afresh I could feel, that in possessing Christ I lacked nothing. Oh, the wonders of His love, that can bear with such weakness and wanderings as mine. Eternal praises to Thee, my covenant God!

November 23rd — This evening I have been favored with a peculiarly sacred season, in sitting alone before the Lord. My soul was drawn out towards my best Beloved, my Ishi, to choose Him, with the cross, rather than a smoother path with a distant Lord. I have had peculiar nearness of spirit to two Christian friends. Surely I found them in the embrace of Jesus, and felt comfort of soul in being knit together in His love, with the privilege of pleading for each of them. Oh, what will glory be, if these foretastes in the wilderness are so rich! I do believe it was a taste of that communion of spirit we shall enjoy above. I cannot express the love of Jesus to these loved ones, as it sweetly flows through my heart to them. This river of love makes glad the city of God above and below. Surely, dear ones, we have blessed you in the house of the Lord, even in "Christ Jesus," where you and I are blessed "with all spiritual blessings in heavenly places." How does all that is of earth recede before the overshadowings of His presence! Precious Lord, draw us each more and more into Thy secret chamber, where worldling never came, where the flesh was never fed. Thou hast a secret chamber below, which is the *ante-room* of glory.

November 25th — The future is quite dark. I have been, and am, as on the top of Carmel, pleading and watching like Elijah and his servant. Oh, my precious Savior, how blessed is Thy presence amidst the storms of this weary land; what will it be to behold Thy unveiled glories, when faith shall be lost in sight? Thou dost give me blessed foretastes in the path of tribulation. Thou hast bid me return from the near view of home above to my kindred in the wilderness, as, in Genesis 32:9, Thou didst bid Jacob return to Canaan. Indeed, I am unworthy of the least of Thy mercies, and I feel it; but Thy mercies are free. Hast Thou not said Thou wouldst do me good? I do find Thee very gracious. I am not tried too much. Help me to trust, and not be afraid.

November 29th, Communion-day — I felt cast down the greater part of yesterday, but had some reviving in the evening. Much blessed this morning. This afternoon I was favored with the felt communion at the Lord's table, although my heart was less melted than at other times. Yet did I truly feed by faith upon the flesh and blood of my blessed Jesus—embracing Him afresh for justification, sanctification, and all I need for time and for eternity. I did cry to the Lord that it might be with me as it is written, John 7:38, "He that believeth on me, out of his belly shall flow rivers of living waters." So I saw at the King's table that it is through the pierced veins and flowing blood of Immanuel that the Father's love flows to us, His younger rebel children. He smote the elder brother to open a way in which He might honorably bless us. May *I* then be hidden and He seen. Let me be employed by Thee as Thou wilt; yea, let my whole self be filled with Thee and used by Thee for Thy glory. Amen. Thou knowest my present strait. "My soul, wait Thou only upon God," for from Him cometh my expectation. This word comes often to my mind when looking at my present position. "Trust in the Lord, and do good, so shalt thou dwell in the land, and verily thou shalt be fed." Thou, Lord, art precious in the trial, although I am sometimes "a day and a night in the deep"; Thou art there unseen, but Thou wilt not leave me. Oh, help me still to watch and pray on Carmel's Mount. While looking out for this temporal token, my soul is earnestly pressing after fuller revelation of Christ, the Father's Beloved.

December 30th —
> "Sweet to lie passive in His hands,
> And know no will but His."

This is what the Lord hath wrought in my soul this morning, and now I am caused to yield myself lovingly to my Beloved, saying to Him, Do with me as seemeth good in Thy sight, only withhold not Thyself; do not be distant towards me; life is a misery without Thee. In other things Thy will be done.

December 31st — An eventful year now closes with praise, adoration, and thanksgiving for the past, and loving trust for the future. Though present things look dark, it shall be well. My beloved and my adorable Lord, I fall into Thine arms for support, guidance, and blessing. Make Thy way plain before me, and give me power to walk in it. Amen. Praise, Ebenezer.

1858

January 1st, New Year's-day, Friday — I seem to have "Looking unto Jesus" for my motto this year; may the Lord make it my daily experience. So early is this year brightened with mercy.

January 3rd, Sacrament-day — I had a blessed communion to-day, and have given up my poor worthless self afresh to my dear Lord for the coming year, that it may be Christ's year, and that to me to live may be Christ. Blessed Lord, do lay us all in the dust at the foot of the cross, and may our precious Jesus in His *crimson* glory *shine us into nothing*, and ever keep us so. What will glory be, if this view of Him through "a glass darkly" is so blessed? Precious, glorious Lord, gather me up into Thyself more fully, that all my life and conversation may praise Thee. I roll my temporal strait upon Thee, but am too happy *with* Thee to think much about it to-day. I am most unworthy of these favors: they are all of grace and love.

January 17th, Sabbath — My soul was richly blest this morning under a sermon from Psalm 26:2, 3, it was Christ-exalting, self-abasing. Mr. B— showed the difference between legal *self*-examination and *Christ*-examination, by which Jesus proves us, discover what self-leaning and self-looking we are the subjects of. He spoke of the Refiner sitting till He sees His own face reflected, and then I thought how, when we all meet in resurrection-glory, He will fully see His image in each. There will be millions of the redeemed made like unto their Lord, who is Himself "the brightness of the Father's glory, and the express image of his person." They will all see Jesus and be like Him, and "He shall see of the travail of his soul, and be satisfied!" This thought was sweet to me, and my heart was filled with the fatness of His house, even of His holy temple.

January 24th — It is the Lord's day—the day of rest—and this morning I desired to lay my burdens at the foot of the Cross and to leave them there; for it is written, "Bear no burden on the Sabbath-day." I enjoyed the exposition of Mark 2; at verse 18 it was said, "If we are the disciples of any *man* we shall fast oft"; but if we are the disciples of Jesus *only*, and follow Him, our fast will be turned into a feast, as when He fed the five thousand with so small a store as a few barley loaves and small fishes.

February 7th, Sacrament-day — I have been again blessed in the House of God. The Dew has fallen, and my soul been refreshed. What can I render? I wonder and adore. The thought was sweet to me that the Tree of Life is on *this* side the river and on *that* side; so that those in grace and those in glory feed on the same heavenly manna. *We* feed by faith, *they* in full fruition. "The Church above and Church below but one communion make."

February 21st, Sabbath-night — How I long "to be in glory! My cup runneth over," my soul is filled with the blessing of the Lord. This evening the text was Deuteronomy 33:11. It was a banquet to my soul. I wanted not to move from the spot, but to sit and feast with the King, or else fly away to Heaven. In quoting Isaiah 43:25, it was said that one way in which the Orientals wrote was on wax tablets, and that when a debt was paid, they passed a hot iron over the tablet, which so melted the wax that no trace of the debt could be seen. This thought was very precious to me, and I saw that there is nothing standing against me in the high court above. As I walked home I was pondering over it with joy, when those words occurred to me in Psalm 22:14. They are the words of Jesus by His servant David, who wrote so fully of His agony in that Psalm. Then I blessedly learned that it was on His heart of love that the debts of His Church were inscribed, and that divine justice was drawing the hot iron of divine wrath over them, to expunge them, when, in anguish of spirit, the Royal Sufferer cried, "My heart is like wax: it is melted in the midst of my bowels"; and not until every sin was atoned for, and cancelled, did the dying Victor say, "It is finished," giving up the ghost as pure and free from sin as though it had never been imputed to Him. For ever praise Him, my pardoned soul. Wrapped up in His perfection, all is well for time and for eternity. Hallelujah! Hosannah to the Son of David!

March 2nd — A wintry day. The ground is covered with snow. I have been to see the mortal remains of dear J. H— laid in the silent tomb. Oh, that I, too, could for one moment behold the glories "within the vail" which she is now enjoying. How is she learning the wonders of His sufferings—the triumphs of His death—the eternal life and power of His resurrection! How does she now give thanks for all the paths of her pilgrimage. How does she praise, and worship, and love, never growing weary. Lord, let Thy love fill my heart, and make me live more like a blood-redeemed soul, like one risen with Christ. Dear Sister, we may still meet and worship together in Him; for we, on earth, are come "to the spirits of just men made perfect" as well as to "the blood of sprinkling." Thy songs are sweeter, and thy notes more melodious, but our joy is *one*, and my lisping Hosannah will not jar at all with thy full Hallelujah. We are one in singing, "Worthy is the Lamb."

March 4th — This morning I went to see an aged friend, and found that the redeemed spirit had fled. How fast the dear saints seem departing. How blissful the exchange of earth for heaven!

"Ah! Lord, with tardy steps I creep,"

and can only say of myself, unprofitable servant, but I have great joy in adding, "Worthy is the Lamb."

March 30th — I have been walking under the deepest abasings of soul. The evil of my fallen nature painfully at work. Oh, what anguish have I felt; but this morning I have had a beam of heavenly light, which, in this dark place is most welcome, while I weep over my native depravity from my heart, saying, "Behold, I am vile." I would also seek with weeping my all-glorious Beloved, and cry, "Worthy is the Lamb."

April 2nd, Good Friday — Blessed Lord Jesus, I hail Thee in the depths. I worship Thee in the shades of my sin and death, for there art Thou my eternal life. Thou didst get the keys of hell and death at a costly price; even by going into their very depths, and enduring all that justice, by them, would have inflicted on Thy Church. And now the keys are Thy *right*, not merely as Creator, but as Surety and Head; seeing Thou hast paid the uttermost farthing, and canst claim the release for the once debtor. As Head Thou wast crowned with the curse in those emblematical thorns, and canst now claim exemption for every one of Thy members. Praised for ever be Thy Name, worthy Lamb. I would for ever be speaking and writing of Thee, from a feeling, sin-pardoned heart.

"Thy presence makes my paradise,
And where Thou art is heaven."

Thou makest *Good* Friday every day. Good *living* and good *dying*, for Thou *art* my goodness, my fortress, and my deliverer, my God, and the Rock of my salvation. For ever blessed be the once crucified Redeemer. Oh, I would always live beneath Thy shadow below, and then, with open face, behold Thy glories above. Jehovah be praised for Gethsemane and Calvary scenes. Oh, do *fire* my soul, and make me a warm living witness of Thy love "which passeth knowledge." Do, Lord, perfume me with Thy fragrance, that I may be a sweet savor of Thee to Thy loved ones. Let us be "as *one* to make one [living] sound" in praising Thee both by lip and life. I love these sacred hours alone, to get into my *sanctum* and *begin* my heaven. My soul panteth for more revelation of Thee.

April 3rd, Saturday — These words were brought with teaching power to my mind, John 12:35, 36, and 9:4. From them I have learned that while we have the light and day of our Lord's power and presence in our souls, we should *walk* and *work* whatever He then puts before us, without consulting fleshly interest or convenience. Dear Lord, seal this instruction on my heart. I would be one of those who "by night stand in the house of the Lord." I have had a great temporal strait and trial to-day. Dearest Lord, still sustain Thy feeble worm, during this night, in Providence. I believe Thou wilt appear for me, and I go on crediting Thy promises.

April 4th, Sacrament-day — I seemed to have my place with holy John, on the bosom of Jesus, and there to plead with my royal Beloved, rolling all my case and care upon Him for soul and body. It was a "time of love"; all praise to my gracious Lord! Oh, I saw what a royal feast it is—with a royal Founder, royal food and guests. It is an *antepast* of the marriage supper of the Lamb.

May 23rd, Sabbath — Much blessed this morning in those words (Jer. 33:16). I cannot express fully what has been conveyed to my mind by the Church being *so* called. I see and feel it to be so separating from everything in self. She, the whole Church, and every individual believer, shall be called by the name of her heavenly Husband, "the Lord our Righteousness" being made "the righteousness of God in him." Here is union, and in that union a *perfection* of righteousness, which nothing of the creature can add to or take from. "Ye are complete in him," is a truth, and the effects will flow out in our life, walk, and conversation. We are called by His name to cut us off from looking for any other righteousness than Himself. All besides are but the *fruits* of righteousness, which do not make us righteous, but manifest us to be so in union to Him: "He that doeth righteousness is righteous, even as He is righteous." Abiding in Him there will be much fruit, yet no rejoicing in *it*, but a continual rejoicing in *Him*, who says, "From me is thy fruit found."

May 30th, Sabbath — I heard blessedly this morning—the text, 1 Peter 1:8—and this evening these words were mentioned, "Give us this day our daily bread." Oh, methought, those words would do to plead every day of my pilgrimage, and, if I should come to have no store in hand, that prayer would be a sweet stronghold for faith. I believe the daily bread will be given. Lord, increase my faith, and keep me from anxious care.

June 6th, Communion-day — This evening, at the Lord's table, it was specially blessed. I did not like to come from the feast; it was a time of love and of freedom at court. While at the banquet, petitions and requests were presented. Oh, I cannot half praise the Lord for His goodness and wonderful works.

July 7th — How sad and sorrowful was my heart yesterday, when the day, and the evening, and the night wore away without one sensible embrace from my precious Lord on my birthday. While I was mourning for want of my birthday portion, my Beloved seemed to say, "I am thy portion," and to give Himself to me afresh; and my heart echoing, "the Lord is my portion, saith my soul." Then came—all the promises of God are in Him, yea, and Amen. So I saw I had them all in having Him, though I had not a special one given. Oh, this is glory in the bud, and the bud also bursting forth a little. I feel it so, and praise the Lord, for, in this sense, no birthday! Oh, my precious second Adam, my Ishi, I am Thy Hephzibah, made for Thee alone. Vile as I feel, Thou seest it not, but viewest me in Thine own beauty, all fair, and without spot or fault. Thou didst withhold Thyself from me yesterday, to bless me superlatively to-day, and give me double in Thyself. In my natural birth I did only inherit sin and shame; but Thou, in love and majesty, would pass that birthday by, and for my shame give me a blessed double, even Thy blood and righteousness, in which I may triumph for ever, and "forget the shame of my youth, and not remember the reproach of my widowhood any more." Surely this night I praise Thee with joyful lips. Being new-born and heaven-bound, an inhabitant of the Rock of Ages, I must sing, and must shout Thy praise from the top of the mountains. Oh, the joy that my first birthday is in one sense blotted out! I am only seen and known on high as a member of Christ— born of incorruptible seed, born in life eternal. No words of earth's providence can half express the blessedness which we have in Christ, and which, this evening, beams anew upon my unworthy soul. Oh, bless my loved ones, my precious Lord. I must plead for them while I banquet with the King. All praise to Thee, my dear heavenly Boaz, from Thy own happy gleaner, who is thankful she had no birthday, and is forgetting her birth in the first Adam, through eternal and experimental union to Thee. Thou art my joy and crown, my holiness and happiness, my heaven and my all. I drink the spiced wine of Thy love, and taste the river of Thy pleasures, oh, glorious Three-in-One, and almost now seem to drink abundantly. We do sing unto Thee, O Lord, the new song. Hosannah to the Son of David. All praise to the Prince of Peace, and, through Thee, glory and honor, and eternal dominion, to Father, Son, and Holy Ghost, my God in covenant for ever.

August 1st, Sacrament-day — Blessed be our God and Father for the bread of heaven, of which whoso eateth shall live for ever. It is blessed to feed upon *Jesus*, not on my *feelings;* but on His flesh and blood. My soul longeth for fresh baptism into His death. Here only is my death to sin, here only my true victory over corruption. Could I subdue it, I should be my own witness; but, since it is only by Jesus that sin is conquered, and only in His death that I die to sin, I must say, "God forbid that I should glory, save in the cross of my Lord Jesus Christ, by whom the world is crucified unto me, and I unto the world."

November 7th, Sacrament-day — The past month has been rich in mercy, though the path has been straight in some things. I think I am like the Israelites at Jericho, they had had abounding mercies and many deliverances, but the one they now needed seemed to be shut out from them by impenetrable walls and massive gates; yet, around those walls they march each day in humble expectation that again the Lord will appear. Contrary, indeed, is this expectation to human appearances, and carnal reason; but still faith renews her daily circuit round the place, and, at the appointed season, those huge walls fall down flat before the mighty God of Israel, as if to do Him homage; and now there is a plain way where before there was none at all. Just so with me in this present strait; there seems no way; but I humbly believe my God will make one, and desire to wait on Him only. Oh, precious Jesus, nourish my faith, that it fail not in this day of adversity. Love in my heart leans on the love in Thine. And hast Thou not said, "Open thy mouth, and I will fill it"? Lord, "do as thou hast said."

November 14th, Sabbath — A day of blessing. My soul has found sweet rest in Jesus amidst the trials of the wilderness. I have been much instructed by this word: "Let not the flocks or herds feed beneath that mount." No food at Sinai, but rich pasture on Calvary. My spiritual Joshua has led me there to feed and to lie down.

November 25th — This morning I was out walking, when the sun suddenly burst upon my view, and, by reason of a mist, I could gaze upon it without being dazzled. It was beautiful, though not shining in its usual refulgence, and I, musing, thought, Why can I look so steadily upon the sun? Only because its brightness is partly obscured by the mist. So, upon Jehovah, its mighty Maker, I could not gaze. His uncreated brightness would confound me; but He has softened that brightness in Jesus. That sun behind the mist reminds me of "God manifest in the flesh." There I can look, and live. While I so thought, the sun gradually became of crimson hue, and then the solemn glories of Calvary came before me. There, again, I could look, and wonder, and adore. I thought, Has my Father revealed Himself so to me in His precious Son? Has He bruised that beloved Son for my sins, so that He was crimsoned with His own pure blood? Then will He not do this lesser thing also? And, as I was thus meditating, my heart melted, my tears flowed, and my soul inwardly sang the praises of my God, feeling glad to have seen the sun in a mist, and to have had my faith encouraged thereby.

November 28th — "Lord, make me to know mine end, and the measure of my days, what it is, that I may know how frail I am." This is the language of my heart this evening. I would see more and more the shallowness, slipperiness, and shortness of all things here, and would live hourly as on the edge of eternity.

December 11th — I have this day been in the deep, and could not see either sun or stars. My poor heart has felt overwhelmed. My trial increases. My dear Lord does not appear. The enemy taunts and provokes me to act in the flesh, and the flesh frets and questions, How can these things be? Why does no help come? Is it no use praying? Dear Lord, rebuke these foes, and help me to endure. I am in the furnace, but I am not *still* enough. I must be kept till tribulation has worked patience through the power of the blessed Spirit. Lord, increase my faith. In Thy time open Thy way of deliverance, and keep me from mine.

December 13th — Oh, Lord, I will praise Thee, for though I thought Thou wast angry with me, Thou dost comfort me in Jesus; and, though not delivered outwardly, I am delivered inwardly, and happy in Him who hath delivered, and I believe He will yet deliver. But, if He still should keep me in the place of straits, Himself will be my enlargement in the midst thereof. As Paul and Silas sang praises in the prison, so, in my trial, I must sing praises, too, to Thee, my God, who hast sustained me.

December 19th — To-morrow comes a crisis from which I hoped Thou wouldst save me; but if not, it must be well. Lord, this very trial shall be a source of praise. Thy way of deliverance is often contrary to ours. For Daniel it was *through* the lions' den, not *from* it; for the three Hebrew children it was *through* the fire, not *from* the furnace.

1859

January 2nd, Sacrament-day — I feel that this is my motto for the year, "The diligent soul shall be made fat." It is very reproving to my slothful soul, but reproofs of wisdom are in the way of life, and I would not shun them. The Lord inspire me with true diligence to know more of Jesus, and make the above word a stimulus to me. *Night*—

> "Sweet the moments, rich in blessing,
>   Which beneath the cross I spend."

March 6th, Sacrament-day — The waters of tribulation have risen high; my bodily suffering and weakness have also been great. It did, indeed, seem as if they would break my frail bark to pieces. But, my Lord, Thou wast very pitiful. "Thou hast considered my trouble; thou hast known my soul in adversities." "Thou sittest King upon the floods. When the waves arise too high, Thou stillest them."

April 17th — My disease has been more painful lately, but, perhaps, I have been a careless daughter, and have not sufficiently heard my Lord's voice; therefore He has sent this fresh messenger. Blessed Lord, sanctify it to my soul's profit and Thy glory. Wouldst Thou gain my ear more closely? Oh, take ear, and eye, and heart, and fill them with Thyself. How much discipline I need. Thou only knowest what trials I pass through, for I cannot burden dear friends, who all seem burdened enough.

April 22nd, Good Friday — But only *good* as Thou, dear Lord, dost make it so. *Half-past Two* — The hours of agony were nearly over: the sun was veiled, and all Nature bedimmed. How could creation look bright when creation's Lord was put to shame? Ah, no, that was an hour too sad and solemn for creation to wear a smile. My precious Lord, I would this day be renewed in the power of Thy death, and, by crucifixion with Thee, would, for ever, have all of earth put into the shade. Then shall I live *for Thee*, seeking Thy glory above all things, through union and dear communion. *Then* shall I cease to desire ease, but shall welcome all that will honor Thee. Do Thou, Lord, renew me in daily dying, that I may daily live and walk in newness of life. Speak Thou to me while I now commemorate Thy agony and death.

May 1st, Sacrament-day — I now go to Thy house and table. Oh, support my poor body. Let it not hinder soul-exercise. Oh, give me a place at the banquet of love, and let Thy bleeding glories afresh ravish my soul, and kill me to all but Thee and Thine. Be Thou known to us in the breaking of bread.

May 22nd — John 6:37. Oh, what sweetness flowed into my soul from those blessed words. Ah, indeed it will be all the way, "unto whom coming," "unto whom coming," and no casting out, no "in no wise." I come, my Savior, for more power to come, to come always and ever, whether it be night or day in my feelings. It was very sweet to weep at the feet of Jesus in His earthly courts; they were tears of love and joy. Bless the Lord, O my soul!

> "Here I'd sit, for ever viewing
>   Mercy's streams in streams of blood:
> Precious drops my soul bedewing,
>   Make and plead my peace with God."

June 12th — The past week have had much bodily suffering, but I have been helped hitherto. All is well. There is no curse in my cup: the bitters are love as well as the sweets. It is not in vain to wait for Him, even while Satan and unbelief are crying, "Ye are idle." Oh, that Thou wouldst, by a revelation of Christ, cause many fleshly leaves to fall off, and make way for spiritual fruit.

July 1st — I have had considerable bodily suffering this week, and have been much shut up in mind. Oh, grant the teaching of the Spirit with every dispensation, and every change of feeling, that I may be instructed, corrected, and comforted. And oh, my precious Lord, sanctify my increasing affliction, that it may be a blessing to myself and others. Yea, let this pain of body be like the rod of Aaron— even bringing forth fruit to Thy praise. Amen. I ask it in the name of my all-precious Jesus. In reading that Solomon was crowned king twice (1 Chron. 29:22), my heart cries to the Lord, that Jesus, the heavenly Solomon, may be crowned afresh in my soul as Lord of all, and, under His blessed reign, I shall enjoy the peace of God, which passeth all understanding; for, though David was a man of war, Solomon was peaceable. In both I see a type of our glorious Christ, and of our experience under His rule. Be Thou exalted afresh, my Beloved, in Thine own right, and reign and rule in me for ever. Thanks and praise for this visitation in a time of trial.

August 11th, Thursday — Dear Mr. T— put off mortality.

August 14th — "The memory of the just is blessed." How embalmed, how fragrant the memory of the members of Christ, with whom we have had communion of soul. His love made them pleasant to us in life, and that same love continues its fragrance and its bond, so that in death we are not divided. Our spirits are one in Jesus, although one body, or both, may be slumbering in the grave. Very sweet communion I have had with him below in years gone by. He had his infirmities, but he has left them behind, and now shines without a spot in the glory of the Sun of Righteousness. Oh, that the Lord would raise up more of His servants to the blessed standing of completeness in Christ, that, heedless of human opinion, they might "speak comfortably to Jerusalem," and "cry unto her that her warfare is accomplished, that her iniquity is pardoned, for she hath received of the Lord's hands double for all her sins." This soul-warming truth is most strengthening to faith, and starving to flesh. Here may I live, here may I die, resting on the Person and work—the sufferings and death—of a glorious Christ. There is no sinking there, except deeper and deeper into the "abyss of love," where our sins, when sought for, can never be found. I feel the blessedness while I write. So completely justified by God in the satisfaction given by Christ, that it is labor in vain for any to try to condemn. "There is therefore now no condemnation to them who are in Christ Jesus, who walk not after the flesh, but after the Spirit," which is to walk in Christ, and in His good works; and, if evil fruits can flow from that, then may "men gather grapes of thorns," and "figs of thistles."

August 25th — I awoke this morning under a deep sense of my sinfulness, but was favored afterwards with a realization of the precious blood of the glorious Lamb of God. How pure, how rich, how efficacious! Every drop is worth more than all the world has in it—the blood of the everlasting covenant, which blotted sin out of God's book, and from my conscience also.

August 28th — Still weak in body, but much blessed in soul. Surely I dwell in the land of Beulah, and wait but the messenger to bid me cross the river to reach the land where are pleasures for evermore. I may yet have much suffering of body, but my precious Lord will sustain me. Oh, may He be magnified in this frail body, by life and death.

September 4th, Sacrament-day — Psalm 98:1. A month of special favor has passed away, and I hail the return of our holy feast-day. It does seem as if home were not far distant; but I have often thought so before, and been disappointed. However, the appointed time must come. The dear Lord is very good to me in this land of Beulah, and He, my glorious Ishi, stands between me and care, and between me and fear, excepting the fear of being burdensome to those I love, which fear my Beloved will sweep away. Oh, He is so gracious, so tender, so supporting! I often marvel with great amazement!

September 25th — The Lord is very gracious to unworthy me. I am often very ill and exhausted, but the precious Rock is most solid, and I am enabled to feel firm footing—all to the praise and the glory of His grace who hath made us accepted in the Beloved.

October 17th, Sabbath — It was very wet this morning, so I could not go up to the house of the Lord, but I had a blessed time at home in the true Temple. The glory of the Lord so filled the house that there was no room for the priests to minister. The great High Priest is here, and His doctrine drops as the rain, His speech distills as the dew. Thy mouth is most sweet, and the opening of Thy lips are right things, "there is nothing froward or perverse in them." Precious Lord, hold my soul in sweet listening to the gracious words which proceed out of Thy mouth, and keep me from the discordant and confusing sounds of the flesh. Exodus 39 was most rich this morning. I saw great beauty in the priestly garments, as being full of a glorious Christ. The stones on the heart and on the shoulders of the priest, typically setting forth the Lord's people as borne by the love and power of our heavenly Aaron. But can I be a precious stone to Thee? Oh, yes; it is Thine own beauty *in* me. And as the stones were enclosed in gold, so Thy bride is enclosed in Thee. Oh, what sweetness there is in that word, "I in them, and thou in me, that they all may be made perfect in one." The whole chapter is full of Christ and His Church. Blessed Jesus! Thou art the living key by which every secret in the Word is opened, as the blessed Spirit uses and reveals Thee in them. Thou art marrow and fatness to my soul to-day. Thirteen years, yesterday, since my dear mother was laid in the tomb. I have since walked through many dark and trying providences, and I am only ashamed of my distrust. I would fly to Thy dear cross, and to Thee, the dear crucified One—my safe hiding-place from all my sins. There would I blush, and weep, and love, and find there "is no condemnation." Oh, what unbounded goodness and mercy have followed me hitherto. "Thy paths drop fatness"; but Thou hast set the day of prosperity and the day of adversity, the one over against the other, while here below. So let it be. Thou art the Joy of prosperity, and the Brother born for adversity. Much pain of body, but the dear Tree of life sweetens Marah's bitter stream.

October 20th — I have been much blessed in these words, "Return unto thy rest, O my soul, for the Lord hath dealt bountifully with thee." The blessed Spirit hath brought me honey out of them, showing them to me as the words of Christ the Bridegroom. He viewed the Father as dealing bountifully with Him in giving Him the Church for His Bride; and His amazing love to her, made Him feel it to be a bountiful dealing also, when the Father laid on Him all her iniquities, and all her stripes and punishment, and then received from Him an obedience on her behalf. Thus He worked, obeyed, and suffered in love, and for the joy which was set before Him. Therefore He counted the Father to have dealt bountifully in delivering Him up to the stroke, that He might be to her a way of escape. So, after laboring for His Bride, He returned to His rest; and the rest of a laboring man is sweet. What is His rest? His Church; of whom He says, "this is my rest for ever, here will I dwell, for I have desired it"; and He will rest in His love to her, saying, "The lines are fallen unto me in pleasant places, yea, I have a goodly heritage." He, the Head, does moreover delight in the Father's gift to His Hephzibah to be His own portion, and also in giving Him the fiery cup of bitters for her sake, and He says, "I will sing unto the Lord, for He hath dealt bountifully with me." "In the midst of the church will I sing praise unto thee," even in the inner temple of the new heart of His Bride. There He rests, and there sings praise unto the Lord, and hence it is her language, too, in union with Himself: "Return unto thy rest, O my soul, for the Lord hath dealt bountifully with thee." He hath dealt bountifully, in not sparing His own Son, but delivering Him up for us all, in bruising Him and putting Him to grief for her sake, and in giving her the cup of blessing because He has drained the cup of curse; and, most of all, in giving her such a Bridegroom to be her rest, and joy, and crown, for ever and ever. Return then unto Him, thy rest, continually, for "His rest is glorious." There all is done, and we lie down in these green pastures, singing praises to the Lord. Though poor as poverty in self, yet

> "Rich to all the intents of bliss,
> Jesus is mine, and I am His."

It is most blessed to see how mutual are the delights between Christ and His Church, and how many portions of Holy Writ, which we apply entirely to one or the other, belong to both in union oneness. We have little conception of our nothingness separate from Jesus: there is no body without the Head, and the Head is never without the body, in God's account. May the blessed Spirit unlock to us these secrets with Christ the key.

November 3rd — What availeth it me to dwell at Jerusalem unless I see the King's face? This has been my language to-day. I long to see Thee, my precious Jesus, and yet, while I see Thee not, but am feeling my poverty and helplessness, I must cleave to Thee. Thou art unchanged, though now it seems winter in my feelings. Thou art my spring, my life, and my liveliness. Be Thou honored by all my changes, and it shall be well. Still do I long for a fresh and fuller revelation of Thy beauty and Thy love. Much bodily suffering.

November 7th, Sacrament-day — Blessed Jesus, be Thou present at Thy table to-day, and let not our eyes or hearts be holden, but be Thou known to us in the breaking of bread. Oh, come, for Thou art the only feast, all is fast besides.

> "I faint, unless I feed on Thee,
> And drink Thy blood as shed for me."

Lord, increase my faith. By faith I apprehend and pursue after Thee when Thou dost seem to fly from me; and by faith I *believe* Thy love when I do not feel it, when Thou seemest to frown, and answer me never a word; and by faith refuse all other rest and comfort when I find them not in Thee. Now, my glorious Beloved, that Thou wilt cause this faith to abound more and more, I humbly ask on this our solemn feast-day, and that, for Thy glory, I may be contentedly nothing.

November 13th — I am still weak and suffering, but blessedly upheld. I have for some time been thinking of having a very loose dress to slip on easily when in great pain and weakness. Yesterday afternoon a dear friend proposed to get me just such a thing; she did not know my thoughts, but our Beloved did, and oh, how it melted my heart to see Him thus stoop and give me a double benefit, a token from Himself and from this loved one too. It is sweet to watch His tender but stately movements.

December 4th, Sacrament-day — Like Jeremiah, "I am shut up, and cannot go up to the house of the Lord"; but He can come to me, and be known of me in sweet communion, as He was at Emmaus to the disciples, in the breaking of bread. For Thee I wait, O precious Beloved! Thou art my feast anywhere. Oh, come, and expound to me in all the Scriptures the things concerning Thy dear Person and work. Thou art the eternal wisdom, and Thy lessons are with clearness and demonstration of the Spirit. "Thy lips drop as the honeycomb," and "the law of Thy mouth is dearer to me than thousands of gold and silver."

1860

January 1st, Sacrament-day, Morning — I am very suffering in body, but I hope the Lord will strengthen me to go up to the feast this evening. Precious Melchizedek, meet us with bread and wine, give it us Thyself, and give Thyself in it. Let the dew of Hermon fall copiously to-day, and may many a dry fleece be refreshingly wet. Oh, remember and visit our souls daily with Thy mercy this new year. I may be nearly at home—Thou only knowest; but do be more honored in and by me. My strong desire this morning is more entire devotedness to Thee and Thy service. Oh, grant it by divine anointing, and let the grape gleanings of my death be more than the vintage of my life, for the glory of Thy precious name, and for the good of precious souls. "The joy of the Lord is your strength," this is sweet, in my suffering state. Let nothing ever come between me and Thee. Be Thou, my precious Beloved, manifestly with us in life and in death, and then receive us to be with Thee for ever. To these poor petitions be Thou the dear "Amen." Praise the Lord, O my soul.

January 2nd — I went up to the house of the Lord, and had some sweet inlet into the sufferings of our precious Lord and Savior. Oh, that this may be a Naphtali year, "full with the blessings of the Lord."

January 7th — I am still in much bodily suffering, but helped on. Dear Lord, renew my faith in looking unto Jesus, and considering Him, instead of pitying myself.

January 8th — For the last five or six weeks I have had acute and trying sufferings, with increasing weakness, but the Lord has graciously upheld me. I have not borne these trials as I would; at times feeling fretful, and often crying out with pain, while my dear Lord was dumb, and opened not His mouth, under far deeper anguish. I have asked the Lord that I might endure more to His glory. At times the enemy has thrust sore at me, and, when hearing of one who spoke sweetly of Jesus with her dying breath, it has darted through my mind, like a spear, that I should not so honor my Lord in death. To-day, however, I feel encouraged that He will arise for my help, and that, though deeper sufferings seem coming on, He will enable me sensibly to triumph in Himself, and be more than a conqueror through Him that loveth me. Yes, though faint and feeble, I humbly now believe that, through my God, I shall "run through [this] troop," "and by my God [shall leap] over [this] wall." I believe Thou wilt bruise Satan under my feet. "Rejoice not then against me, O mine enemy; for, though I fall, I shall rise again." Hallelujah to God and the Lamb.

January 15th — I will mention the mercies of the Lord, and the lovingkindness of the Lord, though in feeble strains. The Lord has fulfilled that good thing for which He caused me to hope. He has rebuked the enemy, and alleviated the severe suffering, giving a precious peace in Himself. I have felt increased weakness, but that is a favor in comparison of the fiery ordeal preceding it. Oh, do Thou be glorified; do be honored; do let souls be edified, and sinners converted unto Thee; my life, my death, are only Thine.

January 20th, Friday — A dark, winterly morning, "but the children of Israel had light in their dwellings." The light of life is here, and my soul is refreshed in Him. Precious Bible, how dear to this heart. How do those streams from the throne of God make me glad, when the blessed Spirit breathes and teaches. And how He does discover a glorious Christ in fresh places, thus dissolving my soul in "wonder, love, and praise." How full of Him are the types, Psalms, and Prophets. He is the joy of my heart, and my portion for ever. Oh, my covenant God, Thou hast given (not lent) me such a "pleasant place," such a "goodly heritage." Hallelujah!

January 29th — I am still growing weaker in body; but I desire to look unto Jesus, and leave myself in His dear hands for life and death. Do help me to endure as seeing Thee. On Friday, a dear friend said to me that my heavenly Father would not lay upon me a stroke too much. I replied, "But I do not feel that He is beating me. I cannot feel so. He has put me into the furnace, but not as a punishment." Afterwards, it came sweetly into my mind, Did the Lord put the three children into the furnace because He was angry with them? No, no! It was for the trial of their faith. And for what else? For the manifestation of the Son of God. That the glorious "Fourth" might be seen by the king and his nobles, walking with His children, in heavenly calmness, amidst the fury of those flames. Oh, this did melt my heart, and make me long that my present furnace may be for the same blessed end. My dearest Lord, so let it be. Oh, come, Lord Jesus, and walk with me by day and by night. Down to the hour of dissolving nature be Thou present, and manifested, and then be glorified in putting me to sleep in Thee. Not in death, as the wages of sin. No, no! Thou hast abolished death for Thy people, and only left the shadow of it as a covenant blessing. My flesh, therefore, shall rest in hope, for Thou art the resurrection and the life, and, through union to Thee, it shall be raised incorruptible. All hail, Thou risen Redeemer!

February 2nd — I had a blessed season before I got up this morning, and enjoyed sweet realization of union to

Jesus, as His bride. For a season I was so absorbed in the blessedness of this union, that all idea of distinct personality seemed swallowed up. The tiny spark seemed blissfully lost in the fire, and the drop in the ocean. The height of enjoyment did not continue long, but the glorious fact remains the same.

February 4th — I have lately had some precious views of the richness and purity of the atoning blood of Jesus, by which I learn, that, though experiencing its efficacy, I know but as nothing of its intrinsic worth. The dignity of the pierced One—the holiness of His Person—and that flaming sword which awoke against Him, and smote His righteous soul in the garden, bringing through the pores of His sacred body drops of the richest blood which had ever flowed—all conspire to make it a wondrous scene to faith and love. I cannot express in words what surpassing value I saw in that blood, compared with which all the glory of creation seemed as nothing. My soul was dissolved in "wonder, love, and praise."

February 5th, Sacrament-day, Afternoon — I had, this morning, a blessed view of the resurrection of our glorious Lord, remembering how that when the Philistines thought they had kept Samson safely enclosed in Gaza for destruction, he arose, and took away in triumph the gates of the city, with the posts and bars; and, in like manner, when the Jews and Romans thought they had got our glorious Head safe in the sepulchre, and had set their seal and their watch to retain Him there, He mightily arose, and opened the doors of the tomb, bearing away all the barriers which could have held Him or His people—not the puny seal and watch of poor mortals, but the arrest of divine justice—the curse of the law—the sting of death—the power of the devil—so that His seed shall come forth from the grave in His own likeness, to be His glorious Hephzibah for ever. All hail, Thou risen Head! Even now, we are virtually risen with Thee, seated in the heavenly places. May it be so experimentally. Oh, for more enlargement into the power of Thy resurrection, not only believing the fact, but enjoying the privilege in union.

February 12th — "How sweet to my heart is the communion of saints." This evening I have had some sweet views of a precious Jesus in the Word, and so I am helped on in the rugged path of suffering, for none but my Lord knows what I pass through.

March 5th — Yesterday was Sacrament-day, but I was too ill to go up to the house of the Lord. I felt it a trial, for "I have loved the habitation of thine house, and the place where thine honor dwelleth." Whilst reading the three last chapters of John, Jesus came in (the doors being shut) and gave me a blessed time. He was truly to me the Master of the feast, and the Substance of it, and I lacked nothing. "Ye have an unction from the Holy One, and need not that any man teach you." The waters of affliction have risen higher this month, but, safe in my living Ark, I remain unhurt. It is painful to flesh and blood, but to faith all is well. I am not always light and bright in my feelings; but oh, what blessed security do I find in my precious Rock. The Lord has shut me in, into this Ark, and into the Rock for ever. Happy, happy, though unworthy R. B—. Angels might envy our mighty joy, for they never knew what it is to rejoice in tribulation and suffering, and to feel safety, and peace, and joy in the flood and in the flame. Oh, it is so real, so very real, because contrary to every grain of the flesh. Hallelujah.

Sabbath, March 11th — The flesh feels keenly the sufferings appointed it; but I am blessedly supported, and comforted, too. My times are in the Lord's hands, and therefore it shall be well. On Friday evening my dear friends came here for our usual prayer meeting. It did rejoice my heart to see them gathered round my bed to read the Word, and pray, and praise; it was a sacred season. Who am I, O Lord, and what is my father's house, that Thou shouldest deal thus bountifully with me? I am still in much suffering, but my glorious Head and Husband will cherish His own flesh. "Praise is comely for the upright."

April 6th, Good Friday — This day did my precious Lord hang on the dreadful cross, where He was made a curse for sinful me, where He had my hell, that I in Him might find eternal heaven. Now, at this time, were the precious drops flowing which were the price of my redemption—what a price! Not earthly gold, or pearls, or diamonds; but purest, richest blood—the blood of Jehovah's Fellow! Here was *heaven's gold paid down on earth* to ransom sinful worms: not for angels were heaven's treasures thus poured out, but for worms. Oh, wonder of wonders, my soul marvels at such matchless love, and at the effects of it. I adore and worship Thee, my glorious Lord, and thank Thee for all Thy sufferings, while I would afresh give myself to Thee for all Thy will, and for more revelations of Thyself. My heart is full, but my body too suffering to go on. Worthy is the Lamb!

May 24th — Hot, indeed, has been the furnace since I last wrote—but not too hot, I know; the gold will not be harmed, it is the dross that does not like it, the flesh loves ease, but our dear Refiner loves us too well to give us all that the flesh desires. I can, from my heart, say, "He hath done all things well," although suffering and weariness have at times made me weep before Him and beg some relief, especially when not seeing or feeling the presence of my Beloved, which has been the case lately. This morning, that word in 1 Peter 1:7, has been sweet, and I believe this is so with me. This poor body seems to be fast sinking into the tomb; but I sink to rise—I die to live—I sleep to wake for ever.

June 11th — I have toiled all night, but caught nothing, yet this morning my adorable Lord was pleased to draw near and refresh my spirit; and oh, what sweetness I felt in that word, *Beloved, my Beloved*. He put it afresh into my heart and mouth. Ever praise Him, O my soul.

June 17th — I am quickly going down into the valley of the shadow of death, that I may rest from pain and weariness. Bodily weakness increases, but the new man is not touched. Jesus is my health, my life, my peace. I am empty and good for nothing, and yet am His fullness, and He is mine. I have a goodly heritage for time and for eternity. I often groan in spirit, and am greatly troubled concerning many of the saints of God who are so eager after the things of time. Oh, it is so sad, they do rob their souls, and know little of rejoicing in the Lord. O Lord, visit Thy vine.

June 21st, Evening — This has been a day of suffering, most trying to flesh and blood, but no cloud on the mind, although I feel quite unable to think, &c. Rather easier now, and I have just had a sweet honey-drop poured into my soul. In speaking of my sufferings now, and of what I am going to, I said, "I am going to be crowned," and then directly I thought, "What have I said?" To be crowned! Why, I never can think of my being crowned. I can love to think of seeing Jesus crowned, but never could I, a poor worm, wear a crown; so I thought, as I have often done before; but immediately the question arose, What is the crown? And the answer flowed into my soul: "The Lord of hosts shall be for a crown of glory and a diadem of beauty to the residue of His people." Oh, I thought, the crown will be the likeness of my Lord, which I shall have. His beauty and glory shall be seen in me to His praise. My heart did leap for joy, and I thought, "Here is the Crown, none other than my glorious Lord." This crown I can wear, I long to wear it. "Then shall I be satisfied when I awake with Thy likeness"; and by Thy own glory in me and on me and shining through me, I shall be Thy crown also. How wonderful this secret of union! It is very sweet to my poor soul.

July 1st — "The light of the King's countenance is as a cloud of the latter rain." I have been asking for "the latter rain" according to that word in Zechariah 10:1. Mr. C— used to say *that* time was at death; so now I seek it, and this evening my dear Lord is as dew to my soul. Precious Jesus, Thou art the rain, and the sun, and all we need. And shall I see Thee face to face? Will this veil of mortality be drawn aside, and Thy open glories burst upon my freed spirit? Glorious prospect! And will sin be done away with for ever? Shall pain and sorrow flee away? Then, Hallelujah to my covenant God! Happy state, though a very suffering one, for the storms of the wilderness are drawing to a close, and before me is eternal rest, in the embrace of my Beloved. I look back, and marvel at the tender mercies of my God all my life long, and now He fails me not, but is the strength of my heart, and my portion for ever.

July 6th — Ebenezer! My birthday. And can it be that I still linger in the shades of mortality to see another birthday? Marvellous are Thy ways, O Lord God of truth; and it is marvellous also to consider what the human frame can bear, when Thou dost afflict and sustain. But I have not a pain, or a wave too much. Flesh and blood is worn and weary many times; but Thou dost renew the "inner man," to "lie passive in Thy hand, and to know no will but Thine." Blessed be Thy divine Majesty, for ever and ever, for thy wonders of love to such a feeble worm. Fifty-five years have I journeyed in this great and terrible wilderness, and none could have borne with me but Thou; neither could any have borne me up but Thou. I can never record fully Thy goodness and mercy. "Eternity will not suffice to utter the half of Thy praise." I wait till Thou shalt fetch me to be with Thee, and behold Thy glory for ever. Oh, my adorable Lord, be manifestly with me in the last river. Thou hast gone through death for me, and taken its sting away. Now let me feel Thee to be my eternal life. O Lord, do bless my beloved friends; and those who will miss me most do Thou baptize abundantly, with Thine own love and joy. Ebenezer! Praise the Lord!

END OF THE DIARY.

Letters, etc.

LETTER I
TO MISS W—

ALAS! my God, that we should be
    Such strangers to each other;
Oh, that as friends we might agree,
    And walk and talk together!
Thou know'st my soul does dearly love
    The place of Thine abode,
No music drops so sweet a sound
    As those two words, "my God."

I long not for the fruit which grows
    Within these gardens here;
I find no sweetness in the rose,
    When Jesus is not near.
Thy gracious presence, O my Christ,
    Can make a paradise;
Oh, what are all the goodly pearls
    Unto this Pearl of price?

May I taste that communion, Lord,
    Thy people have with Thee;
Thy Spirit daily talks with them;
    Oh, may He talk with me.
Like Enoch, let me walk with God,
    And thus walk out my day,
Attended with the heavenly guards,
    Upon the king's highway.

When wilt Thou come unto me, Lord?
    Oh, come, my Lord, most dear;
Come near, come nearer, nearer still;
    I'm well when Thou art near.
When wilt Thou come unto me, Lord?
    I languish for Thy sight:
Ten thousand suns, if Thou art strange,
    Are shades instead of light.

When wilt Thou come unto me, Lord?
    For till Thou dost appear,
I count each moment for a day,
    Each minute for a year.
Come, Lord, and never from me go;
    This world's a darksome place:
I find no pleasure here below,
    When Thou dost hide Thy face.

There's no such thing as pleasure here—
    My Jesus is my *all*;
As Thou dost shine or disappear,
    My pleasure rise or fall.
Come, spread Thy savor on my frame
    (No sweetness is so sweet),
Till I get up to sing Thy name,
    Where all Thy singers meet.

It is the fullness, freeness, and unchangeableness of the love of Jesus which will draw the wandering heart back again. No sense of wandering will draw back; no sense of backsliding will restore. It is Jesus, Jesus only, who is the magnetic stone to draw the far-off one again to Himself and His dear embrace. It is the inflowing of His precious love which will dissolve the heart in true contrition for its wanderings. At a distance from Him it may see its backslidings, and remain hardened, but, under His warm beams, it will feel them, and be melted in adoring wonder, because it has so much forgiven. Oh, wrestle for a fresh revelation of Jesus in your soul; and rest not again till you obtain it. However long you may have to wait for it, wait on; for to them that "look for him, he will appear" unto salvation, even experimental salvation, when needed. "They shall not be ashamed that wait for me." To dear Miss W., affectionately, from an unworthy one, who has been ever bent to backsliding, but has often had to sing that dear wilderness song, "He restoreth my soul." Dear Miss W. will excuse this hasty line, which comes in His warm love from His gleaner who is longing for her joy in the Lord (Jer. 31:18-22).

LETTER II
TO THE SAME

September, 1857

"Take away the dross from the silver,
and there shall come forth a vessel for the finer."
"The fining pot for silver, and the furnace for gold,
but the Lord trieth the heart."

BELOVED IN JESUS,—Your dear line rejoiced my heart; because it shows that the blessed Refiner is dealing with you to take away the dross, and bring you forth again from all besides *to* Himself, and *for* Himself. Oh, fear not the process which may be needful; fear not to see and feel the worst of your case. Cry for faith and patience to endure, while He turns His hand upon you to purge away your dross, and take away your tin (Isa. 1:25). You will keenly feel the smart, and be truly shocked at your own treachery and unfaithfulness; but, oh, it is worth anything to be restored to the simplicity which is in Christ

(2 Cor. 11:2, 3), again to live in endearing communion and fellowship as bosom friends. Tell Him daily that nothing but this will satisfy you. He can easily do it, as He so lovingly showed you on Wednesday. It was gracious of Him so to draw near, and say to you, "Fear not." He gave you afresh the savor of His good ointments (Song 1:3, 4) to draw you on in following Him; and, although, since that, you have seemed to walk in a barren land, allow me to remind you how kindly He takes it when we follow Him "in the land not sown." He condescends to say He remembers it (Jer. 2:2); and, though He speaks this in reproof, it is a reproof in such tender love, that it has often cheered and strengthened my fainting heart to follow Him amidst all felt desolations; while it has also laid me very low, in feeling that I had "left my first love." But "faithful are the wounds of a friend." Oh, may we be enabled to open our bosoms to receive them, and yield ourselves fully to the Lord; entreating Him to separate us from all which separates between our souls and Him. The same dear hand which wounds will heal, and whatever He removes to reveal more of Himself, will be, indeed, a gainful loss. May we each be brought to the spirit of the dear apostle, who counted all things loss and dung (Phil. 3:8) for a precious Christ; and may we not only be *brought* to it, but *kept* to it, for we are ever prone to turn again unto folly.

You do not know how unworthy I am, dearest Miss W., and also "of low degree"; but we are one in Jesus, and that is very sweet.

I must remember you before Him: I seem to get hold of your heart, and present it to Him, that afresh He may "entomb it deeply in His," that you may know nothing but Jesus Christ and Him crucified. I do so long for dear Christians to be brought to walk closely with God, and to live up to their high privileges. May I say that this will not be attained by looking at self or at each other, but by "looking unto Jesus"? When thine eye is single, thy whole body is full of light. The single eye has but one object—"Jesus only" (Matt. 17:8). Oh, may you, by the Spirit's power, so lift up your eyes from all but Jesus, that you will be conformed to His image (2 Cor. 3:18). I shall be most happy to hear from you; but do not expect to receive any better account of yourself—rather a worse one; for, as you get nearer the light, you will see more of your own sinfulness. I do hope, however, to hear you speak well of Him, and that, as you feelingly cry out, "Behold, I am vile," He will melt your heart by responding, "Thou art all fair, my love, there is no spot in thee." May the Spirit be richly poured out upon you, that under His holy anointing you may experience Hebrews 12:1, 2; Colossians 2:6, 7.

—R. B.

LETTER III
TO THE SAME

November 2nd, 1857

MY BELOVED FRIEND,—I rejoice in the token your dear letter contains of the Lord's leading, which I cannot doubt, though oftentimes you are not able to realize the teaching of the Spirit as you desire. It seems to me like that word in Hosea 11:3, 4. All this was done to them of whom it is said, "My people are bent to backsliding from me," even to poor Ephraim, who seems in the Word to be often used as a type of the backslider. In this case he had wandered so long and so far as not at first to recognize the voice of the Good Shepherd, or to realize that He was really "restoring his soul, and leading him again in the paths of righteousness for His name's sake." But nevertheless it was so. The fact remained the same. Ephraim was a sheep, nor could all his waywardness make him a goat, although it robbed him for a time of much of the sheep's privilege, and kept him from feeding and resting in the green pastures; so that, instead of being fat and flourishing, he was lean from day to day. But now the Shepherd of Israel is seeking and searching him out from all the places whither he has been scattered, "in the cloudy and dark day," and, though he has become so bewildered in judgment as not to know where he is, or who is guiding him, yet his faithful Friend will not leave him. He will bring him out from the people, and feed him in a good pasture: on the high mountains of Israel shall his fold be. "Ephraim loved idols." "Ephraim hired lovers." "Ephraim mixed himself among the people." Ephraim's goodness is "like a morning cloud, and as the early dew it goeth away."

Now can my dear Miss W— trace any of her own features in this description of Ephraim? Is she convicted, in her own conscience, of the like evils, as she reads the charges against the backsliding one? Then, let her listen to the sequel, and, though Satan and unbelief may rob her of the comfort of many promises, by insinuating that she is not the character described, and they are not given to her, yet surely she may look for Ephraim-mercies, and plead Ephraim-promises, and hope in Ephraim's pardoning God, who says, "Is Ephraim my dear son? is he a pleasant child? For since I spake against him I do earnestly remember him still; therefore my bowels are troubled for him: I will surely have mercy upon him, saith the Lord" (Hos. 11:8, 9). Ephraim shall say, "What have I to do any more with idols?" "I will heal their backsliding, I will love them freely; for mine anger is turned away from him," even from the Surety on whom their sin was found, and punished. From Him is the divine anger turned away, because He has endured the utmost penalty which justice could require, and therefore a holy God can love us freely (Isa. 53:6).

Oh, my beloved and longed-for, I know your dear heart is fully convicted of backsliding; here you can painfully read your name and character. Well—the Word abounds with rich promises to such; promises of correction, of reviving, and restoration. Search them out: you will wonder at their fullness and freeness. If you dare not think any other breast of consolation belongs to you, this is an abundant one. May you, by faith, drink it in and be satisfied, and may the blessed Spirit bring home these free-grace promises so warmly to your heart, that it shall "dissolve in wonder, love, and praise." May you, by faith, look upon Him whom you have pierced, and mourn for Him, while at the same time you rejoice in His benefits, and receive, by His precious blood, the blotting out of all transgressions. That blood has blotted them out of the book, so that, when sought for, they shall not be found, and it alone can blot them out of the conscience; this also shall be done (Heb. 9:13, 14). Oh, this efficacious blood! Oh, this wondrous Savior! He opens the secret of our wanderings and transgressions, only to declare how entirely He has put them all away by the sacrifice of Himself.

Hear Him speak, Isaiah 43:22-26. Thus "He receiveth sinners, and eateth with them," having been made sin for them, that they "might be made the righteousness of God in Him." Let us join to praise Him, for, if He had meant to destroy us, He would not have shown us such things as these. Oh, what mercy that He did not say, "Let them alone, they have loved idols, after idols let them go." What mercy that by His light He has manifested our darkness, and searchingly said to us, "Is there any secret thing with thee? Has it not been thus with you?" And has He not caused you to reply, Psalm 139:23? Christ is the *Way* (John 14:6). Has He not raised you from the bed of spiritual sloth, to seek your Beloved? And have you not caught some little savor of His good ointments, drawing you on in seeking Him still? Oh, yes; your letter plainly declares it in those little revivings, inflowings of the Word, and encouragements at the mercy-seat; of all which you may say, "It is the voice of my beloved, behold he cometh, leaping upon the mountains, skipping upon the hills." You cannot yet say He is come so as to embrace you, but His tokens are sure, and by them He is saying, "Thou shalt see greater things than these." More of *thine* own heart, and more of *His;* more of *thy* sin, and more of *His* great salvation; more of *thy* deformity, and more of *His* beauty. The blessed Spirit discovers both (John 16:8, 14). Fear not, He will "perfect that which concerneth" you; and, though you may not yet have felt the depth of your nature's evil, as some have, you will learn it more and more as you go on (Ezek. 8:13). Yet remember, this is not salvation, neither will it bring rest to your soul; but, in following Isaiah 45:22, that will be found. It is while beholding Jesus by faith you will be changed into His image (2 Cor. 3:18). I rejoice to hear you say that you are longing above all to know Him. Go on wrestling for it, and may you fully experience Philippians 3:7-16.

I, too, have felt the sweetness of that word, Isaiah 42:8. It is a consolation that when He brought us into the banqueting house, and said, "Yea, I have loved thee with an everlasting love," even then He knew how faithless we should prove; therefore when that faithlessness came out in action, it did not diminish His love, or touch our union, though it did interrupt communion. I am glad, however, that He has so stirred you up, that you cannot rest without it, and that He has made you willing for any trial to the flesh, rather than to follow Him afar off. Do still beg for fuller revelation of Himself and His love. Do not be considering so much how you love Him, as how He loves you. Your love is but the *effect;* His is the *cause;* and the more you have to do with the cause, the more fully will the effect flow from it (1 John 4:19, and St. John 15:9). So with faith; if you would have *it* grow, it must be by looking at *Him*, not at *it*. In short, the more you "consider Him," and are continually coming unto Him, the more lively and healthy will be the graces of the Spirit in your soul, while yet you rejoice, not in your fruitfulness, but only in Him and in what He has done and suffered. If the Holy Spirit open this to you, you will find the secret of peace and power. It is all in Christ, and He says, "Arise, my love, my fair one, and come away." Away from self, away from all besides, to be absorbed in Him. Then shall thy peace flow as a river, and "thy righteousness as the waves of the sea" (Micah 5:5; Jer. 23:6). I am ashamed of writing so much, but know not how to leave off. Jesus is very precious, and you are dear; and I long for your eye and heart to be fixed on Him. Then will your course be steady, and you will not be greatly moved by the many changes you will ever find within. Your letter breathes with tokens of life. You could not feel His blood so precious, and long for His love, unless you were alive; and I believe He is come to you that you may have life more abundantly, and that your heart, which seemed desolate, may be again tilled and sown (Ezek. 36:32 to end).

If it is for the Lord's glory that we meet again, He will bring it about; but if you expect anything from me, you must be disappointed. "He will not give His glory to another." Jesus will be all your need, and, if we ever meet, both looking to Him, it will be a warm meeting indeed.

It has pleased my dear Lord most wonderfully to renew my bodily health. Oh, for grace to spend all in His service. He has been most kind, to open the "upper springs" sweetly since my return home. Oh, press on after a life of faith in Jesus, for it is next in blessedness to a life of glory with Jesus. Beg of the blessed Spirit to draw your faith out continually upon His Person and work. Then will you find that He is a "good land, flowing with milk and honey." I long for you to be brought to rejoice in the Lord, and have sweet fellowship with Him. May He keep you pleading and waiting for it, until He shall say "Be it unto thee even as thou wilt." He loves our importunity, and waits to answer prayer.

—R. B.

P.S — You mention that sometimes all you thought you had enjoyed seems a delusion. You say, "I do not know what to do in such cases." Come to Jesus afresh, in all your emptiness, as if you never had received anything from Him, and He will not cast you out; no, "in no wise." If you fear you were deceived, and think you had false peace and comfort, come and tell Him, and ask Him to take away the wrong, and make you right. Hide nothing from Him. Thus you will get more relief from self, and victory over Satan, than by any other means. Let nothing keep you from Him.

—R. B.

LETTER IV
TO THE SAME

I am so delighted and thankful that you have been enabled to follow your Beloved in a land not sown, still pursuing after Him when He seemed to go away, and still waiting, though He answered you "never a word." I well know the painful feelings when there seems to be no access, and faith is so enfeebled that one can hardly recognize to whom one is speaking. Still it is not in vain. It is for the trial of faith, and though it seem a "fiery trial," faith shall grow thereby, so long as the soul is kept waiting on. "Add to your faith patience"; and see how long the worthies of old had to wait for any promised blessing.

"They who thus sow in tears shall reap in joy" (James 5:7). You must not always measure success by present feelings. Seek to have your heart fixed, trusting in God, and not in what you feel (Isa. 30:18). Wait on, wait ever. One has well said, "If the Lord seem to shut His door against you, it is not to keep you out, but only to make you knock the louder." Therefore, though the vision tarry, wait for it. Ere long the dry fleece shall be wet with the dew of heaven, for the promise is, "I will be as the dew unto Israel." Do not be discouraged by your own dryness and barrenness. You must realize this, that the Lord alone may be exalted, and that you may thankfully say, "All my springs are in Thee."

—R. B.

LETTER V
TO THE SAME (EXTRACT)

September, 1858

You complain of having but little of the sensible love and presence of your Beloved, and that once you enjoyed much more. I do not know sufficient of your experience, to be able to judge whether the Lord is withholding sensible enjoyments to bring you to live more by faith upon Himself than upon His benefits. If so, I am sure the more you are brought so to live upon the precious Person and work of Jesus, the more stability of soul you will experience. Your soul being brought to triumph in Him who is the "Lord our Righteousness." I know not whether it be so, or whether the Lord is saying Revelation 2:4, 5; if so, you will cry Psalm 19:12, and Psalm 51:12. But, however, though no fellow-pilgrim may exactly understand your present exercises and position in the divine life, your dear Lord knows all about it; and, if you closely wait upon Him, He will reveal what He intends, by the change in your experience. Oh, may He cause you to come out of self continually, and find your all in Jesus. The Lord establish, strengthen, and settle you on the Rock, as David sings (Ps. 40:2). My heart longs that it may be thus with you, for this is the victory that overcometh; all faith in Jesus and in His doing and suffering. Excuse all this from one who longs that your heart may be "established with grace." To Him I commend you—may He be revealed more fully in your soul.

—R. B.

LETTER VI
TO A. T.

Ockbrook, May 18th, 1849

My dear A—,—It had already been in my mind to write to you, and now that you have sent me a note, I will try to answer it, feeling most sensibly that the Lord must be my Teacher, or, indeed, I shall darken "counsel by words without knowledge."

You say, "My mouth is shut"—it seems to have been so with one of old (Ps. 88:8; Ps. 2:15; Ps. 142:7). And Jesus says to His Church that she was "a spring shut up, a fountain sealed," so you see this shutting up is old-fashioned work, even in the living family; therefore you must not conclude it to be a black mark against you, though it be a painful one, but rather cry more earnestly to Him "who shutteth and no man openeth"; but, blessed be His name, He also "openeth and no man shutteth." Do not, my dear boy, restrain prayer before God—if you do, I am sure your soul will suffer loss, and Satan will gain the advantage. Perhaps you will say, "My mouth is shut up in prayer, too, I cannot pray." Then that is just a reason for you to go to the Lord, and to be much in secret before Him, who alone can help you. If a spirit of prayer is a blessing, it is worth seeking for, and remember you will not seek in vain! You know the Lord does not expect us to bring *to* Him, but to receive *from* Him. We come empty-handed for a supply, so just bring your prayerless heart (if it should be such) to Him, to put prayer into it. Tell Him, with all simplicity, that you would pray, but cannot; and beg Him to do for you as He promises in Zechariah 10:12; if you cannot utter words, rather stay and groan at His footstool than be driven away. I can say from experience it is good to do so; even if no present answer seem to come, I am sure it is not in vain. You say the Bible is a sealed book; do not on this account cease to search it, for where else can you go to find so purely the words of eternal life? We are to watch daily at Wisdom's gates, and to wait at the post of her doors. They are pronounced blessed who do so, and the words "watch" and "wait" seem to imply that there is not always an obtaining wisdom's lesson. We must be exercised in patience, as well as in knowledge. Well do I know what it is to be without dew and unction, when I seem to have lost old lessons, and to have learnt no new ones. Yet do I always find it best to keep close to that garden of the Word, where I so often have had the showers from heaven; and, however long the season of dryness, they have always come again, and so it will be to you.

Read straight forward, for you know not at which chapter or verse the seal will be broken. Jesus will do for you as in Luke 24:27, 45; and then you will not want my poor encouragement to "search the Scriptures." Proverbs 13:4, 1 Timothy 4:15, are God's own words. You say, "I am as though forsaken," just like the Church of old (Isa. 49:14). But God contradicts her: "They may forget, yet will I not forget thee." Seeming absence and distance are the times for proving our faith, and it is a mercy if we are helped to trust our God in the dark. "If we believe not, He abideth faithful"; and He says, "I will see you again, and your heart shall rejoice, and your joy no man taketh from you" (Isa. 54:7, 8). I trust, ere long, your drooping soul will say, "It is the voice of my beloved, behold, he cometh"; and you will say, "Why should He regard me?" Which question can only be resolved into His own Holy sovereignty. No sinful child of Adam can see why God should love him; each Spirit-convinced soul feels himself the most unlikely one to have been noticed, and can only say, "Even so, Father; for so it seemed good in thy sight." The Scriptures also show us that God's choice and love was of His own will, without one desert or deserving of the creature, for His own glory. And, moreover, we see plainly that He has not taken the most excellent things, but rather those which seem most weak and base to the outward eye (1 Cor. 1:27, 29). Here, therefore, you will find no ground of exclusion, yet look not into your little self for a cause to induce divine love; but look up at the mighty Jehovah, and admire His majestic movements in not stooping to the creature for a motive to move His love, but coming forth in His own sovereignty to love and save freely. How does this thought exalt Him, and abase us! Oh, it is just beautiful, to lay and keep us low.

Now, having looked over all your statement, I can find nothing contrary to the common exercises of the Lord's people, and quite believe you must prepare to "endure with hardness," if you are a soldier of Jesus Christ; for it is His will that they who reign with Him shall also suffer with Him, and also that they shall have many varied exercises in the discipline of the wilderness. We must learn our weakness, as well as His strength; our emptiness, as well as His fullness; our ignorance as well as His wisdom. We must experience that our hearts are like the fallow ground, as well as that He is like the dew unto Israel; and we must have times of shutting up, that we may afresh give Him the glory of opening again, and that we may be kept feelingly saying, "All my springs are in thee." When some new exercise seems painful, it is a mercy if the Lord gives us a desire to go through, rather than to turn away from it. If we are more anxious to learn instruction, than to be relieved from the unpleasantness of it, this is a healthy state of soul, and so walking, we shall understand that the Lord doeth nothing in vain; but that all the humbling and emptying frames that we are brought into are for our establishment in Him, and for His glory. In short, that all is for "the lifting of Jesus on high" in our souls. This is the constant work of the Holy Spirit, to bring us to be experimentally *nothing*, and to make Jesus our "all in all," thereby teaching us to live by faith upon Him. Then does our experience correspond with Jeremiah 17:7, 8; and Psalm 97:11. But do not be discouraged, because you are yet learning your nothingness; this is really needful to make way for the rest. Do not seek to exercise yourself on things too high for you, or be comparing yourself with others, for this will only be an occasion of stumbling to you; but ask to be kept in simplicity, begging of the Holy Spirit to show you how the Lord may be glorified, and how you may be edified by your present state. In this way, you will often find that "out of the eater comes forth meat, and out of the strong comes forth sweetness." Ah, and that the Lord can teach by a dry fleece as well as by one soaked with heavenly dew. May He bless you, and give you understanding in all things. You know that I have been very ill, and at the same time very well. Like 2 Corinthians 4:16-18. Ah, truly I could tell you much of the love, power, and preciousness of my blessed Jesus; but I thought it might be more for your profit to take you upon your own ground, and to talk over your feelings rather than describe mine. But this I must say: I have proved that there is a reality in vital godliness which will stand amid the decay of all that is fleshly, and I have learned that Jesus loveth at all times, and in the depths He is a solid Rock to those who put their trust in Him.

May the weakness of my words throw no confusion over your mind; but may the wind of the Spirit (Job 37:21) pass by and cleanse them. May you, by His power, have the application of the precious blood, and the imputation of the perfect righteousness, and a close walk with God.

So affectionately desires your very sincere friend,

—R. B.

LETTER VII
TO THE SAME

My dear A—,—I feel quite sorry to have been so long without writing to you, but many things in mind and body have seemed a hindrance, so you must excuse it, and not think yours was uninteresting—it is far otherwise. To hear the faintest sigh after heart-acquaintance with Jesus is always deeply interesting to me, and surely it is such "smoking flax" He will not quench, and such "bruised reeds" He will not break. He is a tender Shepherd; He knows the lambs cannot travel very fast, so He will sometimes gather them in His arms, and carry them in His bosom; while, at others, He will suffer even those little ones to feel the roughness of the road and their own weakness, that they may be emptied of self-confidence, and walk humbly, confiding in the Lord alone. All divine leadings are in divine sovereignty, and we cannot mark out any specific line, either for ourselves or others; but this we know, that all who are born of God shall be led and taught by the Spirit, and all such do feel sin hateful and holiness desirable. They hunger and thirst after righteousness—Christ and His manifested pardon is the object, either of their desire or of their enjoyment. To understand the Holy Scripture, and to find a blessing in ordinances, they also seek after, longing at the same time to realize, communion with God and with His saints; such desires are proofs of spiritual life, and where there is life there shall be growth, although, as I before said, the way and manner thereof is sovereign. Some learn war in their youth, and have all their enemies coming out against them, when as yet they scarcely know under whose banner they are fighting. This was my own case; and, though it seemed very hard, I now bless God for it, fully proving that "it is good to bear the yoke in one's youth." We must learn to fight, if we are of the living family, and those who sing and make merry in early days are often very restive when the trumpet calls them from the banquet to the battle; and when, after the green pastures, they have to follow their Lord "in a land not sown." However, all His ways are right ways, and in the end each will say, "He hath done all things well" (Ps. 107:7). They shall all prove that "the end of a thing is better than the beginning." Balaam might well say, "Let me die the death of the righteous, and let my last end be like his"; but, alas, he had never been led forth in the right way—by the footsteps of the flock; he did not hunger and thirst after righteousness, but "loved the wages of unrighteousness," and received them (Rom. 6:23); by the sword of Israel was Balaam the soothsayer sent to his reward.

And now dear A—, there may be nothing in all this that will meet your case. I am sure there will not, unless His hand be in it, whose power levelled the bow which was drawn at a venture, causing the arrow to enter just between the joints of the harness. He knows whether you need a wound or a balsam—remember, He wounds in order to heal, and kills that He may make alive. I covet His workings in your soul (as shall seem best to His godly wisdom), to keep you from false peace and false refuges, and to bring you the true light when you seem to sit in darkness and the shadow of death; to give you also knowledge of salvation by the felt remission of your sins, and to guide you into the way of peace. These things are the work of God (John 6:63); but as He condescends to use instrumentality, and that often of the weakest kind, we are encouraged to write and speak to one another, not knowing when or by what word a blessing may be given or received. On this ground, therefore, I would affectionately encourage you, dear A—, to seek for more openness on this dearest of all subjects. You are restrained in speaking and in writing, partly, perhaps, from natural reserve, and partly from the working of the enemy, who well knows how many blessings the saints got, when in simplicity they speak, "often one to another," of their fears and feelings, and of the things which belong to their everlasting peace. He remembers, also, how many of his snares have been broken and his temptations blunted, when fellow-pilgrims have taken sweet counsel together, and spread each other's hard cases before the Lord. Therefore, while he cares not how much *lip-talk* there is between professors, he will try hard to hinder *heart-talk*, especially between young Christians; he will hold them back with the fear of speaking more than they feel, and professing to be what they are not; and then he will strive to keep them from the helpful encouragements and counsels of those who have tried the road before them, and whose bowels yearn over them in the Lord. Think of these things, and the Lord grant that with the heart you may believe, and with the mouth make confession unto salvation, to the glory of His name. Do not wonder if you are assailed with unbelieving or atheistical thoughts, when reading the Scriptures, or at other times. These are all weapons formed from beneath by the master of black arts, and the iron of them hath entered into many a redeemed soul, making it to cry out in great bitterness, "If the foundations be destroyed, what can the righteous do?" Satan knows he cannot destroy them, although he is permitted at times to envelop them in thick mists, making it to appear as if there were no covenant-keeping God, and no divine authority in the Scriptures, or reality in the religion of Jesus; but he only hurls these fiery darts in order to get the Bible closed, and the footstool of mercy neglected, that the soul may sit down in hopeless gloom, with the eye turned away from the only place of refuge. Though he thus distress, he shall not destroy; and soon the poor heart shall say, as in Micah 7:8, "Rejoice not against me, O mine enemy," &c. These painful things are more or less the lot of Zion's pilgrims; but in all these we are more than conquerors through Him that loved us, and He will bruise Satan under the feet of every one, weak or strong, who put their trust in Him, and who have been caused to fix their hopes upon Jesus, who is entered within the veil. For all such He will arise and rebuke the cruel foe, saying, "Is not this a brand plucked out of the burning?"

You asked about the badgers' skins which covered the tabernacle. I am not wise enough to explain that mystic sanctuary, all of which was full of meaning; but, as both the tabernacle and the temple did prefigure Christ and His Church, and as the tabernacle was covered with rams' skins, dyed red, and with badgers' skins, those beasts must necessarily have been slain before these skins could have been so used. Methinks herein beams upon us, as through a lattice, the death of our gracious Savior, who condescended to be slain as a sacrifice for His Church, whom also His righteousness covers. Do we not here see, in these rams' skins, dyed red, the precious blood of our glorious Surety flowing out from His scourged and pierced body with crimson hue, and also a rich covering of spotless and perfect righteousness to justify? Oh, to be under this red covering, "accepted in the beloved," "complete in him"; oh, to know the value—feel the efficacy of blood divine (Heb. 9:22). All things in the Heavenly Tabernacle—every living vessel in the upper sanctuary has blood applied by the Holy Ghost. No knowledge, or gifts, or feelings, will do in the place of this—no living vessel is too small to experience it, and none so great as not to need it; you may not yet have felt its powerful application, though you may be in the true sanctuary, under the red covering, which betokens that full atonement has been made; but as the rams' skins were hidden by the badgers' skins (Exod. 24:14), we may learn that there must be *personal* revelation and application of the atonement, ere we can feelingly enjoy the benefit; and for this may you be stirred up to pray. And now I commend you to "Him that is able to keep you from falling, and to present you faultless before the presence of His glory with exceeding joy." And, with best wishes,

Believe me, yours very sincerely,

—R. B.

LETTER VIII
TO MISS A—

This letter was written under peculiar circumstances, when the friend to whom it is addressed had just heard that R. B— was suffering from an incurable disease.

Bethel Cottage, December 27th, 1854

"And she said, It is well."

MY PRECIOUS E—, I thank you for your affectionate note, which is very sweet to my heart, because it savors of Him, and He does not let you hang on my skirts, to hold me back from His embrace. I thank you, in His name, for all your tender expressions of love;—I will not say *sympathy*, for you know I need none, even as the betrothed needs no sympathy when her Beloved comes to claim her for Himself. She may have to leave those who are very near and dear, but she is sure to find all more than made up in Himself; and, mark you, the closer you walk with Him, the less will you realize separation. There is such a thing on earth as coming to "the spirits of just men made perfect," and having sweet fellowship in Him with departed saints. I am a living witness of it, and it is no imagination—it is purely spiritual—a holy secret of love, known to those who are least encrusted with earth; and it sweetly proves that the "Church above and the Church below but one communion make." A dear writer has well said, "Surely the spiritual communion should be closer when there is only one body of flesh instead of two to intercept it"; that is, when one is removed to glory, and the other remains in grace. However, I would just say, seek to live very closely with your Beloved, and He will give you many good things, which yet you have no conception of (1 Cor. 2:9, 10). I much feared to tell the nature of my ailment; but, as my health was failing, it did not seem right to hide it longer from my loved ones; and, do you know, since it has been disclosed, my precious Lord has lovingly said to me, when I have felt timid, "Why shouldst thou be ashamed of what I have done?" and I answered Him, that if He will be glorified and revealed in it, I will, for His sake, forget all the rest. Oh, yes; most gladly would I glory in mine infirmity, if He be thereby magnified in this body, whether by life or by death.

As for the affliction itself, I call it a bosom friend, because it tells of home, where every heart will always burn with love, and glow with praise. It seems to me like receiving a card of invitation to go to court. Every line and every letter is love; though the flesh has suffered, the Sun has long since arisen with healing power, and I truly praise Him for it. It has been like the first day; "evening and morning"—the shade first, and afterwards the brightness. My precious Lord distinctly said to me, some months ago, Revelation 3:10, and Isaiah 43:2. Then must I not praise Him? Oh, yes; and here, in the midst of the waters of affliction, would I set up a stone of memorial in honor of His love and faithfulness, who has helped me hitherto. I do cry to Him that my precious friends may have a large rich blessing in this my mercy, and through it they may have a sweet savor of Jesus, to swallow up the ill-savor of this corrupting body, and be so taken up with Him, that, together, we may have a foretaste of that fullness of joy which is in His presence for evermore. I see not an inch of the road before me, and have no stock of strength or ability for the journey; but I must live moment by moment on the Lord God, who will make my feet like hinds' feet, to tread upon very high places—even the God who performeth all things for me. Moreover, to use another figure, I must lie in the arms of my Beloved as a helpless infant—without wisdom or power to do anything for myself, but believing that "the everlasting arms of love" will prove a safe conveyance. I have only one deep, sharp-pointed pang, which makes me daily mourn, and that is, the thought of my unfaithfulness, and the dishonor done to my dearest Lord since I have known His love. I know He has forgiven all, and that His own precious blood has paid the uttermost farthing, but such love makes me hate myself the more, and ever hide my blushing face in His dear bosom, singing, "Sovereign grace o'er sin abounding." Who is a God like unto Thee, multiplying and manifesting pardons to those who have "nothing to pay"?

Oh, what a blessed Jesus we have—who can so soften affliction and so sweeten Marah's bitter stream, making us exceeding joyful even in tribulation, so that I want *power* to praise Him as I would. Oh, that my heart were a ten-stringed instrument, and my life a living epistle, in which all might read *Him;* but, alas, it is so blotted over with unbelief and other sins, that it is hard to pick out His dear name in most of the pages. Oh, when I see Him face to face, and behold those love-prints in His glorious body, what shall I feel? That will be heaven—not one of harps and crowns, or of anything else, but JESUS and the open vision of His unveiled glories, the ineffable glories of Deity, and perfect beauties of humanity ever beaming with new effulgence in the person of our Bridegroom. Then shall we reflect His glory, and show forth His praise.

But I must cease; being still in the body, though sometimes at the gate of heaven.

My dear —, you are young in experience. I feel towards you as 2 Corinthians 11:2, 3, fearing, lest by any means, not Jesus should lose you, but you should lose Jesus, experimentally; lest any should take your crown of rejoicing from you, and cause you to cast away your confidence. May He keep you very close to Himself, and, whatever strange voices perplex, may He cause you to listen to what your Lord says in John 21:22. Remember also 2 Timothy 3:12. There is much which is called godliness which is not *"living godly* in Christ Jesus." To know nothing but Him—to delight in none other—to look nowhere else for holiness, happiness, and fruitfulness—this is the life of faith so fought against by unbelief and carnal reason, both in ourselves and others, as well as by Satan, who knows that hereby he gets more overcome than in any other way (Eph. 6:16; 1 Peter 1:13-15). May the Lord the Spirit open to you this way of faith, and keep you therein to the end of your days, as Galatians 2:19, 20; Proverbs 4:18. I can now testify that it is a solid and blessed reality, notwithstanding my instability. The Lord bless and comfort you (Ps. 87:7). He says, in substance, "All my springs are *for* thee."

Thanks, many, for all kind wishes. I am most unworthy of any love, and often wonder my Lord can bear with me, I am so uncomely in all things, so unlike His handmaids; but it is all His love which flows to me through your heart, and His love is a bottomless, shoreless ocean, in which we shall be absorbed for ever and ever.

Our union is for ever in indissoluble bonds.

Yours, ever in Him,
RUTH, the Happy Gleaner

LETTER IX
TO MISS P—

[To be received, "if the Lord will," on a wedding-day.]

And why does dear Miss — wish for a line from the humble, unworthy Gleaner, when so many tender sensations will be thrilling round her heart? Is it that she thereby desires to forsake all (even when her net is drawn to shore, right full of mercies, Luke 5:6-11), and follow Jesus only? Is it that she longs, on the very day she receives her earthly bridegroom, to give him back to the Lord, and, embracing her heavenly one, to become so absorbed in Him, that He shall ever be between her soul and her heart's best earthly love? If thus it be with her, the Gleaner's heart warmly says, Amen, and may the Lord say so too!

Dear Miss —, as you have requested me to send you a line at this season, it would be unseemly in me to withhold it, but I humbly confess it is not in me to write what you desire. Wherefore, let us look up to the dear Testifier of Jesus, that, under His divine anointing, our meditation of Him may be sweet. It is as the heavenly Lover and Bridegroom of His Church we just now love to think of Him. Oh, what a contrast to the very best earthly husband. They love and choose because of something congenial and pleasing, and in hope of a faithful return of affection. But He, our wondrous Ishi, loved, chose, and determined to betroth and espouse unto Himself, in the certain fore-view of debt, disgrace, and sin. Ah, and of unchaste wanderings, too, for He says, "I knew that thou wouldest deal very treacherously, and wast called a transgressor from the womb." Yet, through all, He loved, and from all He has redeemed with His own precious blood. When His spouse hath "played the harlot with many lovers," His marvellous language is "Return, for I am married unto you"; thereby overcoming His faithless one with the very love which she has slighted—a love, indeed, beyond compare. May its fires afresh be kindled in your soul, that you may now count all things but loss, yea, even as dung, for the sake of such a Beloved. Did Jacob serve seven years for his Rachel, by day in the heat, and by night in the frost, and did they seem but as a day unto him for the love he had to her? Our spiritual Jacob has far exceeded him! He left the throne of His glory for His poor Rachel, and took her humble flesh in the form of a servant, and for her sake served thirty-three years under the Law. He bore the heat of temptation, weariness, and thirst, as well as the cold of reproach and scorn, with the contradiction of sinners against Himself. This He thought not too much; for, when He had finished the work on her behalf, for her He cheerfully entered upon the most bitter part of His sufferings; which made even His mighty heart to thrill with agony, while His dear lips prayed, O my "Father, if it be possible [with the rescue of my bride], let this cup pass from me; nevertheless" (ah, who can tell what was in *that* word?) "nevertheless, not as I will, but as thou wilt." Behold the depth of His unflinching love! The cup of curse must be drunk, or the captive bride must perish. And now He takes it, nor turns away till every dreg was gone, and the same sacred lips which emptied it could say in triumph, "It is finished!" "For the joy that was set before him [of possessing His betrothed], he endured the cross, despising the shame," and is now set down at the right hand of God, till the blissful consummation before assembled worlds; when it will be joyfully proclaimed: "The marriage of the Lamb is come, and his wife hath made herself ready." Then shall the spiritual Jacob and Rachel meet, and embrace, and part no more for ever; she awaking up after His likeness shall be satisfied; and He, seeing her in glory (the very travail of His soul), shall be satisfied likewise.

> "Haste, blissful dawn of endless day,
> When sin shall cease and death shall die,
> And Christ His glory shall display,
> And beam upon our longing eye.
> Then, wrapped in everlasting bliss,
> 'Midst heaven's innumerable throng,
> His love shall all our powers employ,
> And be the theme of every song."

"Wonder, O heavens, and be astonished, O earth," that this most glorious Immanuel—the Prince of Peace, whom angels worship, and before whom the Seraphim bow, should, from all eternity, engage to come and seek His bride from this poor world, and claim her for His own. Yet so it is. But she is filthy and polluted! (Ezek. 16:6; Job 15:14-16; Isa. 60:6.) Then His own precious veins shall pour forth the rich crimson flood to cleanse her (Rev. 1:5), and His Spirit shall open the fountain to her for her sin and uncleanness (Zech. 13:1). But she is naked and bare! (Ezek. 16:22.) Then He will cast His skirt over her (Ezek. 16:8), and will, for her, weave in the loom of the law (Rom. 5:19) fine linen—clean and white—a robe in which she shall be meet to appear at His court. Moreover, the Spirit shall bring near His righteousness (Isa. 46:13), clothing her with "the garments of salvation," and covering her with "the robe of righteousness" "as a bridegroom decketh himself with ornaments, and as a bride adorneth herself with her jewels." But she is diseased (Isa. 1:5, 6). She is a leper (Ps. 51:5)—yet will He bring her health and cure, for He says, "I am the Lord that healeth thee"; and He is actually made to be sin for her (2 Cor. 5:21), that she might be made "the righteousness of God in Him." But she has no personal charms—she is ugly. Then He will put His comeliness upon her; and through it her beauty shall be perfect. But she is poor, so He bestows Himself and His fullness upon her, and thus endows her with a good dowry. But she is unwilling, and has no heart to the match, for she obeys the hostile prince (Eph. 2:2, 3); her delights, too, are in the world and the flesh. A new heart will He give her, and a right spirit will He put within her; the Spirit shall make her willing in the day of His power, and "take away the names of Baalim out of her mouth," so that, prostrate at his feet, she shall say, "Other lords beside thee have had dominion over [me], but by thee only will [I] make mention of thy name." And, now that the Spirit has touched her heart, she feels she is diseased, and discovers her filthiness (Rom. 7:8, 9, 18) and nakedness, knows she is ugly and poor, and cannot think the Bridegroom's heart is towards her, or that she can find favor in his eyes, and therefore she cries out, "I am black"; "behold, I am vile"; my comeliness is turned in me into corruption; but He overwhelms her by responding, "Thou art all fair, my love, there is no spot in thee." Then she exclaims, "Set me as a seal upon thy heart, as a seal upon thine arm, for love is strong as death." He replies, "Fear not, for I have redeemed thee; I have called thee by thy name [Hephzibah], thou art mine." Now she ventures, with a captivated heart, to declare, "My beloved is mine, and I am his. He is the chiefest among ten thousand; he is altogether lovely."

Thus do the matters of this marvellous betrothment and union go on, "which things the angels desire to look into," and devils desire to defeat. The first desire shall be blessedly gratified (Eph. 3:10); but the other shall be disappointed, for none shall be able to pluck His loved one out of His hands; and against her the gates of hell shall never prevail. Praise Him for ever for such love as this!

Well may it be asked, Who is this wondrous Beloved, that would go to such depths for His spouse, and on whom the weak fair one is leaning as she comes up out of the wilderness? Ah, He is the same who, from all eternity, was the great "I AM," the mighty God, by whom all things were created, who is before all things, and by whom all things consist. It is He who, in the fullness of time, scorned not the lowly virgin's womb, but became a babe, and was found in fashion as a man. The same glorious Person who was seen coming from Edom with dyed garments from Bozrah, glorious in His apparel, travelling in the greatness of His strength, who did tread the winepress of almighty wrath alone, and of the people, there was none with Him. It is He whose countenance is as the sun shining in His strength, and yet whose "visage was marred more than any man's," and His form more than the sons of men. He is an Holy One of the Holy Ones, and yet "a man of sorrows, and acquainted with grief; holy, harmless, undefiled, and separate from sinners, and yet numbered with the transgressors." Under the weight of sin and its punishment Jesus agonized in the sacred garden of Gethsemane, and sweat, as it were, great drops of blood, falling down to the ground. (Oh, those rich, rich drops from His precious veins, of more value than all the gold and gems His hands have made!)

This is the matchless Bridegroom of whom we speak. His love has saved, and it does kindle the soul now trying to tell of His worth, who, on Calvary, was stretched on the accursed tree, and there finished the love-scene of His mystic sufferings. Come, sit with me a moment beneath the shadow of His cross. It will not mar, but heighten the joys of your nuptial day. Look up, and remember it is as a Husband He hangs bleeding there. It is the Bridegroom, in love for the bride, enduring those unknown pangs. See how His holy flesh is bruised with scourging, and His precious hands and feet pierced with rugged nails. How is His heavenly brow torn with pricking thorns, and His dear side with the cruel spear; each gaping wound proclaiming man is guilty—God is love. But God is justice, too! Oh, see His precious blood trickling down. It flowed forth for sinners like me—like thee! Look and wonder; look and be comforted; look and adore!

> "Here look, till love dissolve your heart,
> And bid each slavish fear depart."

Say, does not your very soul move towards this glorious Well-Beloved? And will it not join mine in saying

> "Bruised Bridegroom, take us wholly,
> Take, and make us what Thou wilt"?

Oh, glorious Lord, we worship Thee! Thou art fairer than the children of men; grace is poured into Thy lips—

> "Thy beauties we can never trace,
> Till we behold Thee face to face."

We love to meditate on Thy sufferings, but rejoice that they are over. Thou hast suffered, and Thou diest no more! Thou art gone to *our* Father, and to *Thy* Father; and we are expecting Thee to "come again" and receive us unto Thyself, to be with Thee, and behold Thy glory, when, in nobler and sweeter strains, "We'll sing Thy dying [and yet never dying] love, and tell Thy power to save," while, with open face and ravished heart, we gaze upon Thy matchless beauty.... Please excuse my many words. It is to me a thrilling subject, full of blessedness, and the very writing it has been as a lattice, through which my precious Beloved has shown Himself. Oh, may He shine on you; and, when you give your hand and heart to —, may the Holy Ghost come upon you in powerful enablings to give yourself more fully to Jesus than ever before. I come not to you with worldly compliments; they beseem not our holy religion, and the peculiar people. But I come with an honest heart, desiring for you both every choice covenant blessing, with the sweetest mercies of the new estate upon which you are entering, and that these may be to you but as the shadow of a substance, you, *in* and *through* them, coming by the Spirit's power, to fuller enjoyment of union and communion with our all-lovely Immanuel, and with the Father in Him. May your union be of the Lord, in the Lord, and for the Lord. May His name be glorified, and Jesus doubly precious to your souls. The theme wants more than an angel's power to tell all its fullness.

Ever yours in Jesus,
RUTH

Hosea 2:19, 20

THE END

www.ingramcontent.com/pod-product-compliance
Lightning Source LLC
Chambersburg PA
CBHW030258080526
44584CB00012B/360